Computer Security and Penetration Testing

Alfred Basta
Wolf Halton

THOMSON

COURSE TECHNOLOGY

Australia • Canada • Mexico • Singapore • Spain • United Kingdom • United States

THOMSON

COURSE TECHNOLOGY

Computer Security and Penetration Testing

is published by Thomson Course Technology

Vice President, Technology & Trades, Academic Business Unit:
Dave Garza

Director of Learning Solutions:
Sandy Clark

Executive Editor:
Steve Helba

Managing Editor:
Larry Main

Senior Product Manager:
Michelle Ruelos Cannistraci

Marketing Manager:
Guy Baskaran

Print Buyer:
Julio Esperas

Content Project Manager:
Elena Montillo

Art Director:
Marissa Falco

Technical Editor:
Green Pen QA

Copy Editor:
Green Pen QA

Proofreader:
GEX Publishing Services, Inc.

Indexer:
GEX Publishing Services, Inc.

Internal Design:
GEX Publishing Services, Inc.

Compositor:
GEX Publishing Services, Inc.

Disclaimer
Thomson Course Technology reserves the right to revise this publication and make changes from time to time in its content without notice.

ISBN-13: 978-1-4180-4826-6
ISBN-10: 1-4180-4826-7

TABLE OF
Contents

Introduction

This text was written to provide a large number of options for further study for interested individuals or enrolled students who desire an accurate and interesting introduction to the fascinating realm of network security.

This work is designed to give students, professionals, and hobbyists accurate and well-researched examples of current security topics. The field of information security changes quickly, and this text is formulated to provide a solid foundation to enable the reader to understand and differentiate between hype and fact. Readers will acquire a firm grasp of the concepts and history of network development and security as it has evolved. This platform is anchored to real-world examples and techniques to glean the most useful information from the Internet. It is intended to burst the mystique, shine a light into the "how and why" people attack computers and networks, and prepare the reader with the right techniques to begin winning the network security game.

This text is primarily intended for students in the second or third year of programs in:

- Information Technology
- Security
- Network Engineering
- Computer Science

This work is also valuable to upper management of small companies that do not have IT departments, and to bring IT professionals up-to-date on the latest security concepts.

Organization and Coverage

Computer Security and Penetration Testing introduces students to a wide range of topics related to computer security issues. Chapter 1 provides an overview of hacking and cracking and discusses ethical considerations surrounding these often misunderstood activities. Chapters 2 through 6 give a broad overview of the basic concepts that are fundamental to the practice of ethical hacking. Chapter 2 begins with reconnaissance techniques and compares legal and illegal techniques used by hackers to acquire the information necessary to launch attacks. Chapters 3 and 4 cover the use of scanning tools and sniffers, critical tools in the arsenals of both crackers and computer security professionals alike. Chapters 5 and 6 cover the concepts of TCP/IP networking, and encryption and password cracking, topics about which no security professional can afford to be ignorant. Chapters 7 through 13 focus on specific types of attacks and their countermeasures, including spoofing, session hijacking, network device hacking, Trojan horses, denial-of-service attacks, buffer overflows, and programming exploits. In Chapters 14 through 17, the discussion turns to known vulnerabilities in existing software. Chapters 14 and 15 cover vulnerabilities in the protocols and software implementations used for Internet mail and Web servers. Chapters 16 and 17 turn to two popular operating systems—Windows and Linux—and describe some of the vulnerabilities inherent in the systems themselves, as well as those vulnerabilities that result from user error or misconfiguration. Finally, Chapter 18 covers the important topic of incident handling—what steps to take and policies to follow when a security-related incident is detected on a network.

Features

Read This Before You Begin   Technical considerations and assumptions about hardware, software, and lab setup are listed in one place at the beginning of the book to save time and eliminate surprises later on in the book.

Tips   Tips provide additional information, such as background information on a technology, mistakes to watch out for, or Web resources where users can obtain more information.

Chapter Summaries   Each chapter contains a summary of the key content covered in the chapter, which serves as a helpful tool for study and for reinforcing the main ideas presented in the chapter.

Review Questions   Each chapter contains questions that help students evaluate their understanding of the material covered in the chapter.

Hands-On Projects   Projects at the end of each chapter provide students with the ability to apply some of the concepts they have read about in the chapter. The ability to "learn-by-doing" helps students solidify their understanding of the material.

INSTRUCTOR MATERIALS

The following instructor supplements have been prepared to help with classroom preparation. All of the supplements are available on one e.resource CD (ISBN: 1418048275).

Instructor's Manual. The Instructor's Manual includes answers to the textbook's Review Questions.

ExamView. This powerful testing software allows instructors to create and administer printer, computer (LAN-based), and Internet exams. These testing components allow students to take exams at their computers and also saves the instructor time by grading each exam automatically.

PowerPoint presentations. PowerPoint slides are created for each chapter and can be used as a teaching aid for classroom presentation or as chapter reviews for students. Instructors, feel free to customize the PowerPoint slides for your class needs.

Figure Files. All of the figures are reproduced and can be used to customize the PowerPoint slides or made available to students for review.

READ THIS BEFORE YOU BEGIN

This book assumes that the student will have access to networked PC running a current version of Linux. The computer should also have Internet access. In the Hands-On Projects at the end of Chapter 1, general instructions are given for setting up a PC to be used for this book. Note that the specific machine requirements listed are a suggestion, and that other configurations may work as well. In general, any current, standard Linux distribution should work. The steps in this book were written for Fedora Core 6, but other distributions will also work, with minor modifications to the steps.

Throughout the book, students will occasionally need to download software from the Internet and install it. Specific instructions are given were necessary. The text also references a "central Linux server" that the instructor may wish to set up to provide a central location from which students may access software or files. (For example, in Chapter 6, the instructor will need to provide students with a sample "passwd" file that students can use to practice using password-cracking software.) This central server is not required and the instructor may choose to distribute files or software using other methods.

A few parts of the text—for example, Hands-On Project 10-3—are written assuming that the student has access to a Windows computer. If a Windows machine is not available, such sections can be read through without following along at the computer.

Finally, at times it will be necessary for students to access other lab computers. For example, in the project at the end of Chapter 8, the instructor should set up a TCP session between two computers, so that students can observe the session using a sniffer. At the instructor's discretion, virtualization software such as VMware can be used if physical machines are not available.

ABOUT THE AUTHORS

Alfred Basta, PhD

- Professional speaker on topics of Internet Security and Networking
- Member of the Editorial Board for the Norwich University *Journal of Information Assurance*
- Professor of Mathematics, Cryptology, and Information Security

Michael "Wolf" Halton, AB, MSc

- Professional speaker on topics of Internet Security, Linux and open-source adoption, spam-relief strategies, and Painless Grad-School Progress
- CEO, Halton Technical Services—providing security consulting, Web strategy, hardware and software configuration services, project management, and guidance to clients in the medical, real estate, and entertainment industries
- Assisted in developing the curriculum for the Masters of Information Security specialization at Capella University

ACKNOWLEDGMENTS

From Alfred Basta:

To my wife Nadine

"It is the continuing symphony of your loving thoughts, caring actions and continuous support that stands out as the song of my life."

To our daughter Rebecca, our son Stavros

"Fix your hearts upon God, and love Him with all your strength, for without this no one can be saved or be of any worth. Develop in yourselves an urge for a life of high and noble values. You are like little birds that will soon spread your wings and fly."

To my mother

"You are a never ending melody of goodness and kindness. You are without equal in this world."

And to the memory of my father

"If one is weighed by the gifts one gives, your values given are beyond estimation."

From Wolf Halton:

To my wife Helen

"I bless you, I love you, I appreciate you, I am sorry for all the time I had to spend away from you during the research and writing of this book, and I thank you for your encouragement throughout."

To Dr John H. Halton

"Thank you for your unfailing rigour and good ideas about scripting. What I have learned of logical argument and the Monte Carlo Method, I learned from you."

To Yvonne Halton

"The example you set has reverberated through my life in good and surprising ways. Your common-sense approach to problem-solving always seems to come through in the end."

To Dr Jack Kritchen of Capella University

"Your guidance and mentoring have opened doors for me that I never knew existed. Thank you for your patience and your ongoing advise."

To Savannah Nell Rogers

"Thanks for being there. Not just for me, but for so many other people. You will never know how amazing an effect you have on the people around you. Remember, 'I didn't bite nobody!'"

To Robert Anton Wilson, Bob Shea, Steve Arakawa, Rob Breszny, Antero Ali, David Groves, Richard Costello, Bo Weaver, Buckminster Fuller, R. Candler Rogers and a host of others whose insight and assistance have been important to the completion of this work. "The best is yet to come. Network security as a profession is at its infancy, barely undifferentiated. Expect breakthroughs."

1

ETHICS OF HACKING AND CRACKING

> ## After reading this chapter and completing the exercises, you will be able to:
>
> ♦ Understand how the act of unethical computer hacking is a crime
>
> ♦ Classify and identify groups and classes of hackers
>
> ♦ Distinguish the rationale for various types of hackers
>
> ♦ Understand and determine differences in information warfare
>
> ♦ Understand how computer hacking originated and its evolution
>
> ♦ Recognize the importance of ethical hacking and the issues involved in hacker ethics

Hacking and cracking are of great interest to many students of information security as well as to hobbyists and others. This chapter will introduce you to hacking and help you understand the basis of the subcultures of hackers, both criminal and otherwise.

THE IMPACT OF UNETHICAL HACKING

Computer **cracking** is the term for illegally hacking into a computer system without the permission of the system's owner. Despite the motivations of computer **crackers**—whether it be a love of difficult challenges, curiosity, desire for recognition, financial gain, need for revenge, or patriotism—cracking a system is a crime. In the past, it was common for individuals or corporations to fail to prosecute crackers; either because the crime was internal and they didn't want to jeopardize customer confidence, or because they were not sure of the extent of their vulnerability and didn't want to advertise it to other crackers. The trend today is toward prompt prosecution and draconian sentencing for those caught compromising machines owned by others. Due to the growth of computer cracking, many companies have hired, and are hiring more, employees with hacking skills to protect their networks and to identify crackers. According to the FBI in 2005, at least 20% of businesses surveyed had experienced port scans and network sabotage. Nearly 90% said they had experienced some sort of attack and thought viruses (83.7%) and spyware (79.5%) were the most frequent modes of attack. Port scans are not illegal in most states, but systematic port scans are usually the precursor to an attack.

Over 64% of the respondents reported that they had incurred a financial loss. Viruses and worms cost the most, accounting for $12 million of the $32 million in total losses. In 2000, the FBI survey's respondents reported $265 million in losses. This text is designed to assist you in gaining the skills required to defeat computer crackers.

HACKER COMMUNITIES

There are distinct groups of **hackers**; however, the membership between groups is fluid. There are two ways commonly used to categorize them:

- The first is the simplest —White Hat good hackers vs. Black Hat bad hackers.
- The second is based loosely on psychological profiling and is a more complicated and more useful way to understand the motivations of hackers.

Hat Categories

The White Hat/Black Hat model is derived from old Western genre movies where the "good guys" always wore white hats and the "bad guys" always wore black hats. The assumption is that everything the good guys do is right, legal, and justified, while everything the bad guys do is wrong, illegal, and debased. The black/white division is essentially an oversimplification for the purposes of marketing the concept that "some hackers are good guys, and not dangerous" to a market segment perceived as being naive. However, in the world of hackers, there are also "Gray Hat" hackers, evidence that the dichotomy of good and evil is NOT a very good fit to the real world.

Figure 1-1 shows a possible distribution of motivations based on the White Hat/Black Hat model.

	White Hat Hackers	Grey Hat Hackers	Black Hat Hackers
Motivations and Goals	Learning new things, protecting the network in their charge from intrusion or damage, maintaining status quo. Work with official sanction from official organizations.	Fame, credit for solving challenging network puzzles. More interested in damage than pillage. Hacktivists who deface Web sites and networks of target "evil-doers" (e.g., corporations involved in fur trade, tobacco sales, abortion, etc.) are part of this group.	Cash payments, injury to others. May steal trade secrets, credit card numbers, customer lists, employee lists. They want whatever information they can find that will generate a profit. They work with unofficial sanction from official and unofficial organizations.

Figure 1-1   Black Hat/White Hat model

Hacker Profiling

Hacking is similar to criminalistic forensics or martial arts, in that all three disciplines require that the practitioner be intimately familiar with the techniques of the perpetrator or opponent. To be successful as an ethical hacker and network security expert, a person must know not only what to do to protect a network, but also what and whom they are protecting the network from. As Pogo says in the swamp, "We have met the enemy and they is us."[1] The reading and techniques used by both ethical and malicious hackers are identical; what differentiates one from the other is the choice of whether to defend or attack. Figure 1-2 is a list[2], developed by former police detective and cyber-forensics expert Marcus Rogers, of the characteristics of some basic hacker profiles. The profile of a hacker is multifaceted and one cannot just point out the geekiest-looking person in the line-up and say "He's the one!"

Whether one chooses to act in alignment with current regulation or athwart that regulation, whether one chooses to abide by company policy or not, whether one decides to act ethically or not, one must be tireless in researching and practicing to reach the boundary placed by one's environment and predilection. Of the nine types of hackers described in the figure, most are entirely sure that their cause is just or sensible. I venture to say that professional criminals may be entirely aware that they are acting in reprehensible ways, but even the professional criminal likes to think of himself as a pretty nice guy, when he isn't working. A novice with the best of intentions can cause thousands of dollars in damage and loss because she doesn't entirely understand what she is doing.

> *"Are hackers a threat? The degree of threat presented by any conduct, whether legal or illegal, depends on the actions and intent of the individual and the harm they cause." noted hacker Kevin Mitnick*[3]

Hacker Profile	Description
Novices	Limited computer and programming skills. Rely on toolkits to conduct their attacks. Can cause extensive damage to systems because they often don't understand how attacks work. Looking for media attention.
Cyber-punks	Capable of writing their own software. Have an understanding of the systems they are attacking. Many are engaged in credit card number theft and telecommunications fraud. Have a tendency to brag about their exploits.

Internals	a) Disgruntled employees or ex-employees
	     May be involved in technology-related jobs.
	     Aided by privileges they have or were assigned as part of their job function.
	     These hackers pose the greatest security threat.
	b) Petty thieves
	     Include employees, contractors, consultants.
	     Motivated by greed, or need to pay off habits, such as drugs or gambling.
	     Opportunistic; take advantage of poor internal security.
	     Computer literate.

Old guard hackers	Appear to have no criminal intent. Alarming disrespect for personal property. Appear to be interested in the intellectual endeavor.
Coders	Act as mentors to newbies. Write scripts and tools that others use. Motivated by a sense of power and prestige. Dangerous; have hidden agendas, use Trojan horses.
Professional criminals	Specialize in corporate espionage. Guns for hire. Highly motivated, highly trained, have access to state-of-the-art equipment.
Information warriors/ cyber-terrorists	Increase in activity since the fall of many Eastern Bloc intelligence agencies. Well funded. Mix political rhetoric with criminal activity. Political activists.
Hacktivists	Work to eradicate or damage entities or causes they perceive to be evil. Mix political rhetoric with criminal activity. Political activists. Engage in hacktivism.

Figure 1-2 Hacker profiles

As for the Black and White Hats, these are marketing terms that are swapped about depending upon the convenience of the particular hacker. There is a very popular convention called the "Black Hat Briefings," first held in 1997 in Las Vegas. The stated purpose of the convention and its Web site is to "highlight[] breaking security research submitted by leading corporate professionals, government experts, and members of the underground hacking community." Members of the White Hat community claim that they adhere to the hacker ethic, which, according to the online hacker Jargon File, version 4.4.7, is defined as

> *The belief that information-sharing is a powerful positive good, and that it is an ethical duty of hackers to share their expertise by writing open-source code and facilitating access to information and to computing resources wherever possible.*[4]

Hackers themselves disagree as to what is ethical and moral. Many hackers hold that cracking a computer is like cutting across the neighbor's lawn. As long as there is no harm done, the act is not an invasion of the neighbor's privacy or a violation of privacy rights. Another way of looking at this would be, "Anything lying around loose or not tacked down is OK to take. If less than 15 minutes with a crowbar can pry it loose, it is not nailed down." The legal establishment has chosen otherwise.

Hacker Motivations

Regardless of the hacker's profile, knowledge or skills, they are all powerfully motivated by something:

- Curiosity
- Love of puzzles
- Desire for recognition or fame
- Revenge
- Financial gain
- Patriotism or politics

Curiosity

One of the first motivations, and possibly the strongest is curiosity. "What happens when I do this?" or "How do these security measures work?"

We are trained from childhood to be curious, open, and sharing. Crackers take advantage of these tendencies to satisfy their own curiosity about technical blind spots in the systems we build.

Love of Puzzles

Hackers gain great satisfaction in finding the solutions to complicated puzzles. There are many variables that have to be controlled and techniques that have to be mastered to successfully crack systems. These are the same challenges that motivate locksmiths and cat burglars in the physical security realm. Strong passwords, such as "Tr34$>1drU,"(tr) can be devised that block most attack attempts, and locks can be keyed with "024642" pin combinations which are almost unpickable. Think of the fun when you figure out how to solve these difficult puzzles!

Desire for Recognition

Almost all hackers are motivated by a need for acceptance, acknowledgment, and fame—at least among their peers. It takes a person of average intelligence and skill years to become a poor hacker. Acknowledged experts in the field are rare and marvelous in ways that may not be explicable to average citizens. True, hackers may be deficient in social skills or fashion sense, but it is plain that they are as susceptible to the lure of fame as anyone else. As members of an elite group possessing specialized technical skills, hackers believe they deserve recognition.

While ethical hackers believe that they are the last line of defense against malicious individuals, script kiddies and Black Hat crackers enjoy their conquests and the subsequent notoriety in their community of iconoclasts.

Revenge

People who feel that they were wronged, or their cause or group was wronged, can easily talk themselves into performing unethical acts by using the simplistic notion that the badly behaved target person, business, or government deserves to be treated as poorly as possible. It is the cracker's way of getting even for whatever slights they may perceive.

Financial Gain

Making money is a very common motive among all classes of hacker, from the security expert on contract or salary to the script kiddie stealing and selling credit card information. Plainly, the education required and the time spent learning the craft were not without cost, so it makes sense that there is some expectation of remuneration. Many hackers do their best work for free, citing the Hacker's Ethic that information should be free and freely shared to all interested parties, but it is plain that financial health is important to almost all hackers.

Patriotism and Other Moral Causes

Some hackers are motivated by patriotism or nationalism to perpetrate both ethical securing of networks and attacks designed to disrupt services, causing fear among specific "enemy" populations and communities.

Cyber-terrorism, a buzz word intended to cause fear and confusion among target populations, is extremely rare. Though the possibility is there, sacrificial system cracking requires a personality and mindset that is diametrically opposite of all profiles of hacker except that of government agents. The probability of any great influx of real cyber-terrorism remains low.

Ethical Hacking

Ethics are the principles of conduct that govern individuals, groups, and professions. Most professions have a standard or ethical code that binds their members into their shared values. The core values to which a trade or profession adhere are necessary for the good reputation and growth of that professional community. Without a published code of ethics, it is difficult to gain public trust for a profession. The profession of **network security** is emerging from a chaotic set of conflicting ethics from both the hobbyist and student communities and those on the information technology career track. Many individuals involved in the profession, perhaps especially those who have entered the security profession from business rather than technical backgrounds, believe that development of a professional presence and reputation requires distancing themselves from the communities from which they came and from which most of the better penetration tools have come. One of the real causes within the profession is specifically to develop and cultivate differentiation from the bad hackers who are threatening the networks that the good hackers are paid to protect. A good working set of distinctions to separate the ethical hacker from the unethical cracker will determine the frame within which security professionals present the benefits of their profession as it matures.

Evolution of Hacking

In the 1940s, when computers first started to be used in universities, government, and large businesses, few people knew about them. There were no computer science students. Most of the professionals who worked with computers were using them to solve complicated mathematics problems. The modern concept of hacking began in the late 1950s when some of the first students at the Massachusetts Institute of Technology started using their access to the MIT mainframe to work on new languages and experiments outside of sanctioned classes. This was not antisocial or illegal, and the students developed their skills and community of computer hackers at the same time. Students were allowed to access the institute's computers after the formal research and experiments were done. In the 1950s, hacker was another word for a hobbyist in any technical area.

The students used their unsupervised computer time to experiment and find new ways to solve problems and to invent applications to do things in the new computerized way. Those early hackers had no malicious intent. They believed there was always room for improvement, and when a new solution that was simpler and more elegant was found, it was published widely and tested by many. There was little predefined structure to the experimentation. Many took as much pride in their collaborative solutions as they did in their individual achievements. With such open access and freedom, many programmed pranks or discovered ways to access others' personal files to edit their code. These pranks were published just as widely as the more socially acceptable experimental results.

The first password hacks were a response to the Compatible Time Sharing System (CTSS), developed in the early 1960s and first loaded on an IBM mainframe at MIT. This application was intended to enable safe sharing of time by different users so that all cycles of the processor were used, and there was no idle time. One aspect of this application was the use of usernames and logons so that people could not access the computer anonymously. This flew in the face of the freedoms that students had previously enjoyed, and the response of some hackers was to start guessing usernames and passwords. Finally, they broke into the CTSS system.

In the 1970s, phone phreaks, a new sort of hacker, appeared. They used various methods, collectively called **phreaking**, to access telephone networks to make free calls from payphones.

Phreaks eventually began combining traditional phreaking tools with computer programming languages. One popular phreaking program is Blue Beep. It works with MS-DOS and shell prompts of Windows, using PASCAL and other assembly languages. Its features include creating digital tones, controlling trunk lines, and scanning telephone exchanges.

In the 1980s, phreaks started discovering that any server that had a modem could potentially be entered. **War dialers** were developed to search for open modems. Once a hacker had gained access to one server, it was often possible to access another server through the dedicated lines that servers shared. This was one way to access the fledgling Internet and its precursors, the bulletin boards run by Compuserve and AOL. As personal computer prices dropped and users became more common, hacker communities also grew. Hacking started to take on new connotations, and hackers were no longer stereotyped as young, socially inept males with an insatiable curiosity about computers. The stereotype grew to include malicious hackers, who attempted to break into and damage sensitive computers they could access through modems on corporate and government networks.

Automation being the real reason for computers in the first place, it is not surprising that in the 1980s, people started coding applications that could spread themselves automatically, or nearly automatically over the Internet and through e-mail systems. Viruses, worms, and Trojans started appearing in 1988. The thrill of having such simple codes work so well in compromising servers and workstations was intoxicating, and hackers have continued to develop new viruses and worms to this day. More and more disaffected hackers have turned to more hazardous code because it is actually easier to cause harm than it is to make a sophisticated toy. Examples of these harmful viruses are the Bagel virus (with dozens of variants), Nimda, and Code Red.

Viruses are indiscriminate in their damaging effects, and any script kiddie can set one loose. Virus code is available on the Internet, and skilled crackers can use such code as a starting point to develop better ways to break into more specific targets.

The antisocial actions of crackers and script kiddies made it difficult to defend the original concept of hacking, and people started to use the label "computer hacker" to describe computer experts with malicious intent. This stereotype persists today, and has raised the need for security experts to distance themselves from the criminals, in the same way that the official lawmen of the old West used their tin badge to separate themselves from the outlaws.

ETHICS AND ISSUES OF INFORMATION TECHNOLOGY

There is a need for ethics within the hacking profession. Almost all professions have associations that provide legitimacy to their practitioners. The American Medical Association and other associations define the duties and scope of medical practicioners. Teaching professions have extremely strict guidelines to protect students and to provide decision support for employing instructors. Attorneys are members of their state's Bar Association which proctors the "minimum skills" test called the Bar Exam. Accountants are certified by exam and other requirements that vary by state which allow them the title of Certified Public Accountant. All of these certifications and association memberships provide a measure of security for buyers when they hire or contract the services of people practicing those professions. Because there is currently no national certification standard for computer security professionals, and about a dozen certificates available to denote skill levels, the White Hat/Black Hat system has evolved as a way to differentiate security experts from criminal or amateur hackers. White Hats, or conscientious hackers, are employed to strengthen security and prevent attacks. In many cases, they are network engineers and administrators with no specialty in security.

Vendor-Neutral Security Certifications

The list of security certificates and issuing bodies includes:

- CompTIA Security+™ Certification
- Global Information Assurance Certification (GIAC), Security Administration Certifications
    - GIAC Information Security Fundamentals (GISF)
    - Stay Sharp Program – Computer and Network Security Awareness (SSP-CNSA)
    - GIAC Security Essentials Certification (GSEC)
    - Securing Solaris – The Gold Standard (GGSC-0200)
    - Securing Windows 2000 – The Gold Standard (GGSC-0100)
    - Auditing Cisco Routers – The Gold Standard (GGSC-0400)
    - Stay Sharp Program – Defeating Rogue Access Points (SSP-DRAP)
    - Stay Sharp Program – Mastering Packet Analysis (SSP-MPA)
    - GIAC Certified Firewall Analyst (GCFW)
    - GIAC Certified Intrusion Analyst (GCIA)
    - GIAC Certified Incident Handler (GCIH)
    - GIAC Certified Windows Security Administrator (GCWN)
    - GIAC Certified UNIX Security Administrator (GCUX)
    - GIAC Certified Forensics Analyst (GCFA)
    - GIAC Securing Oracle Certification (GSOC)
    - GIAC Intrusion Prevention (GIPS)
    - GIAC Cutting Edge Hacking Techniques (GHTQ)
    - GIAC Web Application Security (GWAS)
    - Stay Sharp Program – Google Hacking and Defense (SSP-GHD)
    - GIAC Reverse Engineering Malware (GREM)
    - GIAC Secure Internet Presence (GSIP)
    - GIAC .Net (GNET)
    - GIAC Assessing Wireless Networks (GAWN)
- ISC2 Certifications
- Associate of $(ISC)^2$
- SSCP Examination

- CAP Examination
- CISSP Examination
- CISSP Concentrations
  - ISSAP Concentration in Architecture
  - ISSEP Concentration in Engineering
  - ISSMP Concentration in Management
- EC-Council Certifications
  - Entry level security certifications
    - Security5 Certification
    - Network5 Certification
    - Wireless5 Certification
  - Graduate level certifications
    - E++ Certified Technical Consultant
    - Fundamentals in Computer Forensics
    - Fundamentals in Information Security
    - Fundamentals in Network Security
    - e-Business certifications
    - Certified e-Business Associate (CEA)
    - Certified e-Business Professional (CEP)
    - Certified e-Business Consultant (CEC)
  - IT Security professional certifications
    - Certified Ethical Hacker (CEH)
    - Computer Hacking Forensic Investigator (CHFI)
    - EC-Council Certified Security Analyst (ECSA)
    - Certified Network Defense Architect (CNDA)
    - Network Security Administrator (NSA)
  - IT Consultant level certifications
    - Licensed Penetration Tester (LPT)
    - EC-Council Tiger Team (ECTT)

- Programming certifications
  - EC-Council Certified Secure Programmer (ECSP)
  - Certified Secure Application Developer (CSAD)
- ISACA Certifications
  - Certified Information Systems Auditor (CISA)
  - Certified Information Security Manager (CISM)

Vendor-Specific Security Certificates

There are almost as many vendor-specific certificates as there are network vendors. Networking certificates such as Cisco's CCNA, and Microsoft's MSCE might be useful to newcomers to the network security industry; they can help newcomers get entry-level jobs that will give them IT experience. However, no one should neglect social networking when searching for an entry-level or intermediate-level job. Many good jobs are not acquired by reading the paper or surfing online job boards.

For more information about vendor-neutral certifications, visit the following Web sites:

- Information Systems Audit and Control Association (ISACA): www.isaca.org
- EC-Council: www.eccouncil.org/Certification.htm
- ISC2: www.isc2.org/cgi-bin/index.cgi
- CompTIA: http://certification.comptia.org/security/
- Global Information Assurance Certification (GIAC): www.giac.org/certifications/security/

For more information about vendor-specific security certification, visit the individual vendors' Web sites.

What Needs to Be Secured

The protection of data provided to organizations or stored on personal computers is a high priority. Medical histories, credit reports, police records, bank accounts, financial and transaction records, and other data are accessible by a cracker with sufficient skill and desire to break into systems, though not all such break-ins are intended to liberate sensitive data.

Some crackers who break into systems do so in order to utilize what they consider wasted computer energy. It is generally known that thousands, if not millions, of computers are idle for 8 to 16 hours or more every day. These hackers do not consider it unethical to use those computers' idle time for their own projects. Consider the peer-to-peer music-sharing industry exemplified by such products as Napster and Kazaa. These systems allow users to access each others' computers for the music and movie files stored therein and also to use free hard-drive space on those computers for other types of storage. Private individuals do not see this as a problem, as they believe they all share equally in the benefit of being able to trade media with 500,000 of their closest peers. Network administrators see the unexpected and unapproved uploads as bandwidth-theft that has the potential to affect network performance. In most commercial networks, peer-to-peer applications such as these are prohibited.

Using bandwidth without permission may seem harmless, but what if accidental damage happens to a system or if alteration to processing information and codes occurs? If the network has been hacked, it doesn't much matter whether the hacker directly caused the error or mischief, they will be blamed for any loss or damage. In many states, unauthorized use of a computer system is a crime, in addition to being unethical.

The majority of hackers employed by organizations understand that they are responsible for the success of the protective measures they use on their employers' networks. Such hackers may take pride in knowing they have an honest career and feel duty-bound to perform all penetration and software testing with diligence and enthusiasm. They strive to uphold the reputation of their profession because they know that to have the profession devalued is to lose both the ground they have advanced and the loyalty and safety of their employers.

Many hackers find it tempting to copy, download, and use proprietary software and other copyrighted works. While hackers typically consider this a harmless activity, it is often illegal (based upon the license with which the software is distributed). There is a philosophical discourse as to whether free access to information is more or less important than a creator's right to protect his or her creations. This is the same sort of debate as that over copyright law, the regulations which govern the distribution and modification of written works. Many feel that proprietary software is a form of elitism that inhibits progress. The argument is that every person has the right to hear, read, see, or learn anything that is available. Proponents of strong intellectual property rights argue that there would be no creation at all if there was not some method of ensuring remuneration or royalty for reproduction of that intellectual property.

Ethical Issues of Hacking

Professional hackers have a responsibility to society that is hard to ignore. Their activities should help to build and improve upon existing technology. Accessing information in a quest for knowledge is valuable, but a hacker's right to free information ought not to infringe on others' rights to their own space and property. It is the responsibility of ethical hackers to ensure that their activities cause no harm to the confidentiality and integrity of information. They should use their skills and interests as opportunities to learn and to teach. Hackers can use their intelligence and experience to invent new solutions that help the overall development of technology.

An ethical hacker is a security professional who applies his or her hacking skills for defensive purposes. This person accesses a computer system or network with the authorization of the system's owner, and without causing damage to the system. Hackers who are conscious of other people's rights are assets to the information technology field. Hackers who act with malicious intent harm the profession, but at the same time they do help security professionals see where their networks are vulnerable.

Ethical Hacking and System Security

Companies would rather pay an ethical hacker to discover their systems' weaknesses and security gaps, than take the risk of waiting for some unknown cracker to make their network vulnerabilities plain. Hackers who commit to improving technology and inventing new security solutions while auditing systems greatly benefit an organization overall.

Ethical hackers work to protect all areas of information technology, from Web servers to shared printers, as well as protecting e-mail from end to end. These hackers must have experience in software engineering, network engineering, and system security. They strive to increase their knowledge of tools and techniques to protect their networks and to forensically check for evidence when those networks are attacked.

CHAPTER SUMMARY

- ❏ Computer cracking is illegally hacking into a computer system without the permission of the system's owner.

- ❏ Hackers are commonly thought of in two groups: White Hat, or "good" and ethical hackers, and Black Hat, or "bad" and malicious hackers. But this is an oversimplified classification, and the hacker community adds the group of Gray Hat hackers.

- ❏ There are nine major profiles of hackers: novices, cyber-punks, internals, old-guard hackers, coders, professional criminals, information warriors, cyberterrorists, and hacktivists.

- ❏ The techniques used by ethical and malicious hackers are similar; what differentiates them is that one group is defending, while the other is attacking.

- ❏ Hackers may be motivated by curiosity, puzzles, fame, revenge, money, or patriotism.

- ❏ The modern concept of hacking began in the late 1950s when some students at the Massachusetts Institute of Technology started using their access to the MIT mainframe to work on new languages and experiments outside of sanctioned classes. With the advent of logon accounts and passwords in the 1960s, hackers went from exploring computers to hacking passwords. The 1970s saw the rise of the phreaks, and the 1980s saw tremendous growth in computer crime and abuse with the introduction of viruses, worms, and Trojan horses.

- ❏ While there are several vendor-neutral and vendor-specific certifications available to computer security professionals, there is no national certification standard.

- ❏ Professional security experts, technologists, and hackers must develop a public code of ethics. Without the assurance a code provides, potential clients may resist employing ethical hackers who could defend their networks and computer systems from crackers.

- ❏ An ethical hacker is a security professional who applies hacking skills for defensive purposes. This person accesses a computer system or network with the authorization of the system's owner, and without causing damage to the system.

REVIEW QUESTIONS

1. Using the W/B Hat model, which hacker is more likely to make up a Web site to teach new hackers how to hack a network?

2. Using the W/B Hat model, which hacker is most likely to work as a network administrator?

3. Using the W/B Hat model, which hacker is most likely to share information?

4. Using the W/B Hat model, which hacker is selling credit card numbers to criminals online?

5. Short Essay: When presenting a talk to a group of business leaders, are you more likely to use the W/B Hat model to explain the dangers posed by hackers or the Hacker Profiles model? If the business leaders were the Chief Information Officers of their respective companies, would you reverse your decision?

6. If your Web site is hacked and all the pages call up the same anti-war slogan and picture, which profile of hacker has hit your site?

7. If it is discovered that the CEO's e-mail browser is set to automatically copy all her outgoing mail to an unknown account called *asmith@thecompany.com*, what profile of hacker is probably responsible?

8. What Hacker Profile tries out attack scripts found on the Internet, "just to see what happens?"

9. Name a trend that has arisen from the hacker mindset of the 1950s.

10. What are the motivations for the Hacker Profile "professional criminal?"

Indicate whether the sentence or statement is true or false.

11. _____ As a security tester, you can make a network impenetrable.

12. _____ An ethical hacker is a person who performs most of the same activities a cracker does, but only late at night.

13. _____ The SysAdmin, Audit, Network, Security (SANS) Institute offers training and IT security certifications through Global Information Assurance Certification (GIAC).

14. _____ The GIAC program offers a certification that focuses on reverse-engineering malware.

15. _____ All states look at port scanning as noninvasive or nondestructive in nature and deem it legal.

16. _____ Old-Guard hackers brag incessantly about their successful exploits.

Match each term with the correct statement below.

    a. script

    b. port scanning

    c. novice

    d. ethical hacker

17. _____ Way to find open ports on a system.

18. _____ Copies code from knowledgeable programmers instead of creating the code himself/herself.

19. _____ Set of instructions that runs in sequence to perform tasks on a computer system.

20. _____ Sometimes employed by companies to perform penetration tests.

Hands-On Project

HANDS-ON PROJECTS

Project 1-1

In this project you will set up the Linux computer that you will be using in many of the projects throughout the book. You will need the following:

❑ An x86 computer with a minimum of 256MB RAM, the equivalent of a Pentium III 900 MHz processor or better, a 20GB hard drive, a 56K phone modem, and a 10/100 Ethernet network interface card. Please note that these specifications should be viewed as minimum requirements; you will get better performance if you have more RAM, a faster processor, and so on.

❑ A current version of a popular, robust Linux distribution, such as Fedora, Red Hat Enterprise, CentOS, Mandriva, SUSE, or Ubuntu. The hands-on projects in this book assume an installation of Fedora Core 6, and the steps are written accordingly. However, other Linux distributions can be used, with minor modifications to the steps, as needed.

❑ An Internet connection

1. Perform a default installation of the Linux OS. For the purposes of this book, you won't need to review or customize partitions, and can accept the default partitioning scheme that the installation program selects.

2. When installation is complete, use the OS's package manager to install any available software updates. This will help ensure that your system contains important security updates and bug fixes. For example, in Fedora, you can start the update process by entering `yum update` at a Terminal window (you'll need to log in as root), or by clicking **Applications**, pointing to **System Tools**, and clicking **Software Updater** to run the Software Updater program.

REFERENCES

1. Kelly, W. 1982, "The Best of Pogo", Edited by Mrs. Walt Kelly and Bill Crouch Jr. *A Fireside Book*, published by Simon & Schuster, retrieved from http://www.igopogo.com/final_authority.htm.

2. Figure 1-2 and its accompanying descriptions of hacker profiles are taken from: Bednarz, Ann. "Profiling cybercriminals: A promising but immature science." *Network World* 29 November 2004, http://www.networkworld.com/supp/2004/cybercrime/112904profile.html, citing Marcus Rogers's original research.

3. Mitnick, Kevin. "They call me a criminal." *Guardian Unlimited* 22 February 2000. http://www.guardian.co.uk/Archive/Article/0,4273,3966123,00.html.

4. *The Jargon File*, version 4.4.7, http://www.catb.org/jargon/html/H/hacker-ethic.html.

2

RECONNAISSANCE

After reading this chapter and completing the exercises, you will be able to:

♦ Identify various techniques for performing reconnaissance

♦ Distinguish and discuss the methods used in social engineering

♦ Discuss the importance of dumpster diving in reconnaissance

♦ Identify a variety of phases of Internet footprinting

There are several techniques to discover viable targets. These techniques fall within three main tactical classes, and in turn these three classes make up the strategies available in the universe of reconnaissance. Figure 2-1 illustrates an organizational model of some of the reconnaissance methods described in this chapter.

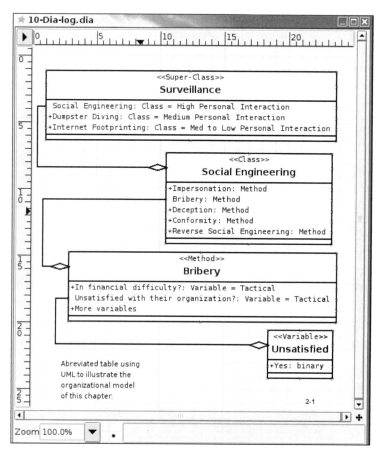

Figure 2-1   Abridged organization chart

Reconnaissance is the act of locating targets and developing the methods necessary to attack those targets successfully. Hackers collect such information as the physical location of the target; data about the users at the facility; administrative short-cuts (such as giving the same password to all new accounts and expecting the user to change the password later); operating systems; network structure; hardware configuration; available services; business strategies; employee phone lists; the staffing structure of the organization; internal newsletters; and all available published information about the company, either on its Web site or by other writers. This information allows a hacker to understand the weaknesses and security vulnerabilities of her targets. This collected information helps hackers identify the best possible techniques, methods, and tools to conduct attacks.

Reconnaissance may be extremely flexible and creative. Reconnaissance is not by definition illegal, and many reconnaissance techniques are completely legal.

Some Legal Reconnaissance

Looking up all of the information about a company available on the Internet, including published phone numbers, office hours, and addresses, is completely legal. Calling with a problem requiring customer service assistance is completely legal (even if it is a made-up problem). Interviewing a member of the staff for a school project is legal. Physical entry of a facility, including attending a tour of the facility, is entirely legal. Making friends with somebody who works there or used to work there is also legal. It would be exceptionally paranoid for company representatives to refuse to answer the phone "just in case it is a hacker performing recon." All of these methods and many others are completely legal and done for various reasons all the time.

Some Questionable Reconnaissance

Local laws vary, but in much of the world, performing a passive port scan is legal. Reading the names on the mail sitting on a mail cart or scanning the document lying loose on a desk may be legal. Picking up trash in the parking lot and looking at it before you toss it out or give it to a company representative is probably legal. Picking up a copy of the company employee newsletter is probably legal. Asking for a phone list or a business card or product specs is probably legal. Looking through a garbage can is probably legal. Physical stake-out to discover the movements of key individuals might be illegal; however, if the hacker is not trespassing or otherwise attracting attention, it may not be. "War driving"—checking for unsecured wireless networks—is legal in some places and not in others. Since you cannot be sure where the information you need may be located, you may find it sensible to attempt many mild tactics rather than attempting a known criminal act that might not net you any more information than a legal or questionable act would.

Some Illegal Reconnaissance

There are a number of plainly illegal reconnaissance techniques. Developing a "front" company and acting as a representative of that company, specifically for the purpose of robbing or defrauding the target company, is probably illegal. Furthermore, being expensive and time consuming, this is probably reserved for the professional intel agencies. Stealing garbage is illegal in many locales. Entering a home or office to look for information is also illegal, but this often goes undetected as no valuables are being removed. Dropping a keylogger—a tool that records users' keystrokes—on a vulnerable machine is illegal. Leaving a sniffer, which can intercept and read data packets, on a network is illegal.

When practicing reconnaissance, it is important to remember that any information about the target is potentially of value. During the collection phase of reconnaissance, hackers are not able to predict how that information can be used. Therefore, hackers strive to gather every detail, all e-mails, passwords, phone numbers, and codes.

Depending upon the technology used and the nature of the investigation, reconnaissance methods can be classified into three types. They are social engineering, dumpster diving, and

Internet footprinting. Each of these reconnaissance classifications are composed of various methods that exist at various levels of risk and legality. Hackers use these methods, together or separately, to collect information about their targets.

SOCIAL ENGINEERING

Social engineering works, for the most part, because people are trusting and helpful. This "flaw" in our social conditioning is at the heart of all social interaction, and we have not yet developed a mindset of security in our children or in ourselves. Suspiciousness and selfishness are not traits we teach our preschoolers, and—not surprisingly—they do not fall in the comfort zone of most adults. Security policies and vulnerability checks provide basic and limited protection for information. The weakest link in any security scheme is the user. Each person must be responsible for guarding his username and complex password; careful with his paperwork, files, and phone conversations; and selective about the circle of people whom he trusts. The fact that people don't wish to be mistrustful is why the social engineer has such an easy time getting information in most organizations.

Kevin Mitnick is a well-known hacker who was known for his social engineering skills. In his book, *The Art of Deception* Mitnick states, "Social engineering uses influence and persuasion to deceive people by convincing them that the social engineer is someone he isn't, or by manipulation. As a result, the social engineer is able to take advantage of people to obtain information with or without the use of technology."[1] While the ILOVEYOU attack was a virus attack, it also used social engineering—exploiting the weakness that curious people are likely to click on an e-mail attachment.

The success or failure of social engineering depends on the ability of hackers to manipulate human psychology, contacts, and physical workstations.

Social Engineering Techniques

To access information about individuals, a social engineer must gain the trust or acquiescence of that person. This is done by deploying any of the following social engineering techniques:

- Impersonation
- Bribery
- Deception
- Conformity
- Reverse social engineering

Impersonation

Impersonation could be at an instance level, such as impersonating Tom Cruise to get into a cool nightclub; or it could be on a role or function level, such as dressing like a service

2

person to get past the controls at the front gate at Disney World. In our usage, an instance-level impostor must know the name of a real employee and have at least some of the ID connected to that person. This is pretty difficult, and has the drawback that one might encounter somebody who knows the person being impersonated. Function-level imposture is easier and might require less preparation for the reconnaissance. In either case, the hacker poses as a legitimate user or an employee who has the authority to collect information.

Examples of this include:

- A social engineer approaches a user, claiming to be a system administrator or an IT support executive, and then asks for passwords.

- An impersonator wearing a baseball cap with the name of a local phone company on it and dressing as a phone company technician could well get into a locked wiring closet unaccompanied.

- A phone call from an impersonator stating that the system is acting erratically and that the victim must authenticate his or her username and password for verification could easily induce a flow of sensitive information.

- A social engineer posing as a flustered, uncertain, but legitimate user makes a phone call to a help desk and asks for information. The information may be given with no security check.

- A social engineer might call the third-shift sysadmin at 6:30 a.m. claiming to be the IT director (who never sees the office until 10:00 a.m.) and request that he or she run a specific line of code on the command line of the mail server.

Before engaging in this kind of social engineering, a hacker usually performs basic research about the target company to avoid creating suspicion.

Bribery

Bribery can be an effective way to collect information. A hacker can pit a person's greed and ignorance against his loyalty to the organization. Blackmail is a common tactic to keep a target employee fruitful. For this technique, a social engineer looks for specific traits in an employee:

- Is he or she of a level in the company that might have useful information?

- Is he or she in financial difficulty?

- Is he or she struggling with an exploitable addiction, such as gambling, alcohol, or drugs?

- Is he or she unsatisfied with the organization?

- Is he or she focused on a short-term gain with the company?

- Is he or she morally elastic?

All of these are excellent target features, and even more so if they appear in groups within a target informant. This is a time-consuming technique, requiring quite a lot of research on the target individual. This technique also carries a potentially expensive front-end. After and during the research, the hacker will probably be required to invest somewhat in the person or persons being bribed. The major risk in this technique is that the employee so primed and ready to perform may be unable to provide useful information or might change his mind—either before or after that segment of the plan is complete. The hacker's risk level stays high, and there is at least one individual within the organization who knows some foul plan is in effect.

Deception

Deception is a method of achieving access to information by actually joining the organization as an employee or a consultant. This system pits the "virtuous" hacker against the "evil" company, and requires a goodly helping of self-delusion on the part of the hacker.

Conformity

This method hinges on the general tendency of people to believe that an *apparent* similarity between themselves and another (unknown) person is an *actual* similarity. The hacker convinces the victim that they have a lot in common and that they share the same values. The hacker becomes the victim's good friend by appearing honest, trustworthy, and friendly. This is a person in whom one may truly confide. Once the information is garnered, the "good friend" just disengages.

Reverse Social Engineering

The hacker projects herself as an authority vested with the power to solve peoples' problems. Reverse social engineering requires quite a bit of planning and research. This is a sting operation, where all of the victim's experiences are manufactured or manipulated by the hacker.

- First the hacker manufactures a problem, such as a DoS attack that shuts down the network for a time.

- Then the hacker advertises himself as an expert who can solve this sort of problem. The victim might be prompted to communicate with the hacker for relief, and the hacker uses this opportunity to solve the victim's problem.

- Now the hacker is believed to be a trusted assistant or expert in the field of network security, and he is given more and more access to the network in question, including many critical systems.

- The hacker collects information from many users and might install hidden running processes on the systems to which he has access.

Most social engineering attacks are opportunistic: the hacker uses whatever technique he or she thinks fits the situation. Impersonating a user and calling a help desk for assistance might not work if the aim is to collect confidential information from a sysop. All social engineering techniques are affected by physical entry into the target organization or by communication with the victims within the organization.

Physical Intrusion

The foremost traditional technique of social engineering is physical intrusion, whereby social engineers physically enter the premises of an organization or the workstations of employees for the sole purpose of collecting information. Any unauthorized entry plan uses the same kinds of research and reconnaissance.

"Casing the joint" before a physical intrusion usually includes:

- Learning the schedules of the organization
- Knowing the floor plan of the building or buildings
- "Baselining" the security procedures

Learning the schedules or pattern of the organization includes knowing which people are likely to be there at all times, their jobs, and their work style. It is good to know who holds which keys and where these people are at various times of the day. The more a hacker knows of the usual behaviors of the people in a building or organization, the less likely the hacker will act in a way that sets off alarms—either intruder alarms or the employees' intuitions.

Knowing the floor plan lets a hacker get to the right place quickly while under stress during the actual intrusion. As in any complex plan, the less left to chance and improvisation, the better the results.

Knowing the security measures that are in place also lets hackers know where the security falls down. A social engineer normally has close contact with an inside employee before entering an organization, and the hacker gets a lot of baseline information from that employee. The friendly employee is likely to be unaware of the useful information she knows, and will consider divulged information to be just "office war stories." These "war stories" let the hacker know the company's physical security, network security, and response policy to intrusion. There is no reason to assume that a single hacker cannot have multiple contacts within an organization; he or she could have a network of interested friends within the firewall of a company.

Once the hacker acquires some information about the organization, he or she can develop fake identification cards. Many companies use a laminated card with the employee's information on it. This is very easy to duplicate with a word processor and a laminator at a copy shop. The social engineer must decide whether to pose as an employee, a contractor, or an authority, and make the appropriate ID. Large companies with lots of employees, contractors, and social churn are the easiest to infiltrate. Since nobody is expecting an attack, no one will challenge a properly dressed individual with authentic-looking identification, confidence, and knowledge of the building and organization. Of course there is a possibility that plain old breaking and entering may be the best tactic, making the ID unnecessary.

The last step is to acquire useful or valuable information. Through the development of a viable backstory, the hacker was able to spend a good amount of time in the building unattended, where he or she acquired all the information available using minimally intrusive methods. Now it's possible to add keyloggers or sniffers to local computers, to jimmy desk-drawer locks, or to break into filing cabinets looking for business documents and passwords. There are several methods for easily gathering information without alarming other employees. Many users write down their passwords and keep them in plain view, or store them in their local computers. A hacker may also just watch users while they type passwords and business documents.

How do social engineers perform these physical intrusion activities without generating any suspicion? They never collect all the required information from a single user or source, and they never hold a position after the value of the position has ended. The more valuable the information is, the more likely hackers are working with a team or with backing that funds their efforts. Corporate espionage is alive and well.

At times when physical intrusion is not a possibility because of a distributed corporate presence or a strong security perimeter, hackers use communication media. Communication media helps social engineers perform their activities remotely, thus causing less suspicion.

Communication Media

Social engineers use postal mail, e-mail, instant messaging, and telephone communication to get useful information from target individuals within an organization. Let us briefly overview these various media and examine how they are used by hackers.

Postal Mail

A venerable medium of communication, postal mail is a powerful tool for social engineers to gather personal information about users. In a typical attack, the victim receives a letter announcing that he or she has won a prize. The content of the mailer is very professional and slick. The user is given several ways to respond with verification details in order to receive the prize. The mailer asks for tax information, phone numbers, e-mail addresses, and other information. The greed engendered by the idea of winning a prize leads the victim to happily surrender all sorts of information, which is then used to further victimize the user. What differentiates this attack from a typical mailing by a genuine mail-order house is that the genuine mailer is a bulk send manufactured to appear less like a bulk send, and a mail attack is probably sent only to the specific victim. This technique is not illegal, but some of the subsequent uses of the information may be.

E-Mail

E-mail is used in a variety of scams and false offerings, but in this chapter we will look at using e-mail for three purposes.

A social engineer can send an e-mail purported to be from a legitimate IT e-mail account, such as from the network administrator, but use a return e-mail address of the hacker. This e-mail claims there is a problem to be fixed, and the user must send his or her password to help with the solution. Most legitimate administrators and technicians are constantly fending off unrequested username and password combinations, volunteered by users who think they need to provide this information to have their problem resolved. A legitimate administrator never needs a password to troubleshoot a user's login issues; nevertheless, the social engineer's trick of asking for this information as though it were needed to fix a problem is often successful.

Another trick is to send e-mail message invitations to join online competitions for receiving prizes. In these cases, a social engineer attaches forms that must be filled out by users for joining the competition. The form requests information such as usernames, phone numbers, passwords, and social security numbers. Users fall for this trick out of the desire to win a prize or money. Many people have the same username and password for multiple online accounts; thus, by providing this information, they jeopardize all of their accounts that use these username/password combinations.

The final ploy is called **phishing**, in which a user is tricked into giving private information about his or her account with a known large organization. Figure 2-2 shows a very obvious phishing form that might be found by following a link claiming to keep a citizen's information safe.

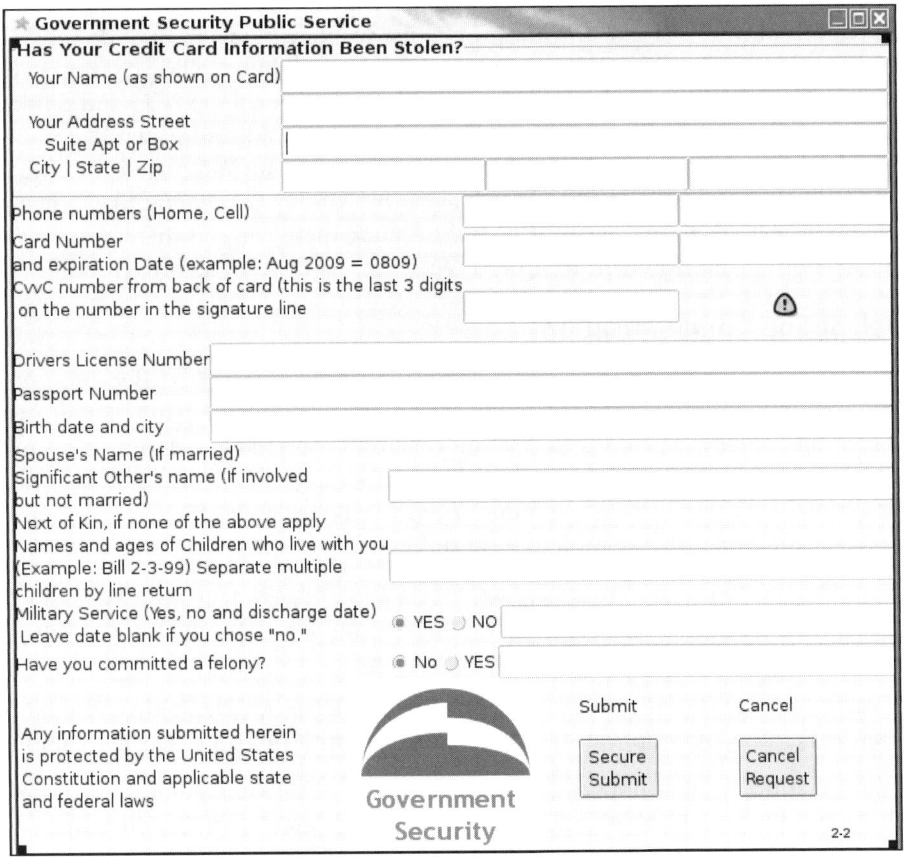

Government Security Public Service

Has Your Credit Card Information Been Stolen?

Your Name (as shown on Card)

Your Address Street

Suite Apt or Box

City | State | Zip

Phone numbers (Home, Cell)

Card Number
and expiration Date (example: Aug 2009 = 0809)

CVVC number from back of card (this is the last 3 digits
on the number in the signature line

Drivers License Number

Passport Number

Birth date and city

Spouse's Name (If married)

Significant Other's name (If involved
but not married)

Next of Kin, if none of the above apply

Names and ages of Children who live with you
(Example: Bill 2-3-99) Separate multiple
children by line return

Military Service (Yes, no and discharge date) YES NO
Leave date blank if you chose "no."

Have you committed a felony? No YES

Submit Cancel

Any information submitted herein
is protected by the United States
Constitution and applicable state
and federal laws

Government
Security

Secure Submit

Cancel Request

2-2

Figure 2-2 An obvious phishing form

Internet sites are used as platforms for phishing expeditions, as well as for phony "prize-distribution" ploys. It is very easy to make plausible, professional Web sites in very little time. It is so easy, in fact, that it is sometimes difficult to tell the phishing sites from the genuine ones. Users should watch for whether their form is an https page, indicating it uses encryption to guard sent data. The fake sites probably don't care if data is at risk during transmission and so will not provide any safeguards. Users should not send sensitive data to sites with which they are not well acquainted. Phishing sites take advantage of users' tendency to employ the same username and password for many similar sites, then they go looking for the other sites to which the users are subscribed.

Instant Messaging

Instant messaging hacking scripts are prevalent in many public IM platforms. Here, the social engineer attempts to befriend the victim to gather information or send the victim to a Web link she might be likely to visit. Usually these sites are pornography-related. Genuine people usually contact each other through mutual friends or by searching profiles for pertinent keywords. Random contacts that are actual people with legitimate interests declare their intentions outright: "I saw on your profile that you like model trains. I do too. How do you make miniature farm animals for your trains?" They might be selling toy horses, but they say that up front. In contrast, there are automated scripts that run on ICQ and YahooIM. These are interesting in that it is possible to have a 20-minute IM session with a set of automated responses, but they are easy to catch, as well. Since they are automated, they are not able to respond to open-ended questions, such as "What kind of tea do you like?" Their responses are noticeably inappropriate, so it is easy to block them early in the conversation. It is also possible to set the IM client to only accept contacts from an approved list.

Telephone Communication

Telephone communication has the advantage of being familiar. Because people are so familiar with telephone communication and often take it for granted, it is easy to use a telephone to mislead people. Social engineers may manipulate background sounds and their own voice to produce a required effect. Hackers with brusque voices and heavy accents may be less effective in eliciting a response from the target individual, so the social engineer's voice is often made to sound feminine and light.

Help desk personnel are vulnerable targets because they are required to give information to people quickly and with a minimum of digression. They are often under time pressure to successfully answer as many calls as they can.

If calling an end user, it is often more effective to call another employee and be transferred. This makes the caller appear more trustworthy than if he had called the victim directly.

Social engineers often impersonate technicians who are contacting target users to inform them that they might have been overbilled for telephone charges. After they convince the user to accept that premise, they ask for more personal information, which can then be used to cost the victim money and time.

Countering Social Engineering

To prevent or mitigate social engineering, you must educate the users. Education must be included in your security policy, and new users must be aware of the policy. All users in a system must take the following steps to counter social engineering attempts:

- Do not provide any information to unknown people.
- Do not disclose any confidential information to anyone over the telephone.
- Do not type passwords or other confidential information in front of unknown people.
- Do not submit information to any insecure Web site.
- Do not use the same username and password for all accounts.
- Verify the credentials of persons asking for passwords, and recognize that authentic administrators often do not need your password to access your files.
- Keep confidential documents locked.
- Lock or shut down computers when away from the workstation.
- Instruct help desk employees to provide information only after they have gained proper authentication.

Dumpster Diving

Dumpster diving is often the mother lode of sensitive information as well as actual hardware and software. Hackers look specifically for sales receipts and paperwork that contain personal data or credit card information. This information can be sold to others who will do damage with it, or it can be used by the hacker himself. Shredded documents can lead to data leaks when all the shredders are strip shredders, and the resultant strips are disposed of in a single bag. Although crosscut shredders are more secure, the complicated jigsaw puzzle they create can be reconstructed by whomever wishes to put in the time. Many people believe that all companies carefully shred and dispose of their personal information, but this is not necessarily true. In many places, documents considered less sensitive are dropped directly into publicly available receptacles. Drafts of letters, even mail-merge documents with hundreds of recipients, are routinely left whole in the trash. Company directory sheets, catalog lists, unused or misprinted labels, and policy manuals are not recognized as sensitive data, so they are loose in the trash. Consider the consequences of a criminal retrieving this misprinted information. They are not concerned with the aesthetics of the documents; they are interested in the names and addresses, phone numbers, and employee IDs that appear there. These documents aid in all sorts of hacking techniques.

Importance of Proper Discarding of Refuse

The security policy must carefully address what is sensitive information and what isn't, and decide how to treat refuse. Some documents may not be considered sensitive, like employee handbooks and company policy statements. But these can often tell hackers what physical and network security to expect when doing intrusion. The best solution to theft of trash paper is to crosscut-shred it and keep it in locked trash receptacles.

Old hardware cannot be shredded and takes up space; thus, these items are frequently thrown out, or given to employees to take home. Hackers search for outdated hardware, such as tapes, CD-ROMs, and hard disks. There are various tools available to hackers, such as forensics programs, that can restore data from damaged data-storage devices.

Prevention of Dumpster Diving

The following guidelines will help prevent these attacks or mitigate their value to the attacker.

- Develop a written recycling and trash-handling policy, connected to other security policies.

- Use the policy to develop a consistent, systematic method for handling trash.

- The trash-handling policy should state that all papers be shredded. Crosscut shredders with narrow cuts are the best because they minimize the possibility of reconstructing documents.

- Erase all data from tapes, floppies, and hard disks. Since data can be recovered even from formatted hard disks and tapes, it is suggested that the policy stipulate that the application employed to erase media use at least government-approved wiping algorithms. This feature overwrites data with other random data more than eight times, therefore minimizing hackers' success in salvaging information.

- Simply breaking CD-ROMs is not sufficient, as data can be recovered from broken disks. Placing them in a microwave and heating them destroys the integrity of the substrate and makes the data irrecoverable.

INTERNET FOOTPRINTING

Internet footprinting is a technical method of **reconnaissance**, which interests budding hackers and network security specialists alike. Hackers like this method because it is clean, legal, and safe, and security students often choose it over all other methods of surveillance. This kind of profiling helps us to understand the Internet, intranet, and remote-access setups of the target system. It is easy to implement and almost undetectable by the victim.

There are four methods used in Internet footprinting.

- Web searching
- Network enumeration

- Domain Name System (DNS)–based reconnaissance
- Network-based reconnaissance

Web Searching

Internet footprinting requires collecting useful information about the target system. These days, the majority of organizations have Web sites containing crucial information. All of the material available from company Web sites is legally available, even if some of it is sensitive.

Hackers use some specific tools to find out about potential targets, such as:

- E-mail
- Search engines
- Hypertext Markup Language (HTML) source code
- Newsgroups
- Security-related Web sites
- Newsletters

None of these sources are protected, except some newsgroups that are "invitation only" and some Web sites that are membership sites, requiring levels of authentication from e-mail and IP address to full name and street address. Some membership sites are "pay sites," meaning that there is a payment schedule to view the site contents. The fact that a site is a pay site does not guarantee that it is also a site requiring a high level of authentication to achieve membership.

Search Engines

Search engines can be used to collect information about any subject or organization. The purpose of search engines is to help people obtain relevant information by submitting simple queries. People with more knowledge can discover far more than basic information. For example, a hacker wants to attack an organization located in Atlanta. The hacker needs to collect as much information about the company as she possibly can, and the basics are available through search engines. Public information, which may seem harmless, can actually aid hackers. There are hundreds of search engines available on the Internet. Some of the famous ones are google.com, yahoo.com, altavista.com, overture.com (acquired by Yahoo), alltheweb.com, ask.com, and ixquick.com.

Using a search engine, such as Google, to find disgruntled employees who might complain about a targeted company might lead to some information that allows the hacker to infiltrate the company. Consider the implications of the following searches:

About 28,700,000 results returned for **Google employer**

About 224,000 results returned for **Google employer terminated**

About 1,190,000 results returned for **Google employer fraud**

If you were using Google as a possible avenue for hacking a company, there might be something here. Any company or organization is vulnerable to innocent searches.

The pages that end up indexed on search engines and the refresh rate of the databases therein vary widely. Many pages stay in the indexes of search engines long after the actual page is taken down, and some specialized search engines, such as www.waybackmachine.org, keep copies of sites going back through many years of changes to those sites.

HTML Source Code

You can view the source code of any Web page from the View, View Source (or Page Source) drop-down menu in your browser. In Firefox, the frames are also displayed on the page. Not all pages are useful, and pages displayed by server-side programming—such as ColdFusion, ASP.NET, JavaServer Pages (.jsp), or PHP Hypertext Processor (PHP)—are absolutely nothing like the code that produced them. How can the HTML source code help a hacker? For a hacker, the area of interest in an HTML source code is its comment entries and the hints of the organization of the site. These may provide critical information about the target. The HTML code for a Submit button on a Web page could contain a comment specifying the database where the information about users is stored, or some hint as to username and password details. Knowing the format of usernames or passwords can be useful, just as knowing the organization of the site can be useful. One helpful hint for you to use on your own Web sites is to have a default or an index page in every subdirectory—for example, ADatabaseSite/Admin/Modules/index.htm—so a blank index.htm page appears when somebody attempts to test a subdirectory, rather than a list of the directory contents. This particular directory structure is from an open source PHP application. The designers put blank index.htm files in all of the code folders, so even if a hacker got into the folder, there would be nothing for him or her to see. Files that tell Web spiders what to index and what not to index are designed to keep search engine spiders from indexing sensitive material, and they do not work if the spider is designed by a hacker to index everything.

Newsgroups

Newsgroups are a relic of the 1980s technology that used to constitute the Web. They are text-based online groups in which users discuss subjects that interest them. Newsgroups are part of an online bulletin board system called USENET, which contains groups covering a huge variety of subjects. Hackers read postings in newsgroups to, among other things, discover information and documents relating to targeted systems, such as their software, hardware, and technical abilities. Google bought deja.com's USENET archives that go back to the beginning of USENET, and these can be found at groups.google.com. To access newsgroups, type in "newsgroups" or "USENET" in any search engine, or subscribe through most e-mail browsers.

Security-Related Web Sites

To say there are several Web sites that provide information about security tools and vulnerabilities would be a slight understatement. Results for a recent search of the phrase "security or hacker Web sites" (without the quotes) returned 60,100,000 entries. Hackers study these Web sites to learn about new developments in information security, especially about new exploits. If a hacker finds an exploit, and she has footprinted a couple of networks that have the hardware or software in which the vulnerability was discovered, then she may well have between a few hours and a few months to exploit the vulnerability before the vendor develops a patch and the administrators deploy the patch. Most of the major exploits in 2004 and 2005 were old vulnerabilities—12- to 30-month-old exploits.

Newsletters

Newsletters, especially security and security alert newsletters, provide cutting-edge developments to hackers. More general-purpose newsletters, like Slashdot and various development bug-tracking newsletters, also provide useful information. In most cases, these newsletters are available free of charge except for the cost of receiving an occasional ad from the site. The newsletters are automatically e-mailed to individuals.

During and after the Web-search and data-acquisition phase, hackers work on identifying IP ranges, domain names, and devices on the network they are attempting to breach. Hackers frequently use network enumeration for this task.

Network Enumeration

Network enumeration is the process of identifying domain names as well as other resources on the target network. Hackers try to gather specific information in the enumeration phase. Items of value are IP addresses of the computers and the contact persons of the target network. Hackers use a tool called WHOIS in order to gather this data.

WHOIS Search

To make a Web site available for Internet users, a domain name must be registered with InterNIC through a certified registrar. InterNIC shows this list on its Web site at www.internic.net/regist.html. To register a domain name, one must fill out a form containing contact details, information about the DNS servers containing the IP address of the Web server, and more. All domain records have a unique identifier field called the handle. If there were no unique identifier, the entire DNS system would be suspect, meaning that there could be more than one specific address for any given Web site.

WHOIS is an Internet tool that aids in retrieving domain name–specific information from the NSI Registrar database. The WHOIS tool has different options that allow individuals to query the NSI Registrar database, based on different fields. It can be accessed from several different Web sites, such as www.netsol.com and www.dnsstuff.com.

Figure 2-3 displays the interface of the WHOIS tool on the Web site www.dnsstuff.com, in addition to other tools.

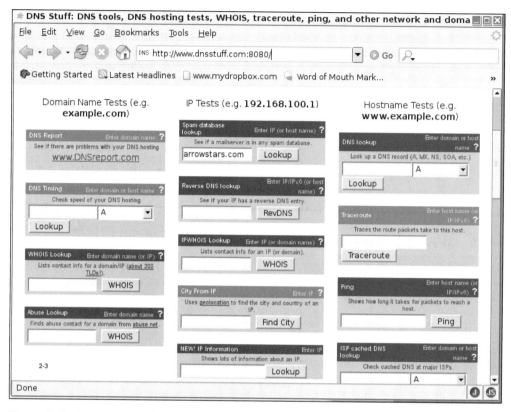

Figure 2-3 WHOIS interface on www.dnsstuff.com

The WHOIS tool allows the InterNIC database to be queried by using the domain name, NIC handle, person's name, IP address, nameserver, or any combination of the fields. The default query option is the domain name field.

When hackers enter the query item in the text box and submit it, these tools search the entire universe of DNS Registrar databases until a match is found. There are, at the time of this writing, 666 certified registrars listed on the InterNIC Web site.

Once the WHOIS tool finds a matching entry in the Registrar database, it displays the information about the searched item. The results may include:

- The address of the registrant
- Domain name
- Administrative contact information, with names, phone numbers, and e-mail addresses
- Technical contact information, with names, phone numbers, and e-mail addresses
- Domain servers, with names and IP addresses

- Date and time of record creation
- Date and time when the record was last modified

Hackers use the WHOIS tool first to extract critical data about their target system and then to conduct hacking activities. If the hacker can find the technical contact on a Web site, he might be able to use that information to conduct social engineering attacks on the company or one of its contractors. Remember, trusted partner companies, clients, and contractors are all potential paths into a target company.

whois CLI Command

The WHOIS Web application is also available at the command-line interface (CLI) of POSIX systems like UNIX, Solaris, and Linux as the command *whois [options] [target]*.

Figure 2-4 shows the options of the *whois* command.

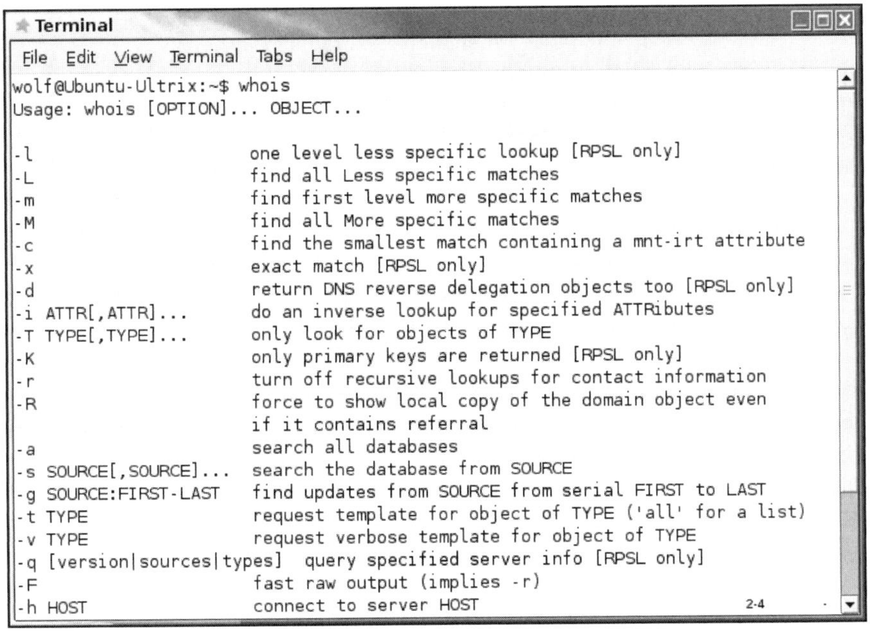

```
★ Terminal                                                          □□▣
 File  Edit  View  Terminal  Tabs  Help
wolf@Ubuntu-Ultrix:~$ whois
Usage: whois [OPTION]... OBJECT...

-l                         one level less specific lookup [RPSL only]
-L                         find all Less specific matches
-m                         find first level more specific matches
-M                         find all More specific matches
-c                         find the smallest match containing a mnt-irt attribute
-x                         exact match [RPSL only]
-d                         return DNS reverse delegation objects too [RPSL only]
-i ATTR[,ATTR]...          do an inverse lookup for specified ATTRibutes
-T TYPE[,TYPE]...          only look for objects of TYPE
-K                         only primary keys are returned [RPSL only]
-r                         turn off recursive lookups for contact information
-R                         force to show local copy of the domain object even
                           if it contains referral
-a                         search all databases
-s SOURCE[,SOURCE]...      search the database from SOURCE
-g SOURCE:FIRST-LAST       find updates from SOURCE from serial FIRST to LAST
-t TYPE                    request template for object of TYPE ('all' for a list)
-v TYPE                    request verbose template for object of TYPE
-q [version|sources|types] query specified server info [RPSL only]
-F                         fast raw output (implies -r)
-h HOST                    connect to server HOST                        2-4
```

Figure 2-4   CLI view of the *whois* command (on Ubuntu Linux)

Domain Name System (DNS)–Based Reconnaissance

When a Web site is launched, normally the Address bar shows the host name, for instance, www.somedomain.com. This is also referred to as a *friendly name* because it is easily readable by human eyes. IP addresses used by TCP/IP are not so easily read. The systems that run the Internet use only the IP address—either dotted decimal IPv4 addresses such as 71.81.18.32 or IPv6 addresses such as 2002:4751:1220::1/48. Therefore, a host name has to be converted into an IP address in order to connect to the requested host. A DNS server is responsible for resolving host names to corresponding IP addresses.

When you type a host name, the Web browser connects to the primary DNS server—either the DHCP-assigned DNS server or a manually assigned DNS server of the LAN administrator's choice—to resolve the IP address. If the primary DNS server is not able to resolve the IP address, it sends the request to a remote DNS server, known as the secondary DNS server. When a secondary DNS server resolves the IP address, the primary DNS server updates its database with that IP address mapping. This allows a primary DNS server to resolve the IP address the next time, without having to contact the secondary DNS server.

There are techniques which assist network troubleshooters and hackers in extracting information about a DNS server and the host names that are resolved by that DNS server. The most important DNS-based reconnaissance techniques are DNS lookup and DNS zone transfer.

DNS Lookup

DNS lookup tools help Internet users discover the DNS names of target computers. Hackers can perform this type of lookup based on either the host name or the IP address. There are several Web sites that provide DNS lookup tools, including the following:

- www.dnsstuff.com

- www.network-tools.com

- www.networksolutions.com

DNS Zone Transfer

Every DNS server has a name space, known as a zone. A zone stores data about domain names. Zone transfer is a DNS feature that lets a DNS server update its database with the list of domain names in another DNS server. The purpose of zone transfer is to permit a secondary DNS server to update its database with the records in the database of the primary DNS server. Zone transfer helps a secondary DNS server provide DNS services to users whenever a primary DNS server is not functioning properly.

An incorrectly configured DNS server may allow any Internet user to perform a zone transfer. The consequences of such activities are critical because an Internet user with malicious intent can transfer the information in the zone and then use it to collect information for hacking purposes.

Hackers use these commands to perform a DNS zone transfer:

- *nslookup*

- *host*

- *dig*

2

nslookup   The program *nslookup* allows anyone to query a DNS server for information, such as host names and IP addresses. The *nslookup* command can be used in both Windows and Linux operating systems. If you execute *nslookup* without arguments or options, the program displays data that is related to the default nameserver. This mode of *nslookup* is the interactive mode.

You can also use the *nslookup* command to gather information about hosts other than the default nameservers. The name or the IP address of the target host must be specified for this activity. This mode of *nslookup* is the noninteractive mode. In noninteractive mode, the *nslookup* program scans the DNS server of the specified host and displays the located entries in the zone. You can use various arguments with *nslookup* to customize this information search. To gather information about hosts and IP addresses in a domain, simply use the following syntax:

```
nslookup -type=any domain_name
```

Figure 2-5 shows an example of the output of this code in action. This is the *nslookup* of one of Network Solutions' nameservers.

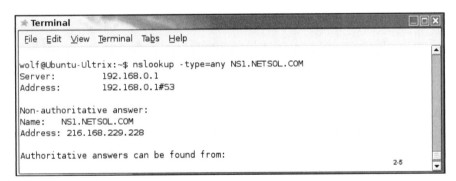

Figure 2-5   *nslookup* for NetworkSolutions.com's NS1 nameserver

In the above syntax, the argument "any" directs *nslookup* to return all types of information about the target. Note that there is no MX or NX information here. That probably means that the mail and news servers are elsewhere. You can store the output of the *nslookup* program, the DNS zone information, on the local computer by storing the output in a text file. To do so, use the following syntax:

```
nslookup -type=any domain_name >file_name
```

host   The *host* command is a utility program that permits you to perform DNS lookup. The base *host* command gives you the information (done in verbose mode), as shown in Figure 2-6.

You must specify the domain name as an argument in this command. A server name on which the *host* utility must search for information should also be specified, but the server name is an optional argument. If the server name is not specified, then the *host* utility checks

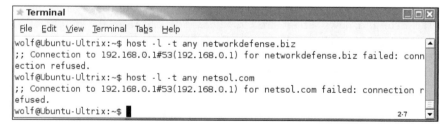

```
 ☀ Terminal                                                        ▢◻▣
File  Edit  View  Terminal  Tabs  Help
wolf@Ubuntu-Ultrix:~$ host -v networksolutions.com                    ▲
Trying "networksolutions.com"
;; ->>HEADER<<- opcode: QUERY, status: NOERROR, id: 16104
;; flags: qr rd ra; QUERY: 1, ANSWER: 1, AUTHORITY: 0, ADDITIONAL: 0

;; QUESTION SECTION:
;networksolutions.com.          IN      A

;; ANSWER SECTION:
networksolutions.com.    300    IN      A       205.178.187.13

Received 54 bytes from 192.168.0.1#53 in 60 ms
Trying "networksolutions.com"
;; ->>HEADER<<- opcode: QUERY, status: NOERROR, id: 21572
;; flags: qr rd ra; QUERY: 1, ANSWER: 0, AUTHORITY: 1, ADDITIONAL: 0

;; QUESTION SECTION:
;networksolutions.com.          IN      AAAA

;; AUTHORITY SECTION:
networksolutions.com.    300    IN      SOA     ns1.netsol.com. dnsadmin.network
solutions.com. 2006042004 7200 3600 604800 3600

Received 94 bytes from 192.168.0.1#53 in 26 ms
Trying "networksolutions.com"
;; connection timed out; no servers could be reached
wolf@Ubuntu-Ultrix:~$                                          2-6    ▼
```

Figure 2-6 *host* lookup for NetworkSolutions.com

the servers listed in the /etc/resolv.conf file. Type in the following syntax to perform a DNS lookup and zone transfer:

```
host -l -t any domain_name
```

In this syntax, the -l option performs the DNS zone transfer activity. The -t any argument helps the *host* utility collect all available information. Figure 2-7 shows an attempted DNS zone transfer.

```
 ☀ Terminal                                                        ▢◻▣
File  Edit  View  Terminal  Tabs  Help
wolf@Ubuntu-Ultrix:~$ host -l -t any networkdefense.biz               ▲
;; Connection to 192.168.0.1#53(192.168.0.1) for networkdefense.biz failed: conn
ection refused.
wolf@Ubuntu-Ultrix:~$ host -l -t any netsol.com
;; Connection to 192.168.0.1#53(192.168.0.1) for netsol.com failed: connection r
efused.
wolf@Ubuntu-Ultrix:~$ ▮                                         2-7    ▼
```

Figure 2-7 Attempted DNS zone transfer

You can also direct the *host* utility to find and gather information about e-mail servers or nameservers. If you want to use the *host* utility to retrieve information about e-mail servers, use the following syntax:

```
host -l -t mx domain_name
```

The following syntax allows you to collect information about nameservers:

```
host -l -t ns domain_name
```

You can store this zone transfer information into a file by using the following syntax:

```
host -l -t any domain_name>file_name
```

dig   Domain information groper (*dig*) is another command that is used to collect DNS-related data. Type the following syntax to collect this DNS information:

```
dig domain_name any
```

DNS-based reconnaissance aids hackers in determining potential computers on the target network. Upon identifying potential target computers, hackers must also identify the network infrastructure of the target network.

Network-Based Reconnaissance

Network-based reconnaissance is the process of identifying active computers and services on a target network. To perform this, hackers use a variety of network utilities, such as *ping, traceroute,* and *netstat.*

ping

This utility is part of the Internet Control Message Protocol (ICMP) and helps to verify whether a host is active. The *ping* utility transmits data packets, known as ICMP echo packets, to the specified host. It then receives packets from that host. If the packets sent and received by the *ping* utility are the same, then the target host is active.

When using the *ping* utility on a host, the host allots some of its memory resources to handle the *ping* query and return packets. This is used by network administrators and users to check if a specific host is reachable while troubleshooting network connectivity. This is also one of the avenues used by hackers to slow down the performance of specific targets by sending thousands of *pings* at the target. The target rises to the occasion by allotting *all* of its memory resources to answering *pings*.

The *ping* command is available for all platforms. There are two *ping* utilities available for a Linux or Unix machine: *ping* and *ping6*. The *ping* utility is the standard IPv4 version, and *ping6* is the IPv6 version. To *ping* on a target host, type the following syntax:

```
ping target_host
```

In this syntax, the `target_host` can be either the host name or the IP address of the target computer. Figure 2-8 shows the basic option sets for *ping* and *ping6*.

You can use three different commands to find a file in UNIX/Linux. The command ***whereis*** shows you where the files appear in your PATH (the directories in which you are allowed to read, write, or execute an application or other file). Another command, ***which***, displays the

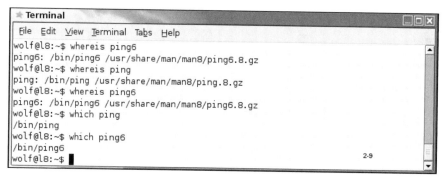

Figure 2-8 Option sets for *ping* and *ping6*

location of the application that will execute when you type its name on the command line. Both of these commands are shown in Figure 2-9. There are many reasons why you might find multiple executable files with the same name—for example, you might be developing an application and have multiple versions in test. However, the default executable (especially those like *ping*, which are installed by default on most POSIX systems) will be in the PATH of almost all users.

```
Terminal
File  Edit  View  Terminal  Tabs  Help
wolf@l8:~$ whereis ping6
ping6: /bin/ping6 /usr/share/man/man8/ping6.8.gz
wolf@l8:~$ whereis ping
ping: /bin/ping /usr/share/man/man8/ping.8.gz
wolf@l8:~$ whereis ping6
ping6: /bin/ping6 /usr/share/man/man8/ping6.8.gz
wolf@l8:~$ which ping
/bin/ping
wolf@l8:~$ which ping6
/bin/ping6
wolf@l8:~$
                                                          2-9
```

Figure 2-9 The *whereis* and *which* commands

The third CLI search command is **locate**. The *locate* command shows all of the displayable file and folder names containing the string designated, including /bin/ping and .../share/isos/ mapping. This can result in lists of hundreds of lines, and is barely useful unless you direct the output to *less, more,* or a named output file, as shown in the following examples:

```
locate [string] | less
locate [string] | more
locate [string] > searchfile_name
```

traceroute

A request for a Web page that resides on a remote server must pass through several servers on its way. In a UNIX–based operating system, you can track all of the intermediate servers by using the **traceroute** command. In Windows operating systems, similar functionality is provided by the **tracert** command. These commands help users and administrators trouble-shoot network connectivity problems. They also help hackers determine the route of data transfer between their computers and their target networks, for the purpose of developing new interim targets and deciding which methods of attack to use.

You can execute the *traceroute* command by specifying the host name or IP address of the target computer, using the following syntax:

```
traceroute target_host
```

To trace the route to a target host while using Windows operating systems, open the Start | Run dialog box, type cmd to open a terminal window, and then type the following syntax:

```
tracert domain_name
```

Figure 2-10 shows an example of the output of *traceroute* and the options of *traceroute*.

TIP In POSIX systems, such as Linux or UNIX, the option -h or --help is about the same as –help or -? in a Windows Terminal emulator running DOS.

In Windows, type *tracert* on the command prompt without any options or target to see the available options.

```
Terminal                                                        _ □ ×
File  Edit  View  Terminal  Tabs  Help
wolf@l8:~$ traceroute 127.0.0.1
traceroute to 127.0.0.1 (127.0.0.1), 30 hops max, 38 byte packets
 1  localhost (127.0.0.1)  0.104 ms  0.057 ms  0.023 ms
wolf@l8:~$ traceroute -h
Version 1.4a12
Usage: traceroute [-dFIlnrvx] [-g gateway] [-i iface] [-f first_ttl]
        [-m max_ttl] [ -p port] [-q nqueries] [-s src_addr] [-t tos]
        [-w waittime] [-z pausemsecs] host [packetlen]
wolf@l8:~$
```

Figure 2-10 Options and sample output of *traceroute* command

netstat

The **netstat** command allows all the Transmission Control Protocol (TCP), User Datagram Protocol (UDP), and IP connections on a computer to be viewed. This command also helps to locate the IP address of computers, the IP addresses of the hosts connected to the computers, and the port of the host to which a computer is connected.

Hackers can use the *netstat* command to extract critical information about an ISP. Further-more, they can discover the IP addresses of the users connected to that ISP.

The *netstat* command provides a variety of options. You can see the options in a UNIX-based operating system by typing either

netstat -h

or

netstat --help

The output is displayed in Figure 2-11 below. To view the *netstat* options in Windows operating systems, simply type the following command at the command prompt:

netstat /?

```
* Terminal                                                              _ □ ×
 File  Edit  View  Terminal  Tabs  Help
wolf@l8:~$ netstat -h
usage: netstat [-veenNcCF] [<Af>] -r         netstat {-V|--version|-h|--help}
       netstat [-vnNcaeol] [<Socket> ...]
       netstat { [-veenNac] -i | [-cnNe] -M | -s }

       -r, --route            display routing table
       -i, --interfaces       display interface table
       -g, --groups           display multicast group memberships
       -s, --statistics       display networking statistics (like SNMP)
       -M, --masquerade       display masqueraded connections

       -v, --verbose          be verbose
       -n, --numeric          don't resolve names
       --numeric-hosts        don't resolve host names
       --numeric-ports        don't resolve port names
       --numeric-users        don't resolve user names
       -N, --symbolic         resolve hardware names
       -e, --extend           display other/more information
       -p, --programs         display PID/Program name for sockets
       -c, --continuous       continuous listing

       -l, --listening        display listening server sockets
       -a, --all, --listening display all sockets (default: connected)
       -o, --timers           display timers
       -F, --fib              display Forwarding Information Base (default)
       -C, --cache            display routing cache instead of FIB

  <Socket>={-t|--tcp} {-u|--udp} {-w|--raw} {-x|--unix} --ax25 --ipx --netrom
  <AF>=Use '-6|-4' or '-A <af>' or '--<af>'; default: inet
  List of possible address families (which support routing):
    inet (DARPA Internet) inet6 (IPv6) ax25 (AMPR AX.25)
    netrom (AMPR NET/ROM) ipx (Novell IPX) ddp (Appletalk DDP)
    x25 (CCITT X.25)
wolf@l8:~$ netstat --help                                          2-11
```

Figure 2-11   Output of the netstat -h command

CHAPTER SUMMARY

- Reconnaissance is the act of locating targets and developing the methods necessary to attack those targets successfully. Reconnaissance techniques are not inherently illegal, and many are completely legal. There are three classifications of reconnaissance methods: social engineering, dumpster diving, and Internet footprinting.

- Social engineering works because people are, for the most part, trusting and helpful. The success or failure of social engineering depends on the hacker's ability to manipulate human psychology, contacts, and physical workstations. Social engineering techniques include impersonation, bribery, deception, conformity, and reverse social engineering. All of these techniques are accomplished through physical entry into the target organization or through communication with users at the target organization.

- To counter social engineering, organizations must establish known security policies and conduct mandatory security training. Users must act as a human firewall against intrusion by protecting confidential information, paying attention to their surroundings, and noting any unusual interactions.

- Dumpster diving can provide hackers with sensitive information, as well as hardware and software. Discarded paper should be shredded, ideally with a crosscut shredder, and kept in locked dumpsters. Data from tape, floppy disks, hard disks, and CD-ROMs should be erased and destroyed before it is discarded.

- There are four methods of Internet footprinting: Web searching, network enumeration, Domain Name System (DNS)-based reconnaissance, and network-based reconnaissance. These are the most frequently used methods of surveillance, attractive to hackers because they are clean, legal, and safe.

- During Web searching, hackers collect information about a target organization by reading Web pages produced by that organization and other online documents about the organization. The hacker's research tools may include search engines, HTML source code, newsgroups, security-related Web sites, and newsletters.

- Network enumeration is the process of identifying domain names and other resources on the target network. Using a tool called WHOIS, hackers can gather information such as IP addresses and contact names.

- DNS-based reconnaissance uses information available from DNS servers about the IP addresses of target network domain names and alternate domains that might be on or connected to the target network. This method uses DNS lookup tools available on specialized Web sites and other tools available on various local machine platforms.

- Network-based reconnaissance is the process of identifying active computers and services on a target network via tools such as *ping, traceroute,* and *netstat.*

REVIEW QUESTIONS

1. What are the three classifications of reconnaissance?

2. Define and discuss legal reconnaissance.

3. What are the methods and tactics of social engineering?

4. How many methods are available in dumpster diving?

5. What are the tactics of the theft method of dumpster diving?

6. What are the tactics of the copying method of dumpster diving?

7. How many methods are available in Internet footprinting?

8. What are the tactics and techniques involved in the Internet footprinting method of Web searching?

9. What are the tactics and techniques involved in the Internet footprinting method of network enumeration?

10. What are the tactics and techniques involved in the Internet footprinting method of Domain Name System (DNS)–based reconnaissance?

11. What are the tactics and techniques involved in the Internet footprinting method of network-based reconnaissance?

12. Short Essay: Define and discuss the respective values of the three classifications of surveillance.

Indicate whether the sentence or statement is true or false.

13. _____ Social engineering is an effective way to discover user passwords.

14. _____ Some IM conversations are initiated by robots for the purpose of enticing users to certain Web sites.

15. _____ It is smart to save time by using the same username and password for all accounts.

16. _____ It is unsafe to dispose of printed drafts of letters in unsecured trash receptacles.

17. _____ Newspapers are useful tools for running exploits on target companies.

18. _____ The WHOIS tool allows the InterNIC database to be queried by using the domain name, NIC handle, person's name, IP address, street address, or school.

19. _____ 71.81.18.32 is an example of an IPv6 address.

20. _____ *Traceroute* and *tracert* are, respectively, the CLI applications for checking all the routers between one Internet node and another on GNU/Linux and DOS platforms.

HANDS-ON PROJECTS

Project 2-1

1. Create a chart that indicates the classification and hierarchy of each of the reconnaissance categories and methods discussed in this chapter. The specific format of the chart is up to you. For example, you can use UML and build upon the incomplete chart shown in Figure 1-2, or you can create a Venn diagram, organizational chart, and so on.

   Whatever format you choose, your chart should indicate which techniques are legal, illegal, or unethical. It should also indicate the level of personal interaction required by each method.

2. Break into three groups. Each group will develop one main class, e.g., social engineering, dumpster diving, or Internet footprinting. The work groups may discover that there are more tactics available within each method. They may also discover tactics that cease being viable as time passes. For example, DNS Zone Transfer has become less valuable as a tactic, as more DNS servers are patched to deny zone transfers from anonymous or uncertified hosts.

Project 2-2

1. **Internet Search Method** Using the Internet search method of Internet footprinting, discover all you can about your school's domain and network.

2. **Network enumeration Method** Using the network enumeration method of Internet footprinting, discover all you can about your school's domain and network.

3. **DNS-Based Reconnaissance Method** Using the DNS-based reconnaissance method of Internet footprinting, discover all you can about your school's domain and network.

4. **Network–Based Reconnaissance Method** Using the network-based reconnaissance method of Internet footprinting, discover all you can about your school's domain and network.

Project 2-3

Review the dumpster-diving classification, and write a template trash and recycling policy. You can use this as you progress in your career as a network security specialist.

HANDS-ON
PROJECTS

Project 2-4

Referring to the methods described within the social engineering classification, develop a game plan to collect information from the following organization:

Bill's Meat Packing plant is a chicken processor at the edge of your town. It has numerous health violations and an enormous turnover of disassembly line employees. It is a publicly traded company, and its stock is generally steady and rising slightly. It has 1000 disassembly line workers who work three shifts. Its office has 20 computers and about 30 administrative and accounting staff members. The company has 12 buildings on a 20-acre campus. The office is open 9:00 to 6:00 on weekdays. The shipping office in Building III is open 24 hours per day in two 12-hour shifts.

REFERENCES

1. Edmead, M. T. "Social engineering attacks: What we can learn from Kevin Mitnick." SearchSecurity.com 18 November 2002. http://searchsecurity.techtarget.com/tip/ 1,289483,sid14_gci865450,00.html, quoting Kevin Mitnick.

3

SCANNING TOOLS

After reading this chapter and completing the exercises, you will be able to:

♦ Comprehend the functioning of scanners

♦ Trace the development of scanners

♦ Identify various types of scanning

♦ Identify different scanners

Network administrators use scanners to find and fix vulnerabilities in remote machines on their network. Hackers do the same thing, but their intention is different. Scanning permits hackers to learn the vulnerabilities of the target system, and this makes ongoing hacking efforts far more effective.

A scanner is a software tool that examines and reports about vulnerabilities on local and remote hosts. Scanners are available as dedicated tools, which are called port scanners; as network scanners; or as part of a networking utility suite. A **port scanner** examines and reports upon the condition (open or closed) of a port as well as the application listening on that port, if possible. Network utilities such as *dig*, *ping*, and *trace* are limited-use port scanners.

Scanners were originally developed to aid security professionals and system administrators in examining networks for security vulnerabilities. The most popular scanners are open source, made freely available across the Internet to speed development and to take advantage of the skills of many developers who are interested in the technology. Open source scanners also allow students, hobbyists, and hackers to test the security of their own networks. The legitimate use of scanners has made many networks safer and less vulnerable to attack. The public availability and quality of their vulnerability reporting has made scanners very popular hacking tools.

Evolution of Scanners

Scanners first appeared even before ARPANET, the precursor to the Internet, appeared in 1969. Prior to ARPANET, the computing world was made up of mainframes and dumb terminals, but even in this limited model, a terminal operator might have occasionally been unable to connect to the mainframe. There were ways to scan for dead terminals from the mainframe even then. As Local Area Networks and the Internet arose, it was a great convenience to be able to *"ping"* it over the network, and across networks segmented by routers and switches not under an administrator's direct control. If a remote computer was not responding to *ping*, it was useful to discover where in the route the breakdown had occurred, so *traceroute* was developed to show the entire list of routers through which the packets were traveling. The more an individual could do without resorting to calling the administrator of the remote system, the more cost effective the whole system could be.

There were many security vulnerabilities in the early days of computing; however, public knowledge about these vulnerabilities was limited. In the early stages of the Internet, only university and government personnel even knew they existed. The Internet was launched in the 1970s, and the first personal computer was not released until 1980. The early UNIX-like languages had no security at all. "Networking is a private club where we are all known to one another," was the prevalent philosophy. This was true at the beginning. There was no "public Internet" and the few people who had access to the Internet were for the most part trustworthy. Vulnerabilities that were found were published in scholarly papers to which criminals and hobbyists did not subscribe. There was no logical reason to publish them more widely than that, nor was there any viable platform from which to do so. The first virus was released in 1988—19 years after ARPANET launched, and 8 years after the first personal computers were shipped. Schools and computer companies were publishing exploits, and eventually students and hobbyists (the hackers of that time) started playing with scanning applications. The hacker community was still working from the philosophical notion that "we are all friends here," but the new group of friends were passing along information about the vulnerabilities they were finding. New vulnerabilities were discovered each year and the old ones patched. When the Internet became mainstream, hobbyist hackers were already publishing these vulnerabilities on the Internet. As with any club that grows too fast, new "members" were arriving each day, with less zeal for the technology and more interest in how they could profit from using the information for their own purposes.

When hackers wanted to crack a system in the 1970s, they would examine the target system for all known vulnerabilities. However, they had to examine all weaknesses and vulnerabilities step-by-step, using various techniques—all of which carried risk of capture. Breaking into a system was time consuming.

Legitimate network users would connect to remote UNIX servers by having their 2K baud modem dial specific telephone numbers. These UNIX-based systems permitted users to access a shell account by providing them with logon names and passwords. At that time, hackers collected and traded telephone numbers of such UNIX servers and tried to establish a successful connection by experimenting with different usernames and passwords. Trying to dial all telephone numbers for a possible connection was time consuming and risky. These drawbacks led the hacker community to the invention of a new tool, the war dialer.

A war dialer is a script that tells the modem to dial a range of phone numbers defined by the user, and then identifies those numbers that connect to remote computers. Automating the process of remote modem discovery made it far easier for hackers to get to the next step, which was guessing a username and password couplet.

War dialers could not reveal the weaknesses of the target system. They were a form of automated scanner, but they were scanning only for open phone numbers, and not attempting to initiate a session or in any other way discover the application listening on the open ports behind the remote server's modem. In the early 1980s, the majority of servers ran on UNIX platforms. System administrators created shell scripts that let them check security weaknesses of their networks and avoid hacking activities. Many of these scripts examined the networks by attempting to connect various ports; they were the first port scanners.

As the Internet increased in availability and popularity, more computers and networks became connected. This enlarged the scope of hacking activities. At the same time, more user-friendly operating platforms appeared, and the ranks of students, hobbyists, and hackers also increased. The development of modern scanners was not primarily a criminal undertaking; however, user-friendly GUI front-ends for scanners have made it easier for relative newcomers to learn how to operate these powerful tools. Today, scanners are available for several popular platforms. Most of them are available on Web sites that allow individuals to download multiple hacking tools, including scanners. These sites are frequented by security professionals, students, hobbyists, and criminal hackers.

How Scanners Work

Scanners automate the process of examining network weaknesses. Scanners are not heuristic; they do not discover new vulnerabilities but check for known vulnerabilities and open ports. A scanner performs these functions:

- Connects to a target host(s)
- Examines the target host for the services running on it
- Examines each service for any known vulnerability

Scanners can be set to target either a single IP address, and search for vulnerabilities on the target host, or a range of IP addresses. In either mode, the scanner attempts to connect with the target (or targets) to find open ports and possible vulnerabilities present on the target host(s).

Types of Scanning

The most important types of scanning are the following:

- Transmission Control Protocol (TCP) connect scanning
- Half-open scanning

- User Datagram Protocol (UDP) scanning
- IP protocol scanning
- Ping scanning
- Stealth scanning

TCP Connect Scanning

Most broadly defined, a TCP connect scan attempts to make TCP connections with all of the ports on a remote system. In this type of scan, the target host transmits *connection-succeeded* messages for active ports and *host-unreachable* messages for inactive ports.

A user does not need root privileges to perform TCP connect scanning; however, even a very poor Intrusion Detection System (IDS) on the target host is likely to recognize this attack. The system log on the target system will log all of these connection requests, and even a very sleepy administrator would notice 65,536 attempts from the same IP. Scanners like Nmap scan only the most useful 1667 ports, which makes the window of exposure smaller for the scan operator—but that is still quite a giveaway.

Half-Open Scanning

Half-open scanning is TCP connection scanning, but it does not complete the connections. In typical TCP connections, a host initially sends a synchronization message, SYN, to the target host. The target host replies back with a SYN and an acknowledgment message, ACK, to the host that requested a connection (SYN/ACK). Next, the host requesting the connection sends an ACK message to the target host. After the target host has the ACK message, the connection is finally established. This describes a successful TCP connection and as such it would be logged to the target host's system log.

In a half-open scan, only the SYN message is sent from the scanner. The reply signal may be a SYN/ACK, indicating the port is open. It also could be an RST/ACK, which means that no listening is done from that port. An open port may be vulnerable to attack. Responding to the target system's reply with an RST flag will often result in no log file being written for the interchange, even though port data was released. IDS programs like Snort can be set to log *all* network activity, and so would record even the anomalous half-open attack signature, however most operating systems do not log these. This makes the half-open scanning technique safe and effective. One obstacle to using this attack is that root or system administrator privileges are required to perform half-open scanning.

UDP Scanning

UDP scanning examines the status of UDP ports on a target system. First, the scanner sends a 0-byte UDP packet to all the ports on a target host. If a port is closed, the target host replies with an *Internet Control Message Protocol (ICMP) unreachable* message to the computer on which the scanner is installed. If the port is active, then no such message is sent back. For this reason, a scanner that performs UDP scanning assumes that a port on the target host is active if it fails to receive an *ICMP unreachable* message. Most operating systems generate UDP messages very slowly. This makes UDP scanning impractical, compared to other types of scanning.

IP Protocol Scanning

IP protocol scanning examines a target host for supported IP protocols. In this method, the scanner transmits IP packets to each protocol on the target host. If a protocol on the target host replies with an *ICMP unreachable* message to the scanner, then the target host does not use that protocol. If there is no reply, then the hacker assumes that the target host supports that protocol. Unfortunately for the hacker, firewalls and computers that run operating systems such as Digital UNIX (now replaced with Compaq Tru64 Operating System) and HP-UX do not send any *ICMP unreachable* messages. Consequently, the IP protocols supported by such hosts cannot be determined by using IP protocol scanning. Fortunately for the script kiddie population, the number of Digital UNIX, Tru64, and HP-UX servers is relatively small.

Ping Scanning

A ping scan demonstrates whether a remote host is active by sending *ICMP echo request* packets to that host. If the target host sends back packets, it can be assumed that the host is active. However, sometimes hosts block or drop *ICMP echo request* packets. This results in a false negative reading on that specific host. This is a shortcoming of ping scanning. Figure 3–1 shows two Nmap displays to show a situation where a remote host is dropping *pings*.

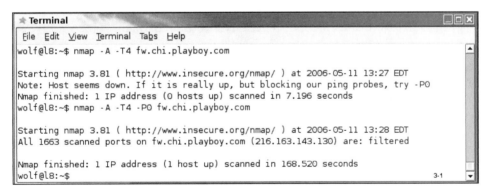

Figure 3-1 How it looks when a target host is dropping *pings*

Stealth Scanning

Stealth scanning lets you examine hosts behind firewalls and packet filters; in some ways it is similar to half–open scanning in that most stealth scanners do not allow target hosts to log the scanning activities.

CATALOG OF SCANNER TECHNOLOGY

The majority of scanners are written in the C or Perl language; therefore, in-depth knowledge of these complex programming languages is required to create a scanner. Extensive knowledge of TCP/IP routines is also necessary for developing a scanner. However, it is unnecessary to design and build a scanner from scratch. There are many outlets for source code and compiled binaries of scanning tools with open source, freeware, and shareware licenses. Although the earliest scanners were based on UNIX platforms, they are currently available for Windows and Macintosh platforms. Some popular scanners that can be easily found are:

- Nessus
- Network Mapper (Nmap)
- Security Auditor's Research Assistant (SARA)
- Security Administrator's Integrated Network Tool (SAINT)
- Strobe
- Cheops

Nessus

Formerly an open source vulnerability assessment tool, Nessus is a remote security scanner designed to be run on Linux, BSD, Solaris, and other versions of Unix. It generates reports in HTML, XML, LaTeX, and ASCII text, and suggests solutions for security problems. It was open source for many years, but Tenable Network Security, the sponsor of Nessus, decided to make further code proprietary in late 2005.

Nessus was developed with a client/server architecture. The Nessus client is the front-end application of the program, while the Nessus server performs the actual scanning activity. The Nessus server and client programs can be installed on a single computer or on different computers on a network. The Nessus server examines the services on the network when the Nessus client requests scanning. This program examines weaknesses of a network by utilizing a security vulnerability database that contains updated information of all known vulnerabilities.

In this program, each security test is written as an external plug-in. There are over 1200 different test plug-ins for Nessus. Tests can be very tightly customized to specifically fit the environment being tested. Whenever Nessus performs a security test on a service, the program simulates an environment of the target service and attempts to communicate with that client by using the necessary protocols. For instance, to examine the security of a mail server, Nessus acts as a mail client and tries to communicate with it. Most scanners examine only one service if there are multiple services of the same type running on a computer. Nessus examines all available services of the same type.

Tenable chose to turn away from the General Public License (GPL), but there is some evidence that the 2.x version (still under GPL) is being maintained and supported by somebody other than Tenable. The Nessus 3.x program may be downloaded for Linux, Mac OSX, and BSD. There is also an available client for Windows platforms. The 2.2.7 Installer for all UNIX systems is also available from this site, along with a separate GUI client for UNIX and full source code. All of this is free of charge from www.nessus.org/download.html, along with a free Registered Feed for updates and plug-ins. There is a seven-day lag from when the plug-ins enter the "Direct Feed," which is a paid feature. It is not too expensive, but to some people, any price for software is too high. Figure 3-2 is the completion screen after installation on an Ubuntu Linux platform.

Figure 3-2   Successful Nessus 2.2.7 installation

Nmap

Nmap is probably the best all-around network scanner to date. Fyodor, the developer of Nmap, has one of the most interesting and useful security sites on the Internet, especially for newcomers to the field of network security. Nmap is powerful, yet easy to use. It's also very flexible in that it supports many different operating systems, including Unix/Linux, Windows, and MacOS; can use a variety of techniques to map out complex networks; and, because it's open source, can be modified and customized as necessary.

- **Flexible**: Nmap supports dozens of advanced techniques for mapping out networks filled with IP filters, firewalls, routers, and other obstacles. These include many port scanning mechanisms (both TCP & UDP), OS detection, version detection, ping sweeps, and more.

- **Powerful**: Nmap has been used to scan huge networks of hundreds of thousands of machines.

- **Portable**: Nmap supports most operating systems: Unix compilation from source; RPM-based distributions (Red Hat, Mandrake, SUSE, Fedora); Red Hat, Fedora, Mandrake, and Yellow Dog Linux using Yum; Debian Linux and derivatives such as Ubuntu; Gentoo Linux; Windows—from zipped binaries, or compiled from source (the latter requires you have C++ loaded on your PC); Sun Solaris; Apple Mac OS X; FreeBSD / OpenBSD / NetBSD; Amiga; HP-UX; IRIX; Sharp Zaurus PDA; Compaq iPAQ PDA; and several other PDAs. Surprisingly, there is no version (yet) for PalmOS.

- **Easy**: You can start out as simply as `nmap -v -A targethost` and progress through a large set of advanced features designed for expert users. Both traditional command line and **graphical user interface (GUI)** versions are available to suit your preference. Binaries are available for those who do not wish to compile Nmap from source.

- **Free**: The primary goals of Nmap are to help make the Internet a little more secure and to provide administrators/auditors/hackers with an advanced tool for exploring their networks. Nmap is available for free download, and also comes with full source code that may be modified and redistributed under the terms of the license.

- **Well Documented**: The documentation for Nmap is extensive. You will not feel lost in the sauce when you have access to Nmap's online help as well as extensive man pages, whitepapers, and tutorials.

- **Supported**: While Nmap comes with no warranty, it is well supported by the community and appreciates bug reports and patches.

- **Acclaimed**: Nmap has won numerous awards, including "Information Security Product of the Year" by *Linux Journal*, *Info World*, and *Codetalker Digest*. It has been featured in hundreds of magazine articles, several movies, dozens of books (including this one), and one comic book series.

- **Popular**: Thousands of people download Nmap every day, and it is included with many operating systems (Red Hat Linux, Debian Linux, Gentoo, FreeBSD, OpenBSD). It is among the top ten (out of 30,000) programs at the Freshmeat.net repository. This is important because it lends Nmap its vibrant development and user support communities.
Download Nmap at www.insecure.org/nmap/download.html.

Using Nmap in Red Hat Linux

Many Linux distributions (distros) come with Nmap installed. This section describes how to verify the installation of Nmap in Red Hat Linux; the steps for other versions of Linux may vary somewhat, but will be similar. For example, to check for an installation of Nmap in Red Hat Linux, use the following syntax:

```
rpm -q nmap
```

If the program is already installed on the computer, the operating system will display output similar to the following (the version number may be different):

```
nmap-3.50-3
```

The Nmap program has a GUI-based interface, *nmap-frontend*. To see whether *nmap-frontend* is installed on a Red Hat Linux operating system, type the following syntax:

```
rpm -q nmap-frontend
```

If it is installed, then the operating system will display output similar to the following:

```
nmap-frontend-3.50-3
```

If the program is not installed, simply download the program from a Web site such as insecure.org. After completion of the download, you can install Nmap on Red Hat Linux by using this syntax:

```
rpm -ivh nmap-3.50-3.i386.rpm nmap-frontend-3.50-3.i386.rpm
```

You can use Nmap either from the command prompt or the GNU Network Object Model Environment (GNOME) session. In order to scan a target host from the command prompt, type the following syntax below:

```
nmap
```

Figure 3-3 depicts a sample output of the *nmap* command without arguments or target. This always results in a basic list of arguments (options).

```
┌─────────────────────────────────────────────────────────────────┐
│ ✳ Terminal                                            □□⊠         │
├─────────────────────────────────────────────────────────────────┤
│ File  Edit  View  Terminal  Tabs  Help                            │
│ wolf@l8:~$ nmap                                                 ▲  │
│ Nmap 3.81 Usage: nmap [Scan Type(s)] [Options] <host or net list> │
│ Some Common Scan Types ('*' options require root privileges)      │
│ * -sS TCP SYN stealth port scan (default if privileged (root))    │
│   -sT TCP connect() port scan (default for unprivileged users)    │
│ * -sU UDP port scan                                               │
│   -sP ping scan (Find any reachable machines)                     │
│ * -sF,-sX,-sN Stealth FIN, Xmas, or Null scan (experts only)      │
│   -sV Version scan probes open ports determining service & app names/versions │
│   -sR RPC scan (use with other scan types)                        │
│ Some Common Options (none are required, most can be combined):    │
│ * -O Use TCP/IP fingerprinting to guess remote operating system   │
│   -p <range> ports to scan.  Example range: 1-1024,1080,6666,31337│
│   -F Only scans ports listed in nmap-services                     │
│   -v Verbose. Its use is recommended.  Use twice for greater effect.│
│   -P0 Don't ping hosts (needed to scan www.microsoft.com and others)│
│ * -Ddecoy_host1,decoy2[,...] Hide scan using many decoys          │
│   -6 scans via IPv6 rather than IPv4                              │
│   -T <Paranoid|Sneaky|Polite|Normal|Aggressive|Insane> General timing policy │
│   -n/-R Never do DNS resolution/Always resolve [default: sometimes resolve] │
│   -oN/-oX/-oG <logfile> Output normal/XML/grepable scan logs to <logfile> │
│   -iL <inputfile> Get targets from file; Use '-' for stdin        │
│ * -S <your_IP>/-e <devicename> Specify source address or network interface │
│   --interactive Go into interactive mode (then press h for help)  │
│ Example: nmap -v -sS -O www.my.com 192.168.0.0/16 '192.88-90.*.*' │
│ SEE THE MAN PAGE FOR MANY MORE OPTIONS, DESCRIPTIONS, AND EXAMPLES │
│ wolf@l8:~$ █                                                      │
│                                                            3-3 ▼  │
└─────────────────────────────────────────────────────────────────┘
```

Figure 3-3   Sample output of the *nmap* command without arguments

Figure 3-4 shows a very simple scan using *nmap*:

```
nmap -A -P0 ip_address
```

The -A enables OS detection, the -P0 disables *ping*. (That is -P[zero], not P0 as in Post Office.) The IP address in the following figure is my local router. The initial few lines are the result of a *ping* command (to prove that the router is there), and the next command is:

```
nmap -A 192.168.0.1
```

The result of that scan is a statement that the host appears to be down or blocking *pings*.

So next I typed the command as:

```
nmap -A -P0 ip_address
```

This scan gave me a fair bit of information about the router, but not much of interest. Next, I tried a very basic command:

```
nmap -P0 mit.edu
```

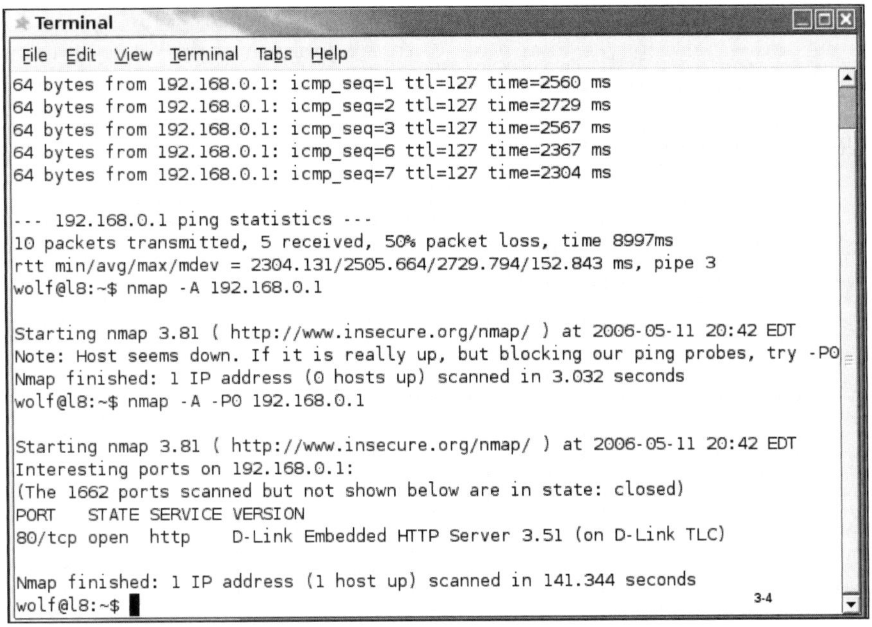

```
Terminal                                                              [_][□][x]
File  Edit  View  Terminal  Tabs  Help
64 bytes from 192.168.0.1: icmp_seq=1 ttl=127 time=2560 ms
64 bytes from 192.168.0.1: icmp_seq=2 ttl=127 time=2729 ms
64 bytes from 192.168.0.1: icmp_seq=3 ttl=127 time=2567 ms
64 bytes from 192.168.0.1: icmp_seq=6 ttl=127 time=2367 ms
64 bytes from 192.168.0.1: icmp_seq=7 ttl=127 time=2304 ms

--- 192.168.0.1 ping statistics ---
10 packets transmitted, 5 received, 50% packet loss, time 8997ms
rtt min/avg/max/mdev = 2304.131/2505.664/2729.794/152.843 ms, pipe 3
wolf@l8:~$ nmap -A 192.168.0.1

Starting nmap 3.81 ( http://www.insecure.org/nmap/ ) at 2006-05-11 20:42 EDT
Note: Host seems down. If it is really up, but blocking our ping probes, try -PO
Nmap finished: 1 IP address (0 hosts up) scanned in 3.032 seconds
wolf@l8:~$ nmap -A -PO 192.168.0.1

Starting nmap 3.81 ( http://www.insecure.org/nmap/ ) at 2006-05-11 20:42 EDT
Interesting ports on 192.168.0.1:
(The 1662 ports scanned but not shown below are in state: closed)
PORT    STATE SERVICE VERSION
80/tcp open  http    D-Link Embedded HTTP Server 3.51 (on D-Link TLC)

Nmap finished: 1 IP address (1 host up) scanned in 141.344 seconds
wolf@l8:~$ █                                                          3-4
```

Figure 3-4 Basic *nmap* scan

and got the following response:

```
wolf@l8:~$ nmap -PO 18.7.22.69
            Starting nmap 3.81 (
            http://www.insecure.org/nmap/ ) at
            2006-05-11 20:45 EDT
            Interesting ports on WEB.MIT.EDU
            (18.7.22.69):
            (The 1651 ports scanned but not shown
            below are in state: closed)
            PORT       STATE     SERVICE
            43/tcp     open      whois
            79/tcp     open      finger
            80/tcp     open      http
            135/tcp    filtered  msrpc
            136/tcp    filtered  profile
            137/tcp    filtered  netbios-ns
            138/tcp    filtered  netbios-dgm
            139/tcp    filtered  netbios-ssn
            443/tcp    open      https
            445/tcp    filtered  microsoft-ds
            593/tcp    filtered  http-rpc-epmap
            4444/tcp   filtered  krb524
```

This was far more interesting, especially since I was not using anything beyond TCP connect scanning and was not logged in as root. With the addition of the -A argument, my results were all of the above plus a string of useful information about the architecture of the machine (x86 Pentium or above), the operating system (Linux), the Web Server (Apache 1.3.26) with openSSL, and so on. You can see that the SF: notation is a new line in the output (and that the output is not formatted to fit the page you are reading) and x20 is a blank space. Backslashes are used to comment out the character following so that it is not mistaken by the program to be an argument for execution. The last part of the block is a pair of Web pages returned as error messages.

```
1 service unrecognized despite returning data. If you know
the service/version, please submit the following
fingerprint at http://www.insecure.org/cgi-bin/servi cefp-
submit.cgi :
SF-Port80-TCP:V=3.81%D=5/11%Time=4463E0A5%P=i686-pc-linux-
gnu%r(GetRequest
SF:,111C,"HTTP/1\.1\x20200\x20OK\r\nDate:
\x20Fri,\x2012\x20May\x202006\x20
SF:01:11:09\x20GMT\r\nServer:\x20MIT\x20Web\x20Server\x20
Apache/1\.3\.26\x
SF:20Mark/1\.4\x20\(Unix\)\x20mod_ssl/2\.8\.9\x20OpenSSL/0\
.9\.7c\r\nLast-
SF:Modified:\x20Thu,\x2011\x20May\x202006\x2003:59:
19\x20GMT\r\nETag:\x20\
SF:"71e13e8-42d3-4462b697\"\r\nAccept-Ranges:
\x20bytes\r\nContent-Length:\
SF:x2017107\r\nConnection:\x20close\r\nContent-Type:\x20text/
html\r\n\r\n<
SF:!DOCTYPE\x20HTML\x20PUBLIC\x20\"-//W3C//DTD\x20HTML\x204\
.01\x20Transit
SF:ional//EN\">\n<html>\n<head>\n\x20\x20<title>Massachusetts\
x20Institute
SF:\x20of\x20Technology</title>\n\x20\x20<meta\x20http-
equiv=\"Content-Typ
SF:e\"\x20content=\"text/html;\x20charset=iso-8859-
1\">\n\x20\x20<meta\x20
SF:http-
equiv=\"Expires\"\x20\x20\x20\x20\x20\x20content=\"12\x20Ma
y\x2020
SF:06\">\n\x20\x20<!--
\x20Copyright\x20\(C\)\x202003\x20Massachusetts\x20I
SF:nstitute\x20of\x20Technology\x20--
>\n\x20\x20<meta\x20name=\"date\"\x20
SF:content=\"Thursday,\x20May\x2011th\x202006\">\n\x20\x20<
meta\x20name=\"
SF:keywords\"\x20content=\"Massachusetts\x20Institute
\x20of\x20Technology,
SF:\x20MIT\">\n\x20\x20<meta\x20name=\"description\"\x20con
tent=\"MIT\x20i
```

3

```
SF:s\x20devoted\x20to\x20the\x20advancement\x20of\x20knowle
dge\x20and\x20e
SF:ducation\x20of\x20students\x20in\x20areas\x20that\x20con
tri")%r(HTTPOpt
SF:ions,D3,"HTTP/1\.1\x20200\x20OK\r\nDate:\x20Fri,\x2012\x
20May\x202006\x
SF:2001:11:12\x20GMT\r\nServer:\x20MIT\x20Web\x20Server\x20
Apache/1\.3\.26
SF:\x20Mark/1\.4\x20\(Unix\)\x20mod_ssl/2\.8\.9\x20OpenSSL
/0\.9\.7c\r\nCon
SF:tent-
Length:\x200\r\nAllow:\x20GET,\x20HEAD,\x20OPTIONS,\x20TRAC
E\r\nCo
SF:nnection:\x20close\r\n\r\n")%r(RTSPRequest,25B,"HTTP/1\.
1\x20400\x20Bad
SF:\x20Request\r\nDate:\x20Fri,\x2012\x20May\x202006\x2001:
11:20\x20GMT\r\
SF:nServer:\x20MIT\x20Web\x20Server\x20Apache/1\.3\.26\x20M
ark/1\.4\x20\(U
SF:nix\)\x20mod_ssl/2\.8\.9\x20OpenSSL/0\.9\.7c\r\nConnecti
on:\x20close\r\
SF:nContent-Type:\x20text/html;\x20charset=iso-8859-
1\r\n\r\n<!DOCTYPE\x20
SF:HTML\x20PUBLIC\x20\"-
//IETF//DTD\x20HTML\x202\.0//EN\">\n<HTML><HEAD>\n
SF:<TITLE>400\x20Bad\x20Request</TITLE>\n</HEAD><BODY>\n<H1
>Bad\x20Request
SF:</H1>\nYour\x20browser\x20sent\x20a\x20request\x20that\x
20this\x20serve
SF:r\x20could\x20not\x20understand\.<P>\nThe\x20request\x20
line\x20contain
SF:ed\x20invalid\x20characters\x20following\x20the\x20proto
col\x20string\.
SF:<P>\n<P>\n<HR>\n<ADDRESS>MIT\x20Web\x20Server\x20Apache/
1\.3\.26\x20Mar
SF:k/1\.4\x20Server\x20at\x20web\.mit\.edu\x20Port\x2080</A
DDRESS>\n</BODY
SF:></HTML>\n");
```

```
Nmap finished: 1 IP address (1 host up) scanned in 146.683
seconds
```

Nmap supports all the types of scan listed above. You can select a scan type by adding the required option in the *nmap* command. Table 3-1 explains options for some of the important scan types.

Table 3-1 Important scanning options of the *nmap* command

Option	Description
-sT	Performs TCP connect scanning
-sS	Performs half-open scanning
-sP	Performs ping scanning
-sU	Performs UDP scanning
-sO	Performs IP protocol scanning

You can use *nmap* in a different way to determine the operating system of the target host. Type the following syntax for this procedure:

```
nmap -O ip_address
```

Figure 3-5 shows the result of this scan. Please note that this scan has to be done with root privilege.

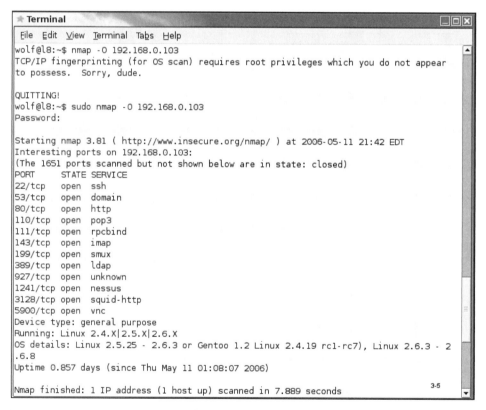

Figure 3-5 Operating system information section of an *nmap* scan

The fourth line from the bottom in this figure shows the operating system is Linux, but *nmap* is not completely sure which specific distro or kernel version it is running.

You can also scan multiple hosts by using *nmap*. The following example will scan the hosts between 100 and 110 within the 192.168.0.x subnet:

```
nmap -O 192.168.0.100-110
```

This example scans for all IP addresses from 192.168.0.100 to 192.168.0.110.

You can use a wildcard to scan networks. The * character can be used anywhere in an IPv4 address to specify all numbers within the expected set from 1 to 255. Consider the following examples:

```
A)  nmap -sS *.10.10.10
B)  nmap -sS 10.*.10.10
C)  nmap -sS 10.10.*.10
D)  nmap -sS 10.10.10.*
E)  nmap -sS *.*.*.*
```

They all perform "half-open" TCP connect scans, but they would certainly return different results.

A through D would potentially return 254 nodes (the 255th is a broadcast IP), each from a very wide number of source subnets to a single IP subnet. Luckily, the first example doesn't work because the first IP queried would be 0.10.10.10, and there is no IPv4 address with 0 as the first octet. By the same logic, Example E won't work either. Example B might work but it might take two million hours. Example C completed within less than 21 seconds because there appear to be no available 10.10.*.* addresses. Learn to put sensible limits on the search parameters.

NmapFE

NmapFE is a graphic interface for the GNOME Linux Desktop. You can run the *nmapfe* command in the "Run a Program" dialog box of the GNOME session to view the *nmap front-end* window. Figure 3-6 shows the GNOME "Run as.." dialog box. Figure 3-7 shows the NmapFE interface.

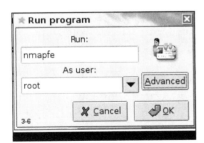

Figure 3-6   GNOME "Run as.." dialog box

You can specify the host or hosts to be scanned in the Target(s) text box.

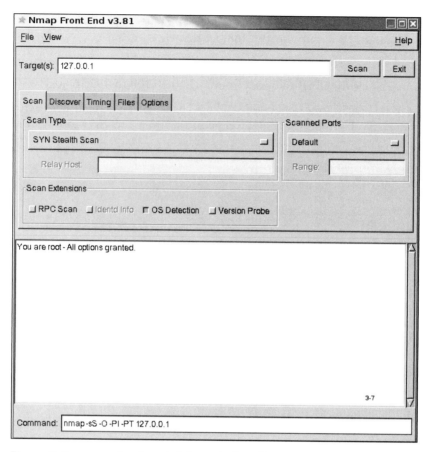

Figure 3-7 *nmap front-end* dialog window (NmapFE)

Scan Tab   You select a scan type from the Scan options section. The Scan Ports drop-down box lets you specify ports.

Discover Tab   You can set which kind of ping (echo packet) you send. You can also specify how many (from zero to six) and to which ports the pings will be sent.

Timing Tab   You can manually set Nmap's timing options, or use one of several built-in timing options, which range from "paranoid" (a very accurate but slow scan) to "insane" (not as accurate but a much faster scan). The timing is a way to make your attack, or scan, harder to discover (by the target system[s]).

Files Tab   This is where you designate both the input files—the downloaded files from the DHCP server that list all the DHCP address leases—and the output files—the logs of this search—so you can send them to the auditors or use them to help you fix the vulnerabilities you found.

3

Options Tab   The Options tab is where you set the verbosity; choose whether Reverse-DNS resolution is done; choose what spoofed IP you will use as the from field on the ping packets you send; choose whether you are sending to IPv6 addresses; and choose whether you attempt to fool Network IDS by fragmenting the packets.

Figure 3-8 illustrates a sample output of the scanning performed by *nmap-frontend*.

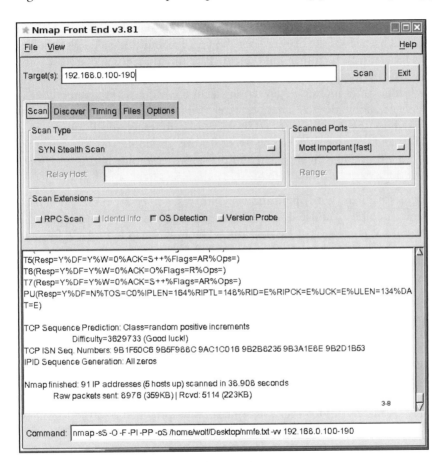

Figure 3-8   Output of an *nmap-frontend* scan

Please note that the line that NmapFE automatically placed in the text box at the bottom of the dialog contains exactly the options and arguments that you would use in the command line, presuming you changed the filename and path for the output file.

```
nmap -sS -O -F -PI -PP -oS /home/wolf/Desktop/nmfe.txt -vv 192.
168.0.100-190
```

KNmap

This program was developed by Alexandre Sagala and is a GUI for Nmap, to be used with the KDE desktop environment. It has all the features of Nmap, just as NmapFE does. In the UNIX environment, front-end applications are almost always afterthoughts and often produced by third-party developers. Windows applications almost always come bundled with (and sometimes integrated with) their respective front-end graphic interfaces, so a person skilled in the use of the Windows operating system might think that it is obvious that a GUI would have all of the features that the CLI has, but this isn't always the case. Usually the GUIs have at least beginner and intermediate functionality, and at least some advanced capability. The tricky thing about relying entirely on the GUI is that if the GUI developers didn't have time for or interest in developing all of the features of the underlying application, then they just didn't do so. There is rarely any mention of which features were *not* incorporated in the GUI. As a GUI Warrior, you may not think to read the CLI information, and so you will not know what features the application programmers designed into the application. This might include useful information for hacking, such as a development back door.

As sometimes happens with applications, KNmap seems to have died at version 0.9. The program has not been updated since 2002, while QT (one of the required underlying technologies) has continued to be developed. Thus, KNmap is available for download, but probably won't work. This is not necessarily a bad thing—in fact, it could be an opportunity. It might be possible to take over the maintenance of the project and start developing a name for yourself and your company by working on KNmap or a similar project.

SARA

The Security Auditor's Research Assistant (SARA) is a third-generation network security analysis tool developed by Advanced Research Corporation and based on a program called the Security Administrator's Tool for Analyzing Networks (SATAN). SATAN was developed in 1995 by Dan Farmer and Weitse Venema and was the benchmark for network security analysis for several years. However, few updates were provided, and the tool slowly became obsolete in the growing threat environment.

SARA was designed to complement and interface with other security tools, such as Nmap. It runs on a variety of operating systems, including Unix/Linux, MacOS, and—using the coSARA package based on Cooperative Linux—Microsoft Windows. A host of features—including SQL injection tests, CVE standards support, integration with the National Vulnerability Database, support for user extensions, and frequent updates—make SARA an effective network analysis tool.

SAINT

SAINT, or Security Administrator's Integrated Network Tool, has a downloadable application, which works on UNIX, Linux, and Mac OS X operating systems. Saint also produces an appliance to scan networks and an online "over-the-Internet" scanning application.

A free trial of the software can be downloaded from download.saintcorporation.com. SAINT is a viable commercial product suite and is not a popular hacker's tool.

Strobe

Strobe is a TCP port scanner for BSD and Red Hat that was developed by Julian Assange. This program scans for all open ports on the target host. Its scanning activity is reputed to be very fast compared to other port scanners, yet it is many years old with no apparent live project page. It has almost undoubtedly been superseded by more modern applications such as Nmap and Nessus. If desired, download a copy of Strobe from linux.maruhn.com/sec/strobe.html.

```
root@l8:~/Desktop/tools # strobe -v -s 192.168.0.3
strobe 1.05 (c) 1995-1999 Julian Assange <proff@iq.org>.
attempting port=1 host=192.168.0.3
...[visualize similar lines for the other 65633 available
ports here]
attempting port=65535 host=192.168.0.3
stats: hosts = 1 trys = 97 cons = 0 time = 67.27s trys/s = 1.44
```

Cheops

Cheops, a port scanner for Linux operating systems, was developed for the GNOME interface by using the GTK+ kit. The most important differentiating feature of Cheops is its graphical nature. This application uses a dramatically large percentage of cpu cycles and slows all other applications to a crawl, which probably has something to do with the complexity of its graphical interface. This is a popular application, but Nessus and Nmap do more useful work without this beautiful GUI. This program can be downloaded from ftp://ftp.marko.net/pub/cheops.

 CAUTION The scanners discussed in this chapter are just some of the scanning tools available on the Internet. Scanning outside your own network can get you blocked by your own ISP if the target servers are running IDS systems. When you are contracted to scan a public IP, make sure you first have a signed contract and a permission form in hand. Do not make the naïve assumption that anyone would thank you, or hire you as a network security consultant, because you found and told him about a vulnerability that you were not asked to scan for in the first place. There are civil and sometimes even criminal codes in place for people who make this mistake.

CHAPTER SUMMARY

❑ Scanning permits hackers to learn the vulnerabilities of the target system. A scanner is a software tool that examines and reports about vulnerabilities on local and remote hosts. Scanners are available either as dedicated tools, which are called port scanners; as network scanners; or as part of a networking utility suite.

❑ The most popular scanners are open source or freeware, made freely available across the Internet. The legitimate use of scanners has made many networks less vulnerable to attack. The public availability and quality of their reporting have made scanners very popular hacking tools.

❑ In the early days of computing, security vulnerabilities, while abundant, were not well known. Scanners were first used in the 1960s to scan for dead terminals from the mainframe. As Local Area Networks and the Internet arose, *traceroute* was developed to show the entire list of routers through which packets were traveling.

❑ When hackers wanted to crack a system in the 1970s, they would examine the target system for all known vulnerabilities, starting with finding a server's modem phone number and getting or guessing a usable signon. The time-consuming and risky practice of dialing all telephone numbers for a possible connection led to the development of the war dialer, a type of automated scanner that scanned for open lines.

❑ As students and hobbyists started playing with scanning applications, new vulnerabilities were discovered. When the Internet became mainstream, hackers were already publishing these vulnerabilities on the Internet.

❑ In the early 1980s, most servers ran on UNIX platforms. System administrators created shell scripts that let them check security weaknesses of their networks and avoid hacking activities. These shell scripts were the first port scanners.

❑ Scanners automate the process of examining network weaknesses, and check only for known vulnerabilities and open ports. They attempt to connect to a target host, examine the target host for the services running on it, and examine each service for any known vulnerability.

❑ Scanners can be set to target a single IP address or a range of addresses. They can perform the following scan types: Transmission Control Protocol (TCP) connect scanning, half-open scanning, User Datagram Protocol (UDP) scanning, IP protocol scanning, ping scanning, and stealth scanning.

❑ Scanners are available on UNIX, Windows, and Macintosh platforms. Popular scanners include Nessus, Network Mapper (Nmap), Security Administrator's Research Assistant (SARA), Security Administrator's Integrated Network Tool (SAINT), Strobe, and Cheops.

❑ Scanning outside your own network can get you blocked by your own ISP, if the target servers are running IDS systems.

3

REVIEW QUESTIONS

1. Can you use a scanner to check open ports on a computer on another LAN?

2. Are the following entries valid *nmap* command syntaxes?

```
nmap -sS -sT -P0 192.168.2-222.256
nmap -A http://randomdomain.com
nmap -P1 /home/nmap/file2 10.10.10.1-224
nmap -sS -P0 10.10.10.1-200 | less
nmap -s 192.168.155.45 > /home/nmap/file2
```

3. What is the difference between a ping scan and a Ping of Death?

4. What useful information comes from port scans?

5. Can you stop a port scan if you discover you are being scanned?

6. Name two port scanners.

7. In the NmapFE program, where do you set the spoofed IP you will use as the from field on the ping packets you send?

8. Can Cheops be used to scan the entire Internet? Some "security experts" used to scan various companies' networks and then send them e-mails informing them of their shortcomings and offering to fix these for a fee. Is this a reasonable and ethical marketing technique? Does it make us safer to legislate port scans as illegal?

9. Is the Strobe scanner under development currently?

10. Can you use Strobe on a Windows machine?

Match each term with the correct statement below.

    a. -sT

    b. -sP

    c. -sS

    d. -sU

    e. -sO

11. _____ *nmap* option that performs TCP connect scanning

12. _____ *nmap* option that performs half-open scanning

13. _____ *nmap* option that performs UDP scanning

14. _____ *nmap* option that performs IP protocol scanning

15. _____ *nmap* option that performs ping scanning

HANDS-ON PROJECTS

Project 3-1

1. It's possible that the Nmap and Nessus programs are already installed on your computer. Check to see if these programs are installed by entering the following command at a terminal window:

```
which nmap nessus
```

A response that looks like this says that Nmap and Nessus are already installed, in the directories listed:

```
/usr/local/bin/nessus
/usr/bin/nmap
```

2. If you do not get a similar response, then type the following command to install Nmap:

```
yum install nmap
```

Yum is an automated updater for rpm systems that is far easier to use than rpm or tar. The above command will install Nmap and all needed dependencies.

3. Next, enter the following command to install Nessus:

```
yum install nmap
```

4. If you get an error message, try downloading the latest Nessus rpm from www.nessus.org, and save it to your home folder. Then, in your home folder, type the following command (substituting your rpm filename for the one that appears here):

```
rpm -ivh Nessus-3.0.5-fc6.i386.rpm
```

This should install Nessus and any needed dependencies.

Project 3-2

1. Run the following *nmap* commands and note the differences in the output. (As with all commands used in this book, if the directory containing the program you want to run is not in your path, either specify the full pathname when running the command, cd to the correct directory and use ./ to run the command, or modify your PATH environment variable.)

```
nmap -sT -F IP-address          TCP connect scan
nmap -sS -F IP-address          SYN scan
nmap -sU -F IP-address          Scan UPD ports
nmap -sF -F IP-address          FIN scan
nmap -O  -F IP-address          Determine OS
nmap -p22 -O  IP-address        Determine OS on port 22
nmap -p 1-30,40-65535 IP-address Scan given port ranges
```

2. Did you get the output you expected?

Project 3-3

Although Nessus is commonly run at the command line, a GUI is also available. In this project, you experiment with downloading, installing, and using the Nessus GUI client.

1. Go to www.nessus.org and download the most recent version of the NessusClient GUI for Linux. (As of this writing, the current version is–3.0.0.beta2.) Select the appropriate file for your system. For example, for Fedora Core 6, you would download NessusClient-3.0.0.beta2-fc6.i386.rpm.

2. Change to the directory containing the file you just downloaded and type the following command to install the GUI client:

   ```
   NessusClient-3.0.0.beta2-fc6.i386.rpm
   ```

3. Start the Nessus client using the appropriate command on your desktop's programs menu. Refer to the Help command on the menu bar in the Nessus client for information on using the GUI client. Experiment with some commands and run a few different scans to get an idea of how to use GUI client.

4

SNIFFERS

After reading this chapter and completing the exercises, you will be able to:

- Identify sniffers
- Recognize types of sniffers
- Discover the workings of sniffers
- Appreciate the functions that sniffers use on a network
- List types of sniffer programs
- Implement methods used in spotting sniffers
- List the techniques used to protect networks from sniffers

A sniffer, or **packet sniffer,** is an application that monitors, filters, and captures data packets transferred over a network. As with any network monitoring tool, a sniffer can be used for legitimate purposes, such as checking for bottlenecks or anomalies within network traffic, or for unethical purposes, such as trolling for plaintext passwords or series numbers to use in a **spoofing** attack. Sniffers are nearly impossible to detect in operation, and can be implemented from nearly any computer. There are three classes of sniffer, two of which will be discussed in detail. The three types of sniffer are bundled, commercial, and free.

Bundled Sniffers

Bundled sniffers come bundled with specific operating systems. It is possible, but not likely, that you might need to get a copy of a bundled sniffer for your operating system separate from the one that came on your installation media. You may need a copy if you have implemented an extremely minimized server installation and discovered later that you wanted sniffer functionality. A copy might also be necessary if you have damaged installation media, customized installation media, or corrupted or missing files after installation. Examples of bundled sniffers include the following:

- Network Monitor comes bundled with Windows. Network Monitor, a component of Microsoft® Systems Management Server (SMS), enables you to detect and troubleshoot problems on LANs, WANs, and serial links running the Microsoft Remote Access Server (RAS). Network Monitor provides real-time and post-capture modes of network data analysis.

- Tcpdump comes with many open source UNIX-like operating systems, like Linux. Tcpdump is an open source application. If you are running a standard install of many Linux systems, you can find out if Tcpdump is present on your system by typing which tcpdump in a terminal window. Figure 4-1 shows the output from a command line check for Tcpdump.

```
root@l8: /root                                              [_][□][✕]
 File  Edit  View  Terminal  Tabs  Help
wolf@l8:~$ tcpdump
tcpdump: socket: Operation not permitted
wolf@l8:~$ which tcpdump
/usr/sbin/tcpdump
wolf@l8:~$ su -
Password:
root@l8:~ # tcpdump --help
tcpdump version 3.9.1
libpcap version 0.8.3
Usage: tcpdump [-aAdDeflLnNOpqRStuUvxX] [-c count] [ -C file_size ]
               [ -E algo:secret ] [ -F file ] [ -i interface ] [ -M secret ]
               [ -r file ] [ -s snaplen ] [ -T type ] [ -w file ]
               [ -W filecount ] [ -y datalinktype ] [ -Z user ]
               [ expression ]
root@l8:~ # █
                                                              4-1
```

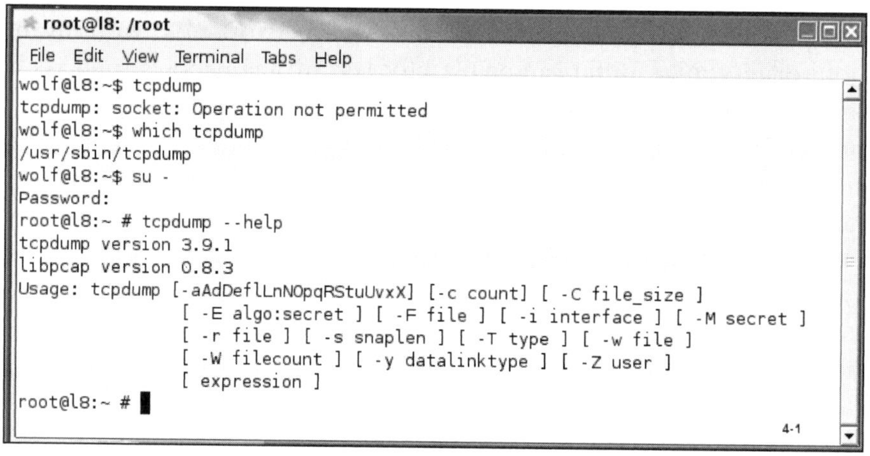

Figure 4-1   Command line check for tcpdump

- Snoop is bundled with the Solaris operating systems. Snoop captures packets from the network and displays their contents. Snoop uses the network packet filter and streams buffer modules to provide efficient capture of packets from the network. Captured packets can be displayed as they are received, or saved to a file (which is *RFC 1761*–compliant) for later inspection.

- The nettl and netfmt packet-sniffing utilities are bundled with the HP-UX operating system.

Commercial Sniffers

Commercial sniffers observe, monitor, and maintain information on a network. Some companies use sniffer programs to detect network problems. Commercial sniffers can be used for both fault analysis, which detects network problems, and performance analysis, which detects bottlenecks.

Free Sniffers

Free sniffers are also used to observe, monitor, and maintain information on a network. These sniffer programs are used, just like their commercial brethren, to detect network problems. Free sniffers can also be used for both fault analysis, which detects network problems, and performance analysis, which detects bottlenecks. The two major differences between commercial and free sniffers are:

- Commercial sniffers generally cost money, but typically come with support.

- Support on free sniffers has the reputation of being scant, meaning it is difficult to find anyone who will offer support; incomplete, meaning that the information was never recorded; or fiendishly expensive, compared to support for commercial products. This reputation is not always deserved.

Hackers, students, and experimenters are often ill-funded, and the outlay of $2995.00 for a copy of EtherPeek may be out of the question. The Internet tradition of "free everything" is another draw toward using open source and free tools when they are available. However, you may have a specific network, such as gigabit Ethernet, that you cannot sniff with any of the current free sniffers, which would require that you spend cash on a commercial product. (But the fact that you are playing with a gigabit network places you in a different category from most hackers, students, or experimenters.)

SNIFFER OPERATION

To do packet sniffing, you will have to obtain or code a packet sniffer that is capable of working with the type of network interface supported by your operating system.

TCP/IP supports the following types of network interfaces:

- Standard Ethernet Version 2
- IEEE 802.3
- Token-ring
- Serial Line Internet Protocol (SLIP)
- Loopback
- FDDI
- Serial Optical

- ATM
- Point-to-Point Protocol (PPP)

Sniffers look only at the traffic passing through the network interface adapter on the machine where the application is resident. That means that you can read the traffic on the network segment upon which your computer resides. It takes a series of steps to be able to sniff other network segments, including introducing a Trojan to open a back door so you can introduce a sniffer and get the information back through the intervening routers, switches, and firewalls.

If you are on an Ethernet LAN or a commercial "fast Ethernet" service like cable, satellite, or DSL access, the most common wired network interface adapter is an RJ-45 10/100BASE-TX NIC. The second most common interface adapter is a USB connection from the cable or DSL modem to the computer. The wireless network interface card is built into many laptops and desktop PCs. There are packet sniffers designed for wireless networks, but they are not covered in this text.

If your PC does not have a "fast Ethernet" RJ-45 port or a USB connection to a cable or DSL modem, and you are not using a wireless Internet connection, then you are not on a LAN. You are probably dialing up using a telephone modem. Your sniffer will probably work just fine on that segment of your ISP's network. The majority of nodes on a commercial ISP network segment are most likely residential customers. These are the standard fare of network hackers looking for unsophisticated users and unpatched machines to load Trojans onto and to sniff for plaintext passwords and credit card numbers.

Components of a Sniffer

As shown in Figure 4-2, sniffers use the following components to capture data from a network:

- Hardware
- Capture driver
- Buffer
- Decoder
- Packet Analysis

Hardware

A NIC is the hardware most needed for much of what a hacker, student, or experimenter will be doing with a sniffer. Certain conditions require specialized hardware to diagnose. Hardware faults, such as **Cyclic Redundancy Check (CRC)** errors, voltage problems, or cable problems, require such specialized equipment as network analyzers and **time domain reflectometry (TDR).**

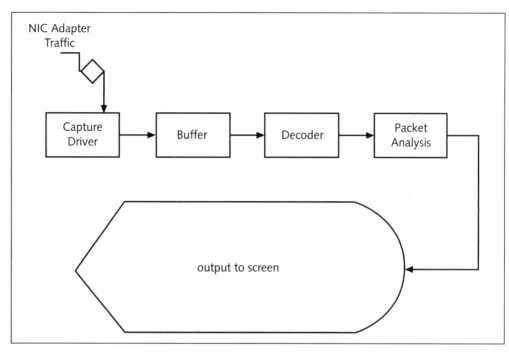

Figure 4-2 Sniffer components

Capture Driver

The capture driver captures the network traffic from the Ethernet connection. It filters out the information that you don't want, and then stores the filtered traffic information in a buffer. Why would you filter the traffic? A small LAN like your lab setup transmits over 108 packets per second. If you run your sniffer, or analyzer, for 10 minutes on that network, you could presumably have 64,800 packets to consider. You might want to filter out the ARP requests and BIOS notifications, or the SIP protocol packets (VoIP), or use some other choice of filter. Without some filter in place, you are likely to fill your buffer with useless (for you) packet information.

Buffer

When a sniffer captures data from a network, it stores the data in a buffer—a dynamic area of RAM that holds specified data. There are two ways of storing captured data.

In the first method, data is stored until the buffer is filled with information. If the full buffer does not trigger the sniffer to stop collecting data, there might be a resultant "buffer overflow" condition. The second way to store information is the round-robin method. This method stores data until capacity is reached. At this point, the oldest data is replaced by the newest data captured. If you have a buffer capable of taking in 60,000 lines of data, you will start overwriting lines in a little over nine and a quarter minutes, based on the network example above.

Decoder

Information traveling across a network is typically in binary format, which is not human-readable. Decoders interpret this information and then display it in a readable format. A decoder helps analyze what information is passed from computer to computer.

Packet Analysis

The final major feature of a sniffer is packet analysis. Sniffers usually provide real-time analysis of captured packets. Some advanced sniffing features enable editing and retransmitting of the data.

Figure 4-3 shows an example of network traffic recorded through Tcpdump.

```
12:45:21.998838 IP 8.8.194.14.sip > 192.168.0.103.sip-tls: SIP, length: 455
12:45:22.048750 IP 192.168.0.103.sip-tls > 8.8.194.14.sip: SIP, length: 323
12:45:22.056791 IP 192.168.0.103.sip-tls > 8.8.194.14.sip: SIP, length: 893
12:45:22.122257 IP 8.8.194.14.sip > 192.168.0.103.sip-tls: SIP, length: 277
12:45:22.126593 IP 8.8.194.14.sip > 192.168.0.103.sip-tls: SIP, length: 377
12:45:22.273404 IP 192.168.0.103.sip-tls > 8.8.194.14.sip: SIP, length: 352
12:45:33.933227 IP 192.168.0.104.1176 > ipt-rtca08.dial.aol.com.5190: UDP, length 32
12:45:33.933524 IP 192.168.0.104.1176 > ipt-rtca08.dial.aol.com.5190: UDP, length 4
12:45:33.933684 IP 192.168.0.101.34634 > 192.168.0.1.domain:  57459+ PTR? 8.5.163.152.in-addr.arpa. (42)
12:45:33.961221 IP ipt-rtca08.dial.aol.com.5190 > 192.168.0.104.1176: UDP, length 4
12:45:33.963608 IP 192.168.0.1.domain > 192.168.0.101.34634:  57459 1/0/0 PTR[|domain]
12:45:38.507445 IP 192.168.0.1.1900 > 239.255.255.250.1900: UDP, length 252
12:45:38.507815 IP 192.168.0.1.1900 > 239.255.255.250.1900: UDP, length 270
12:45:38.508244 IP 192.168.0.1.1900 > 239.255.255.250.1900: UDP, length 324
12:45:38.509121 IP 192.168.0.1.1900 > 239.255.255.250.1900: UDP, length 316
12:45:38.510259 IP 192.168.0.1.1900 > 239.255.255.250.1900: UDP, length 246
12:45:38.510473 IP 192.168.0.1.1900 > 239.255.255.250.1900: UDP, length 288
12:45:38.511472 IP 192.168.0.1.1900 > 239.255.255.250.1900: UDP, length 320
12:45:38.512840 IP 192.168.0.1.1900 > 239.255.255.250.1900: UDP, length 266
12:45:38.513303 IP 192.168.0.1.1900 > 239.255.255.250.1900: UDP, length 318
```
4-3

Figure 4-3   Tcpdump traffic

The general pattern in Tcpdump starts out with the time stamp of each frame down to the 10-thousandth of a second. Following that is the originating IP and port or protocol, then the recipient IP and port or protocol (SIP is a voice-over IP protocol). The last item is the packet size, or length, in bytes.

Placement of a Sniffer

- A sniffer can be implemented anywhere within a network; however, it is best to load your sniffer on a node in the network segment that is to be inspected. Consider the following example network, shown in Figure 4-4: This network has e-mail and Web servers in its **DMZ** area, and a firewall between the gateway router and the main network. Inside the main network there is a possibility of 24 subnets, depending on the switch in use there. The two subnets shown are for the Accounting and Research & Development (R&D) departments. The information available from sniffing the traffic to the Accounting and the R&D subnets would be valuable to a hacker for different reasons. We will assume you have enough access to place your sniffer anywhere in this network. As an intrusion tester, you will have to think like a hacker to monitor what a hacker would want to do. To get all of the information from the main network, the sniffer would have to be mounted on the gateway router or on a computer in that segment.

- To get all of the mail and Web server usernames and passwords, the sniffer could be placed on a machine in the DMZ. This would get the remote users who VPN as well as the local users.

- To get outgoing and incoming traffic from all subnets but not the traffic that would be dropped at the inner firewall, you would want to put your sniffer on the subnet between the inner firewall and the switch.

- You might be able to get the same information by placing your sniffer on the switch itself.

- You could get all of the network usernames and passwords by putting your sniffer on the radius server, which runs authentication for the network.

- You could get all the traffic to and from the Accounting Department by placing your sniffer on a machine in the Accounting subnet. You will not get any internal chatter from R&D or any of the traffic to or from R&D.

- You could get all the traffic to and from the R&D Department by placing your sniffer on a machine in the R&D subnet. You will not get any internal chatter from Accounting (or any other subnet) or any of the traffic to or from Accounting.

Figure 4-4 shows the network and various places where a sniffer could be placed to return useful data.

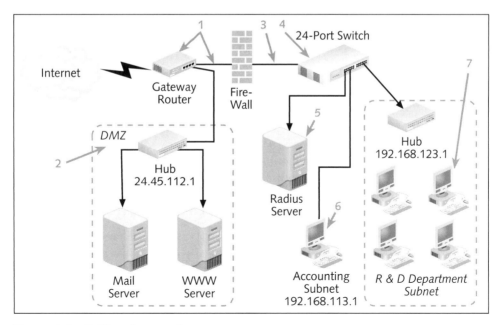

Figure 4-4   Sniffer placements

A sniffer is best strategically placed in a location where only the required data will be captured. In the above example, the R&D subnet probably transmits about 1000 packets per hour, whereas the entire network, with 24 subnets and Web and e-mail servers, is probably transmitting and receiving over 100,000 packets. Placing your sniffer at point 1 with no filters on the traffic will result in a full hard drive in short order (100K * 64K per packet fills the storage space at a rate of 6.4 GB per hour).

TIP

This is an approximate figure. What is generally called 64K is really 65,536 bytes. A kilobyte is really 1024 bytes. All modern computers use binary coding, base 2, whether it is explicitly stated or not. IP addresses are binary, whether they are displayed in dotted decimal (192.168.0.101); in hexadecimal, which is rare but important to consider (C0.A8.00.65); or in binary (11000000 .10101000.00000000.01100101).

This might look suspicious to **Tripwire** or an attentive security administrator. If you were testing to see what kind of traffic runs through the network before you filter out the traffic you do not need, you might well be discovered. To avoid this possibility, you probably want to place your sniffer at point 2, 6, or 7 and filter the collected data packets to capture only required information, such as authentication information like usernames and passwords.

Sniffers are normally placed on:

- Computers
- Cable connections
- Routers
- Network segments connected to the Internet
- Network segments connected to servers that receive passwords

MAC Addresses

To understand how sniffers operate, you must be familiar with the idea of a **Media Access Control (MAC)** address and the process of how data is transferred across a network. As you know, Ethernet cables connect computers on a network with one another. In order to identify a particular computer on a network, computers are assigned a unique identifier called a MAC address. This identifier, associated with the NIC attached to most networking equipment, is important. When data is transferred over a network, each computer requires a unique address that distinguishes it from the other computers on the network.

The Arp table shown in Figure 4-5 displays the MAC addresses associated with the IP addresses of the nodes on the local subnet.

```
root@l8: /root
Terminal
File  Edit  View  Terminal  Tabs  Help
Address            HWtype  HWaddress          Flags Mask      Iface
192.168.0.1        ether   00:0D:88:A7:97:1C  C               eth0
192.168.0.100      ether   00:B0:D0:95:38:0A  C               eth0
192.168.0.104      ether   00:07:95:29:99:32  C               eth0
wolf@l8:~$
                                                               4-5
```

Figure 4-5 Arp table

TIP MAC addresses are sets of hexadecimal numbers. If you ever see a MAC address with alphabetic characters beyond the letter F, you have caught a text error. No computer would be able to handle a spoofed MAC with a G in it.

Data Transfer over a Network

Figure 4-6 illustrates the concept of data transfer over a network. If a data packet is sent from Alice to Bob, this packet must pass through many routers. These various routers will first examine the destination Internet Protocol (IP) address, in order to direct the data packet to Bob.

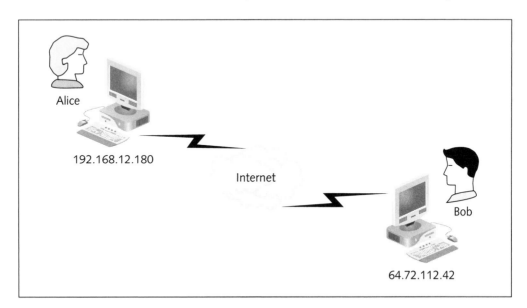

Alice

192.168.12.180

Internet

Bob

64.72.112.42

Figure 4-6 Imaginary message from Alice to Bob

In this example, Alice is on a private 192.168.x.x network, of which there can be unlimited numbers attached to the Internet. As this is known to be a private LAN subnet, no IP address starting with 192.168 can be searched over the Internet, and no duplicate private IP addresses can conflict with each other, as long as there are two routers with a public IP interface between them. In Figure 4-7, the destination is a public IP address.

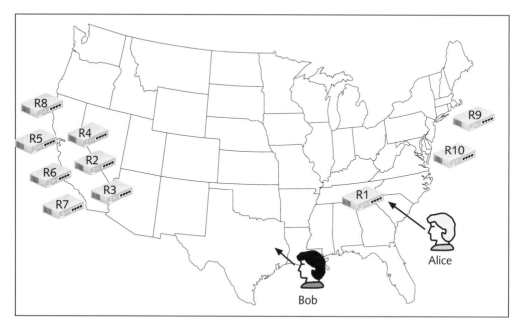

Figure 4-7 A packet travels from Alice to Bob

This example packet goes through 10 routers. (Though this is only an example, all of these public IP addresses are real and owned by the listed owners.)

- 192.168.12.180   Originator (Alice's computer in North Metro Atlanta)

- R1   192.168.12.1   Gateway Router with an outward-facing IP in the 10.136. 192 subnet

- R2   10.136.192.1   Router in the Charter Cable Internet Network in California

- R3   209.186.118.17 Router owned by CERFNet on an AT&T network in San Diego

- R4   172.26.96.249 Backbone Router - NetName: IANA-BBLK-RESERVED

- R5   atlnga1wcx1-pos4-0.wcg.net (64.200.231.245) Owner Level 3 Communications

- R6   drvlga1wcx1-pos14-0-oc48.wcg.net (64.200.127.150) A gateway router into a commercial network owned by Williams Communications on a Level 3 network

- R7   * drvlga1wcx3-pos6-0-oc48.wcg.net (64.200.127.134) Router within the subnet, maybe a firewall or a repeater

- R8 drvlga1wcx3-cogent-peer.wcg.net (64.200.127.234) Gateway router out of the Williams network into another commercial network

- R9 p10-0.core01.iah01.atlas.cogentco.com (154.54.5.89) Leased to Cogentco by Performance Systems International in Washington, DC

- R10 38.99.206.186 Another Cogentco server in Washington, DC

- 64.72.112.42 Owner Alpha Red Inc. This is the outward-facing address of Bob's PC, but it may be only the gateway router's public IP address. Bob's real IP address may never be knowable from a trace.

Alice has the information about the first router and the IP address of Bob's PC. Alice knows nothing about all the intervening routers and would be surprised that her packet has to go through San Diego *and* Washington, DC, to get to Bob in Houston. Her computer communicates with R1 to transmit the data packet. To do this, Alice's computer employs an Ethernet frame to communicate with that router. The format of an Ethernet frame is shown below in Figure 4-8.

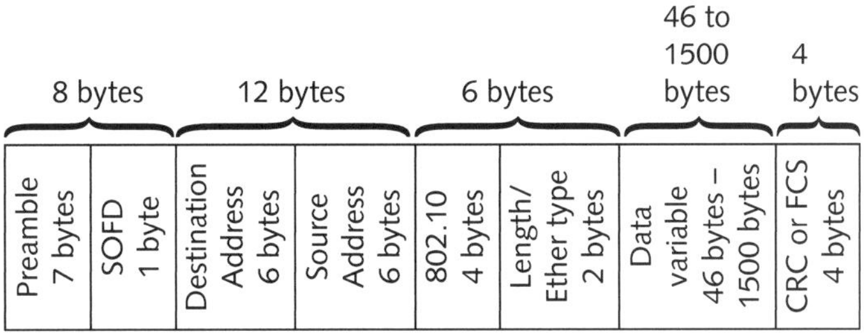

Figure 4-8 Ethernet frame

The Transmission Control Protocol/Internet Protocol (TCP/IP) stack in Alice's computer generates a frame to transmit the data packet to Bob in Houston. The TCP/IP stack then transfers it to the Ethernet module. Now it can attach 18 bytes for the destination MAC address, source MAC address, 802.1Q VLAN Information, and EtherType 0x0800. The frame also contains the origin and destination IP addresses. This data is sent so that the TCP/IP stack at the opposite end is able to process the frame. In addition, the Ethernet module attaches four bytes at the end, with a checksum or CRC. CRC checks to verify that the Ethernet frame reaches the destination address without being corrupted.

Next, the frame is sent to the Ethernet cabling within the network or (in this case) the private LAN. Now all of the hardware adapters on the LAN can view the frame, including the adapter attached to R1. Every adapter then compares the destination MAC address in the frame with its own MAC address. If they do not match, then the adapter discards the frame. This comparison of MAC addresses is created at the Open System Interconnection (OSI) Data Link layer. The R1 router has an ARP table that includes at least one router outside of the network, for which it has both MAC and IP addresses, and that is where it sends unknown IP address requests. Router R2 gets a packet with the source MAC address of R1, and a destination MAC of whatever its MAC is. The packet is then passed across the country twice, and this has the beneficial effect of updating all the route tables in all the routers to get addresses from Atlanta to Houston, as well as opening a session between Alice and Bob.

The Role of a Sniffer on a Network

When you transmit information in a data packet to a computer on a network, the request is sent to every computer on that network that uses the same Ethernet cable or wireless LAN. Although all computers receive the request, only the computer to which the data packet was sent will respond. All the other NICs examine the destination address in the data packet and then drop it. If Computer C transmits data packets to Computer A, then Computer B and D will drop these data packets. Only Computer A will accept the data.

A NIC can be set up to retrieve any data packet being transferred throughout the Ethernet network segment. This mode is known as **promiscuous mode**. A sniffer on any node on this network can record all the traffic that travels across the network by using the NIC's built-in ability to examine packets. A sniffer puts a network card into the promiscuous mode by using a programmatic interface. This is how an administrator or a hacker can use a sniffer in the promiscuous mode to capture all network traffic.

The majority of operating systems provide an interface by which a user-level program has the capacity to turn on the promiscuous mode and capture data packets. This interface can bypass the TCP/IP stack operating systems. The traffic is then passed on to the application layer of the TCP/IP stack, where the sniffer application collects, filters, and analyzes that traffic. Figure 4-9 shows MAC addresses and their corresponding IP addresses for each frame (or packet) transferred.

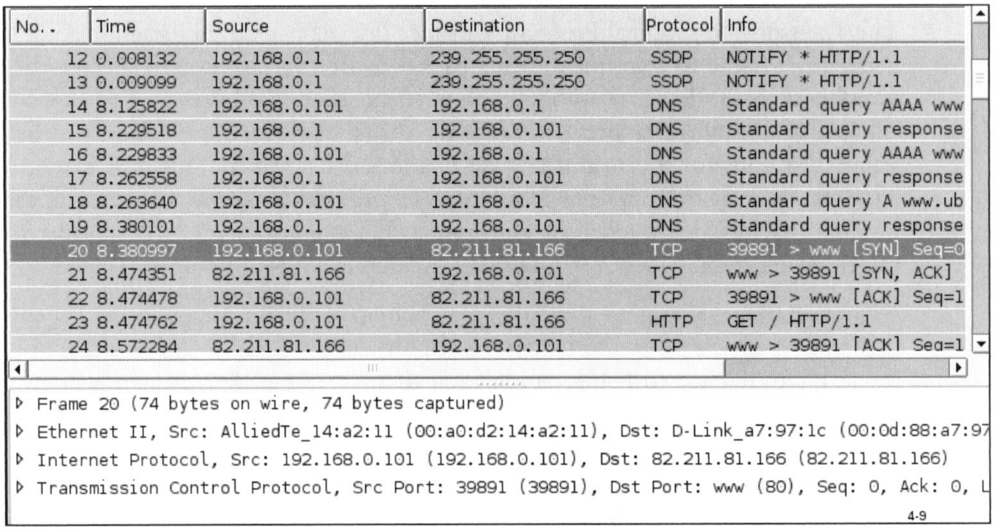

No. .	Time	Source	Destination	Protocol	Info
12	0.008132	192.168.0.1	239.255.255.250	SSDP	NOTIFY * HTTP/1.1
13	0.009099	192.168.0.1	239.255.255.250	SSDP	NOTIFY * HTTP/1.1
14	8.125822	192.168.0.101	192.168.0.1	DNS	Standard query AAAA www
15	8.229518	192.168.0.1	192.168.0.101	DNS	Standard query response
16	8.229833	192.168.0.101	192.168.0.1	DNS	Standard query AAAA www
17	8.262558	192.168.0.1	192.168.0.101	DNS	Standard query response
18	8.263640	192.168.0.101	192.168.0.1	DNS	Standard query A www.ub
19	8.380101	192.168.0.1	192.168.0.101	DNS	Standard query response
20	8.380997	192.168.0.101	82.211.81.166	TCP	39891 > www [SYN] Seq=0
21	8.474351	82.211.81.166	192.168.0.101	TCP	www > 39891 [SYN, ACK]
22	8.474478	192.168.0.101	82.211.81.166	TCP	39891 > www [ACK] Seq=1
23	8.474762	192.168.0.101	82.211.81.166	HTTP	GET / HTTP/1.1
24	8.572284	82.211.81.166	192.168.0.101	TCP	www > 39891 [ACK] Seq=1

▷ Frame 20 (74 bytes on wire, 74 bytes captured)
▷ Ethernet II, Src: AlliedTe_14:a2:11 (00:a0:d2:14:a2:11), Dst: D-Link_a7:97:1c (00:0d:88:a7:97
▷ Internet Protocol, Src: 192.168.0.101 (192.168.0.101), Dst: 82.211.81.166 (82.211.81.166)
▷ Transmission Control Protocol, Src Port: 39891 (39891), Dst Port: www (80), Seq: 0, Ack: 0, L

4-9

Figure 4-9   MACs in a frame

SNIFFER PROGRAMS

Sniffer programs have been written for use with many different operating systems. Some sniffer programs are used for monitoring purposes; others are written specifically for capturing authentication information. Many of the common commercial and free sniffers are described below. The "bundled-only" sniffers mentioned above will not be described in detail. Several of these entries are essentially for historical interest rather than for download and use. With the advent of faster networks, CPUs, and RAM over 128MB, the partially functioned sniffers have fallen out of favor. In the year 2000, 10Mbps Ethernet was the norm for enterprise LANs that were not running token-ring BNC networks, and dial-up was the only sensible choice for home users of Internet services. The average home machine was a Pentium II with a 333mHz Processor and 64Mb RAM.

Wireshark (Ethereal)

Previously known as Ethereal, Wireshark is probably the best-known and most powerful free network protocol analyzer for UNIX/Linux and Windows. It allows you to capture packets from a live network and save them to a capture file on disk. You can interactively browse the captured data, viewing summary and detail information for each packet. Ethereal has several powerful features, including a rich display filter language and the ability to view the reconstructed stream of a TCP session.

Data can be captured off the wire from a network connection and can be read from Ethernet, FDDI, PPP, token-ring, or X.25 interfaces. Detailed information on every data packet can be viewed. The information is displayed in a readable format. Captured data can be edited or altered by using command-line switches.

Figure 4-10 shows the options available for capturing data using Ethereal. As the figure details, you can capture data in promiscuous mode. You can also capture data in standard mode, but the collected data will be only broadcasted requests or packets sent directly to the NIC upon which the sniffer is installed.

When network traffic is captured, you get information about the source and destination IP addresses, the protocol being used, and the data contained in the packet. All of this data is shown in Figure 4-11. The highlighted packet is an AOL Instant Messenger (AIM) message from which there was no human response. As you can see, there is much information to glean from a few minutes of sniffing.

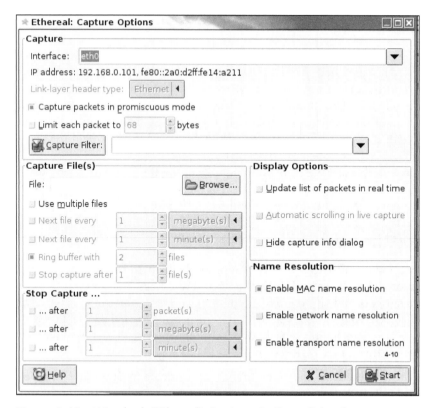

Figure 4-10 Wireshark (Ethereal) Capture Options dialog box

Tcpdump/Windump

Tcpdump, mentioned above as the most commonly bundled sniffer with Linux distros, is also widely used as a free network diagnostic and analytic tool for UNIX and UNIX-like operating systems. Tcpdump is configurable to allow for packet data collection based on specific strings or regular expressions. Tcpdump can decode and monitor the header data of the following protocols:

- Internet Protocol (IP)
- Transmission Control Protocol (TCP)
- User Datagram Protocol (UDP)
- Internet Control Message Protocol (ICMP)

Tcpdump also monitors and decodes application-layer data and can be used for tracking network problems, detecting ping attacks, or monitoring network activities, including network infrastructure protocols.

When the *tcpdump* command is executed at the command line, or *windump* (the separate Microsoft Windows port of Tcpdump) is executed at the MS-DOS prompt, the operator

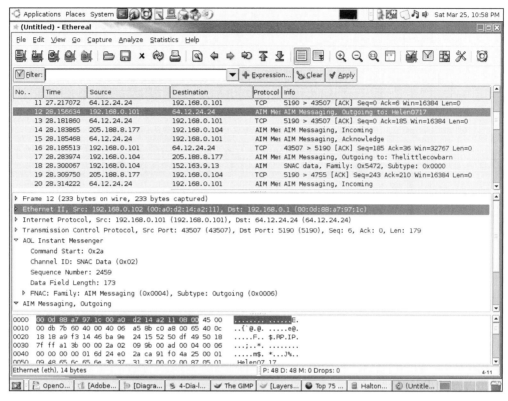

Figure 4-11   Wireshark (Ethereal) packet capture data

receives information about the data packets being transferred over the network. Figure 4–12 shows the options available in Tcpdump, and Figure 4–13 shows a segment of the packet data displayed using the command *tcpdump*. One option that is not entirely obvious is that -v or -vv will put Tcpdump into "verbose mode," causing the packet data stream to be richer in information.

```
Terminal
File  Edit  View  Terminal  Tabs  Help
wolf@l8:~$ tcpdump --help
tcpdump version 3.9.1
libpcap version 0.8.3
Usage: tcpdump [-aAdDeflLnNOpqRStuUvxX] [-c count] [ -C file_size ]
               [ -E algo:secret ] [ -F file ] [ -i interface ] [ -M secret ]
               [ -r file ] [ -s snaplen ] [ -T type ] [ -w file ]
               [ -W filecount ] [ -y datalinktype ] [ -Z user ]
               [ expression ]
wolf@l8:~$
                                                                        4-12
```

Figure 4-12   Tcpdump options

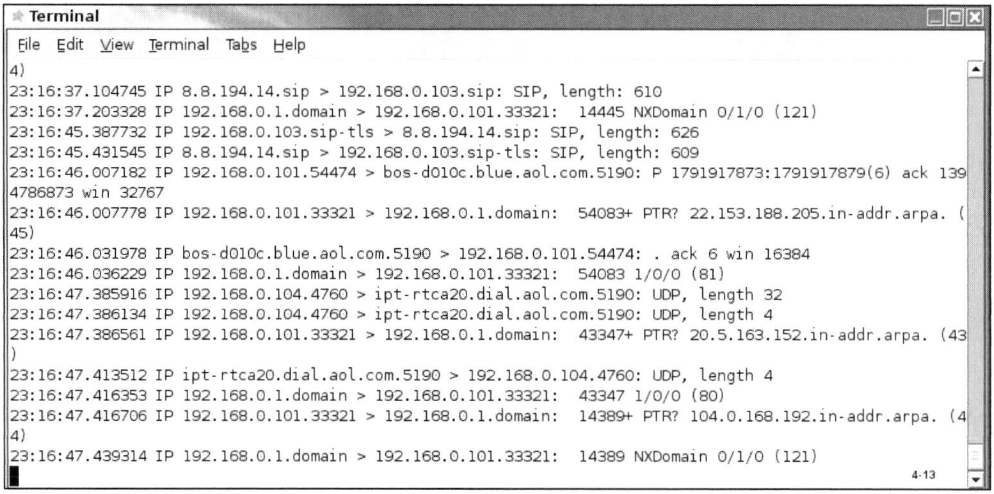

```
Terminal                                                                    _ □ ×
File  Edit  View  Terminal  Tabs  Help
4)                                                                               ▲
23:16:37.104745 IP 8.8.194.14.sip > 192.168.0.103.sip: SIP, length: 610
23:16:37.203328 IP 192.168.0.1.domain > 192.168.0.101.33321:  14445 NXDomain 0/1/0 (121)
23:16:45.387732 IP 192.168.0.103.sip-tls > 8.8.194.14.sip: SIP, length: 626
23:16:45.431545 IP 8.8.194.14.sip > 192.168.0.103.sip-tls: SIP, length: 609
23:16:46.007182 IP 192.168.0.101.54474 > bos-d010c.blue.aol.com.5190: P 1791917873:1791917879(6) ack 139
4786873 win 32767
23:16:46.007778 IP 192.168.0.101.33321 > 192.168.0.1.domain:  54083+ PTR? 22.153.188.205.in-addr.arpa. (
45)
23:16:46.031978 IP bos-d010c.blue.aol.com.5190 > 192.168.0.101.54474: . ack 6 win 16384
23:16:46.036229 IP 192.168.0.1.domain > 192.168.0.101.33321:  54083 1/0/0 (81)
23:16:47.385916 IP 192.168.0.104.4760 > ipt-rtca20.dial.aol.com.5190: UDP, length 32
23:16:47.386134 IP 192.168.0.104.4760 > ipt-rtca20.dial.aol.com.5190: UDP, length 4
23:16:47.386561 IP 192.168.0.101.33321 > 192.168.0.1.domain:  43347+ PTR? 20.5.163.152.in-addr.arpa. (43
)
23:16:47.413512 IP ipt-rtca20.dial.aol.com.5190 > 192.168.0.104.4760: UDP, length 4
23:16:47.416353 IP 192.168.0.1.domain > 192.168.0.101.33321:  43347 1/0/0 (80)
23:16:47.416706 IP 192.168.0.101.33321 > 192.168.0.1.domain:  14389+ PTR? 104.0.168.192.in-addr.arpa. (4
4)
23:16:47.439314 IP 192.168.0.1.domain > 192.168.0.101.33321:  14389 NXDomain 0/1/0 (121)
                                                                              4-13
```

Figure 4-13   Tcpdump packet data flow

Snort

Snort can be used as a packet sniffer, packet logger, or network intrusion detection system, although it is generally used as the latter. It logs packets into either the binary format or the decoded American Standard Code for Information Interchange (ASCII) format. The functions of Snort include:

- Performing real-time traffic analysis
- Performing packet logging on IP networks
- Debugging network traffic
- Analyzing protocol
- Searching and matching content
- Detecting attacks, such as buffer overflows

It works on the following platforms:

- Linux
- Solaris
- Windows NT
- Windows 2000
- Sun
- IRIX

4

The Snort options list is much longer than the Tcpdump list; it has an available Windows GUI front-end; and it is user-friendly, even for a Command Line Interface (CLI) application.

```
wolf@l8:~$ snort

   ,,_        -*> Snort! <*-
 o"   )~    Version 2.3.2 (Build 12)
  ''''      By Martin Roesch & The Snort Team:
http://www.snort.org/team.html
            (C) Copyright 1998-2004 Sourcefire Inc., et al.

USAGE: snort [-options] <filter options>
Options:
        -A          Set alert mode: fast, full, console, or
none   (alert file alerts only)
                    "unsock" enables UNIX socket logging
(experimental).
        -b          Log packets in tcpdump format (much
faster!)
        -c <rules>  Use Rules File <rules>
        -C          Print out payloads with character data
only (no hex)
        -d          Dump the Application Layer
        -D          Run Snort in background (daemon) mode
        -e          Display the second layer header info
        -f          Turn off fflush() calls after binary log
writes
        -F <bpf>    Read BPF filters from file <bpf>
        -g <gname>  Run snort gid as <gname> group (or gid)
after initialization
        -h <hn>     Home network = <hn>
        -i <if>     Listen on interface <if>
        -I          Add Interface name to alert output
        -k <mode>   Checksum mode
(all,noip,notcp,noudp,noicmp,none)
        -l <ld>     Log to directory <ld>
        -L <file>   Log to this tcpdump file
        -m <umask>  Set umask = <umask>
        -n <cnt>    Exit after receiving <cnt> packets
        -N          Turn off logging (alerts still work)
        -o          Change the rule testing order to
Pass|Alert|Log
        -O          Obfuscate the logged IP addresses
        -p          Disable promiscuous mode sniffing
        -P <snap>   Set explicit snaplen of packet (default:
1514)
        -q          Quiet. Don't show banner and status
report
        -r <tf>     Read and process tcpdump file <tf>
```

```
        -R <id>      Include 'id' in snort_intf<id>.pid file
name
        -s           Log alert messages to syslog
        -S <n=v>     Set rules file variable n equal to value v
        -t <dir>     Chroots process to <dir> after initialization
        -T           Test and report on the current Snort
configuration
        -u <uname>   Run snort uid as <uname> user (or uid)
after initialization
        -U           Use UTC for timestamps
        -v           Be verbose
        -V           Show version number
        -w           Dump 802.11 management and control frames
        -X           Dump the raw packet data starting at the
link layer
        -y           Include year in timestamp in the alert
and log files
        -z           Set assurance mode, match on established
sessions (for TCP)
        -?           Show this information
<Filter Options> are standard BPF options, as seen in TCPDump
```

Figure 4-14 shows an example of the output available from using Snort as a packet sniffer.

Network Monitor

Network Monitor, mentioned in the Introduction as a bundled-only sniffer, is part of the Microsoft Windows NT, Windows 2000 Server, and Windows 2003 Server. Earlier versions of Network Monitor captured only the traffic entering or leaving the server on which it was installed, similar to the functionality of Windows 2000. Current versions capture all of the data traffic. Network Monitor performs the following functions:

- Captures network traffic and translates it into a readable format

- Supports a wide range of protocols, including the most widely used Internet and Microsoft protocols

- Maintains the history of each network connection, making it easier to detect errors and their causes

- Supports high-speed as well as wireless networks

- Provides advanced filtering capabilities, which allow the filtering of information at any level and the use of one or more filters at a time

Gobbler

Gobbler is an antiquated MS-DOS-based sniffer that can run on any system with Windows 95 or Windows NT. Gobbler is not in the top 75 hacking tools at insecure.org; however, it is still possible to download a copy of this application. If you are running Win95 or WinNT, you might

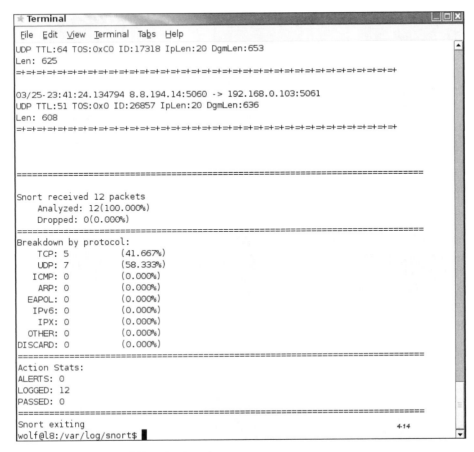

Figure 4-14 Snort CLI output and summary

want to look at what it can do. Once the application has begun, press the F1 key to view information about the various functions it provides. Functions that are supported by Gobbler include packet filtering and event triggering.

Ethload

Another MS-DOS terminal-based application, which may also have a port to Novell systems, is Ethload—a freeware packet sniffer that was written in the C language for Ethernet and token-ring networks. The Ethload program cannot be used to sniff rlogin (UNIX-style remote access) and Telnet sessions. This is unlikely to be in your network analysis toolkit, even if you are running a Windows-only shop. You are much more likely to be using Snort or Wireshark (Ethereal).

Ethload analyzes the following protocols:

- TCP/IP
- DECnet
- OSI
- XNS
- NetWare
- NetBios Extended User Interface (NetBEUI)

Esniff

Esniff is a sniffer program that was written in the C language by the hacker known as "rokstar." The last update of the source file was April 1994. Esniff was designed to sniff packets on SunOS by Sun Microsystems and is coded to capture only the first 300 bytes of each packet, including the username as well as the password. For this reason, hackers frequently used this program. Though a very old program, hackers are probably still able to use it, as there are still many networks where plaintext passwords are the norm. Esniff can support the following protocols:

- Telnet
- FTP
- rlogin

Dsniff

Dsniff is a suite of powerful network auditing and penetration-testing tools last updated in May 2002. This popular and well-engineered suite by Dug Song includes many tools that allow you to passively monitor a network, using filesnarf, dsniff, mailsnarf, msgsnarf, urlsnarf, or Webspy; intercept network traffic, using Arpspoof, dnsspoof, and macof; and perform man-in-the-middle attacks, via sshmitm and webmitm. Dsniff is available for a variety of different Unix/Linux platforms, and has also been ported to Windows.

Sniffit

Sniffit is a network protocol analysis and monitoring tool last updated in February 2005. It captures Transmission Control Protocol (TCP), User Datagram Protocol (UDP), and Internet Control Message Protocol (ICMP) packets, and can be configured to filter incoming packets. It provides detailed technical information about the captured packets—such as information on SEQ, ACK, or TTL fields. It can also decode packets in hex or plain text.

By default, Sniffit can handle Ethernet and Point-to-Point Protocol (PPP) devices and can also be configured to capture data from other devices. While monitoring packets, this program operates in an interactive mode. Sniffit can be used with the following operating systems:

- Linux
- Solaris
- SunOS
- IRIX

Sunsniff

Sunsniff, written in the C language, is a sniffer program written specifically for Sun Microsystems operating systems, such as SunOS. The antispyware sites reiterate that this is not easily portable to other operating systems, so it could presumably be used for experimental purposes if you are running SunOS on your SPARC workstation and are unable to upgrade to Solaris 10.

 SunOS emerged in 1982 and came to an end in 1998 at version 5.7. Solaris is an offshoot of SunOS.

TIP

Linux_sniffer

Linux_sniffer is a Linux-specific sniffer, hence the name. This program is also written in the C language and is of interest mostly for historical reasons. It may still be accessible on some hacking sites, but for the most part, you will find information about it on antispyware sites and security software providers' sites as one of the dangers from which they protect you. Wireshark or Tcpdump are both still being maintained and are more flexible.

Sniffer Pro

Sniffer Pro is a commercial product created by Network Associates, Inc. This program offers an easy-to-use interface for capturing and viewing network traffic. It captures important authentication information, like usernames and passwords. Sniffer Pro is a little like Esniff with a Windows GUI.

EtherPeek NX

WildPackets' Windows-based expert Ethernet network analyzer provides network engineers with the expert diagnostics they need to deploy, secure, and troubleshoot Ethernet networks. This is a commercial sniffer and has a clean and useful interface. It offers a great many features and technological innovations, including real-time expert analysis on multiple adapters, Application Response Time (ART) analysis, extensive application protocol decoding, packet generation, alarms, triggers, notifications, monitoring, and reporting. WildPackets offers a good range of sniffers for various niches.

Fluke Networks Protocol Analyzers

Fluke Networks is a provider of network tools. Its focus is on selling physical tools for network analysis rather than selling only software. There is real value in having an appliance, in that it is impossible to mishandle the installation of the software if it is on a dedicated appliance with only one purpose or user. The downside is that the purchase locks you into the appliance designer's architecture and vision. There is no bouncing around from software to software, looking for the one that is just right for you. There is also very little chance of customizing the interface on the fly with a dedicated tool.

DETECTING A SNIFFER

Since sniffer technology is passive—a byproduct of the way TCP/IP works—it is difficult to detect sniffers. Rather than transmitting information, they merely collect information across networks. No trace of their presence is left on a system, nor is there a record of their use. There are several detection techniques and methods that vary in accuracy; however, you can only detect whether or not the suspect is running his or her NIC in promiscuous mode. You might detect promiscuous mode and falsely assume a sniffer is operative, as there is no law that says that a user cannot run in promiscuous mode without running a sniffer. There are several tools available to check for sniffers, including the following:

- AntiSniff—A project from the L0phtCrack group; runs on Windows NT/98/95 GUI and is also available for CLI on Solaris and OpenBSD. Available at http://packetstormsecurity.nl/sniffers/antisniff.

- SniffDet—Modern, current project, performs ICMP test, ARP test; DNS test; and LATENCY test; runs on UNIX. Available at http://sniffdet.sourceforge.net.

- Check Promiscuous Mode (cpm)—Available at ftp://ftp.cerias.purdue.edu/pub/tools/unix/sysutils/cpm.

- Neped.c—Available at 202.115.128.130/pub2/linux/security/stiff/unix/network-scanners.

- Ifstatus—Works in BSD, HP-UX, SunOS4, and SunOS5; might run in Linux with some tweaking to the source code. Available at ftp://ftp.rediris.es/volumes/vol3/ftp.cert.dfn.de/pub/tools/net/ifstatus.

DNS Test

Some sniffers perform DNS lookups in order to replace IP addresses in their logs with fully qualified host names. Packets sent to an obscure IP address such as 203.115.23.144 would not be as interesting to an attacker as packets sent to mail.thibadeaux.com.

Many tools exist to detect sniffers using this method. Using a tool to generate packets destined for random IP addresses causes your computer to make requests for reverse DNS lookups. The sniffer will make its presence known by generating its own DNS lookup requests on the IP address. Your tool sniffs these requests, which then points to the sniffer program.

Network Latency Tests

4

Several methods use the delay in network latency to determine a host's likely sniffer activity. It is possible to "measure" which of the machines are working harder (in CPU terms), by combining different packet configurations and flooding the network to saturation point with stray packets. The "hard workers" are potential sniffer hosts. The disadvantage of this method is that it significantly degrades network performance. It is essentially a flood attack with a purpose.

Ping Test

Use AntiSniff to perform this test. All sniffers operate on devices that have a TCP/IP stack installed on them. When a computer sends a message to another computer, the receiving computer responds to it by sending a confirmation. When a network card is in promiscuous mode, the OS examines all packets passed on the network to see whether they should be processed. But in some versions of the Linux kernel, only the IP address is examined. Antisniff can take advantage of this by sending a packet that contains a legitimate IP address, but a fake MAC address. If a host responds to a ping with a fake MAC address, it must mean that that host is in promiscuous mode.

ARP Test

An ARP test takes advantage of the way certain Windows operating systems—Windows 95, 98, and NT—handle broadcast ARP packets. When in promiscuous mode, the driver for the network card—that is, the default Microsoft driver that comes with the OS—examines only the first octet of the MAC address to determine whether it is a broadcast packet. Antisniff can exploit this flaw by sending a packet with a MAC address of ff:00:00:00:00:00 and the correct destination IP address of the host, causing the Microsoft OS to respond while in promiscuous mode.

Source-Route Method

The source-route method uses a technique known as the loose-source route. This method may be used to locate sniffers on nearby network segments. This technique adds the source-route information inside the IP header of packets. In this technique, the routers ignore the destination IP address and forward the packet to the next IP address in the source-route option.

In order to understand the loose-source network technique, consider this example. Computers A, B, and C are all on the same network segment, and routing has been disabled on Computer C. Computer A has to send a message to Computer B, but configures the message so that it can only reach Computer B through Computer C. When Computer A transmits the message, it will initially be sent to the router.

When the message is sent from the router to Computer C, Computer C drops the message because its routing has been disabled. If Computer B, on the same segment as Computer C, responds, then it will be evident that it has sniffed the packet from the Ethernet wire.

If Computer C does appear to have sent the message to Computer B, the Time to Live (TTL) field of the message can be used to verify whether Computer B has responded through Computer C or directly from sniffing the Ethernet traffic. Consider the following example to help you understand how the TTL field helps in detecting a sniffer on a computer over a network: Whenever a packet is transferred from Computer A to Computer C, the TTL field of the packet has a preliminary value of 30. At this point, with each hop over the network, this value will decrease by 1. For this reason, if a packet is actually sent from Computer A to Computer B through Computer C, the TTL value will be 29. If Computer B has sniffed the packet from Computer A, obviously the TTL value will not change. Therefore, the presence of a sniffer on Computer B is easily detected.

Decoy Method

The decoy method involves setting up a client and a server on either side of a network. The server is configured with accounts that do not have rights or privileges, or the server is virtual. The client runs a script to log on to the server by using the Telnet, POP, or IMAP protocol. Hackers can grab the usernames and passwords from the Ethernet wire because all of these protocols allow plaintext passwords. The hacker will then attempt to log on to the server by using the captured username and password. This will give network administrators a good idea of which PC is involved in the login attempt.

Whenever a hacker captures information using this method, you can configure standard intrusion detection systems or audit trails in order to log information about the hacker. This method could use a honeypot server. The decoy method works across network segments, whereas ping and ARP methods do not.

Commands

The following commands can be used to detect sniffers on a network from a Linux or UNIX platform. This command may tell you if you are running in promiscuous mode:

```
ifconfig -a
```

And the following command can tell you if you are running a sniffer on your own computer or on any computer to which you have SSH access:

```
ps aux
```

When hackers break into systems, they often leave sniffer programs running in the background. On some UNIX and Linux systems, you can run `ifconfig` to see if the NIC is running in promiscuous mode. You can query the interface simply by employing the `ifconfig -a` command. The parameter "RUNNING PROMISC" indicates that the computer is running in promiscuous mode. This does not work on Debian or Fedora Core versions of Linux.

In the UNIX and Linux operating systems, you can execute the `ps -aux` command for detecting a sniffer. The output of this command displays in a standard table format on the terminal.

This command displays a list of all processes, shows the computer that initiated these processes, and tells the percentage of the processing time as well as the percentage of memory that is being used. In the example below, Ethereal is running as root, plainly showing that you are running a sniffer. Unfortunately, it is not a foolproof method. A hacker could change process arguments on a seemingly valid process to execute a sniffer. Figure 4-15 shows a portion of the output of the `ps aux` command.

TIP Learn what is normally running on your Windows, Linux, or UNIX box. If you aren't sure, then you will not be able to tell if something is out of place. For instance, if you see the process `ultrapossum` and you aren't running an LDAP server on your machine, you may need to look into it.

```
cupsys   24712  0.0  0.4    7652  3564 ?      SNs  07:50  0:02 /usr/sbin/cu
syslog   24991  0.0  0.1    1772   804 ?      SNs  07:57  0:00 /sbin/syslog
wolf     27896  0.0  0.2    4328  1620 ?      S    08:35  0:00 /bin/sh /usr
wolf     27914  7.3  1.5   20752 11924 ?      Sl   08:35  0:49 gnome-system
wolf     27920  2.7  8.1  165708 63476 ?      Sl   08:35  0:18 /usr/lib/ope
wolf     27957  0.1  0.8   12468  6956 ?      S    08:37  0:00 gksudo /usr/
root     27960  0.2  2.8   44696 21788 ?      Ss   08:37  0:01 /usr/bin/eth
root     27964  0.4  2.4   33292 19300 ?      S    08:38  0:02 ethereal-cap
wolf     27968  0.7  1.6   30788 12760 ?      Sl   08:38  0:03 gnome-termin
wolf     27971  0.0  0.0    2280   712 ?      S    08:38  0:00 gnome-pty-he
wolf     27972  0.0  0.2    4696  2060 pts/0  Ss   08:38  0:00 bash
root     28077  0.0  0.1    2692  1540 pts/0  S    08:44  0:00 -su
root     28103  0.0  0.1    2556   884 pts/0  R+   08:46  0:00 ps aux
root@Ubuntu-Ultrix:~ #
```

Figure 4-15   Output of the `ps aux` command

Time Domain Reflectometers (TDR) Method

Time domain reflectometry, TDR, is based on the principle that distance can be measured by computing the time required for reflected energy to be measured at the source. These principles are also the premise for SONAR and RADAR systems. A TDR sends an electrical pulse in the wire and creates a graph based on the reflections that emanate. It also provides distance information in a numerical format. An expert is able to study the graph of the response and then determine the presence of devices that should not be attached to the wire. In addition, the graph can display the distance along the Ethernet wire where the wiretap is located. TDR can detect hardware packet sniffers attached to the network that are otherwise silent.

PROTECTING AGAINST A SNIFFER

The heart of defense against a sniffer is to make the data inconvenient to use. If the hacker cannot use any of the information she collects, then to you as a security administrator it doesn't particularly matter if *all* of your nodes are running sniffers. It is as irrelevant as plugging an RJ-11 phone cable into the RJ-45 Ethernet port and making an audio recording of what comes through the telephone earpiece. The primary way to make the data inconvenient to use is to enrypt it. Encryption is easy to implement; however, it comes with a price: it takes time to encrypt and to decrypt a message. There are lots of encryption models used for specific applications. Encourage the use of applications that use standards-based encryption, such as:

- Secure Sockets Layer (SSL)
- Pretty Good Privacy (PGP) and Secure/Multipurpose Internet Mail Extensions (S/MIME)
- Secure Shell (SSH)

Secure Sockets Layer (SSL)

Designed by Netscape, SSL provides data security between application protocols, such as HTTP and NNTP. This security protocol is called the **Secure Sockets Layer,** or **SSL**. SSL is a nonproprietary protocol providing data encryption, server authentication, message integrity, and client authentication for a TCP/IP connection.

SSL is built as a security standard into all Web browsers and servers that are on the Internet. It permits encrypted Web surfing and is used in e-commerce. SSL allows users to securely enter personal information such as Social Security numbers or credit card information.

SSL comes in two forms, 40-bit and 128-bit. These forms represent the length of the session key generated by all encrypted transactions. As the length of the key increases, it becomes more difficult to break the encryption code. The longer the session key, the more time it takes to encrypt and decrypt.

Pretty Good Privacy (PGP) and Secure/Multipurpose Internet Mail Extensions (S/MIME)

E-mail messages can be sniffed at various points in their travel from sender to receiver. An e-mail message passes through corporate firewalls monitoring network traffic. The message may be held at the sender's mail server for both traffic and security issues. Since your corporate e-mail account belongs to the company and not to you, there is sufficient reason for the company to archive all messages. The message may also be held at a number of intermediate servers, where it is logged and saved. Finally, at the receiving end, a mail server logs and saves the message for retrieval as well as possibly archiving the message for security reasons. Though it is unlikely, the message may mistakenly become misdirected during this period, thus reaching the incorrect mailbox. In this case, the privacy of an e-mail message can be ensured by encryption. The two basic requirements for securing e-mail messages are privacy and authentication. Privacy indicates that only the intended recipient reads the message, and authentication indicates the process that confirms the identity of the sender.

There are two methods that will ensure the security of e-mail messages: **PGP** and **S/MIME**. PGP may be purchased as an optional add-on to many products. It is also available free of cost for personal use. S/MIME is built into several popular e-mail programs, like Eudora, Calypso, Netscape Messenger, Microsoft Outlook, and Outlook Express.

Secure Shell (SSH)

Secure Shell (SSH) is a program used to log on to another computer across a network, execute commands from a remote computer, and transfer files from one computer to another. SSH is the secure alternative to Telnet, an older cleartext protocol.

SSH protects against:

- IP spoofing
- Spoof attacks on the local network
- IP source routing
- DNS spoofing
- Interception of cleartext password
- Man-in-the-middle attacks

More Protection

At OSI layer-2: Enabling port security on a switch or enforcing static ARP entries for certain hosts helps protect against arpspoof redirection, although both countermeasures can be extremely inconvenient.

At OSI layer-3: IPSEC paired with secure, authenticated naming services (DNSSEC) can prevent dnsspoof redirection and trivial passive sniffing.

Firewalls can be a mixed blessing. Since they protect sensitive private networks from the public Internet, they encourage a perimeter-defense model of network security. Sniffers are most effective behind a firewall, where Telnet, FTP, POP, and other legacy cleartext protocols are often allowed by corporate security policy.

CHAPTER SUMMARY

- A sniffer, or packet sniffer, is an application that monitors, filters, and captures data packets transferred over a network. Sniffers are passive technology that exploit the basic operation of network interface cards and network protocols such as TCP/IP.

❏ Bundled sniffers come built into operating systems. Some are free, like Tcpdump, but the commercial bundled sniffers are usually reduced versions of what is available as a separate download.

❏ Nonbundled sniffers are either commercial sniffers with a cost of ownership or free sniffers. Not all free sniffers are open source, especially the historical ones like Gobbler.

❏ The components of a sniffer are hardware, capture driver, buffer, decoder, and packet analysis.

❏ Sniffers need to be placed where they will get the smallest aggregate network traffic but the largest part of the traffic from a targeted node.

❏ The standard behavior in a TCP/IP network that sniffers exploit is that all packets are passed to all the nodes in the subnet before being transferred out to the Internet. All standard NICs examine the packets to compare their MAC address with the destination of the packet. Packets that do not match are discarded or dropped.

❏ Sniffers change the NIC operation mode to promiscuous mode, which allows the capture driver to buffer all packets on the network. That makes it easy to collect cleartext usernames and passwords.

❏ Wireshark (Ethereal), Tcpdump/Windump, Snort, and Network Monitor are all modern packet sniffers and are readily available for UNIX, Linux, and Windows operating systems.

❏ Sniffit works on SunOS, Solaris, UNIX, and IRIX.

❏ Gobbler, Ethload, eSniff, Dsniff, Sunsniff, and Linux_sniffer are essentially of interest for historical reasons.

❏ Sniffer Pro, EtherPeek NX, and Fluke Networks Protocol Analyzers are examples of commercial packet sniffers.

❏ Several tools exist, or have existed, to detect a sniffer. All tests performed by these tools are designed to check for a NIC in promiscuous mode. The tests include: DNS test, network latency tests, Ping test, ARP test, source-route method, decoy method, time domain reflectometer (TDR) method, and certain Linux (UNIX) commands to see if your own machine (or one you can shell into) has been compromised by a hacker and is running a sniffer.

❏ All tools for protecting your network from a packet sniffer involve some level of encryption. Currently the best defenses include Secure Sockets Layer (SSL), Pretty Good Privacy (PGP), Secure/Multipurpose Internet Mail Extensions (S/MIME), and Secure Shell (SSH).

REVIEW QUESTIONS

1. Are there cases where a network sniffer is a legitimate application to be running?

2. What operating systems will support a packet-sniffing application?

3. Name four Linux-based packet sniffers.

4. Name four Windows-based packet sniffers.

5. What is a good way to keep sniffer technology from discovering your e-mail passwords?

6. What protocol would you consider for encrypting passwords?

7. What does a time domain reflectometer do?

8. What are the components of an average packet sniffer?

9. What is a MAC address?

10. What equipment uses a MAC address?

11. What feature of a NIC on a TCP/IP network does a sniffer exploit?

Indicate whether the sentence or statement is true or false.

12. _____ Sniffers are made for AppleTalk Networks.

13. _____ Ethernet networks can be made sniffer-proof.

14. _____ Running a sniffer in promiscuous mode is a class VI misdemeanor in many states.

15. _____ Snort is not a sniffer.

16. _____ EtherPeek only runs on SunOS.

17. _____ You can detect a sniffer from its characteristic sound.

18. _____ SSL is a protocol that makes data transmissions unintelligible to a hacker using a sniffer.

19. _____ Sniffers that are not resolving host names are almost impossible to detect.

20. _____ Strict control of who has administrative privileges can wipe out illicit use of sniffers on your LAN.

HANDS-ON PROJECTS

HANDS-ON PROJECTS

Project 4-1

Ethereal/Wireshark is a useful sniffer which gives you the ability to look at raw network packet information so you can monitor items like sequence numbers and timing. Like most complex software packages, Wireshark has dependencies. If you are compiling Wireshark from source code, you may need to ensure that the required external libraries—including GLib/GTK+, libpcap, Net-SNMP, PCRE, and GNU ADNS—are installed. In this project, you will install Wireshark using Fedora's automated package installer, yum. This will automatically install any required dependencies. If using another Linux distribution, use the appropriate package installer for your system.

TIP

Ethereal and Wireshark? In mid-2006, Gerald Combs, founder of the Ethereal project, announced on the Ethereal development mailing list that he was changing jobs, moving to a new location, and taking the project and its core developers with him as he left. This is essentially a trademark issue, but it is unknown how long the Ethereal site will remain active. Combs specifically said that his previous employer, www.netisinc.com, would be in charge of the further progress of Ethereal Inc. Wireshark is a fork of the Ethereal project, a situation not uncommon in the free/open source software universe. Since the main developer is moving to the new project named Wireshark, the maintainers of Linux distros are already making the changes in their software repositories. Since there is no Windows repository, the Windows version may have to be obtained from Wireshark.org.

1. To install Wireshark in Fedora, make sure you are logged in as root, and then type the following command in a Terminal window:

   ```
   yum install wireshark-gnome
   ```

2. After the appropriate repositories have been set up and dependencies have been resolved, you'll see a prompt asking whether you want to continue. Type **y** and press **Enter**. The Wireshark package will be downloaded and installed, and `Complete!` will be displayed when installation is complete.

HANDS-ON PROJECTS

Project 4-2

Many Linux distributions include *tcpdump* as part of the standard installation. If *tcpdump* is not included with your distro, you can install it as shown in this project.

1. Make sure you are logged in as root and enter the following command in a Terminal window:

   ```
   tcpdump
   ```

   You will either see a `command not found` error or you will observe the basic *tcpdump* behavior, which is a scrolling list of all the packets going past on the network. On very small networks, this will not be a lot of traffic. This is the same information that Ethereal stores to a RAM buffer. Figure 4-16 shows the output of the *tcpdump* command.

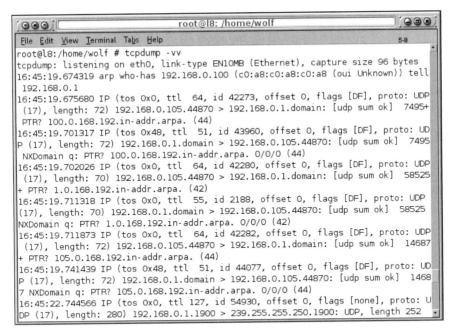

Figure 4-16 *tcpdump* output

2. If you get a `command not found` error, which indicates that tcpdump is not yet installed on your system, type the following command:

```
yum upgrade tcpdump
```

3. When the *tcpdump* package is located, you will be prompted to continue. Type **y** and press **Enter** to begin the installation process. *tcpdump* will be installed on your Fedora system. To install *tcpdump* on a different Linux distribution, use the appropriate package installer. (For example, on a SUSE Linux box, use YaST.)

5

TCP/IP VULNERABILITIES

After reading this chapter and completing the exercises, you will be able to:

♦ Give a definition of TCP/IP

♦ Know the steps of TCP/IP communication

♦ Recognize weaknesses in TCP/IP

♦ Identify steps in protecting information from vulnerabilities in TCP/IP

TCP stands for Transmission Control Protocol, and IP is the abbreviation for Internet Protocol. **TCP/IP** is a suite of protocols that underlie the Internet. The TCP/IP suite comprises many protocols and applications that focus on two main objectives. IP has the tools to provide the correct routing of packets and any device-to-device communications. TCP is responsible for safe and reliable data transfer between host computers. TCP/IP is the common language of networked computers and makes transferring information fast and efficient. However, the developers of this protocol did not take into account the rapid growth of the Internet, and many vulnerabilities of TCP/IP have become apparent. Illegitimate users take advantage of TCP/IP vulnerabilities by exploiting what is known as the "three-way handshake." Unauthorized users may launch a **denial-of-service attack** on the destination computer—this is an assault on a network that floods it with so many additional requests that regular traffic is either slowed or completely interrupted. Denial-of-service attacks will be discussed in greater detail later in this text.

Chapter 5 covers some basic information on TCP/IP and delves into data encapsulation, timers, SYN attacks, spoofing, and other attacks. Figure 5-1 shows the most important protocols within the TCP/IP suite.

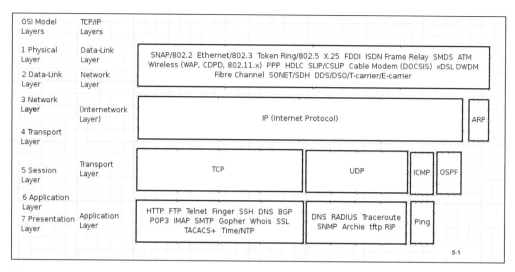

Figure 5-1   TCP/IP

Notice that the OSI Model and the TCP/IP Model are not entirely aligned. The OSI Model has seven layers and the TCP/IP Model has four—or five, if the useful Internet-working layer is added. There has always been a disconnect between these two models.

Data Encapsulation

The TCP/IP Model uses data encapsulation to transfer data from one machine to another (or from one process to another). **Data encapsulation** is the process of enclosing higher-level protocol information in lower-level protocol information. For instance, source–address and destination-address data are unusable to programs at the OSI Presentation layer level. The Presentation layer is involved with display of data on screen and the interaction with the keyboard and mouse, as could be illustrated by a simple word-processor document. The OSI Application layer and TCP/IP Application layer are more concerned with properly saving the document to disk and tracking changes in the document than in transferring the information between nodes. That kind of information doesn't show up as useful until the data is passed to the Transport layer. There, it is broken into packets suitable for processing on the Network layer protocol of TCP, which adds data verification information and numbering for the packets. The packets are then handed off to the Internetworking-layer IP protocol, where they are prepared for the physical transfer by data-link protocols operating on the physical networks that exist between the sender and receiver. Data encapsulating, also called data hiding, is the mechanism where the implementation details of a class remain hidden to the user. Each successive layer hand-off adds at least one new layer of headers to each packet.

The Application layer takes user data and converts it into a format that permits it to be sent when data is transmitted over the network. Control information is added, and that data is passed to the Transport layer. This layer will organize the data into pieces, add its own header information, and pass it on to the Internetworking (IP) layer. The IP layer provides logical addressing as it works with the data in packet format. After the packet addressing information is added, it is sent to the Network layer. There the data is delivered to the Data Link layer, where it is broken down into Ethernet frames or packets. The final headers and trailers are added, and these frames are added to the data stream formats that take it to its end recipient. Figure 5-2 is an illustration of the data encapsulation of a document as it goes from one host to another over a network.

		Frame(Ethernet)		Frame(Ethernet)	
Data Link Layer	Sent out to gateway router and on to described recipient	Header IP Header TCP Header Application Header Data.doc Frame(Ethernet) Footer		Header IP Header TCP Header Application Header Data.doc Frame(Ethernet) Footer	Received from gateway router and checked as to whether this is proper recipient
Network Layer	Prepared for transfer and loaded to NIC queue	IP Header TCP Header Application Header Data.doc		IP Header TCP Header Application Header Data.doc	Frame header and trailer stripped, then packets passed to TCP Transport Layer
Transport Layer	Divided into packets	TCP Header Application Header Data.doc		TCP Header Application Header Data.doc	Packets checked for data-integrity and reassembled in proper order, then TCP Headers stripped
Application Layer	Saved as a document type	Application Header Data.doc		Application Header Data.doc	Verified as a document of specified type, and opened by that application
User Data	the contents of a document	Data		Data	Read by recipient
Layers	Process	Image		Image	Process
	Encapsulation Process			De-Encapsulation Process	

Figure 5-2 Data encapsulation

This process may seem extremely complicated and unmanageable, but in fact, the modular nature of this process greatly simplifies the problem of getting data of various types to successfully transfer over local networks or the Internet.

IP (Internet Protocol)

The Internet Protocol (IP) is responsible for transmitting data from the source computer to the final destination computer. IP is a network protocol operating at layer 3 of the OSI Model (and layer 2 or 3 of the TCP/IP Model). IP is connectionless and so does not guarantee the delivery of packets to the destination. The IP process is responsible for routing packets over network hardware. IP packets may pass by many routes over the network before reaching their final destination. IP addresses come in one of the following formats: IPv4, a 32-bit address, which is usually written as a dotted-decimal number such as 192.168.100. 201; and IPv6, a 128-bit address, which is usually written as eight groups of four hexadecimal digits such as 2001:0db8:85a3:08d3:1319:8a2e:0370:7334. The reason IPv6 exists is that IPv4 allows for only 16,777,216 (1.677216×10^7) possible unique addresses, while IPv6 allows for 3.402823669×10^{38} addresses. This is required by the necessity that each device has a unique address upon the network. IPv6 has not taken over the IP addressing space because of several advances based on IPv4. Industry experts have advanced the date of **IP address exhaustion**—the theoretical time when the number of unallocated IP addresses equals zero—to approximately the beginning of 2011 due to factors such as Dynamic Host Configuration Protocol (DHCP); network address translation (NAT); name-based virtual hosting, tighter control by Regional Internet Registries on the allocation of addresses to Local Internet Registries; network renumbering to reclaim large blocks of address space allocated in the early days of the Internet; and the use of private networks.

IP packets often arrive out of sequence because they are not all taking the same route in sequence, as do the pulses over a standard telephone connection (although even standard telephone connections are routed differently now that many calls travel over the Internet fiber-optic backbone). This is a vulnerability that attackers can exploit. Table 5-1 illustrates the composition of an IP header.

Table 5-1   IP header

Version	IHL	Type of Service	Total Length		
Identification			Flags		Fragment Offset
Time to Live		Protocol	Header Checksum		
Source Address					
Destination Address					
Options				Padding	
TCP header, followed by data					

When a large IP packet is sent over a network, it is broken down. This process is called fragmentation. At its destination, the fragments are reassembled to form a single packet.

Table 5-2 illustrates the possible contents of the fields within an IP header.

Table 5-2   Components of the IP header

Fields within an IP Header	Size in Bits	Description
Version	4	Set to 4 to specify IPv4 packets or to 6 to specify IPv6 packets.
IHL	4	Internet Header Length (IHL) is the length of the Internet header; normal value=5.
Type of Service	8	Points out the quality of the requested service; the quality of service specifies trade-offs between low delay, high reliability, and high throughput, and specifies the precedence level of a packet.

Table 5-2 Components of the IP header (continued)

Fields within an IP Header	Size in Bits	Description
Total Length	16	Specifies the total length of the datagram packet that is being relayed; because this is a 16-bit field, the maximum size of the IP datagram is 65,535 bytes.
Identification	16	Specifies an identity assigned to all of the packets in a datagram so that if the datagram is fragmented, it can be reassembled at the destination.
Flags	3	Three flags are used in the fragmentation of the datagram. The first is reserves. The second is Don't Fragment (DF), which is used for testing purposes, and is ignored by most higher-level protocols. Setting DF to 1 means the packet should not be fragmented. The third flag is More Fragments (MF). If MF is set to 0, it is the last piece. If set to 1, it will be followed by others.
Fragment Offset	13	Specifies the sequence of the fragment in the datagram.
Time to Live	8	Specifies the maximum time the datagram can remain on the network, stated in terms of how many router hops it can make.
Protocol	8	Specifies the next-level protocol to which the datagram belongs.
Header Checksum	16	Specifies the checksum on only the datagram header. It is a simple 16-bit checksum calculated by dividing the header bytes into words (a word is two bytes) and then adding them together. It is needed because the header changes when the value in the Time to Live field changes. At that point, it is recalculated. Each router performs this checksum, and if the calculated figure and the contents of the Header Checksum field are found to be dissimilar, then that router discards the packet as corrupted.
Source Address	32	Specifies the source IP address of the datagram; this is always the original sender, even if the intervening sender was a router or bridge.
Destination Address	32	Specifies the destination IP address of the datagram; this is always the final destination of the packet, even if the intervening destination is a router or a bridge.
Options	Varies	May or may not be present in a datagram; these options are related to routing packets over the network.
Padding	Varies	Adds extra "0" characters to pad out the header to a multiple of 32 bits.

TCP

TCP uses a connection-oriented design, meaning the participants in a TCP session must initially create a connection. The TCP connection is called the three-way handshake. TCP is responsible for providing connection-oriented services between a source and destination computer and for guaranteeing the delivery of packets. The packets reach the application layer in the right order because TCP identifies and assembles packets based on sequence numbers. The sequence number guarantees proper delivery of packets to the destination computer.

The source and destination computers exchange the **initial sequence number (ISN)** when a connection is made. These packets are accepted within a particular range that is specified during the establishment of a connection. TCP rejects packets that contain sequence numbers that are outside the ranges specified by the window size. The TCP header is illustrated in Figure 5-3 below.

16-bit source port number									16-bit destination port number		
32-bit sequence number											
32-bit acknowledgement number											
4-bit header	Reserved (6-bits)	U R G	A C K	P S H	R S T	S Y N	F I N		16-bit window size		
16-bit TCP checksum									16-bit urgent pointer		
Options (if any) plus Padding											
Data (if any)											

Figure 5-3   TCP header

Table 5-3 explains various fields within a TCP header.

Table 5-3   Components of the TCP header

Fields in a TCP Header	Size in Bits	Description
Source port number	16	Can be any port number from 1 to 65,535; there is no reason for a source port for a Web-page request to be port 80.
Destination port number	16	The port number of the destination; can be any port number from 1 to 65,535.
Sequence number (ISN)	32	Sequence number of the first data octet in this segment.
Acknowledgment number	32	If the ACK bit is set, this field contains the value of the next sequence number that is expected by the sender.
Header	4	Offset where data begins in the packet.
Reserved	6	Reserved for future use.
URG	1	Urgent pointer field.
ACK	1	Acknowledgment field.
PSH	1	Push Function.
RST	1	Reset the connection.

Table 5-3 Components of the TCP header (continued)

Fields in a TCP Header	Size in Bits	Description
SYN	1	Synchronize sequence numbers.
FIN	1	No more data from the sender.
Window size	16	Number of data octets starting from one.
TCP checksum	16	Checksum for error-checking of the header and data in the packet.
Urgent pointer	16	When the URG bit is set, this field is interpreted; it contains the value of the urgent pointer, which is higher than the sequence number in this segment.
Options (if any)	Varies	Routing options for the packet.
Padding	Varies	Pads the header to achieve a multiple of 32 bits.
Data (if any)	Varies	Data to be transmitted.

5

Connection Setup and Release

As mentioned above, TCP uses a three-way handshake to set up and release a connection. This means that participants in a TCP session build a connection using three packets in a specific order. There are six possible **TCP packet flags**: URG, ACK, PSH, RST, SYN, and FIN. Packets can have more than one flag set, and this is indicated by the flag names being separated by a slash, such as SYN/ACK, or a comma, such as ACK,FIN. SYN/ACK says the packet is attempting to both synchronize with the sender and acknowledge the received packet. Normally a packet will have only one flag sent, except in the case of SYN/ACK or FIN/ACK. You will never see an RST/FIN packet because these flags signal the same result. Packets with three or more flags set are probably attempts to crash your machine. A packet with all six flags set is called a "Christmas Tree Packet," or a "Nastygram." Newer implementations of TCP/IP usually drop packets like this.

The three packets in a TCP connection are SYN --> SYN/ACK --> ACK. They must update one another on progress by sequencing (ISN) and acknowledgment from both sides. This process is intended to ensure data reliability.

Connection Setup

First, the source computer delivers a SYN packet to the destination computer. This packet has the initial sequence number (ISN) that the destination computer must use in order to send a response (ACK) to the source computer. The ISN is indicated by whether the SYN bit is "set." For example, if the SYN bit is set to 1, the 32-bit sequence number represents ISN. However, if the SYN bit is not set, meaning the value of the SYN bit is zero (0), the 32-bit number represents the (ongoing) sequence number.

Upon receipt of the SYN packet, the receiving computer transmits a SYN with an acknowledgment, ACK. Finally, the source computer sends an ACK to the destination computer as a response with an "in-range" sequence number. Figure 5-4 illustrates a connection setup.

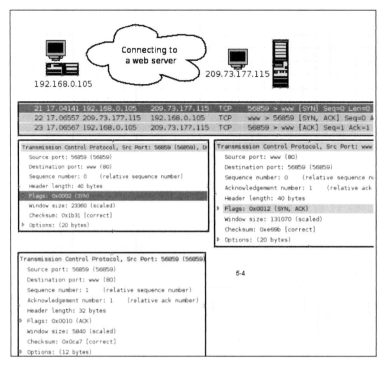

Figure 5-4   Connection setup

Connection Release

When releasing the connection between two computers, the source computer sends a FIN packet to the destination computer. The destination computer then sends a FIN/ACK packet, and the source computer sends an ACK packet. Either computer could send an RST and close the session (reset) immediately.

TCP Timers

All TCP sessions are tracked with timers built into the TCP protocol. Listed below are some of the timers used by TCP/IP:

- Connection establishment: This timer establishes a session. The connection establishment initializes once the source computer transmits a SYN to the destination computer. This occurs during the connection setup. Seventy-five seconds is the default value for the majority of operating systems. A session will not be established if it takes longer than 75 seconds for the destination server to respond.

- FIN_WAIT: This timer waits for FIN packets. Its default value is 10 minutes. If a FIN packet is received within this time, the timer will stop and the connection will close. If that timer runs out, then it is reset for 75 seconds, after which the connection will close.

- TIME_WAIT: The default value for this timer is two minutes. Time_Wait specifically waits for packets to arrive at the destination computer. This timer is uncomplicated because the connection is closed as soon as the timer ends.

- KEEP_ALIVE: This timer checks to see if the destination computer is active. After establishing a connection in a network, the source or destination computer may turn off without informing the other computer. Either computer may send a test packet every two hours to verify whether the other computer is alive and idle. The connection is terminated if there is no response to these packets.

5

VULNERABILITIES IN **TCP/IP**

During the development of TCP/IP in the 1980s, security was not a priority, because almost everybody involved either knew each other or worked for the government, a major corporation, or a university. Since 1990, security has become a serious problem because of the vulnerabilities of TCP/IP, and much work has been done to tighten up network security.

Some of the vulnerabilities that have been exposed are IP spoofing, connection hijacking, ICMP attacks, TCP SYN attacks, and RIP attacks.

IP Spoofing

IP spoofing is a technique attackers use in which they send packets to the victim or target computer with a false source address. The victim is unaware that the packet is not from a trusted host, and so it accepts the packet and sends a response "back" to the indicated source computer.

Since the attacker sending the spoofed packet cannot see the response, he must guess the proper sequence numbers to send the final ACK packet as if it had come from the "real" source. If this attempt is successful, the hacker may have a connection to the victim's machine and be able to hold it for as long as the computer remains active. There are two methods for resolving these problems: sequence guessing and source routing.

Sequence Guessing

During the three-way handshake, the source computer sends a sequence number to the destination computer as part of the initial SYN packet. The destination computer produces its own sequence number and delivers it to the source computer. Then, the source computer sends the ACK packet along with the sequence number that was created by the destination computer.

The hacker sends a few connections to the victim and gets a feel for how quickly the sequence number is incrementing. When the hacker sends the spoofed SYN, and the victim replies to the "real" source, that computer usually lets the SYN/ACK packet drop, since it didn't send the original contact packet. The attacker then sends a spoofed ACK packet with a "best guess" victim's sequence number, based on knowing how busy the victim appears to be, and by what set increment the victim is incrementing its sequence number. Ultimately, the hacker can guess the sequence number because the number is generated using a global counter and is incremented in fixed units.

Source Routing

Each router that receives the packet will examine the destination IP address as packets travel through the network. It then chooses the best destination to route the packet for its next "hop." A sender using **source routing** can specify the return path through which the destination computer will send its reply. Typically, this feature is used for either trouble-shooting a network or improving its performance. Historically, attackers used source routing to gain access to a target computer on the Internet, but they were sometimes unable to reach the target due to the use of private addressing. In this eventuality, the attacker looked for an intermediate computer or router on the Internet that could forward packets to the target computer. At this point, the attacker could reach the target computer from the Internet by source routing through that intermediate computer. This could be called a historical hack because most newer routers and firewalls are configured to drop source-routed packets.

Connection Hijacking

An attacker may be able to control an existing connection between source and destination computers using **connection hijacking**. To do this, an attacker desynchronizes a series of packets between the source and destination computer. Extra packets sent to one of the victims with the same sequence numbers as authentic packets force the victim to choose which packet to accept. If the victim chooses to discard the authentic packets and interacts with the spoofed packets, the attacker has hijacked the connection and now authentic packets will be ignored. The attacker then communicates with the victim computer as if he were the authentic source computer, and that source computer, being ignored, will close its own connection to the victim.

ICMP Attacks

ICMP stands for Internet Control Messaging Protocol. In an **ICMP attack**, packets are used to send fraudulent or deceptive connection information among computers. ICMP is used to test for connectivity using utilities such as the *ping* command. ICMP does not authenticate packets, so it is easy to intercept them and transmit spoofed ICMP packets.

Denial-of-service (DoS) attacks can be formulated by using ICMP packets. Destination Unreachable and Time to Live Exceeded are ICMP packets that reset existing connections between a source and a destination computer. A Destination Unreachable ICMP packet specifies that, because of a problem within the network, packets cannot be sent to the destination computer. The Time to Live field in the TCP header states the duration of time that the packet is valid. Attackers transmitting spoofed packets can successfully reset existing connections.

TCP SYN Attacks

A **TCP SYN attack** takes advantage of the way that most hosts implement the TCP three-way handshake. When Host B receives the SYN request from A, it must keep track of the partially opened connection in a queue for at least 75 seconds. Most systems are limited and can keep track of only a small number of connections. An attacker can overflow the listen queue by sending more SYN requests than the queue can handle. This is why SYN attacks are also called SYN flooding. If large quantities of SYN packets are received without acknowledgment, then all the connections will be busy. Since no new connection can be established, legitimate users will be unable to connect to the computer. This is not always a bona fide attack. When a lot of legitimate users go to a popular site, the same result occurs. There is no way of tracking how many legitimate users are turned away by an overflow of traffic, other than to have load-balancing software and multiple servers to handle that overflow.

RIP Attacks

RIP attacks take advantage of RIP, or Routing Information Protocol. This information protocol is an essential component in a TCP/IP network and is responsible for distribution of routing information within networks.

A RIP packet is often used without verification. Attacks on RIP change the destination of data. An attacker can change the routing table on routers and specify that the route through the hacker's designated collection node is the fastest route for packets to or from a sensitive machine. Once the router is modified, it transmits all of the packets to the hacker computer. They can then be modified, read, or responded to.

SECURING TCP/IP

Data in packets is not encrypted nor are the packets authenticated. This is the two-holed vulnerability in TCP/IP. Since data is not encrypted, a packet sniffer can be used to observe the contents of the packets. It is interesting to watch the user account names and cleartext passwords of POP3 e-mail clients, like Outlook Thunderbird, running over the network at predictable 10-minute intervals. Since computers do not verify whether or not the packets were actually sent from the apparent source computer, attackers can send spoofed packets from any computer.

These flaws cannot be eradicated without changing the architecture of the TCP/IP protocol suite. There is no magic bullet or "killer app" to resolve the security issues in TCP/IP. One must employ many methods simultaneously to achieve success in this area. These solutions are not all global. One solution may have to be implemented again and again on all of the PCs in a network.

These methods can be implemented to decrease vulnerabilities in TCP/IP:

- Modifying default timer values can be used to disrupt or avoid TCP SYN attacks.
- The number of simultaneous connections that a computer can handle may be increased.
- The time limit used to listen for replies to the SYN/ACK in the three-way handshake can be reduced.
- The method used to generate sequence numbers can be changed, using a Random Number Generator (RNG) to generate part of an algorithm that would arrive at the ISN, to make sequence guessing more challenging.
- Firewall rules could be implemented to block spoofed packets from entering the intranet through the Internet or vice versa. The rules could block suspicious packets from moving back and forth from the local network to the Internet.
- Avoid using the source address authentication. Implement cryptographic authentication systemwide.
- If an operator allows outside connections from trusted hosts, enable encryption sessions at the router.
- Packets that are transmitted on the network can be encrypted first or sent using an encrypted VPN. Encryption makes it very challenging for an attacker to get any useful information from employing a sniffer on a network.

IP Security Architecture (IPSec)

IP Security Architecture (IPSec) is a collection of Internet Engineering Task Force (IETF) standards that define an architecture at the Internet Protocol (IP) layer that protects IP traffic by using various security services. Table 5-4 shows some of the protocols included in IPSec.

Table 5-4   Some IPSec protocols

RFC Number	Name	Description
2401	Security Architecture for the Internet Protocol	The main IPSec document, describing the architecture and general operation of the technology, and showing how the different components fit together
2402	IP Authentication Header	Defines the IPSec Authentication Header (AH) protocol used for ensuring data integrity and origin verification
2403	The Use of HMAC-MD5-96 within ESP and AH	Describes a particular encryption algorithm for use by AH and ESP called Message Digest 5 (MD5)
2404	The Use of HMAC-SHA-1-96 within ESP and AH	Describes a particular encryption algorithm for use by AH and ESP called Secure Hash Algorithm 1 (SHA-1)

Table 5-4   Some IPSec protocols (continued)

RFC Number	Name	Description
2406	IP Encapsulating Security Payload (ESP)	Describes the IPSec Encapsulation Security Payload (ESP) protocol that provides data encryption for confidentiality
2408	Internet Security Association and Key Management Protocol (ISAKMP)	Defines methods for exchanging keys and negotiating security associations
2409	The Internet Key Exchange (IKE)	Describes the Internet Key Exchange (IKE) protocol used to negotiate security associations and exchange keys between devices for secure communications; based on ISAKMP and OAKLEY
2412	The OAKLEY Key Determination Protocol	Describes a generic protocol for key exchange

IPSec provides the following services for network users:

- Encryption of user data for privacy

- Authentication of the integrity of a message

- Protection against certain types of security attacks, such as replay attacks

- An ability for devices to negotiate the security algorithms and keys required to make secure authenticated connections

- Two security modes, tunnel and transport, to meet different network needs

CHAPTER SUMMARY

- Internet Protocol (IP) is responsible for sending data from a source computer to a destination computer. It is connectionless and does not validate packets. IP does not ensure the delivery of packets to the destination.

- TCP guarantees the delivery of packets. TCP/IP uses the three-way handshake to set up or release a connection. The three-way handshake is SYN --> SYN/ACK --> ACK.

- Some of the timers that are important for TCP/IP security are Connection Establishment, FIN_WAIT, TIME_WAIT, and KEEP_ALIVE.

- Vulnerabilities in TCP/IP include TCP SYN attacks, IP spoofing, connection hijacking, RIP attacks, and ICMP attacks.

- Vulnerabilities in TCP/IP can be decreased by modifying the default timer values, generating random sequence numbers, using properly configured firewalls, using TCP wrappers on UNIX and Linux boxes, using authentication, or using encryption.

❏ IP Security Architecture (IPSec) is a collection of Internet Engineering Task Force (IETF) standards that define an architecture at the Internet Protocol (IP) layer that protects IP traffic by using various security services.

❏ IPSec provides the following services for network users:

   ❏ Encryption of user data for privacy

   ❏ Authentication of the integrity of a message

   ❏ Protection against certain types of security attacks, such as replay attacks

   ❏ An ability for devices to negotiate the security algorithms and keys required to make secure authenticated connections

   ❏ Two security modes, tunnel and transport, to meet different network needs

REVIEW QUESTIONS

1. What does TCP/IP stand for?

2. What does TCP handle on the Internet?

3. What does IP handle on the Internet?

4. What is data encapsulation?

5. What are the layers of the TCP/IP stack?

6. What are the three flags in the IP header, and what are they for?

7. What does the Header Checksum do in the IP header?

8. What does the TCP Checksum field do in the TCP header?

9. What is the three-way handshake?

10. What is a SYN flood?

11. What is a Christmas Tree Packet?

12. What are three ways to reduce or eliminate TCP/IP vulnerabilities?

Indicate whether the sentence or statement is true or false.

13. _____ RIP attacks take advantage of RIP, or Routing Information Protocol.

14. _____ Firewall rules should be implemented to block spoofed packets from entering the intranet through the Internet.

15. _____ Firewalls can be software-based, on any local computer, or hardware-based, in an appliance that sits on the network.

16. _____ The IPSec Authentication Header (AH) protocol is used to ensure that packets get to the receiver in no time at all.

17. _____ IKE stands for the Internal Key Export protocol used to negoti-ate salary associations and export keys to a new office.

18. _____ ACLs provide protection against certain types of security attacks.

19. _____ IPSec provides an ability for devices to negotiate the security algorithms and keys required to make secure authenticated connections.

20. _____ In IPSec, tunnel security mode is less prone to dissection than transport security mode.

5

HANDS-ON PROJECTS

Project 5-1

EtherApe is a graphical network traffic monitor. It is a fun and easy-to-understand sniffer that many network administrators have running all the time as it will run on a very limited machine. It is GNOME- and libpcap-based.

Automated package installers such as yum, apt, and YaST will all check for and install dependencies. In the following steps, you use yum to install EtherApe on a Fedora system.

1. Open a Terminal window when logged in as root (or, if logged in as a regular user, enter su to become root), and then enter the following command:

   ```
   yum install etherape
   ```

2. The EtherApe package will be found and any dependencies will be resolved. When prompted as to whether you want to continue with the installation, type **y** and press **Enter**.

   This will install EtherApe and all of its dependencies. EtherApe will be found in the GUI menu under "Network" and will be available as "EtherApe as root" and simply "EtherApe." If you run EtherApe as a standard user, the results are not very interesting, as you need root access to see any of the NIC card's traffic. To start EtherApe as root, enter the following when logged in as a regular user:

   ```
   sudo etherape
   ```

   or switch the user to root and enter

   ```
   etherape
   ```

Figure 5-5 shows an instance of the EtherApe program when it is running.

Project 5-2

Using Tcpdump

1. Tcpdump is an interesting command-line application. To use it, enter

   ```
   tcpdump
   ```

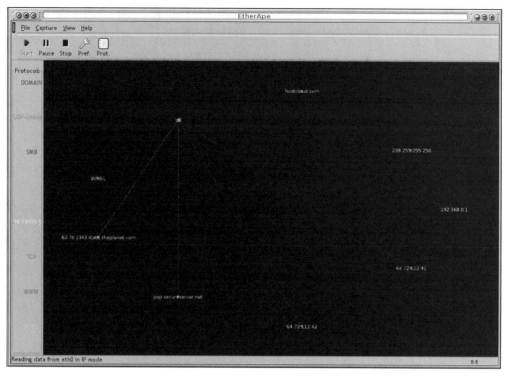

Figure 5-5   EtherApe display

(If the directory in which *tcpdump* is installed is not in your path, include the full pathname when typing the command.)

A description of the many available options appears in the man (manual) page, which you can view by entering the following:

man tcpdump

if you want to read it inline, or

man tcpdump > ~/Desktop/tcpdump.txt

to send the manual to a text file that you can read later or print out for offline reading.

You can also type

tcpdump --help

to view concise information about available options, as shown here:

tcpdump version 3.9.4
libpcap version 0.9.4

```
Usage: tcpdump [-aAdDeflLnNOpqRStuUvxX] [-c count] [ -C file_
size ] [ -E algo:secret ] [ -F file ] [ -i interface ] [ -
M secret ] [ -r file ] [ -s snaplen ] [ -T type ] [ -
w file ] [ -W filecount ] [ -y datalinktype ] [ -
Z user ] [expression ]
```

Read the man file for detailed information regarding the options and switches available.

1. Enter the following command to write all collected packets' information to a file in the current directory named "tcpdump1.txt", in extremely verbose mode.

   ```
   tcpdump -vvv > tcpdump1.txt
   ```

2. Next, enter the following command to record the same information in the tcpdump2.txt file—except that this time, only IP addresses, not hostnames, will be listed:

   ```
   tcpdump -nvvv > tcpdump2.txt
   ```

3. Using a text editor, open and compare the tcpdump1.txt and tcpdump2.txt files. Note that the second method—using the -n switch to avoid DNS lookups—is harder for a system administrator to notice, as it is passive.

HANDS-ON PROJECTS

Project 5-3

Using Wireshark

1. At the GNOME desktop, start Wireshark by clicking **Applications**, pointing to **Internet**, and clicking **Wireshark Network Analyzer**. (Type in the password for root if you are so prompted.) You can also start Wireshark from a Terminal window by logging in as root, typing `wireshark` at the command line, and pressing **Enter**.

2. Click **Capture** on the menu bar, and then click **Interfaces** to display the Capture Interfaces dialog box. On the right side of the row corresponding to your Ethernet adapter (probably named "eth0"), click the **Options** button to display the Capture Options dialog box.

3. Click the **Capture Filter** button to display the Capture Filter dialog box. In the list of filters, click **No Broadcast and no Multicast**, and then click **OK**.

4. In the Capture Options dialog box, type /*home*/*user*/test.cap (substituting your home directory as appropriate). Click the **Use multiple files** check box, and accept the default of **Next file every 1 megabyte**. See Figure 5-6.

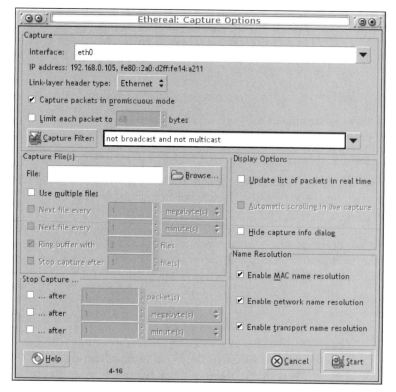

Figure 5-6   Capture options in Linux

5. Click the **Start** button to start the capture. Figure 5-7 shows a capture in progress. (Note that your screen may look different, depending on the versions of Linux and Wireshark that you are running, and the display options set in Wireshark.)

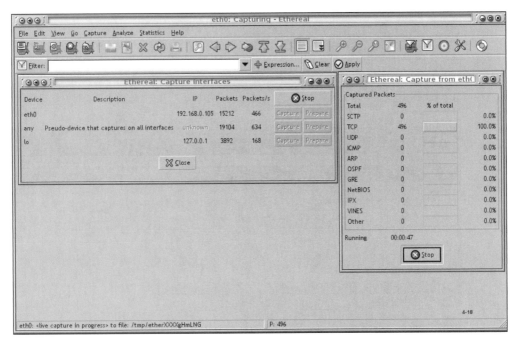

Figure 5-7   Capture in progress

6. After a few minutes, click the **Stop the running live capture** button on the toolbar. Figure 5-8 shows some of the captured packets. Note that Wireshark marks suspicious packets in black. These duplicate ACKs and retransmissions could be a sign of a session hijacking in progress. In this case, the situation is a software update from a server in Europe. This is probably a benign network traffic issue, but it could be an attack on the server from an attacker within the 192.168.0 subnet. If the attacker had been in another subnet, the sniffer would not have seen the duplicate ACKs.

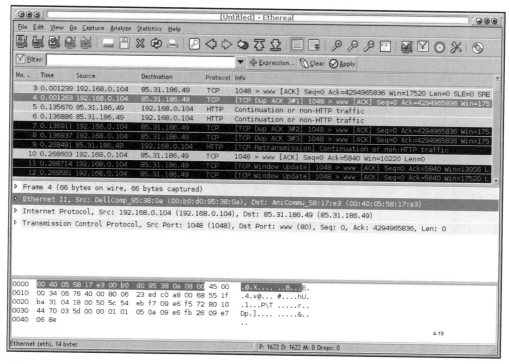

Figure 5-8   Wireshark capture log

What does normal traffic look like in your network? What are the protocols in use there?

6

ENCRYPTION AND PASSWORD CRACKING

After reading this chapter and completing the exercises, you will be able to:

♦ Understand basic cryptographic principles

♦ Understand the fundamentals of encryption

♦ Describe the most common ciphers in use today

♦ Identify the most common attacks on passwords

♦ Use various programs for cracking passwords

One of the best defenses against unwanted entry into a computer or a network is a collection of strong passwords based upon a personal or organizational policy requirement. This standard is the foundation of adequate security. The challenge is that guessing, stealing, or **cracking passwords** is the foundation of defeating any kind of security.

Sadly, there is a tendency among all users to discount the value of their data access and so most people, even those in the security industry, make elemental errors when choosing or protecting their passwords and usernames. Crackers have no shortage of poorly protected systems against which to test their skills and ingenuity.

Cryptography

Cryptography is a common way of protecting passwords. **Cryptography** uses an algorithm to **encrypt** a ciphertext document from a **plaintext** document, and when the information is needed again, the algorithm is used to **decrypt** the ciphertext back into plaintext.

Transposition

Transposition is a change in the position or order of letters or words, as in an anagram. Transposition does not rely on length of password, as the longer the document, the more likely that some regularity of character usage will help a hacker crack a word or two. Transposition is based on probabilities. There are 26 letters in the alphabet, and there are 10 digits in the common base-10 numbering system. If all 36 of these characters are used, there are $3.7199(10^{39})$ possible alternatives. This is 37,199 followed by 35 zeros. This probability is based on the fact that the first character in the ciphertext can be anything from a–z plus 0–9 (36 characters), but the next can be only all of that minus the first character. This would be shown as $36*35*34*...*1$, or 36! The user is starting at $3.7199(10^{39})$ to 1 against a hacker guessing the entire transposed character-set. Another way to look at this is that a user would have a 1:36 chance of guessing the correct initial letter or number if handed a document encrypted by transposition. If he or she guessed correctly the first time, the user would have a 1:35 chance of choosing the next one correctly. No matter how long the document or how complicated, anyone can break a transposition cipher based on frequency of letters in the language in which the code was written.

Devising codes based on transposition requires that both parties know each other's trans-positional formula. Choosing to transpose forward three characters, as in the **Caesar Cipher** devised by Julius Caesar, a becomes d, b becomes e, c becomes f, and so on until the end is reached. Then the letters wrap back around and x becomes c. This is a fairly simple cipher to crack because of the relative frequency of letters in English words. For example, the most common vowel in English sentences is e and the most common consonant is t. Knowing this, one can assume that there is a good chance that those letters that appear most frequently in the encrypted message. Not all messages share the exact frequency occurrence, but it is certainly a place to start.

Substitution

Substitution is the replacement of a letter or group of letters with another letter or group of letters. The simplest form would to be to reverse the alphabet so that Z stood for A as in the chart below:

```
A    B    C    D    E    F    G    H...
Z    Y    X    W    V    U    T    S...
```

Possibly the most famous substitution cryptography machine was **Enigma**, the most secure encryption method of its time. Enigma worked similarly to a mechanical word processor, in that it could be configured to print a substitute character for the character typed. During World War II, the German Army used this machine to send commands and orders from headquarters to the battle lines. The recipient would use an identical machine set up with the proper configuration to decrypt the messages. Using information from Nazi defectors and from errors in some coded German documents, Alan Turing, a member of the British government's Code and Cypher School at Bletchley Park, developed the **Turing Bombe,** a machine to crack the "Enigma Code."

Influenced by Alan Turing's work in cracking Enigma's codes, and his idea of a machine that would assist in decryption, Max Newman came up with Colossus, a programmable computer, in 1943.

Using computers for cryptography differs from earlier efforts because of the speed with which computers can crunch numbers. Transposition and substitution are still in use, but the basis might be extended character tables with 256 possible characters, such as the ASCII codes that computers use to translate letters and symbols into numeric codes that are used by the computers themselves.

The following are common terms when dealing with cryptography:

- Cleartext is a readable or decoded version of an original message.
- **Ciphertext,** the opposite of cleartext, is an unreadable or encoded version of an original message.
- **Key** is the use of a number, word, or phrase generated in an algorithm to both encrypt and decrypt.
- An **algorithm** is a mathematical function used to make a key.
- A hash is a one-way function that converts messages into unique strings of digits.

Cryptography involves changing text from a readable format to an unreadable format and back again. Encrypting a message before transmitting it is supposed to make the message impossible to decode within a useful period of time; however, even this level of security may be vulnerable as computers get faster. An encrypted page that would have taken a brilliant mathematician 10 days to decode might take a computer with a 386 processor, running at 33 MHz, approximately two hours. On a Pentium 4, running at 3 GHz, it might take three seconds.

SYMMETRIC AND ASYMMETRIC KEY ENCRYPTION

Encryption can be performed with either a symmetric key or an asymmetric key.

Symmetric Key Encryption

Sometimes called secret key algorithms, **symmetric key algorithms** use the same key to encrypt and to decrypt the data. Both the sender and the recipient must have a copy of the key. The inherent vulnerability of secret key algorithms is that the key must be transmitted somehow, and often in plaintext. If the key is somehow intercepted, then the message is easy to decipher. The best aspect of symmetric key algorithms is that they are much faster than symmetric key algorithms. Table 6-1 shows the relative strengths of some well-known secret key algorithms.

Table 6-1 Secret key ciphers

Cipher	Security	Speed (Pentium PC)	Key length
DES	low	4.0 Gb/s	56 bits
3DES	good	1.5 Gb/s	112 bits
IDEA	good	2.0 Gb/s	128 bits
3IDEA	very good	1.0 Gb/s	256 bits
Skipjack	good	4.0 Gb/s	80 bits
CLIPPER chip	good	-	80 bits

The two kinds of symmetric key algorithms are block and stream ciphers.

Stream Cipher

Stream ciphers use a key stream to encrypt and decrypt a plaintext message. A key stream is similar to a one-time pad. A **one-time pad** consists of a list of random numbers from 1 to 25 (all the letters of the alphabet minus one). If the first word of the plaintext is "Try" and the first three numbers on the one-time pad are 4, 3, and 10, then the algorithm takes the letters and adds the number to them. T+4 is X, R+3 is U, Y+10 is I (if you get to the end of the alphabet, then you start at the beginning of the alphabet again). This makes the ciphertext. When the message gets to the agent, she uses the one-time pad and subtracts the number from the ciphertext to get the message. This one-time pad uses a random number equal to the alphabet minus one because it avoids the possibility of the random number coming up as letter + 26. That would make the ciphertext the same as the plaintext.

The algorithm XORs the key stream with the plaintext message. Key streams are composed of random numbers from 1 to 254. The ASCII table used by computers to give users all the characters on an English-language typewriter keyboard contains 255 numbers. **XOR** mean "exclusive OR." An OR manipulation says that in comparing 2 bits, if one or the other is *set* (set means it equals 1) then the result is set. The "exclusive OR" manipulation says, if either one of the bits is set, then the result is set, but if both bits are set, then the result is not set. This is useful in cryptography because sometimes the key stream affects the result and sometimes it does not.

Block Cipher

Block ciphers operate on blocks of data. The algorithm breaks the plaintext document into blocks (usually 8 or 16 bytes long) and operates on each block independently. For example, the first 16 bytes are converted to a 16-byte block of encrypted text using the key table, then the next block is encrypted, and so on, until the whole document is encrypted. If the last block contains fewer than 16 bytes of plaintext, then the block is padded with some characters. The most popular block cipher algorithm uses the following convention: if the last block is only 6 bytes long, then the algorithm pads the block with 10 repetitions of the character 10. If the last block contains 12 bytes of plaintext, then the pad is 4 repetitions of the character 4. The plaintext will always be padded; so if the plaintext works out evenly, then the last block is padded with 16 repetitions of the character for the number 16[1]. Block ciphers allow you to reuse keys.

Asymmetric Key Algorithms

6

Also called public key algorithms, **asymmetric key algorithms** use two keys for encrypting and decrypting data. Each user has a public key and a private key. Public key algorithms effectively solve the biggest drawback to secret key schemes: the distribution of the proper keys to the proper people. Public key algorithms allow public keys to be sent unencrypted over unsecured media. Table 6-2 compares some popular asymmetric key algorithms.

Table 6-2 Asymmetric ciphers compared

Cipher	Security	Speed	Key length
RSA	good	fast	varies (1024 safe)
Diffie-Hellman	good	slower than RSA	varies (1028 safe)
DSS	low	—	512 bits

Assuming Alice wants to send an encrypted message to Bob, she gets and verifies Bob's public key, uses it to encrypt the message, and then sends the message to Bob. He uses his private key to decrypt the message. Anybody can have anybody else's public key. If Sylvia intercepts the message from Alice to Bob, she cannot decrypt the message with the public key, only with the private key.

DSA (Digital Signature Algorithm)

In the **Digital Signature Algorithm**, a digital signature connects documents with the holder of a specific key. This algorithm is considered too slow for general encryption.

Digital Time Stamps

A **digital time stamp** connects the document with a specific time of origination.

Cryptanalysis

A cryptanalyst decodes messages to make them readable. The first and most important step in **cryptanalysis** is detecting the key values. Only after detecting the key values can a cryptanalyst decipher all encrypted messages with that specific key value.

DESCRIPTIONS OF POPULAR CIPHERS

Though there are many ciphers available, the average Internet user is aware of few or none of them. The average user tends to confuse the categories within the cryptographic taxonomy.

Symmetrical Key Ciphers

Symmetric key ciphers use a single key to encrypt and decrypt the text in a document.

DES (Data Encryption Standard)

DES, a block cipher, is a popular secret key encryption standard, developed in the early- to mid-1970s. The Data Encryption Standard (DES) in a FIPS-approved cryptographic algorithm as required by FIPS 140-1. FIPS is an acronym for **Federal Information Processing Standards**, and is published by NIST, the National Institute of Standards and Technology.

As a symmetric cipher, DES uses the same 56-bit key to encrypt and decrypt a given plaintext message. (It actually uses a 64-bit key, but 8 of these bits are used for parity checking, so only 56 bits are used for the actual encryption and decryption.)

DES works by breaking the plaintext into 64-bit blocks, and applying a series of permutations to each of these blocks. First, an initial permutation is applied to the entire 64-bit block, and then the resulting block is split into two 32-bit blocks. Each of these blocks undergoes a series of 16 identical operations, including expansion permutation, compression permutation, s-box substitution, and p-box permutation. (A detailed description of these operations is beyond the scope of this text.) After this, the 32-bit blocks are rejoined into a 64-bit block, and a final permutation is applied. This final permutation is the inverse of the initial permutation.

The particular selection of substitutions and permutations used by DES was designed such that the same algorithm can be used for both encryption and decryption. The operations were also designed to be fast.

Security of DES

The security of DES is dependent upon the chosen key. Many people contend that DES is inherently insecure because the 56-bit key is not long enough, which makes it susceptible to brute-force attacks. In fact, in 1998, the Electronic Frontier Foundation, a group concerned with Internet users' rights and privacy, cracked DES in less than three days using a machine built for less than $250,000[2]. Also, a number of theoretical attacks are known, but none of these is considered feasible. Still, because of the time and expense needed to perform a brute-force attack on a well-chosen key, many believe that DES is safe for everyday use, even if it is not appropriate for critical security applications.

6

3DES (Triple DES)

3DES (Triple DES) is the technique of encrypting plain text with DES and then taking the ciphertext and encrypting it again, with another DES key, and then taking the result and encrypting it yet again, with yet another DES key. The reader may ask why there is no such thing as Dexa DES, where the results are encrypted ten times. The answer is that each encryption takes time at both ends, and industry is unhappy to multiply the time spent encrypting and decrypting a document between three and ten times. Still, 3DES is faster than any secure asymmetric key algorithm.

Speed of 3DES   As might be expected, Triple DES is almost three times slower than DES.

Security of 3DES   3DES is much more secure than DES, and is estimated to be equivalent to the security of single DES using a 112-bit key[3]. A successful attack would require approximately 2^{108} computational steps, not to mention huge memory resources, and is thus infeasible given current technology[4].

AES (Advanced Encryption Standard)

The **Advanced Encryption Standard (AES)**, also known as Rijndael, is a block cipher adopted as an encryption standard by the U.S. government. It superceded Data Encryption Standard (DES) in 2001 and is one of the most popular algorithms used in symmetric key cryptography.

AES uses a block size of 128 bits, and can use either 128-, 192-, or 256-bit keys. At the start of the cipher, the input bit sequence is copied to a 4×4 array of bytes known as the State array. This State array is then transformed via a series of substitution and transposition operations. Finally, the State array is copied back to a bit sequence, representing the output.

Speed of AES   The encryption speed of AES is faster than DES, but slower than Blowfish. Hash-function performance on a Pentium processor, using a 128-bit key, came out as follows[5]:

- Rijndael (AES)   34 clock cycles per byte
- Blowfish   20 clock cycles per byte
- DES   43 clock cycles per byte
- IDEA   74 clock cycles per byte

Security of AES   So far, all successful attacks upon AES have been through side-channel attacks. **Side-channel attacks** are attacks based on factors other than the strength of the algorithm.

IDEA (International Data Encryption Algorithm)

IDEA (International Data Encryption Algorithm) is an algorithm developed at ETH Zurich, in Switzerland. It uses a 128-bit key, and operates on 64-bit blocks. Like DES, IDEA employs a series of identical operations that are applied to the data, and which are used for both encryption and decryption. Instead of using the permutations and substitutions of DES, IDEA transforms the data using three different types of arithmetic operations. These operations are applied to sets of four 16-bit blocks, derived from the 64-bit blocks of input data.

Speed of IDEA The encryption speed of IDEA is somewhat faster than 3DES, but slower than DES. A Pentium 4 PC can encrypt about 2.0 Gbps.

Security of IDEA IDEA was designed to be resistant to differential cryptanalysis, and to date has proved to be so. Although some weak keys are known, this is not considered to be a practical vulnerablity, due to the huge number of available keys. In general, IDEA is considered very secure.

Skipjack

Skipjack is an NSA-developed encryption algorithm that was developed for use in the Clipper chip. The **Clipper chip** was a cryptographic device developed by the U.S. government and designed to enable the use of "key escrow" in telecommunications devices. This arrangement was intended to provide secure encryption in Clipper-enabled devices, but would allow government agencies to decrypt conversations, provided they proved their legal authority. The classified Skipjack algorithm and Clipper chip met strong opposition from privacy and civil liberties groups, and the project was effectively dead by 1996.

The Skipjack algorithm was declassified in 1998. It uses an 80-bit key size and operates on 64-bit blocks, using a process not unlike DES. Shortly after declassification, Skipjack was shown to be at least partially vulnerable to differential cryptanalysis.

RC4

RC4 is a cipher designed by RSA Data Security, Inc. It was a trade secret until someone posted the source code in Usenet News. The main benefit of RC4 is its speed; the algorithm is very fast. Several GB per second can be encrypted on a Pentium 4 PC. Although it has some known vulnerabilities, it can be useful where moderate security is needed. For example, RC4 is used in such popular protocols as WEP (Wireless Encryption Protocol) and SSL (Secure Sockets Layer).

Other Symmetric Key Ciphers

The following are some other, less well-known symmetric ciphers:

Quantum Cryptography

Quantum cryptography is a method for secure key exchange over an insecure channel based on the nature of photons. Photons have a polarization, which can be measured in any basis consisting of two directions orthogonal to each other. The base assumption of quantum cryptography is the Heisenberg uncertainty principle, which states that if a particle's speed is measured and known exactly, then its mass cannot be known exactly. The converse is also true. The Heisenberg principle derives from quantum mechanics. In quantum cryptography, when measuring the polarization of a photon, the choice of what direction to measure affects all subsequent measurements. For instance, if one measures the polarization of a photon by noting that it passes through a vertically oriented filter, the photon emerges in a vertically polarized direction, regardless of its direction of polarization before it went through the vertical polarization filter. If one places a second filter oriented at some other angle q to the vertical, there is a certain probability that the photon will pass through the second filter as well, and this probability depends on the angle q. As q increases, the probability of the photon passing through the second filter decreases, until it reaches 0 at $q = 90$ deg (i.e., the second filter is horizontal). When $q = 45$ deg, the chance of the photon passing through the second filter is precisely $1/2$. This is the same result as a stream of randomly polarized photons impinging on the second filter, so the first filter is said to "randomize" the measurements of the second.

If a photon's polarization is read in the same basis twice, the polarization will be read correctly and will remain unchanged. If it is read in two different bases, a random answer will be obtained in the second basis, and the polarization in the initial basis will be changed randomly.

The following protocol can be used by Alice and Bob to exchange secret keys:

1. Alice sends Bob a stream of photons, each with a random polarization, in a random basis. She records the polarizations.

2. Bob measures each photon in a randomly chosen basis and records the results.

3. Bob announces, over an authenticated but not necessarily private channel (for example, by telephone), which basis he used for each photon.

4. Alice tells him which choices of bases are correct.

5. The shared secret key consists of the polarization readings in the correctly chosen bases.

Quantum cryptography has a special defense against eavesdropping: If an enemy measures the photons during transmission, he will use the wrong basis half the time, and thus will change some of the polarizations. That will result in Alice and Bob having different values for their secret keys. As a check, they can exchange some random bits of their key using an authenticated channel. They will therefore detect the presence of eavesdropping, and can start the protocol anew.

Blowfish

Blowfish is an algorithm developed by Bruce Schneier of Counterpane Systems, author of *Applied Cryptography*.

Enigma

Enigma was used by the German forces in World War II, and was eventually broken by the Allies during the war.

Vigenère

Vigenère is a historical and easy-to-solve substitution cipher.

Asymmetric Key Ciphers

Asymmetric key ciphers use one private key to encrypt the message and a second public key to decrypt it. The public and private keys both belong to the sending or originating party.

RSA (Rivest, Shamir, and Adleman)

The **RSA** public-key cryptosystem is currently the most popular public key encryption standard. RSA develops keys that are the product of two 1024-bit prime numbers. RSA was invented in 1977 by Ron Rivest, Adi Shamir, and Leonard Adleman and gets its name from the initials of their last names.

RSA is based on the fact that it is very difficult to factor large numbers. That is, given a number with, say, 150 digits, it is extremely hard, even for a computer, to figure out two specific numbers that were multiplied to produce that number. An overview of the algorithm is as follows:

1. Generate two large random prime numbers, p and q, of roughly equal size, such that n = pq, and n is 1024 bits.

2. Choose an encryption key, e, such that e and (p - 1)(q - 1) are relatively prime (that is, they share no factors with each other besides 1).

3. Compute a decryption key, d, such that $d = e^{-1} \mod ((p-1)(q-1))$.
   The numbers e and n are considered the public key and can be shared with anyone. The number d is the private key and should be kept secret. It is difficult to compute the private key, d, given only the public key (e, n).

4. Now, someone wanting to send a message M can turn it into the encrypted message C by using the following formula: $C = M^e \mod n$. (Of course this is all done automatically, via the software.) Note that the public key, e along with n, is used to encrypt the message.

5. To decrypt the message C (thereby recreating the original message M), the recipient uses the following formula: $M = C^d \mod n$. Note that only the private key, d, is used to decrypt the message.

Security of the RSA Algorithm   The security of RSA is based on the difficulty of factoring large prime numbers. So far, there is no known way to do this quickly, and RSA is considered very secure. However, some progress has been made in factoring large (300+ digit) numbers, and there is speculation that it won't be too long before 1024-bit RSA encryption is vulnerable. Note that larger key sizes, such as 2048 and 4096, can also be used with RSA, increasing security profoundly.

Diffie-Hellman

As noted earlier, a weakness of symmetric-key cryptography is that the shared key must be exchanged between the two parties before they can encrypt and decrypt their communications. **Diffie–Hellman** is an algorithm that was developed to solve this problem, as it allows two parties who do not have prior knowledge of each other to establish a shared secret key over a public, insecure channel. Diffie Hellman is currently considered secure, an assumption that rests upon the difficulty of solving the *Diffie Hellman problem*, a mathematical problem proposed by Whitfield Diffie and Martin Hellman. To date, no easy solutions have been found for this problem.

6

DSS (Digital Signature Standard)

DSS stands for the United States government's **Digital Signature Standard**, which is based on the Digital Signature Algorithm (DSA). It is used to generate digital signatures for authentication of electronic documents, and works via a combination of public key cryptography and a hash function to create a condensed version of the text, called a message digest. This message digest is used to create a digital signature that is sent to the recipient with the message itself. Using the sender's public key and the same hash function, the recipient is able to verify the authenticity of the message.

Elliptic Curve Cryptosystems

One problem with cryptographic solutions is that faster computers are always being developed, which leads to the use of longer keys to ensure that they can't be cracked in a reasonable amount of time. If a 64-bit key is good, then a 128-bit key should be better. Keys of 1024-bit length are common and the next step up in a binary progression is 2048-bit. The problem is that increasing key length leads to slower encryption times, which is undesirable. One possible solution is to use elliptic curve problems, which are harder to solve than factoring the products of large prime numbers. This means that shorter keys can be used with elliptic curve cryptography than are used in RSA.

Elliptic curves, as used in cryptography, are mainly defined over finite fields. An elliptic curve consists of all elements $(x; y)$ satisfying the equation $y^2 = x^3 + ax + b$, together with a single element denoted by O, called the "point at infinity," which can be visualized as the point at the top and bottom of every vertical line. A detailed discussion of elliptic curve cryptography is beyond the scope of this book.

Neo for Java

NTRU's **Neo for Java** uses a matrix of 251 8-bit numbers, said to be the equivalent of RSA-1024. This system purportedly runs as much as 2,000 times faster than the hallmark RSA.

Lattice-Based Cryptosystems

Lattice-based cryptosystems are based on NP-complete problems involving geometric shapes built of lines or vectors. A lattice might be a two-dimensional grid of all integral coordinates. This lattice is generated by integral linear combinations of two vectors. Lattice-based systems have not proven to be effective for cryptography, as they are too slow in practice.

Cryptographic Hash Functions

Hash functions are used in cryptography to transform variable length data (such as a message or file) into a fixed-size hash value. This key concept underlying hash functions is that, if you have two different hash values, it is extremely unlikely that they were made using the same input values. Thus, hashes are often referred to as "digital fingerprints", because they allow recipients to verify that received files are in fact genuine. Cryptographic applications often employ one-way hashes, in which it is easy to create the hash from the input data, but very difficult to recreate the input data from the hash.

MD5 (Message Digest Algorithm 5)

Message Digest Algorithm 5 (MD5) is a secure hash algorithm developed in 1992 by Ron Rivest, one of the inventors of RSA. It operates on input data using 512-bit blocks, and produces a 128-bit hash value (or message digest) as output. Since the publication of MD5, a number of weaknesses have been uncovered and, while it is still considered secure for most everyday applications, many experts recommend hash algorithms that use longer hash values, such as SHA.

SHA, SHS (Secure Hash Algorithm)

Secure Hash Algorithm (SHA), also **Secure Hash Standard (SHS)**, is a hash algorithm that was developed by the U.S. government and adopted as a FIPS standard. Several variations of SHA hash functions exist, and they operate on either 512-bit blocks or 1024-bit blocks. SHA-1 hashes are 160 bits long, while a set of four stronger variants, collectively known as SHA-2, produce larger hashes (224, 256, 384, and 512 bits, respectively). Although some potential vulnerabilities have been reported in SHA-1, it is still considered superior to MD5. As of this writing, SHA-2 is believed to be secure.

ATTACKS ON PASSWORDS

Whether or not encryption is used, the use of password protection is open to various kinds of attack, from dictionary attacks to sheer guesswork. The strength of a password is based on a number of factors, including how long it will take to crack the password using various tools and techniques, and the extent to which the user keeps the password secure. A very strong password will not be of much help if it is written on a piece of paper and taped to the user's monitor.

Dictionary Attacks

The process of guessing passwords by using a list of common words is called a **dictionary attack**. This method of password cracking systematically enters every word in a dictionary in order to deduce the password by comparing each word in the dictionary against the user's password. Dictionary attacks have the capability to determine the key necessary to decrypt an encrypted document. Using this type of program is illegal, but that fact rarely stops a determined cracker, even though if convicted of using such a program the cracker could spend five years in prison.

As mentioned earlier, most people do not form complex passwords, therefore these dictionary attacks work surprisingly well. However, they usually do not work against complex passwords that contain numbers and are case sensitive.

Crackers need the file that contains the passwords of the target; in order to get this, they usually examine the vulnerability of the target system by using scanners and social engineering. Since administrative privilege is almost always required to read the file (in Windows, the SAM database, or in Linux, the /etc/shadow file), a cracker has a two-fold task before him. When, through a combination of skill, daring, and luck, the cracker gets a copy of the password file, his work gets much easier. Knowing the usernames reduces more than half of the work of preparing a break-in. Crackers make use of a default dictionary, which is part of dictionary attack software, and this allows them to include information about the target such as names, names of family members, pet names, birthdates, addresses, and any other information that may exist about a target.

One good defense against an attack to acquire a password file is to limit the number of guesses allowed before the user is locked out. Another is to add numbers to the password or mangle the word in some other way, but these passwords are vulnerable to hybridization attacks.

Hybridization

Hybridization attacks guess passwords by creating new words; they work by adding letters and/or numbers to every word in a dictionary. The most common hybridization practice is to add a range of numbers—for instance, 0 to 100—to both the beginning as well as the end of a word in the dictionary. The program compares the new word with the password, after the addition of a combination of numbers and words.

Some hybridization methods use a number spread, which is the process of inserting numbers into passwords, for example, presi254dent. Duplication is simply duplicating a word to form a new word, for instance, cat becomes catcat. Substituting with symbols is replacing letters in words with symbols that look similar to the missing letters. An example of this is money, changed to M0ney. The zero replaces the letter o. To reverse a word is to spell it backwards, so BillMonroe would become eornoMlliB. Appending characters is the process of adding suffixes such as ed, ing, 4u, or 3b, so one could convert the password Cherry into Cherry4u, or Cherryed, or Cherry3b.

Hybridization methods are more complex than dictionary attacks because passwords that are common names may sometimes have a number attached to them. For example, a user's password may be the name of his dog. After realizing that this is an easy password to crack, the person decides he must make it more difficult. However, he is afraid of forgetting his password. In order to make the password more complex, yet memorable, the user simply adds the number 1 to his dog's name. Many people also add a special date or their house number to a common name. Some examples are Wilbur12, 2006thomas, 4856Jessica.

Table 6-3 describes some important hybridization methods.

Table 6-3   Important hybridization methods

Hybridization Method	Description	Example
Appending characters	The process of adding endings, such as ing or 4u, to the words in the dictionary	Alfred+4u=Alfred4u
Reversing words	The process of reversing the letters in a word	Alfred=derfla
Duplication	The process of duplicating a word to create a new word	Randy=RandyRandy
Number spread	The process of inserting numbers into the password	Corey=Co4r5ey

A dictionary attack has trouble cracking this sort of password; but a hybridization program will probably succeed.

To reduce the possibility that dictionary and hybridization attacks will succeed, users should follow basic guidelines when creating passwords:

- Avoid using the same password for everything
- Avoid using one's own name in a password, as well as that of a child, spouse, friend, or pet
- Avoid using common words or names for passwords
- Include random letters, numbers, and characters in a password
- Avoid writing down difficult passwords where they might easily be found

Brute-Force Attacks

Brute-force attacks use all possible combination of letters, numbers, and special characters to determine the target password. It is very time consuming and requires patience, yet the use of brute force can extract the most difficult passwords, given sufficient time. Brute-force attacks are slow compared to dictionary attacks. The speed of the operation depends on several factors, but most important is the length of the password. Each character in a password is tested against 256 possible ASCII codes, for instance, so a five-character password (a very unsafe length) requires 256*256*256*256*256 tries to cover all possible combinations. That is 1,099,511,627,776 tries. Compared to a dictionary attack that might look only for all five-letter words, this can't help but seem slow. Brute-force attacks need a large amount of RAM and a fast processor in order to work efficiently. Cryptographic keys or encryption algorithms aid in the success of cracking codes. This kind of attack will fail if the login system allows only five tries before lockout, or if the Intrusion Detection System (IDS) is set to fire an alarm at an unusually large number of login attempts.

The brute-force attack is most effective when the encrypted document or password hash file can be extracted from the target system and tested on an anonymous offline location.

Observation

Other names for this method include "snooping," "eavesdropping," or "shoulder-surfing." This method is used whenever an attacker has physical proximity and can literally watch the victim type in their username and password. Though low-tech, this is a very common method for attackers who have close connections to the victim. Family members, friends, or co-workers might use this method.

Keyloggers

A **keylogger** program can easily be installed on a computer by an inside cracker or by trickery through an e-mail attachment. The unsuspecting user does not realize that a program on his or her computer is recording every key pressed. The hacker or cracker then examines the file generated by the program and determines the passwords by examining the keylogger log. Commercially available keyloggers are used by parents to monitor children's Web use, and sometimes by systems administrators to discern nonbusiness use by company employees. Keyloggers are generally invisible to the victim. They often do not show up in the task manager as a running process and are very difficult for the monitoring subject to remove or disable.

Social Engineering

A cracker can pretend to be a legitimate user of the target system and extract information simply by asking. Users are often willing to assist the cracker who has posed as an authority with whom one must comply, or as another user who needs help. This method of tricking people has been in use since the dawn of time—not all confidence swindles involve computers. Computer cons take advantage of a lack of understanding among average users. Social engineers rely on human nature and basic trust.

People behave naively when a so-called computer expert questions them. Users will give out personal, highly sensitive information to the cracker pretending to be a technician who must run tests, check security, or restore a system.

Another form of social engineering is called phishing. Phishing relies on mass-exposure of ads, pop-ups, or e-mails purported to be from legitimate companies. These notices warn of impending issues and request that users click a link to "verify" their account information. The verification site collects the information and uses it to steal from the victim, or to perpetrate identity theft to steal from a business. Legitimate companies never ask users to give out credit card information, passwords, or Social Security numbers. A bank or credit card company already has that information on file.

Sniffing Methods

Crackers use packet sniffers to catch cleartext passwords from protocols such as Telnet, FTP, and POP3. All a cracker has to do is run a sniffer to extract the username and passwords from network traffic. If the passwords and usernames are encrypted, the cracker can use a dictionary or brute-force attack on the network traffic log to get the passwords.

Password File Stealing

A cracker trying to find a password can often simply steal or copy the files where the password hashes are stored from the victim's computer. It is far safer to spend one's time cracking passwords on a remote computer than on the victim's. IDS and login lockout programs are no threat on the remote computer. A cracker can take all the time necessary to perform a brute-force attack. Sometimes passwords are not stored in the main system but in a shadow file that is readable only by users with administrative privileges. This reduces the chance of the file being found at all. Most UNIX and Linux systems use shadow files.

PASSWORD CRACKERS

Programs that guess and crack passwords are widely available on the Internet, even to a novice cracker, and they are available for both Windows and UNIX/Linux platforms. Password crackers are wonderful when passwords are lost or key personnel are fired or not available. (Sometimes, the last thing an outgoing administrator does is change the root passwords on the servers.) Security administrators also use password crackers to check for weak passwords on their networks. Some widely used cracker programs are:

- Cain and Abel
- Crack
- John the Ripper
- Telnet_crack
- THC Hydra
- L0phtCrack

Cain and Abel

This was the top password-recovery tool for the Windows platform listed on insecure.org in 2006. It was developed for Windows systems, and it has lots of entertaining options, especially if the attacker has some time to play with Windows as an administrator. This tool handles an enormous variety of tasks and is user-friendly. It can recover passwords by sniffing the network;

crack encrypted passwords using dictionary, brute-force, and cryptanalysis attacks; record VoIP conversations; decode scrambled passwords; reveal password boxes; uncover cached passwords; and analyze routing protocols. It can also do ARP poisoning. Figure 6-1 shows a screenshot of the Cain and Abel NTLM hash table with one decoded password.

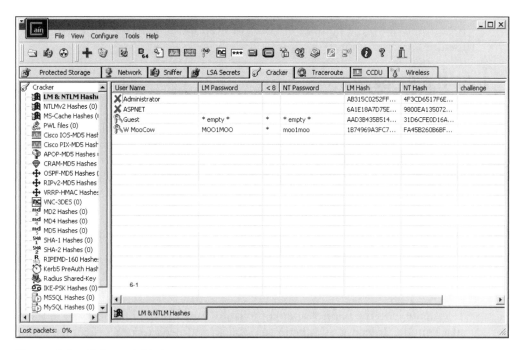

Figure 6-1 Cain and Abel

Crack

Alec Muffet designed Crack for UNIX-based systems in 1991. The program and components are freely available. It scans UNIX password files and then extracts weak logon passwords. The Crack program can also detect encrypted ciphertext by using the Crypt (3) algorithm. Similar to brute-force attacks, the performance of Crack depends on both the computer's processing speed as well as its memory. Crack can be found at www.crypticide. com/alecm/security/c50-faq.html. The basic requirements for running Crack are a UNIX-based operating system, a C compiler, and root access.

To compile Crack in Linux, the contents of the file src/util/Makefile must be replaced with the text from the following page: www.crypticide.com/alecm/ security/c50-linux-util-makefile.txt.

To find word lists, ftp://ftp.ox.ac.uk/pub/wordlists/ is an excellent source for word lists in many languages and based on many categories of words. It is worth a visit, to see the wealth of word lists available.

When the Crack program is finished executing, it immediately displays the message "DONE" and then exits. An application called crack-pwc is launched, which runs in the background for some number of hours or even months. To view the results, users need to use the Reporter utility.

John the Ripper

John the Ripper is a fast password cracker. As the second-ranked password cracking utility in the insecure.org top 100 list, John the Ripper is currently available for many versions of UNIX (11 are officially supported, not counting different architectures), DOS, Win32, BeOS, and OpenVMS. Its primary purpose is to detect weak UNIX passwords. It supports several crypt(3) password hash types which are most commonly found on various UNIX versions, as well as Kerberos AFS, and Windows NT/2000/XP LM hashes.

It has its own optimized modules for different ciphertext formats and architectures. It can detect ciphertext encrypted by programs utilizing algorithms, such as the standard DES, the double-length DES, the extended DES, MD-5, and Blowfish.

John the Ripper v1.7.0.2 is the latest stable version. The distribution is in source code and it must be compiled for use.

To execute John the Ripper: after compilation, run it in the dictionary or in the brute-force attack mode. To run it as a dictionary attack, you need to run a dictionary. Conveniently, John the Ripper has a default dictionary. This file is password.lst and is stored in the /john-1.6/run directory.

It is possible to edit the password.lst file to add words that are more common. You may also create new dictionary files. In order to create a new dictionary file, follow these instructions:

1. Create a new text file.

2. Open the file in an editor and add the required words to the dictionary.

3. Save the dictionary file in the /john-1.7.0.2/run directory.

After creating the dictionary file, the attack can begin. Follow these instructions to perform the dictionary attack:

4. Change the directory to john-1.6/run by using the following command:
   cd ../run

5. From the run directory, execute the following command to check the shadow file. Doing this allows you to crack the logon passwords that are similar to the words in the dictionary file:
   ./john -wordfile:password.lst /etc/shadow.

In order to use John the Ripper in the brute-force attack mode, you need to execute the following code:

```
./john /etc/passwd
```

Check the progress of the program by pressing the SPACEBAR.

The program may be terminated by pressing CTRL+C, or it can be restored by using the `./john -restore` command.

Modes

John the Ripper supports several modes for cracking passwords:

- The wordlist mode is the simplest mode supported by John the Ripper and compares passwords against a list of words in a text file.

- The single-crack mode is faster than the wordlist mode, and it uses logon or GEOCS information for cracking passwords. It limits the cracking process to the accounts related to the logon information. If more than one user has the same password, it repeats the comparison of guessed passwords.

- The incremental mode is the most powerful mode used by John the Ripper. It attempts all possible combinations of letters, numbers, and special characters as passwords. This mode is used for conducting brute-force attacks.

- The external mode is the user-defined mode. An external mode may be defined by using the section [List.External: Mode] in the john.ini file. Here, mode is the name of the external mode. You can use an external mode to specify customized functions for trying passwords. You should add these functions to the [List: External: Mode] section.

Telnet_Crack

The password cracker Telnet_crack uses a dictionary attack to crack Telnet account passwords. Crackers may use Telnet_crack from UNIX and Linux platforms.

Hackers must specify the Telnet account name and the IP address of the computer holding the user's account to crack passwords and establish a connection. Specifying the name of the dictionary file is necessary. To run this program in Linux, type the following command:

```
./telnet_crack <user name> <IP Address> <dictionary file name>
```

System administrators are able to detect logon attempts made by hackers by checking log files where logon attempts are stored. This is a useful security measure; however, very weak passwords may be cracked before the administrator can see what is happening.

THC Hydra

THC Hydra is a very useful network authentication cracker which supports many different services. Available from THC at http://thc.segfault.net/thc-hydra/, Hydra (hydra-5.3-src.

tar.gz – last updated 5/5/2006) is a brute-force cracker for testing remote authentication services. It can perform rapid dictionary attacks against more then 30 protocols, including Telnet, FTP, HTTP, HTTPS, HTTP-PROXY, SMB, SMBNT, MS-SQL, MySQL, REXEC, RSH, RLOGIN, CVS, SNMP, SMTP-AUTH, SOCKS5, VNC, POP3, IMAP, NNTP, PCNFS, ICQ, SAP/R3, LDAP2, LDAP3, Postgres, Teamspeak, Cisco auth, Cisco enable, LDAP2, and Cisco AAA (incorporated in Telnet module).

L0phtcrack and Lc5

L0pht Heavy Industries developed L0phtCrack as a security tool, to help system administrators and security professionals check password weaknesses of the Windows NT operating system. In 2006, the company that owned L0phtCrack, the @Stake company, was purchased by Symantec. Symantec has chosen to discontinue support of this application. It is still available from various sources on the Internet, but only as a 15-day trial. Since Symantec declines to send out the licensing keys, the application is rendered useless after the trial period. Cain and Abel or John the Ripper seem like better candidates for a security toolbox. L0phtCrack is included here for historical interest. It was considered an important application for many years, but it is essentially dead now.

CHAPTER SUMMARY

- Requiring the use of effective, strong passwords is one of the best ways to secure a network against attackers. A common method of protecting passwords is to use cryptography to disguise the actual plaintext password.

- Basic types of cryptography include transposition and substitution ciphers. In transposition, the position of words or letters is altered. In substitution, letters or groups of letters are replaced with alternate letters.

- Encryption can be performed using either symmetric key algorithms (secret key algorithms) or asymmetric key algorithms (public key algorithms). Symmetric key cryptography uses the same key to both encode and decode plaintext. Asymmetric key cryptography uses one key to encode the plaintext, and a different key to decode it.

- Popular symmetric key ciphers include DES, 3DES, AES (Rijndael), IDEA, Skipjack, and RC4.

- Popular asymmetric key ciphers include RSA, Diffie-Hellman, DSS, and elliptic curve cryptography.

- Cryptographic hash functions generate a fixed-size hash value from a message of any length. The two most popular secure hash algorithms are MD5 and SHA, which produce 128-bit and 160-bit hash values, respectively.

- Effective password security depends upon choosing strong passwords and making sure they are kept secret.

❏ Common attacks on passwords include technical measures, such as dictionary attacks, hybridization attacks, brute-force attacks, keyloggers, and packet-sniffers; and physical techniques, such as social engineering and theft.

❏ Password-cracking programs are readily available on the Internet. Popular password crackers include Cain and Abel, Crack, John the Ripper, Telnet_crack, THC Hydra, and L0phtCrack. These tools can be used for both legitimate purposes, such as recovering an authorized user's lost password, and unethical purposes, such as stealing passwords from other users.

REVIEW QUESTIONS

1. Short Essay: What is the difference between transposition and substitution in cryptography?

2. Writing Exercise: Write a paragraph of 25–40 words, using a transposition or substitution code. On a separate sheet of paper, explain the formula (or algorithm) for your code as well as the plaintext of your paragraph.

3. List and discuss the symmetric key encryption algorithms based on algorithm and security level.

4. List and discuss the asymmetric key encryption algorithms based on algorithm and security level.

5. Summarize a few of the methods used to acquire passwords.

6. What are the positive uses for password-cracking utilities?

Indicate whether the sentence or statement is true or false.

7. _____ Cain and Abel is used on Linux platforms to crack passwords.

8. _____ When a password hash is present, a Rainbow Table could be used to crack the password.

9. _____ It takes such a long time to crack strong passwords like "199!2GfrRRb9(e)woP," that it should be used for every account.

10. _____ The strong password "199!2GfrRRb9(e)woP" could be cracked with a dictionary attack.

11. _____ The strong password "199!2GfrRRb9(e)woP" could be cracked by using a dictionary attack with a word file that has been run through a script used to mangle words.

12. _____ The strong password "199!2GfrRRb9(e)woP" could be cracked with a brute-force attack.

13. _____ The process of creating new words through the addition of letters and/or numbers to every word in a dictionary is called hybridization.

14. _____ Crackers use packet poodles to catch cleartext passwords from protocols such as Telnet, FTP, and POP3.

15. _____ Poodles cannot read whether the protocol uses cleartext or ciphertext.

16. _____ Cain and Abel is used from the command line or GUI.

17. _____ Crack was first released in 1991.

18. _____ John the Ripper uses word files to make dictionary attacks.

19. _____ Telnet_crack is used to read encrypted mail or voice traffic.

20. _____ THC Hydra was developed by an organization called "The Hackers Choice."

HANDS-ON PROJECTS

These lab exercises will familiarize you with four different crackers for different uses.

HANDS-ON PROJECTS

Project 6-1

Crack the passwords in the `passwd` file supplied by your instructor using John the Ripper.

1. Download the `passwd` file that contains encrypted passwords from the central Linux server (or ask your instructor where to obtain the file).

2. Download the John the Ripper software from www.openwall.com/john (or your central Linux server). The name of the file to be downloaded is john–1.7.0.2.tar.gz, or the latest free "stable" release.

3. Unzip the file john–1.7.0.2.tar.gz by entering the following command:

```
tar –zxvf john-1.7.0.2.tar.gz
```

4. Change to the directory that is created when the files are unzipped, by entering the following command:

```
cd john-1.7.0.2
```

5. Change to the source directory by entering the following command:

```
cd src
```

6. Compile the source files by entering the following command:

```
make generic
```

7. After the program has compiled successfully, change to the `run` directory present under the `john-1.7.0.2` directory and copy the file `passwd` into the current directory.

8. Execute the following command to crack passwords from the `passwd` file:

```
./john –wordfile:password.1st passwd
```

The preceding command uses the dictionary file `password.lst` to attempt to crack the passwords in the `passwd` file.

Were you able to crack the passwords? How long did it take?

Project 6-2

Crack the passwords present in the `passwd` file, using the `thunk` program.

1. Download the software `thunk` to your local Linux computer from http://sourceforge.net/projects/thunk/, or from the central Linux server. The name of the file to be downloaded is `thunk-0.5.tgz`.

2. Unzip the file by entering the following command:

   `tar -zxvf thunk-0.5.tgz`

3. Change to the directory `thunk-0.5`, using the following command:

   `cd thunk-0.5`

4. Execute the following command to locate the file php:

   `whereis php`

   The location may be `/usr/bin/php` or it may return something like `php`:

   `/usr/bin/php /usr/bin/X11/php /usr/local/bin/php /usr/local/lib/php /usr/share/php /usr/share/man/man1/php.1.gz`.

5. Type the following to find out which php is being used.

   `which php`

6. Whatever the answer is, change the first line of the file `thunk`, using a text editor, from:

   `#!/usr/local/bin/php -q`

   to whatever the `which` command returned, for instance:

   `#!/usr/bin/php -q`

7. Save the file, and exit the text editor.

8. Copy the `passwd` file that contains the encrypted passwords, downloaded from the central Linux server, to the thunk-0.5 directory.

9. Execute the following command to crack the passwords present in the `passwd` file:

   `./thunk k dictionary_2416_words passwd`

   If successful, the passwords will be cracked and displayed. Did it work? How long did it take?

6

Project 6-3

Use `Telnet_crack` to connect to a target Linux server from a source Linux machine.

1. Download the Telnet_crack.tar.gz file from the central Linux server, or from http://packetstormsecurity.nl/Crackers/.

2. Copy the file, `Telnet_crack.tar.gz`, to the `thunk-0.5` directory, using the following command:

   ```
   cp Telnet_crack.tar.gz thunk-0.5
   ```

3. Change to the thunk-0.5 directory and uncompress the file by entering the following command:

   ```
   tar -zxfv Telnet_crack.tar.gz
   ```

4. Change to the Telnet_crack directory and execute the *Telnet_crack* command to attack another computer, using the brute force method. (Your instructor will provide you with the IP address of a target computer.) Enter the following command:

   ```
   ./ Telnet_crack.pl  user1 192.168.0.1 dictionary_2416_words
   ```

   A successful attack will let you connect to the target computer and work on it.

Project 6-4

Use Cain and Abel to crack passwords in Windows 2003 Server.

1. Log on to a Windows 2003 Server machine.

2. Create two users, Billionaire and Clara. Do not assign any password to Billionaire. Assign 'Starburst' as the password to Clara.

3. Download the file, ca_setup.exe, from the central Linux server or from www.oxid.it/cain.html.

4. Doubleclick `ca_setup.exe` and extract it into the default directory, C:\Program Files\Cain.

   If the installer attempts to load WinPCap, choose "yes" and install it.

5. Start Cain and Abel from the Start menu.

6. Click the **Cracker** tab.

7. Click **LM & NTLM Hashes**. The Add NT Hashes dialog opens.

8. Choose **Import Hashes from local system**.

9. Right-click **Billionaire** and choose **Dictionary attack**, then **NTLM**.

10. Add Wordlist.txt from \Cain\Wordlists\.

    Did the attack succeed? Try Brute Force NTLM - Min 8, Max 10 (about an 8-hour process).

Project 6-5

1. Download THC Hydra from the central Linux FTP server, or www.thc.org/thc-hydra.

2. Using tar, uncompress the downloaded file into your Desktop folder. Change to the hydra–5.3-src/ folder.

3. Type ./configure and then press **Enter**.

4. Type make and then press **Enter**.

5. Type make install and then press **Enter.**

6. To use the GUI front-end, type xhydra and press **Enter**.

You will note that there is no username or password file included. The makers of Hydra expect you to handle that part yourself. Normally, this is not a problem, because you would likely be using this program to check a list of ftp usernames and passwords for weak passwords (the legal reason to run this utility). You could use the dictionary files from various password crackers, such as John the Ripper, or find them in various places on the Internet. The following is a script for making a very basic word list without word-mangling:

7. In the following script, copy the content between the `<script>` tags and paste it into a new text document, named `wordlist`, with no extension.

```
<script>
#!/bin/sh
# Written by Michal Kosmulski <mkosmul _at_ users
_dot_ sourceforge _dot_ net> edited by Wolf Halton
<wolf_at_networkdefense_dot_biz>
# This script is hereby put in the public domain.
#
# THIS SOFTWARE IS PROVIDED BY THE AUTHOR "AS IS"
AND ANY EXPRESS OR IMPLIED
# WARRANTIES, INCLUDING, BUT NOT LIMITED TO, THE
IMPLIED WARRANTIES OF
# MERCHANTABILITY AND FITNESS FOR A PARTICULAR PURPOSE
ARE DISCLAIMED. IN NO
# EVENT SHALL THE AUTHOR BE LIABLE FOR ANY DIRECT,
INDIRECT, INCIDENTAL,
# SPECIAL, EXEMPLARY, OR CONSEQUENTIAL DAMAGES
(INCLUDING, BUT NOT LIMITED TO,
# PROCUREMENT OF SUBSTITUTE GOODS OR SERVICES;
LOSS OF USE, DATA, OR PROFITS;
# OR BUSINESS INTERRUPTION) HOWEVER CAUSED AND ON ANY
THEORY OF LIABILITY,
# WHETHER IN CONTRACT, STRICT LIABILITY, OR TORT
(INCLUDING NEGLIGENCE OR
# OTHERWISE) ARISING IN ANY WAY OUT OF THE USE OF THIS
SOFTWARE, EVEN IF
# ADVISED OF THE POSSIBILITY OF SUCH DAMAGE.
```

6

```
#
# Generate a list of words (e.g.
for use by John the # Ripper) from aspell
# dictionaries.
# Use English and Polish words by default
languages=(en)
echo "Generating wordlist from aspell dictionaries:
${languages[@]}" >&2
echo "Please wait..." >&2
export LC_ALL=C
{
    for ((i=0; i < ${#languages[@]}; i++)); do
        aspell --lang="${languages[$i]}" \
            dump master "${languages[$i]}"
    done
} | tr -d \'- | tr [:upper:] [:lower:] | sort -u
echo "Done." >&2
echo "It is a good idea to additionally use John the
Ripper's -rules" >&2
echo "option to generate extra word variants." >&2
</script>
```

You can also copy the script from networkdefense.biz, at http://networkdefense.biz/wordlist.htm.

8. Open a terminal window, change to the directory where you saved the file, and type:

```
./wordlist > list.txt
```

then use the list to fill the field for password list in xhydra on the telnet port of the central Linux server where you have an account. Figure 6-2 shows the xHydra target dialog. You enter the IP address of the target device.

Figure 6-3 shows the screen where you would enter a known username and the location of your password file.

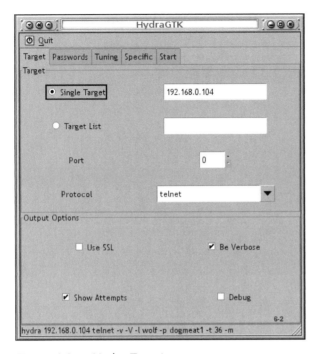

Figure 6-2   xHydra Target screen

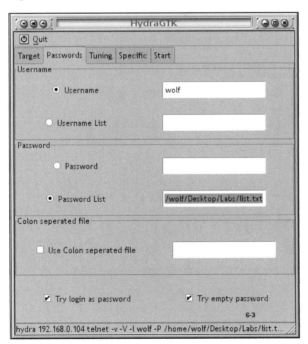

Figure 6-3   xHydra Username and Password screen

Figure 6-4 shows the output of the test. Bigger dictionaries and hybridizing scripts could make success more likely.

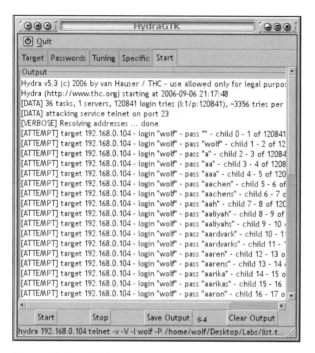

Figure 6-4   xHydra output

In Figure 6-4, you cannot see the end of the list, but the unmangled word list did not break the tester's password. How did it do with yours?

REFERENCES

1. Burnett, S., Paine, S., 2001, *RSA Security's official guide to cryptography*. Berkeley CA: RSA Press, Osborne/McGraw Hill.

2. http://www.eff.org/Privacy/Crypto/Crypto_misc/DESCracker/.

3. Frösen, J., "Practical cryptosystems and their strength." http://www.tml.hut.fi/Opinnot/Tik-110.501/1995/practical-crypto.html.

4. Lucks, S., "Attacking Triple Encryption." http://th.informatik.uni-mannheim.de/People/Lucks/papers/pdf/3des.pdf.

5. Schneier, B., et al., "Performance Comparison of the AES Submissions." *Proc. 2nd AES Conf., Nat'l Inst. Standards and Technology*, 1999, pp. 15—34.www.counterpane.com/ aes-performance.html.

6

7

SPOOFING

After reading this chapter and completing the exercises, you will be able to:

- ◆ Understand the mechanics of spoofing
- ◆ Describe the consequences of spoofing
- ◆ Define various types of spoofing
- ◆ List and describe some spoofing tools
- ◆ Learn how to defend against spoofing

Spoofing can be defined as (1) a sophisticated way to authenticate one machine to another by using forged packets, or (2) misrepresenting the sender of a message (e-mail, IM, letter, resume, etc.) in a way that causes the human recipient to behave a certain way.

Figure 7-1 depicts a TCP/IP internetwork. At the heart of internetworked systems are two critical issues:

- Trust

- Authentication

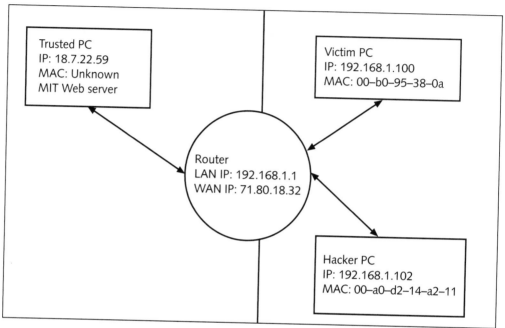

Figure 7-1 A TCP/IP internetwork

Authentication is less critical when there is more trust. For instance, if two communicating machines on the same table are the only two nodes on the network and are operated by a single user or two relatives, there is little reason to look for ways to authenticate the identity of either party. Conversely, the less trust there is, the greater the need for authentication. This is why you must type in a username and a password to log into an FTP server, Telnet accounts, or your school's online student resources. A computer can be authenticated by its IP address, IP host address, or MAC address.

IP address—An IPv4 address is a set of dotted numeric figures such as 66.37.227.194 (this particular address is in the Cox Communications Omaha NE network).

IP host address—This is the "friendly URL" for a machine, e.g., mail.yahoo.com.

MAC address—MAC stands for Media Access Control and is a 12-character hexadecimal number that every network appliance or PC has. MAC addresses are usually notated like this: 00-09-D5-00-DB-BA. Each MAC address contains the code for the manufacturer. You can look up MAC addresses on the Internet at www.techzoom.net/nettools-macdecode.asp.

TCP/IP has a basic flaw that allows IP spoofing. This is due to the fact that trust and authentication have an inverse relationship. Initial authentication is based on the source address in trust relationships, but IP source address authentication is not reliable because most fields in a TCP header can be changed (forged). This opens up the possibility of an attacker changing header fields to make bogus packets look legitimate.

THE PROCESS OF AN IP SPOOFING ATTACK

A successful attack requires more than simply forging a single header. On the contrary, there must be a complete, sustained dialogue between the machines for a minimum of three packets: the initial request from the originating machine, the return acknowledgment (ACK) from the recipient machine, and a final acknowledgment from the originating machine. Table 7-1 shows an IP header with sizes of field.

Table 7-1   IP header

4 bits	8 bits	16 bits		32 bits
Version	IHL	Type of service	Total length	
Identification			Flags	Fragment offset
Time to live		Protocol	Header checksum	
Source address				
Destination address				
Option + Padding				
Data				

IP takes care of the transport between machines. But IP is unreliable, and there is no guarantee that any given packet will arrive unscathed. When the packets arrive at the receiving host, TCP takes over. TCP is more reliable and has features for checking received packets and sending ACKs to the sender to verify that the packets were properly received and processed. For a detailed treatment of the contents of an IP packet header.

TCP uses an indexing system to keep track of packets and put them in the right order. This is the 16-bit "Identification" field in the header. This index is used for error checking by both machines.

To spoof a trusted machine relationship, the attacker must:

- Identify the target pair of trusted machines
- Anesthetize the host the attacker intends to impersonate
- Forge the address of the host the attacker is pretending to be
- Connect to the target as the assumed identity
- Accurately guess the correct sequence

Identifying a trust relationship from your network to an outside machine is a passive activity. You can use any network protocol analyzer to monitor your LAN and its connections. Figure 7-2 shows a Capture Interfaces dialog box from Ethereal/Wireshark. As you saw in an earlier chapter, when using Wireshark, you need to choose the capture interface (in this case, the Ethernet card is the best choice). The other two choices are the loopback or the pseudo-device that captures all network and loopback traffic.

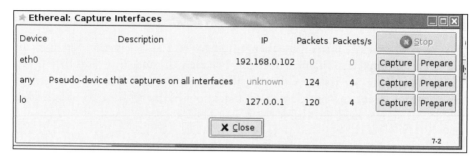

Figure 7-2   Wireshark (Ethereal) Capture Interfaces dialog box

The next screen is the Capture dialog. This sits and collects packets until you manually hit the "Stop" button (not shown here). Then the main Ethereal window populates with the packet information. Figure 7-3 shows the Wireshark (Ethereal) Capture in Progress dialog.

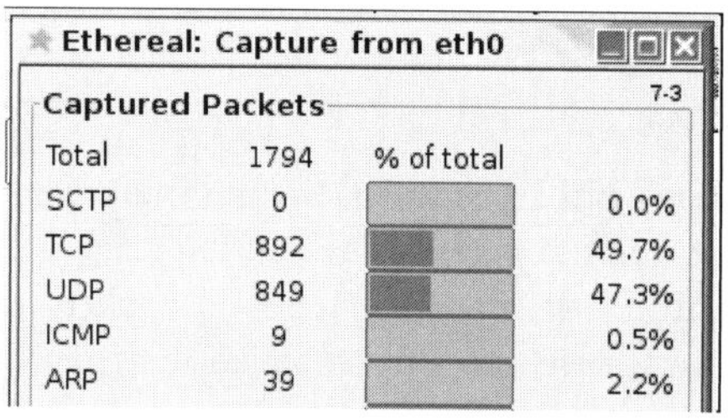

Figure 7-3   Wireshark (Ethereal) Capture in progress

Figure 7-4 shows filtered output. The filter used to capture these packets collects only the transactions between 192.168.0.100 (a local Linux box) and 18.7.22.69 (MIT's Web server).

Note that, in the Ethernet II row in the packet details pane, the MAC address for the local machine is known; that is, the MAC address 00:b0:d0:95:38:0a appears in parentheses next to the IP address, 192.168.1.100. In contrast, in the Internet Protocol row, the MAC address for the destination computer ("Dst") is not known; rather, the IP address, 18.7.22.69, is repeated.

As noted above, when carrying out a spoofing attack, it is necessary to first anesthetize, or stun, the host that you want to impersonate by performing a SYN flood (or SYN attack), Ping of Death, or some other denial-of-service attack. The idea is to keep the machine so

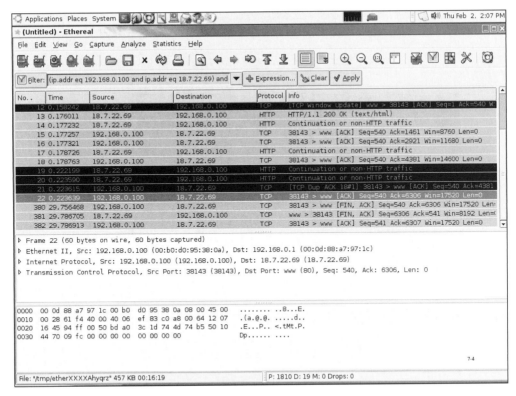

Figure 7-4   Wireshark (Ethereal) filtered results

busy answering bogus connections that it is unable to respond when the victim sends out a NAK (which it would do because it did not actually initiate the contact).

Forging the address of the stunned host could be done with the same utility used to stun the trusted machine. The big problem is guessing something close to the correct incremented victim-side sequence number to put into the second packet you send to the victim machine. Theoretically, that machine knows the ISN it responded with, and there is some specific method by which sequence numbers are incremented. ISNs are not random, so the guess you make is not random either. In the last four lines of Figure 7-5, the SEQ from the victim machine is 540 and the ACK is 6306, both in the ACK and the [FIN, ACK] from the victim machine. The trusted machine answers with its own [FIN, ACK], but the SEQ and ACK numbers are swapped, since that's how it looks from the other end. Look closely and you will notice that the ACK flag from the local machine did not increment, but the [FIN, ACK] flag did increment.

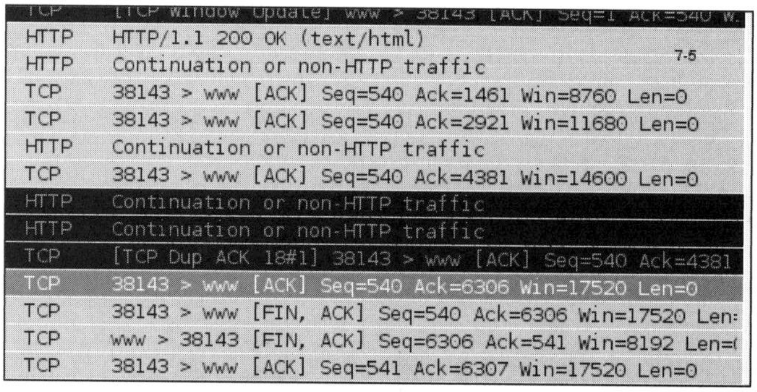

Figure 7-5   Wireshark (Ethereal) detail of sequence number incrementation

Sequence numbers start at 1 when the machine is booted up, and every second thereafter, the number increases by 128,000. Every connection increases the ISN by 64,000, and certain data types advance the number by 1.

Table 7-2   ISN incrementation

ISN Increments	
One second passes	128,000
One connection established	64,000
ACK Packet	0
FIN Packet	1
SYN Packet	1
FIN/ACK Packet	1
SYN/ACK Packet	1

A continuously running system with no established connections will roll over from 1 to 4,294,967,297 approximately every 9.32 hours.

Once the hacker has put the trusted machine to sleep with a SYN attack, she sends a SYN packet to the victim machine. This packet ISN number will be equal to the source ISN plus 1. The acknowledgment from the victim shows the same source ISN, and its ACK number shows the sequence number the victim machine expects to get from the source system. Figure 7-6 shows a spoofing attack.

The hacker should connect to the victim machine several times on port 23 or 25 to get an idea of how quickly the ISN advances. The attacker also needs to deduce the packet's round-trip time (RTT) by sending several packets and recording the times. The time to the victim system can be approximated by averaging several *ping* times and dividing that number by 2 to get the one-way time. Figure 7-7 shows the result of a *ping* command in a Linux terminal. *ping* in a Windows terminal would look similar.

In Figure 7-7, the average RTT is 35.32 ms (0.03532 seconds). With $\frac{RTT}{2} * 128,000$ and a general idea of how many connections per second may be occurring, the attacker can

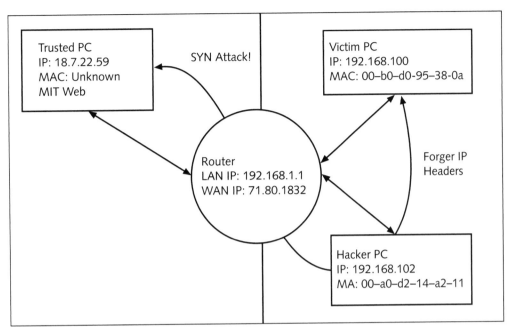

Figure 7-6 Diagram of a spoof attack

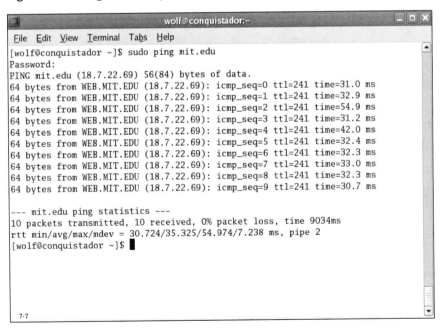

Figure 7-7 ping command results (Linux terminal)

begin to estimate what sequence number might be on the attacker's blind acknowledgment of the victim machine's response to the first packet sent. All of this must happen very quickly. The attacker cannot maintain an attack on the off-site machine for hours while testing forged headers on the victim. It is important to have the next step in place when the spoof works. If you cannot capitalize on the opening, you have just spent hours performing a felonious attack with no chance of recompense and a good chance of being discovered by the logs. The attacker probably won't get caught, but if the IDS in the network is logging the behavior, the victim and the trusted machine will probably be hardened against spoofing attacks, so repeated attempts are unlikely to succeed.

When the attack is done, the trusted machine must be released and returned to normal by sending a string of FIN packets.

COSTS OF SPOOFING

The costs to the victims of successful spoofing attacks are tied to the amount of information that was copied and the sensitivity of the data. There are both tangible and intangible losses. The tangible loss of 100,000 credit card numbers and the client information attached is traceable and in many ways controllable, assuming the company moves quickly. But the company might have to tell many more customers than were actually affected by the theft. The resulting publicity, the impact on the company's reputation, and possible litigation against the company are examples of intangible losses that can be very costly indeed.

What the attacker left behind may be just as important as what he or she stole away. A successful spoof attacker is probably going to leave a back door so he or she can get back in later. The attacker may leave several back doors, so even a careful security administrator might not find them all. The hacker could change settings on the router to allow a particular back door to work. He or she could hack the network administrator's password or the root password, and augment an unused username with administrator group membership to get in after the furor has died down. An experienced hacker would then doctor the logs or erase them to make detection more difficult.

Kinds of Tangible Loss

There are several categories of loss possible as a result of a successful spoofing attack, including economic loss, strategic loss, and general data loss.

Economic Loss

Economic loss may occur when valuable data is lost or duplicated. Distributing the bank account numbers, balances, and accounting data of a large conglomerate might have an impact upon a large number of people, including both employees and competitors of the victim. Knowing exactly where things stand with the company can lead to unforeseen opportunity for others at the expense of the victim. There are other ways to get this sort of data, and industrial espionage is still a growth industry. But the surreptitious nature of a successful spoofing attack makes it possible that the company never knows exactly what happened or when.

Strategic Loss

Strategic loss is a loss of, or the untimely publication of, strategic data that outlines events planned for the future. More specifically, from an organization's point of view, strategic loss provides competitors with very specific knowledge of the company's plans. This allows competitors to accurately and efficiently plan their own business goals. An example of this would be when a hacker uses a spoofed IP address to retrieve the marketing strategy of Company A. Company B buys this information from the hacker and uses it to disrupt Company A's plans and develop a competitive advantage. This could lead to loss of both money and goodwill for the spoofed company. If the victim is a government agency, the loss of strategic secrets can lead to anything from losing an election to losing a war. For example, the loss of secrecy of the Nazi Enigma cipher was a significant factor leading to the Allied victory in World War II.

General Data Loss

General data loss usually has less of an impact than the first two categories of losses. General data often comes from unsecured documents used by employees working on various projects or engaged in the day-to-day business of the company. This information is not crucial or irreplaceable, and if a hacker acquires this type of data, it will usually take a great deal of imagination to make the acquisition valuable to information buyers or to cause much injury to the victim company.

Types of Spoofing

Hackers employ several different types of spoofing, depending on factors such as the intended target and how much information about the network is available. The main categories of spoofing include the following:

- Blind spoofing

- Active spoofing

- IP spoofing

- ARP (Address Resolution Protocol) spoofing

- Web spoofing

- DNS (Domain Name System) spoofing

Blind Spoofing

Blind spoofing is any kind of spoofing where only one side of the relationship under attack is in view. It involves a situation in which the hacker is not aware of all network conditions and still uses various means to gain access to the network. Figure 7-8 describes blind spoofing.

Figure 7-8   Blind spoofing

Active Spoofing

In **active spoofing**, the hacker can see both parties, observe the responses from the target computer, and respond accordingly. The hacker in this position can perform various exploits, such as sniffing data, corrupting data, changing the contents of a packet, and even deleting some packets. A hacker in this kind of spoof is probably involved in misdirection instead of simply "smash and grab."

IP Spoofing

Discussed at length above, this technique consists of a hacker accessing a target disguised as a trusted third party. IP spoofing can be performed by hackers through either blind or active methods of spoofing.

ARP Spoofing

Modifying the Address Resolution Protocol (ARP) table for hacking purposes is called **ARP spoofing**. An ARP table stores the IP address and the corresponding Media Access Control (MAC) address of the computer that would be notified to send data. When a packet arrives on the network, the router searches the ARP table for the destination computer's MAC address. If the address is not detected, the IP address is broadcast, and the computer with the matching IP address replies with its MAC address. After the MAC address has been received, the packets are transmitted to the destination computer. An ARP spoofing attack involves detecting broadcasts, faking the IP address, and then responding with the MAC address of the hacker's computer. After the router has received the MAC address, it assumes that the received MAC address is correct and sends the data to the hacker's computer. This concept is referred to as ARP poisoning. A tool called Arpoison and another called Ettercap are used to perform ARP poisoning. Figure 7-9 shows an example of an ARP table.

Static DHCP Client List			
Host Name	IP Address	MAC Address	
Dynamic DHCP Client List			
Host Name	IP Address	MAC Address	Expired Time
	192.168.0.102	00-A0-D2-14-A2-11	Feb/09/2006 11:49:29
	192.168.0.101	0009D500DBBA01	Feb/09/2006 11:49:22
unknown	192.168.0.104	00-07-95-29-99-32	Feb/09/2006 11:48:59
unknown	192.168.0.100	00-B0-D0-95-38-0A	Feb/09/2006 20:45:21

Figure 7-9   Example ARP table

Web Spoofing

When a hacker spoofs an IP address through a Web site, it is known as Web spoofing. After spoofing the Web site, a hacker can either transfer information, such as pieces of malicious code, or get information, such as credit card numbers and passwords.

The hacker can spoof using a strategy that ensures that all communication between the Web site and the user is directed to the hacker's computer. The hacker may also falsely acquire a certificate used by a Web site to prove that it is trustworthy and authentic. Thus, the victim believes that a reliable source is being accessed. An example of a dangerous exploit would be if a hacker retrieved a certificate assigned to a popular news-based Web site. With this certificate, the hacker could successfully respond whenever the Internet browser of a user's computer sent a request to visit that site. Because the certificate itself is valid, the user's browser would validate the response, assuming that it was a reliable Web site. This would allow the user to interact with the site (when, in fact, it is a Web site controlled by the hacker). After gaining access to the network through the Web site, the hacker could then perform various actions, such as transferring malicious code or Trojan horses along with the Web page.

DNS Spoofing

In a DNS spoof, the hacker changes a Web site's IP address to the IP address of the hacker's computer. Consequently, whenever a user from the target subnetwork sends a request for that Web site, DNS servers convert the host name to the incorrect IP address. Altering the IP address directs the user to the hacker's computer. Since the user is accessing the hacker's computer under the impression that he or she is accessing a different, legitimate, site, the hacker can then send malicious code to the user's computer. The hacked site might show an alert message suggesting that all users download a specific program to protect their computers from the dangerous W32/Willies Virus. Users might actively assist in their own demise, believing they are on the real site. DNS spoofing puts the spurious IP information into a cache on a DNS server, and this needs to be frequently refreshed if the spoof is to be long-running. While the spoof is in place, anybody who uses that specific DNS server will be directed to the bogus site. Figure 7-10 depicts a DNS spoof exploit.

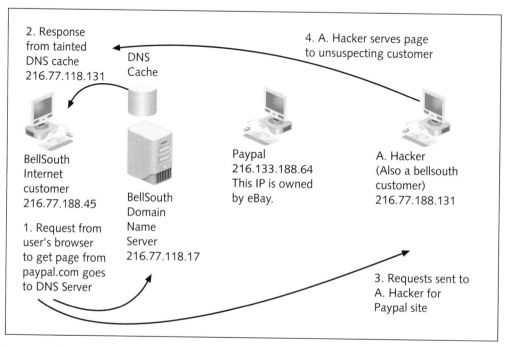

Figure 7-10 DNS spoofing

SPOOFING TOOLS

This section covers the following spoofing tools and their uses:

- Apsend
- Ettercap
- Arpspoof

Apsend

Apsend is a spoofing tool that provides a variety of options to perform different spoofing attacks. It supports the following protocols: TCP, IP, User Datagram Protocol (UDP), and Internet Control Message Protocol (ICMP). Apsend is used to test firewalls as well as other network applications. It can perform a variety of spoofing attacks, including a SYN flood attack, a DoS attack against *tcpdump* running on a UNIX-based system, a UDP flood attack, a *ping* flood attack, socket functions, a time-to-live (TTL) attack, and a type-of-service (ToS) attack. Figure 7-11 shows the command options for Apsend.

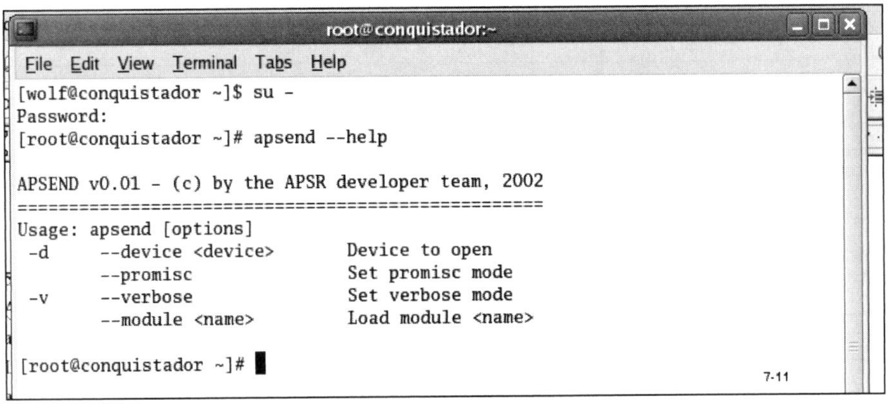

```
root@conquistador:~
File  Edit  View  Terminal  Tabs  Help
[wolf@conquistador ~]$ su -
Password:
[root@conquistador ~]# apsend --help

APSEND v0.01 - (c) by the APSR developer team, 2002
======================================================
Usage: apsend [options]
 -d      --device <device>      Device to open
         --promisc              Set promisc mode
 -v      --verbose              Set verbose mode
         --module <name>        Load module <name>

[root@conquistador ~]#
                                                    7-11
```

Figure 7-11   The command options of the Apsend tool

To perform a task, the hacker needs to first specify the destination IP address, the spoofed source IP address, and the character assigned to the task that the hacker intends to perform.

If a hacker desires to transmit packets to the destination computer with the intention of generating a SYN flood on the destination computer, the command line would be as follows:

```
APSEND -d 142.15.162.12 -s 142.15.162.15 -sf
```

The above command assumes that the IP address of the destination computer is 142.15.162.12 and the IP address of the source computer is 142.15.162.15. The variables assigned to the creation of the SYN flood attack are -sf on the menu of the Apsend tool. This command line creates SYN flood packets and sends them to the destination computer, which in turn assumes that the computer with the IP address 142.15.162.15 is transmitting the packets. The destination computer accepts the packets only because it trusts the source computer. Subsequently, these packets create a SYN flood on the destination computer.

Ettercap

As shown in Table 7-3, Ettercap provides a list of options that can be used to perform various spoofing operations. Examples of these are sniffing, intercepting, and password logging. After the tool is deployed, the preliminary step that the Ettercap tool must perform is creating a list of all the active IP addresses on the network. Next, the hacker selects the source and destination IP addresses of the computers on which the actions must be performed.

Table 7-3   Ettercap options

[root@conquistador ~]# ettercap --help	
ettercap NG-0.7.3 copyright 2001-2004 ALoR & NaGA	
Usage: ettercap [OPTIONS] [TARGET1] [TARGET2]	
TARGET is in the format MAC/IPs/PORTs (see the man for further detail)	
Sniffing and Attack options:	
-M, --mitm <METHOD:ARGS>	perform a mitm attack
-o, --only-mitm	don't sniff, only perform the mitm attack
-B, --bridge <IFACE>	use bridged sniff (needs 2 ifaces)
-p, --nopromisc	do not put the iface in promisc mode
-u, --unoffensive	do not forward packets
-r, --read <file>	read data from pcapfile <file>
-f, --pcapfilter <string>	set the pcap filter <string>
-R, --reversed	use reversed TARGET matching
-t, --proto <proto>	sniff only this proto (default is all)
User Interface Type:	
-T, --text	use text only GUI
-q, --quiet	do not display packet contents
-s, --script <CMD>	issue these commands to the GUI
-C, --curses	use curses GUI
-G, --gtk	use GTK+ GUI
-D, --daemon	daemonize ettercap (no GUI)
Logging options:	
-w, --write <file>	write sniffed data to pcapfile <file>
-L, --log <logfile>	log all the traffic to this <logfile>
-l, --log-info <logfile>	log only passive infos to this <logfile>
-m, --log-msg <logfile>	log all the messages to this <logfile>
-c, --compress	use gzip compression on log files
Visualization options:	
-d, --dns	resolves ip addresses into hostnames
-V, --visual <format>	set the visualization format
-e, --regex <regex>	visualize only packets matching this regex
-E, --ext-headers	print extended header for every pck
-Q, --superquiet	do not display user and password
General options:	
-i, --iface <iface>	use this network interface
-I, --iflist	show all the network interfaces
-n, --netmask <netmask>	force this <netmask> on iface
-P, --plugin <plugin>	launch this <plugin>

Table 7-3 Ettercap options (continued)

-F, --filter <file>	load the filter <file> (content filter)
-z, --silent	do not perform the initial ARP scan
-j, --load-hosts <file>	load the hosts list from <file>
-k, --save-hosts <file>	save the hosts list to <file>
-W, --wep-key <wkey>	use this wep key to decrypt wifi packets
-a, --config <config>	use the alterative config file <config>
Standard options:	
-U, --update	updates the databases from ettercap website
-v, --version	prints the version and exit
-h, --help	this help screen

After choosing the destination and source IP addresses, the hacker selects the action to perform from multiple options that are provided by the tool. A few of these options are listed below.

- ARP poisoning—This option alters the values of the source computer in the ARP table. Once executed, it modifies the MAC address assigned to the IP address of the destination computer. These adjustments ensure that whenever the packets are transferred from the source computer to a specific destination computer, they are initially sent to the hacker's computer. The source computer believes that the packets are being sent to the correct destination because the ARP table reflects the hacker's computer address as the destination computer's address. ARP poisoning allows the hacker to observe the packet transfer between the source and destination computer. It can also place some extra packets in between. Nevertheless, the likelihood of continuous acknowledgment code (ACK) transfers between the source and destination computers is high in the ARP poisoning method.

- Viewing interface—This interface supplies the hacker with the option of viewing the commands being executed by the source and destination computers, as well as the results, in the same window.

- Packet filtering/dropping—This option permits filtering of the packets to look for a particular string. It can then be replaced by the hacker to perform actions.

As of this writing, Ettercap works on the following platforms:

- Linux 2.0.x – 2.4.x
- FreeBSD 4.x
- OpenBSD 2. [789] 3.0
- NetBSD 1.5
- Mac OS X (Darwin 1.3. 1.4 5.1)

Arpspoof

Arpspoof, part of the dsniff suite, can be used to spoof ARP tables. The general syntax for running Arpspoof is

```
arpspoof [-i interface] [-t target] host
```

This tool changes the MAC address specified for the IP address of the destination computer in the ARP table of the source computer. The MAC address allocated to the IP address of the destination computer is the MAC address of the hacker's computer. After the packets are transferred from the source computer to the destination computer, they are initially redirected to the hacker's computer. At this point, the hacker may or may not send the packets back to the destination computer.

PREVENTION AND MITIGATION

To avoid or defend against IP spoofing:

- Wherever possible, avoid trust relationships that rely upon IP address only.
    - On Windows systems—If you cannot remove it, change the permissions on the $systemroot$\hosts file to allow read only access.
    - On Linux systems—Use TCP wrappers to allow access only from certain systems.
- Install a firewall or filtering rule disallowing access from external sources with internal IP addresses and also denying access to internal sources with external IP addresses. For example, the following ACLs will work for a network with an internal source address of 192.168.x.x:
  ```
  access-list 101 deny ip 192.168.0.0 0.0.255.255 0.0.0.0
  255.255.255.255access-list 101 permit ip 0.0.0.0 255.255.255.255
  0.0.0.0 255.255.255.255
  ```
- Use encrypted and secured protocols like IPSec.
- Use random ISNs to avoid the predictable way sequence numbers are implemented.

To avoid or defend against ARP poisoning:

- Use methods to deny changes without proper authorization to the ARP table.
- Employ static ARP tables.
- Log changes to the ARP table.

CHAPTER SUMMARY

❏ Spoofing can be defined as (1) a sophisticated way to authenticate one machine to another by using forged packets, or (2) misrepresenting the sender of a message (e-mail, IM, letter, resume, etc.) in a way that causes the human recipient to behave a certain way.

❏ Trust and authentication are at the heart of internetworking. The more trust there is, the less the need for authentication. Machines can be authenticated by their IP address, IP host address, or MAC address.

❏ A successful IP spoofing attack requires a complete, sustained dialogue between the machines for a minimum of three packets: the initial request from the originating machine, the return acknowledgment (ACK), and a final acknowledgment from the originating machine.

❏ To spoof a trusted machine relationship, the attacker must identify the target pair of trusted machines; anesthetize the host the attacker intends to impersonate; forge the address of the host the attacker is pretending to be; connect to the target as the assumed identity; and accurately guess the correct sequence.

❏ The costs to the victims of successful spoofing attacks are tied to the amount of information that was copied and the sensitivity of the data. Tangible losses include economic loss, strategic loss, and general data loss. Intangible losses include negative publicity, damage to your company's reputation, and the threat of litigation.

❏ Types of spoofing include blind spoofing, active spoofing, IP spoofing, ARP spoofing, Web spoofing, and DNS spoofing.

❏ Apsend, Ettercap, and Arpspoof are three common spoofing tools. Apsend supports TCP, IP, User Datagram Protocol (UDP), and Internet Control Message Protocol (ICMP), and is used to test firewalls as well as other network applications. Ettercap provides various spoofing operations including sniffing, intercepting, password logging, ARP poisoning, viewing interface, and packet filtering/dropping. Arpspoof can be used to spoof ARP tables.

❏ To avoid or defend against IP spoofing, avoid IP-address-based trust relationships, install a firewall, use encrypted protocols, and use random ISNs.

❏ To avoid or defend against ARP poisoning, use methods to deny changes without proper authorization to the ARP table, employ static ARP tables, and log changes to the ARP table.

REVIEW QUESTIONS

1. What is spoofing?

2. What is IP spoofing?

3. What is the difference between active spoofing and blind spoofing?

4. Can ARP spoofing be accomplished if the target computer is a Mac running OS X?

5. Is it common to use "phishing" e-mails to entice a victim to a DNS spoof site?

6. Can you use Ethereal to send spoofed IP packets?

7. Does Ethereal run on Mac computers?

8. What is a static ARP table and what is the disadvantage of using one?

9. What do you do with this formula? $\dfrac{RTT}{2} * 128,000$

Indicate whether the sentence or statement is true or false.

10. _____ Apsend, Ettercap, and Arpspoof are three common spoofing tools.

11. _____ Ettercap works on any Windows machine.

12. _____ Cain & Abel is a common spoofing tool that works on Windows platforms.

13. _____ Arpspoof, part of the dsniff suite, can be used to spoof MAC tables.

14. _____ Authentication and trust have an inverse relationship.

Match these types of spoofing with their definitions below.

 a. IP

 b. Web spoofing

 c. Blind

 d. Active

 e. Domain Name System (DNS)

 f. Address Resolution Protocol (ARP)

15. _____ Spoofing where only one side of the relationship under attack is in view.

16. _____ The hacker can see both parties and is in a position to observe the responses from the target computer.

17. _____ The hacker changes the IP address assigned to a Web site to the IP address of the hacker's computer.

18. _____ Spoofing that consists of a hacker accessing a target disguised as a trusted third party.

19. _____ Modifying the ARP table for hacking purposes.

20. _____ A hacker spoofs an IP address through a Web site. Phishing e-mails and fraudulent ads draw the victim to the spoofed site.

HANDS-ON PROJECTS

Spoofing is probably illegal if done on the public Internet. Practice on your lab computers.

Project 7-1

1. Using the model below, fill in the field names and the size (in bits) of a TCP header.

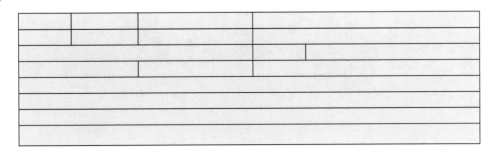

Project 7-2

1. Using WireShark on either the Linux or Windows platform, develop a filter that will allow you to capture the packets going between a specific computer in your classroom and the Internet. (Ask your instructor what computer you should use as your target.) Then, create a report that includes a printout of a selection of captured packets, and identify on your report all the TCP header fields that you listed in Project 7-1.

8

SESSION HIJACKING

After reading this chapter and completing the exercises, you will be able to:

- ◆ Define session hijacking
- ◆ Understand what session hijacking entails
- ◆ Identify the styles of session hijacking
- ◆ List some session-hijacking tools
- ◆ Explain the differences between TCP and UDP hijacking
- ◆ Note measures that defend against session hijacking

Hijacking occurs when an unauthorized individual takes control of a vehicle away from those who are authorized to operate that vehicle. In session hijacking, the vehicle is the network transaction itself. Though the attacker may pose as either the sender or the receiver, hijacking differs from spoofing in that the takeover occurs during an authenticated session. Hackers hijack a session in order to send and execute commands that cannot be implemented by an outside agent.

If one of the parties in the active session has administrative privileges, then the hacker might be in a position to act as an administrator while the session lasts. Session hijacking is often compared to sniffing because the sole purpose of sniffing is to retrieve and observe data while it is being transmitted. In session hijacking, hackers first sniff out the session to be hijacked, then sniff the identification data, and then use that data to inject themselves into the session as either party or both parties.

TCP Session Hijacking

TCP session hijacking occurs when a hacker takes control of a TCP session between two hosts. A TCP session can be hijacked only after the hosts have authenticated successfully. This is illustrated in Figure 8-1.

Figure 8-1   Hacker intervention in an authenticated TCP connection

The hacker cannot hijack a session while the authentication procedure between a host and a recipient is in progress. This is because a session cannot be initiated until the authentication process is finished. To understand TCP session hijacking, it is important to be aware of the procedure followed by TCP to build a connection and interact. The authentication process followed by TCP is defined as a three-way handshake method. The TCP three-way handshake uses TCP packet flags in a special way.

In the three-way handshake authentication method of TCP, a SYN packet is sent to the server by the client in order to initiate a connection. Then the server sends a SYN/ACK packet as an acknowledgment that the synchronization request by the client has been received, and awaits the final step. The client sends an ACK packet to the server. At this point, both the client and the server are ready to transmit and receive data. The connection ends with an exchange of Finish packets (FIN), or Reset packets (RST).

If a hacker tries to hijack the session while the authentication is in progress, that authentication will stop, and no connection will be established.

Session Hijacking – Hacker's Point of View

TCP works with IP to manage data packets on the network. IP is unreliable and may lose or change the sequence of packets during transmission. TCP must ensure that all data packets have been transmitted, and the session is closed only after all the packets have been received. TCP ensures that this happens successfully by tracking the packets sent to the recipient. The host and the recipient both keep a copy of the number and sequence of data packets that would be transferred in the transaction. Only after the host receives an ACK packet from the recipient (the third piece of the three-way handshake) are the details regarding the packet sequence numbers deleted from the host. Once the packet sequence numbers are no longer being read, the stage is set for a hijacking.

One popular method of session hijacking is using source-routed IP packets. Most routers are configured to deny passage of source-routed packets. Source routing is a debugging technique that allows packets to explicitly state the route they will follow to their destination rather than follow normal routing rules. This allows a hacker at point C on the network to participate in a conversation between A and B by encouraging the IP packets to pass through its machine. If source routing is turned off, the hacker can use blind hijacking, whereby he or she guesses the responses of the two machines. As in blind spoofing, the hacker can send a command but can never see the response. However, a common command would be to set a password allowing access from somewhere else on the net.

A hacker can also be inline between B and C, using a sniffing program to follow the conversation. This is a man-in-the-middle attack strategy, as shown in Figure 8-2. A common component of such an attack is to execute a denial-of-service (DoS) attack against one end point to stop it from responding. This attack can be either against the machine itself to force a crash, or against the network connection to force heavy packet loss.

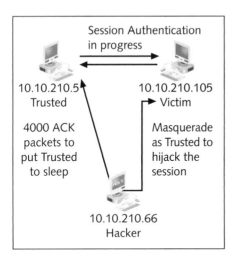

Figure 8-2   Denial of service

A successful hijacking takes place when a hacker intervenes in a TCP conversation and then takes the role of either host or recipient. Then the hacker receives the packets before the actual host. The hacker could find problems for two reasons:

- The host computer that has been hijacked will continue to send the packets to the recipient and expect an ACK packet in return. Yet once the recipient receives the packets that have been delivered by the hacker's computer, the packets will be classified as received and then an ACK will be sent to the actual host.

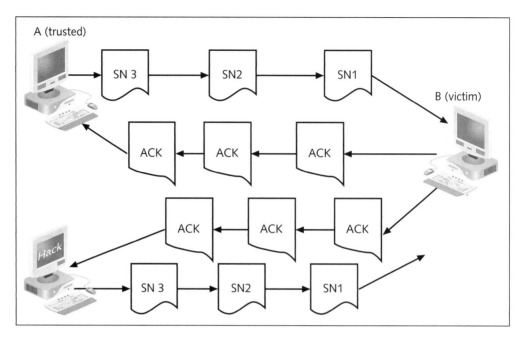

Figure 8-3   ACK attack

When the host sends the same packet to the recipient, the recipient server will automatically assume that it is a duplicate copy. For this reason, it will be ignored. These two packets will not be compared.

The recipient will then send an ACK with a correct sequence of packets to the host, even if the two packets have different contents. The results will be out of order. This will send another ACK to the recipient with the proper sequence of packets.

- The recipient gives an ACK to the host computer after receiving packets from the hacker's computer. The host computer receives an ACK for a packet that has not been sent until that exact time. Consequently, the host will send an ACK with a copy of the sequence where the packets will be transferred between the two computers.

Whatever the case may be, the result will be a large quantity of ACK transmissions between the two computers. This will disrupt the network traffic and data transfer.

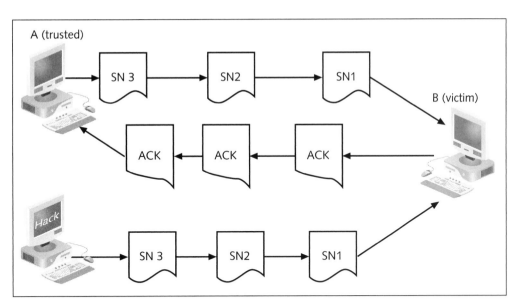

Figure 8-4   ACK attack without DoS

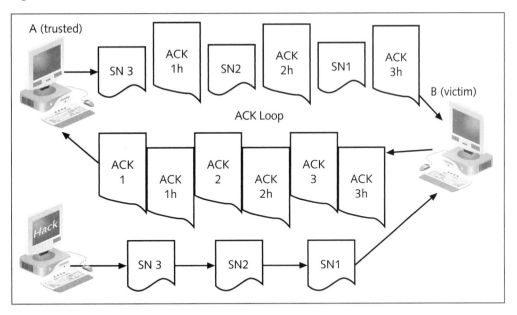

Figure 8-5   ACK loop

Continuous ACK Transfer

There are three ways to stop a continuous ACK transfer. They are losing the ACK packet, ending the connection, and resynchronizing the client and server.

If an ACK packet from either the host or the recipient is lost during transmission, then one computer will time out, thereby terminating the transmission. This would be the case whether a hijacking was in progress or not.

The second way a hacker can stop a continuous ACK transfer is by breaking the TCP connection. As noted previously, a TCP connection can be broken either by exchanging the FIN packets or by sending RST packets. A FIN packet aborts the connection in the same way that the three-way handshake started the session. If the attacker sends a FIN packet to the victim, that host will send a FIN/ACK to the trusted computer, expecting a return ACK to verify the FIN. If the trusted computer maintains the connection, then the response from the victim will not be validated. This means a FIN packet might not end the session. However, an RST packet will end the session abruptly, regardless of its origin. This will allow the hacker, who is pretending to be the trusted machine, to terminate the session. Once the session has ended, the ACK storm will cease. For the actual host, the only log entry will be an end-of-session record. This will not reflect that the session was hijacked. No clues about the hijacker will be left.

Resynchronizing the actual trusted computer with the victim server is performed because both computers have information regarding the quantity of packets that must be transferred. Whenever the hacker inserts additional packets to the stream of data between the actual client and the server, the victim server receives more packets than the trusted client actually sent. To avoid the loop of ACK packets between the client and the host, the hacker should synchronize the number of packets that are sent, which leads both valid members of the session to believe that the packet count is right. If this is done correctly, there will be no ACK storm because neither the trusted computer nor the victim will have too high or too low of a packet count. The hijack will be a complete success and the malicious code transfer from the attacker's machine will be considered a success.

TCP Session Hijacking with Packet Blocking

Packet blocking solves the ACK storm issue and facilitates TCP session hijacking. The ACK storm happens because the attacker was not in a place to stop or delete packets the trusted computer sent. An ACK storm will not occur if the attacker can place himself in the actual flow of the packets, but it takes a certain amount of daring to set up the situation so that you can put yourself in the flow. The attacker would have to be in control of the connection itself so that the session authentication takes place through the attacker's chosen channel, as shown in Figure 8-6.

Following authentication, the trusted computer indicates to the server that 200 packets are to be transferred for the session. The server, as well as the client, keeps a copy of the number and sequence of packets to be transferred in the session. They both have a record that 200 packets and their subsequent ACKs are expected. In typical TCP session hijacking, the hacker can either wait for the ACK packet to drop or manually synchronize the server and client records by spoofing. This is done to avoid problems. If a hacker can block the packets, the hacker will be able to drop the exact number of packets that are desired for transfer. In this manner, the

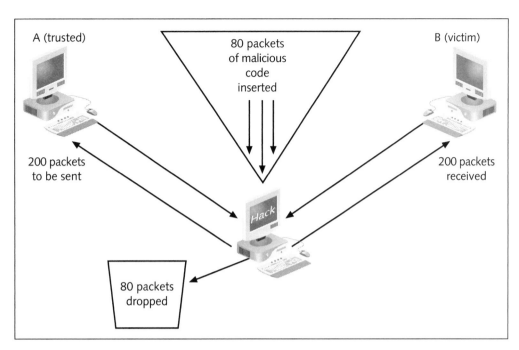

Figure 8-6   Packet blocking

generation of incorrect ACK packets in the data transfer procedure is easily avoided. If the hacker is unable to drop the packets, then the hacker may have the option to stop the extra ACK packets from being generated by the victim.

Methods

TCP session hijacking with packet blocking can be performed in two ways. One way is route table modification and the other is an Address Resolution Protocol (ARP) attack.

Route Table Modification

Before you can understand what a hacker can do with a route table, you have to understand how a route table is structured and what is done with the information.

All computers that use a TCP/IP protocol keep a route table. The simplest explanation of a route table is that it shows the way to the address sought, or the way to the nearest source that might know the address. In the Linux route table shown in Figure 8-7, there are only two entries (the two lines immediately below "Destination"). The first shows the way to all of the nodes within the LAN, and the second shows the way to all of the addresses not on the LAN. There is no gateway listed for the computer addresses within the LAN (anything with an IP address starting with 192.168.0) and there is only one gateway listed for everything else. The latter is called a default route and is used if there are no other ways to get there. If there was a second subnet in this network with a router address of 192.168.0.2 and an internal IP address of 192.168.100.0 (all nodes that start 192.168.100), there would be a third entry in the route table as follows:

```
192.168.100.0192.168.0.2255.255.255.0UG000eth0
```

A route table has two sections: the active routes and the active connections. These will be explained in greater detail below. A route table can be seen by giving the following command at the console prompt in either the Windows or Linux/UNIX operating system:

```
netstat -nra
```

Figure 8-7 shows an example of a route table.

```
wolf@l8:~$ netstat -nra
Kernel IP routing table
Destination     Gateway         Genmask         Flags  MSS Window  irtt Iface
192.168.0.0     0.0.0.0         255.255.255.0   U        0 0          0 eth0
0.0.0.0         192.168.0.1     0.0.0.0         UG       0 0          0 eth0
wolf@l8:~$ netstat -n
Active Internet connections (w/o servers)
Proto Recv-Q Send-Q Local Address        Foreign Address        State
tcp        1      0 192.168.0.102:44714  69.45.64.163:80        CLOSE_WAIT
tcp        1      0 192.168.0.102:44706  69.45.64.163:80        CLOSE_WAIT
tcp        0      0 192.168.0.102:49148  64.12.24.26:5190       ESTABLISHED
tcp        0      0 192.168.0.102:56944  207.46.4.53:1863       ESTABLISHED
tcp        1      0 192.168.0.102:49980  69.45.64.171:80        CLOSE_WAIT
tcp        0      0 192.168.0.102:58298  64.12.165.67:5190      ESTABLISHED
tcp        0      0 192.168.0.102:39341  152.2.210.65:80        ESTABLISHED
tcp        0      0 127.0.0.1:32769      127.0.0.1:57156        ESTABLISHED
tcp        0      0 127.0.0.1:49129      127.0.0.1:631          ESTABLISHED
tcp        0      0 127.0.0.1:57156      127.0.0.1:32769        ESTABLISHED
tcp        0      0 127.0.0.1:631        127.0.0.1:49129        ESTABLISHED
tcp        0      0 192.168.0.102:36909  216.155.193.170:5050   ESTABLISHED
tcp        0      0 192.168.0.102:36935  205.188.2.80:5190      ESTABLISHED
tcp        1      0 192.168.0.102:53510  208.254.57.141:80      CLOSE_WAIT
Active UNIX domain sockets (w/o servers)
Proto RefCnt Flags     Type      State       I-Node Path
unix  7      [ ]       DGRAM                 4611381 /dev/log
unix  3      [ ]       DGRAM                 3979    @udevd
```

Figure 8-7 Linux route table

If the route table is not able to locate a perfect match of the IP address, it has to search for the closest possible match in the list of network addresses. After the match is found, the IP address of Computer A sends the packets to the IP address. The IP address is the gateway address in the netstat -nr output, and is assigned to the host computer. Even though the packets are not directly transferred to the IP address of the destination computer, the source computer assumes that the IP address of the routing computer will have a perfect match for the IP address of the destination computer. In the table above, there are only two route table entries and almost all of the active routes (that are not loopback connections) for eth0 are to the HTTP port (80) of various servers. The UNIX domain sockets in the truncated list at the bottom of the figure are all connections from one application or process to itself or to another application or process through the **loopback address (127.0.0.1)**. See Figure 8-8 for an illustration of a route table in action.

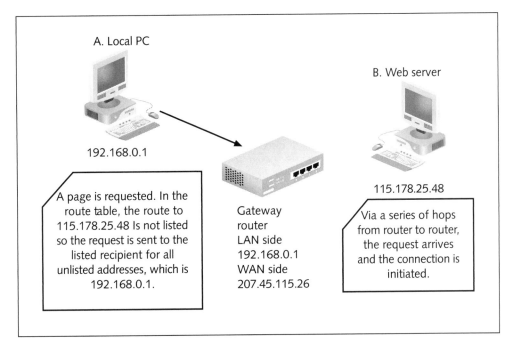

A. Local PC

B. Web server

192.168.0.1

A page is requested. In the route table, the route to 115.178.25.48 Is not listed so the request is sent to the listed recipient for all unlisted addresses, which is 192.168.0.1.

Gateway router
LAN side
192.168.0.1
WAN side
207.45.115.26

115.178.25.48

Via a series of hops from router to router, the request arrives and the connection is initiated.

Figure 8-8   Route table in action

TIP If you are interested in what all the port numbers mean and what applications use which ports, go to www.iana.org/assignments/port-numbers. Port 80 is for HTTP, 1863 is for MSN Messenger, 5190 is for AOL Instant Messenger and ICQ, and 5050 is for a multimedia conference control tool (probably Yahoo Messenger in this case).

Figure 8-9 illustrates the situation in which the computer above would send packets by using the nearest match in the route table.

If the route table cannot find a match, it uses the default network address option of 0.0.0.0. This option specifically refers the request to the network gateway. The gateway router has a register of network addresses and is capable of finding a match. The route table uses the netmask in combination with the network address to decide if the destination computer belongs to a LAN (local area network) or an external network.

The active connections section is the second section of the route table on a Windows box, and netstat -F (or netstat -n) on the Linux box. It shows the network addresses of the computers that are connected with the host computer. Note: On a *nix system, most of the traffic is through the lo interface, 127.0.0.1, which is the loopback. A Linux box

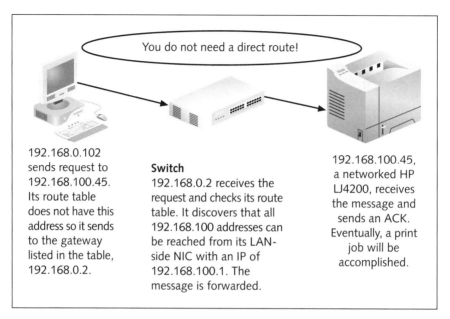

You do not need a direct route!

192.168.0.102 sends request to 192.168.100.45. Its route table does not have this address so it sends to the gateway listed in the table, 192.168.0.2.

Switch
192.168.0.2 receives the request and checks its route table. It discovers that all 192.168.100 addresses can be reached from its LAN-side NIC with an IP of 192.168.100.1. The message is forwarded.

192.168.100.45, a networked HP LJ4200, receives the message and sends an ACK. Eventually, a print job will be accomplished.

Figure 8-9   Route discovery

perceives itself as *being* the network and many processes talk to each other through the lo interface. This explains the bottom section of Figure 8-7.

A hacker is able to change the route table in such a way that the host computer will assume that the best possible path for the transfer of data packets is through the hacker's computer. A hacker can do this by altering the gateway address that is assigned to a particular network address. For instance, if a hacker wants to receive all the packets sent from Computer A to Computer B, he or she can modify the gateway address assigned to the network address of Computer B in the route table of Computer A. Whenever Computer A searches its route table for the network address of Computer B, the gateway address provided to Computer A will then be the address of the hacker's computer. This action sends the packets to the hacker's computer. At this point, the hacker can transfer the packets to the actual destination computer. This arrangement could go on indefinitely as long as the hacker does not alter anything substantial in the packet flow.

Figure 8-10 illustrates the concept of a route table modification attack.

Hackers can modify a route table using two methods. One method is to erase all of the necessary records from the route table of a computer and then provide the hacker's own IP address as the default gateway address in the route table. This will guarantee that all packets sent from that computer will be transferred to the hacker's computer. Another method is to change the corresponding route in the route table of the gateway router. That allows hackers to receive packets sent to a specific server from a client computer. It is probably easier to adjust the route table on the local computer.

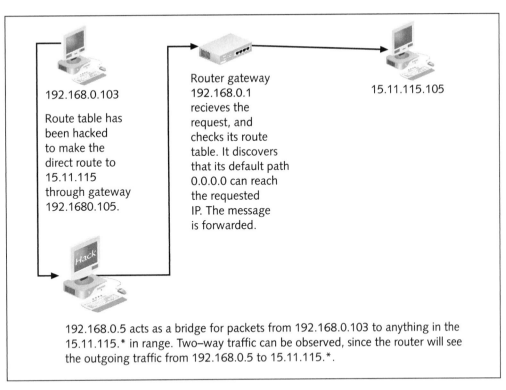

192.168.0.103

Route table has
been hacked
to make the
direct route to
15.11.115
through gateway
192.1680.105.

Router gateway
192.168.0.1
recieves the
request, and
checks its route
table. It discovers
that its default path
0.0.0.0 can reach
the requested
IP. The message
is forwarded.

15.11.115.105

192.168.0.5 acts as a bridge for packets from 192.168.0.103 to anything in the
15.11.115.* in range. Two–way traffic can be observed, since the router will see
the outgoing traffic from 192.168.0.5 to 15.11.115.*.

Figure 8-10   Route table hack

CAUTION

Session hacking is yet another reason not to operate your computer as Administrator or root during standard sessions. How fast do you think a hacker could
type one or two lines in at your command line if he or she had a couple of
minutes alone on the machine? How fast do you think a script could run that
would do the same things?

```
route add -p 172.16.0.0 mask 255.255.255.0 192.168.0.3
route add -p 192.168.5.0 mask 255.255.255.0 192.168.0.3
```

This would add two direct routes to make the hacker's Windows PC the default route
between the local private subnet and the nonlocal IP range 172.16.0.1 – 172.16.0.254.

If you have a Linux machine:

```
route del -host 0.0.0.0 mask 255.255.255.0 192.168.0.1 eth0
route add -host 0.0.0.0 mask 255.255.255.0 192.168.0.101 eth0
```

would delete the current gateway and add the IP 192.168.0.101 as the new gateway.

ARP Attacks

Every computer has a unique IP address and a MAC, or physical address. An ARP table on
a computer stores the IP address and the corresponding MAC address. This is used to

transfer data packets. As shown in Figure 8-11, the ARP table of a computer can be viewed by typing `arp -a` at the console prompt.

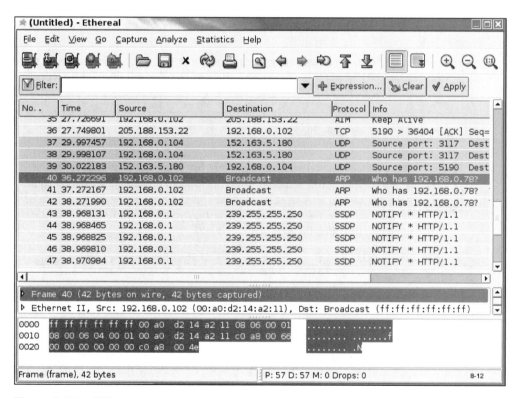

```
root@l8:~$
wolf@l8:~$ arp
Address                  HWtype  HWaddress           Flags Mask       Iface
192.168.0.100            ether   00:B0:D0:95:38:0A   C                eth0
192.168.0.1              ether   00:0D:88:A7:97:1C   C                eth0      8-11
```

Figure 8-11   ARP table

When a computer has to send data to another computer, the host computer can find the MAC address of the destination computer by referring to the ARP table. If the host computer does not have the MAC address of the destination computer, it transmits a broadcast message called an ARP request on the network to identify the destination computer's MAC address. This is shown in Figure 8-12. In order to send a broadcast message, the host computer gives the MAC address as FF-FF-FF-FF-FF-FF.

Figure 8-12   ARP request

The destination computer with an IP address that matches the IP address mentioned in the ARP request sends the MAC address to the host computer in an ARP reply packet. This creates a fresh entry in the ARP table of the host computer. After the MAC address of the destination computer has been received, the host computer will send the packets to the destination computer by employing the MAC address.

If the host computer already has the MAC address of the destination computer, then no separate broadcasts are released. Therefore, the packets are sent directly to the destination computer. If the local trusted target computer already has the ARP of the victim server in its ARP table, the attacker has to edit the ARP table for that entry. This is easiest to do while sitting in front of the target computer:

```
arp [-v]           [-i <if>] -d  <host> [pub]<-Delete ARP entry
arp [-v]    [<HW>] [-i <if>] -s  <host> <hwaddr> [temp]<-Add entry
example:
arp -d 192.168.0.102

or

arp -d dcheney
arp -s 192.168.0.102 01:23:a1:b2:ff:09
or
arp -s dcheney 01:23:a1:b2:ff:09
```

NOTE In the case of editing the ARP table for the purpose of session hijacking, helpful details like the interface and verbose response are not chosen.

If the host computer does not have an entry of the MAC address of the destination computer, it will send a broadcast message. The destination computer that has the matching IP address can respond to the host computer. As shown in Figure 8-13, an attacker can interrupt the response from the destination computer and change its MAC address to the MAC address of the hacker's computer. This procedure adds an entry, with the hacker's MAC address, in the ARP table of the host computer. Consequently, all the packets that are sent to the destination computer will instead be sent to the hacker's computer.

There may be a situation whereby the host computer already has the corresponding MAC address of the destination computer's IP address. In this situation, the hacker can change the ARP entry for the destination computer and specify the MAC address of the hacker's computer in the ARP table of the host computer. This may also result in the transfer of the packets to the hacker's computer, rather than to the actual destination computer.

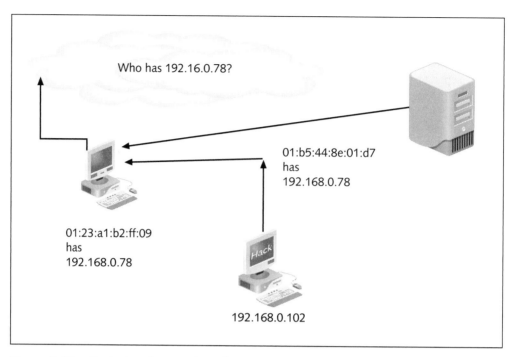

Who has 192.16.0.78?

01:b5:44:8e:01:d7
has
192.168.0.78

01:23:a1:b2:ff:09
has
192.168.0.78

192.168.0.102

Figure 8-13   Capturing the ARP broadcast response (ARP race)

SESSION HIJACKING TOOLS

There are several tools that can be used for session hijacking. Here, you will read about one of these tools: Hunt.

Hunt

Hunt was developed by Pavel Krauz. Inspired by Juggernaut, another session hijacking tool, Hunt also performs sniffing in addition to session hijacking. The Hunt tool provides the following menu options: listing, watching, and resetting connections. See Appendix D for Hunt's entire menu list.

Specifying the letter that is assigned to the options at the prompt performs the assigned function. The Hunt tool is able to hijack a session through ARP attacks. As you have read previously, ARP attacks help to avoid continuous ACK exchange between the actual client and server. This tool also allows ways for the hacker to synchronize the connection among the host and the server during session hijacking.

UDP Hijacking

User Datagram Protocol (UDP) is a connectionless protocol that, like TCP, runs on top of IP networks. Unlike TCP/IP, UDP/IP provides very few error recovery services, offering instead a direct way to send and receive datagrams over an IP network. It's used primarily for broadcasting messages over a network.

Since UDP does not have many error recovery features, it is more vulnerable to hijacking because the hacker needs only to sniff the network for a UDP request for a Web site and drop a spoofed UDP packet in before the Web server responds. The victim in this case would be the local computer, and not the server. The victim assumes that the spoofed UDP package is the authentic one and carries on its session with the hacker's machine. The hacker then sends UDP packets across with malicious code, Trojans, worms, or whatever. The victim might get a "page cannot be displayed" error, but the user would not consider that they had been attacked.

8

Prevention and Mitigation

To defend against session hacking, use encrypted protocols and practice storm watching.

Encryption

A hacker needs to be authenticated on the network to be able to successfully hijack a session or retrieve data. If the data transfer is encrypted, it is far too complicated and time consuming to get authenticated.

Standard protocols like Post Office Protocol (POP3), Telnet, Internet Message Access Protocol (IMAP), and Simple Mail Transfer Protocol (SMTP) are excellent targets because they transfer data as plaintext. This data can be picked up from the network and used later as required. Use encrypted protocols like Secure Shell (SSH) or Transport Layer Security (TLS). These programs encrypt the complete session, prolonging the amount of time needed to even get the general information about the session. This is really the heart of encryption. If the data is of no value after five minutes, you only need to use an encryption system that makes the data uncrackable for six minutes.

Table 8-1 Replace or enhance insecure protocols with secure protocols

Insecure protocols	Encrypted Protocols
Post Office Protocol (POP3)	POP3 over TLS
Simple Mail Transfer Protocol (SMTP)	SMTP over TLS
Internet Message Access Protocol (IMAP)	HTMLS, SSL
Telnet	Secure Sockets Layer (SSL), SSH
File Transfer Protocol (FTP)	SSL, SSH
Hypertext Transport Protocol (HTTP)	Secure Hypertext Transport Protocol (HTTPS), SSL

As shown in Figure 8-14, the encryption method involved in SSH and TLS uses two keys, the public key and the private key. The public key can be accessed by all computers and is also used to encrypt data. The private key is available only for the server to decrypt data. The server identifies the private key to be used for decryption on the basis of the public key that is attached to the encrypted packets.

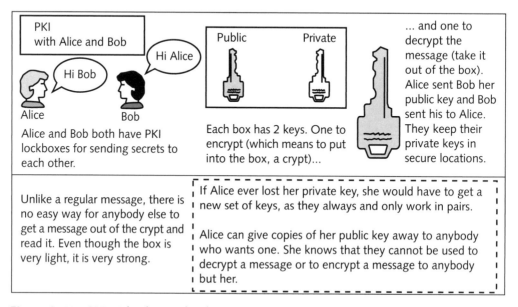

Figure 8-14 PKI with Alice and Bob

The hacker must have the algorithm of the encryption method and a lot of time, or the server's private key, in order to properly decrypt the data. A wise administrator shuts down unnecessary services and open ports on the server where the private key is stored. If an attacker is successful and manages to hack that server and get the private keys, any session encrypted with the complementary public keys can be read and hijacked. However, there are more effective hacks if you have root access to the server.

Storm Watching

Storm watching refers to setting an IDS rule to watch for abnormal increases in network traffic and to alert the security officer when they occur. Duplicate packets and retransmission of data are rare events on most TCP/IP networks. Quality of service is much higher than in the average cellular phone network. An unexpected increase in traffic could be evidence of an ACK storm like those created by TCP session hijacking. Packet size can also be cached for a short period. Two packets with the same header information but of different sizes could be evidence of a hijacking in progress.

Even if there is no hijacking in process, increased network traffic could be a sign of some other sort of attack or a sign of equipment failure somewhere in the network.

CHAPTER SUMMARY

- TCP session hijacking takes place when a hacker takes control of a TCP session between two hosts; this can only occur after the hosts have authenticated successfully.

- A successful hijacking takes place when a hacker intervenes in a conversation, takes the role of either host or recipient, and then receives packets before the actual host.

- Session hijacking can be accomplished by using source-routed IP packets, which allows a hacker to participate in a conversation by encouraging IP packets to pass through its machine; blind hijacking, whereby a hacker guesses the responses of the two machines; or a man-in-the-middle attack strategy, using a sniffing program to follow the conversation.

- There are three ways of stopping a continuous ACK transfer: losing an ACK packet, ending the TCP connection, and resynchronizing the client and server.

- Packet blocking places the hacker in the actual flow of packets, solving the problem of the ACK transmission storm.

- TCP session hijacking with packet blocking can be performed in two ways: modifying the route table and initiating an ARP attack.

- A popular tool used for session hijacking is Hunt.

- UDP has a small number of error recovery features and is therefore more vulnerable to hijacking.

- Two methods used to prevent session hijacking are encryption and storm watching.

REVIEW QUESTIONS

1. What is session hijacking?
2. Why is session hijacking done?
3. What is the difference between session hijacking and IP spoofing?
4. How would an attacker use source routing to hijack a session?
5. How can continuous ACK transfer be stopped?
6. How would an attacker perform TCP session hijacking with packet blocking?
7. What does the command `netstat -nra` do at a Windows command prompt?
8. What is the default loopback address?
9. Where does a packet go if the address in its destination field is unknown in the route table?
10. What are the two main functions of Hunt?
11. Name five encryption protocols.

12. How common are duplicate packets and retransmission on most TCP/IP networks?

Indicate whether the sentence or statement is true or false:

13. _____ The encryption method involved in SSH and TLS uses three keys.

14. _____ TCP is more vulnerable to hijacking than UDP.

Match these unsafe network protocols with their safer encrypted counterparts:

    a. Post Office Protocol (POP3)

    b. File Transfer Protocol (FTP)

    c. Telnet

    d. Internet Message Access Protocol (IMAP)

    e. Hypertext Transport Protocol (HTTP)

    f. Simple Mail Transfer Protocol (SMTP)

15. _____ POP3 over TLS

16. _____ SMTP over TLS

17. _____ HTMLS, SSL

18. _____ Secure Sockets Layer (SSL), SSH

19. _____ SSL, SSH

20. _____ Secure Hypertext Transport Protocol (HTTPS), SSL

HANDS-ON PROJECT

The act of session hijacking is illegal on public networks and probably illegal on your school or organization's LAN, so this project will be done by setting up three VMware virtual servers on the lab's central server. The instructor will set up a TCP session between two of them, and will attempt a session hijacking from the third virtual server. (Alternately, at the discretion of the instructor, three designated lab computers can be used for this project.) The students' job will be to watch the packet traffic for signs of the attack.

Project 8-1

1. Using Wireshark as root on your Linux box, or as an administrative user on your Windows box, set the basic filter to ignore broadcasts, and start the sniffer before the instructor begins the exploit.

2. Start Tcpdump or WinDump so you can watch the scrolling network events while the instructor sets up the exploit. For example, type the following to start Tcpdump on a Linux box:

```
tcpdump -v -i eth0
```

3. Watch the attack as it takes place. Make note of the packets as they scroll past. (*Hint:* Since the first section of the line in Tcpdump is the time, based on your own system clock, you can just note that time as where to look on the Wireshark output.) In the following code snippet, the time is highlighted:

```
"18:28:58.041892 IP (tos 0x20, ttl  46, id 65434, offset 0,
flags [DF], proto: TCP (6), length: 40)
xmlrpc.rhn.redhat.com.https > constantine.local.39315: .,
cksum 0xc418 (correct), ack 1189 win 2532"
```

8

9

HACKING NETWORK DEVICES

> ## After reading this chapter and completing the exercises, you will be able to:
>
> ♦ Identify the vulnerabilities of proxy servers
> ♦ Identify the vulnerabilities of routers and switches
> ♦ Identify the vulnerabilities of firewalls
> ♦ Identify the vulnerabilities of virtual private networks (VPNs)

This chapter will show you the basics of hacking network devices such as proxy servers, routers, switches, firewalls, and virtual private networks (VPNs). These are all used as outward facing devices, and the challenge to hacking all of these devices is to hack them from outside the network.

A network can be divided into two main areas, either of which a hacker can use as a corridor to attack a target computer. These are:

- Networking software
- Networking devices

Networking software can be divided into three categories: security software, such as firewalls; connection software, such as VPN software; and transport software, such as proxy servers and router operating systems.

Networking devices allow the computers on a network to interact with each other. For example, a network card allows a computer, a printer, a closed circuit camera, or any other device to access the network. A combination of software and hardware devices completes a network and builds an interactive framework that can be used to access the network.

This chapter covers various hacking techniques and methods used to execute attacks on a network. The networking components detailed in this chapter are:

- Proxy servers
- Routers and switches
- Firewalls
- Virtual private networks (VPNs)

PROXY SERVERS

Proxy servers, such as the one shown in Figure 9-1, perform various functions in an organization's network.

- Proxy servers restrict users from accessing specific Web sites using Internet access rules, such as those that a firewall would enforce.
- Proxy servers mask the IP of the users' PCs within the network from outside connections.
- Proxy servers maintain logs of the requests and the details of users that are accessing the Internet.
- Proxy servers also maintain a cache of the sites that users on the network have visited. For example, when a request is made for a Web site, the proxy then searches the cache for its availability. If there happens to be a cache entry available for that Web site, the proxy does not send a request on the Internet. Instead, it displays the site from the cache itself.

A proxy server is simple to install. It is often part of the operating system of a server that performs file storage, WWW services, or mail services, and it does not require separate hardware to function. A proxy server is simple to use and is often included in router and firewall software. Whenever a user sends a request for a Web site, the proxy server will store details about the user, such as IP address and time of request. Next, the proxy server checks to

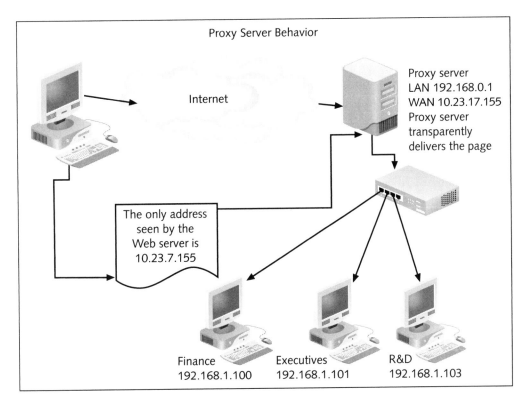

Figure 9-1 Proxy server in place

make sure that the user has access permission to visit that site. Upon validation, the proxy server checks the cache for the availability of that Web site. If that site is available, the proxy server uses the cache to display the Web site. It does not send a request on the Internet. If the proxy server does not have a cache entry, it sends out a request on the Internet and locates the Web page. The IP address sent from the proxy server to the remote Web server is the same IP address of the proxy server. The user interacting via the proxy server is hidden, but can be traced through the log stored on the proxy server.

Categories of Attacks

The attacks related to proxy servers are classified into two groups: attacks made *upon* proxy servers and attacks made *through* proxy servers.

The attacks made through proxy servers include buffer overflow attacks, denial-of-service attacks, and session-hijacking attacks. A key method used by hackers to attack via proxy server is to keep their identities concealed by accessing the Internet through the proxy server.

Concealed Identity

When users access the Internet through a proxy server, their identities are hidden and the remote Web server interacts with the proxy server's IP address. Hackers use this model to perform hacking operations anonymously. Using a proxy server on some network, a hacker accesses a Web site and subsequently performs the hacking actions. This obscures the real IP address of the hacker in the Web server's log files. The hacker's IP and time of attack is, however, maintained on the proxy server. If the Web server's administrator sees that the proxy server at xyz.com hacked her computer at a specific date and time, she can contact the administrator at xyz.com, who can examine his proxy server logs to see who was listed as the user in that case. This might put our hacker at risk, as system administrators can use this log file to track the IP address of the hacker's computer. There are two ways that an attacker can work around this automatic logging problem.

A hacker might use a chain of proxy servers to put a long list of long and dull log files between the administrators and himself. Due to the large size of log files, it might be very difficult to track the hacker through a series of high-volume networks. Figure 9-2 shows how hackers use a chain of proxy servers to conceal their identities.

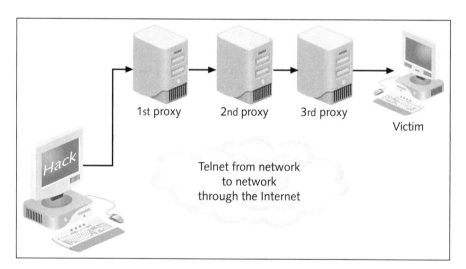

Figure 9-2   Using a chain of proxy servers to conceal identities

Another method a hacker can use is spoofing the valid authentication details of a network. By using the IP address of a valid user, a hacker can perform operations on the target computer through the proxy server of that network. In this type of case, any attempt to track down the hacker will lead to the IP address of an innocent user. Figure 9-3 depicts how hackers hide their identities by using valid authentication details.

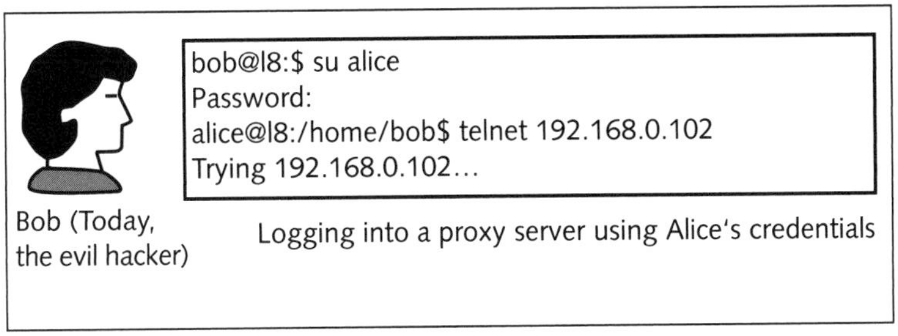

```
bob@l8:$ su alice
Password:
alice@l8:/home/bob$ telnet 192.168.0.102
Trying 192.168.0.102…
```

Bob (Today,
the evil hacker)   Logging into a proxy server using Alice's credentials

Figure 9-3 Hacking through a proxy server using valid authentication details

ROUTERS AND SWITCHES

Routers and switches both segment a network, and most can filter packets. Switches are considered to have lower security than routers, so switches are often thought of as internal network components; however, with the advent of VLAN technology on switches, some networks are being designed with gateway switches, as shown in Figure 9-4. Since routers are basically OSI Layer 2 switches, it makes sense to use a switch as a gateway device. VLANs are a form of logical network segmentation. Because switches almost always have multiple inward-facing ports, what could be more natural than being able to designate specific subnets for each port? This is an undeniable cost savings, as one 24-port switch is far cheaper than eight or three switches (depending on how many network segments you are designing). The first danger is that there is only one switch between the outside world and your whole kingdom. You cannot run the same level of IDS, and with only one password to crack, an attacker can dice up your network much more quickly than if you had multiple internal switches with different passwords.

CAUTION You are not doing yourself any favors in terms of security if all of your routers and switches have the same admin password. Having different passwords adds a layer of difficulty before the potential attacker. If your network administrator from the New York office quits, then you will only have to change the passwords on the routers and switches that she had control over, rather than all of the passwords. Note to hackers: If a company is running multiple locations and using one global admin password, it is unlikely to change the password globally, as that is a big hassle. This is not proper security policy, but it is how the real world works.

Attacks on Routers and Switches

If the attacker has access to the console port of the router, he can easily set a remote user for the router or switch. This is the hardest step, after which the attacker can get into the router by Telnet until either the Telnet port is shut down or the bogus user is discovered.

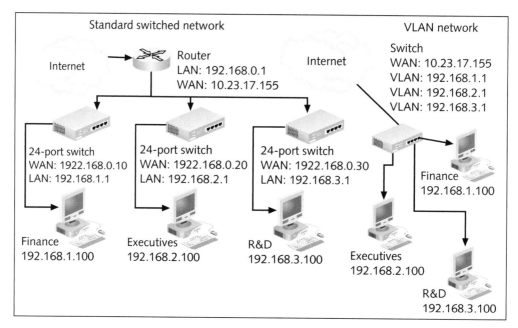

Figure 9-4 VLAN architecture

Configuration Procedure

In this example, passwords are configured for users attempting to connect to the router on the VTY lines using Telnet. The following example is specifically for a Cisco 2610 router.

From the privileged EXEC (or "enable") prompt, enter configuration mode and enter your username/password combination. You can add more than one user.

```
router#configure terminal
Enter configuration commands, one per line. End with CNTL/Z.
router(config)#username evilhacker password boom
router(config)#username fakeadmin password tricky
```

Switch to line configuration mode, using the following command.

```
router(config)#line vty 0 4
router(config-line)#
```

Configure password checking at login.

```
router(config-line)#login local
```

Exit configuration mode.

```
router(config-line)#end
router#
%SYS-5-CONFIG_I: Configured from console by console
```

Verify the configuration if you have time.

Examine the configuration of the router to verify that the commands have been properly entered.

```
show running-config - displays the current configuration of the
router.
router#show running-config
Building configuration...
!
!-- some lines omitted
username evilhacker password boom
username fakeadmin password tricky
!-- some more lines omitted

line con 0
line 1 8
line aux 0
line vty 0 4
 login local
!
end
```

To test this configuration, a Telnet connection must be made to the router. This can be done by connecting from a different host on the network, but you can also test from the router itself by Telnetting to the IP address of any interface on the router that is in an up/up state as seen in the output of the show interfaces command.

Here is a sample output if the address of interface ethernet 0 was 10.23.17.155:

```
router#telnet 10.23.17.155
Trying 10.23.17.155 ... Open
User Access Verification
Username: evilhacker
Password:
router
```

Now the attacker has a great back door. Other routers are similar, but if an attacker is going to make a career of cracking routers, he had better learn as much as possible about the possible routers out there. Things to learn include configuration snippets such as the above example, as well as default passwords and current exploits.

The default password for Cisco routers is admin/admin. See Table 9-1 for a selection of default passwords.

9

Router Exploits

Table 9-1 Sample default password list

Manufacturer	Product	Username	Password
Cisco	CiscoWorks 2000	admin	cisco
Cisco	BR340	n/a	(none)
Cisco	Content Engine	admin	default
Cisco	PIX firewall	(none)	cisco
Cisco	BBSM MSDE Administrator	sa	(none)
Cisco	GSR	admin	admin
Cisco	3600	Administrator	admin
Cisco	1721	n/a	(none)
Cisco	VPN Concentrator 300	admin	admin
Cisco	Cache Engine	admin	diamond
Cisco	Netranger / secure IDS	netrangr	attack
D-Link	DWL 1000	admin	(none)
D-Link	DI-804	admin	(none)
D-Link	DI-624	admin	(none)
D-Link	DI-624+	admin	admin
D-Link	hubs/switches	D-Link	D-Link
Linksys	Router DSL/Cable	(none)	admin
Linksys	BEFSR41	(none)	admin
Linksys	BEFW11S4	admin	(none)
Linksys	WRT54G	admin	admin
Netgear	DM602	admin	password
Netgear	FM114P	(none)	(none)
Netgear	FR114P	admin	password
Netgear	WGT624	admin	password
Netgear	RT314	admin	(admin)

As shown in Figure 9-5, port scans are used to discover whether ports are open, what applications are using the ports, and even the operating system of the system being scanned. If you are scanning IP ranges over the Internet, you are as likely as not to get network routers among your live nodes.

In the figure, there is only one port open port: 80, the HTTP port. D-Link D-604 routers use an HTTP page for configuration, and the default port is 192.168.0.1, as shown in the figure.

Hackers can perform many attacks on routers and switches even if they cannot get into the building and set themselves up as a system administrator. The sheer complexity of router configuration affects their vulnerability. Sometimes adding protection to one area can actually open another area to attack.

```
root@l8:~ # nmap -sS -O -v 192.168.0.1

Starting nmap 3.81 ( http://www.insecure.org/nmap/ ) at 2006-02-16 16:21 EST
Initiating SYN Stealth Scan against 192.168.0.1 [1663 ports] at 16:21
Discovered open port 80/tcp on 192.168.0.1
The SYN Stealth Scan took 0.55s to scan 1663 total ports.
For OSScan assuming port 80 is open, 1 is closed, and neither are firewalled
Host 192.168.0.1 appears to be up ... good.
Interesting ports on 192.168.0.1:
(The 1662 ports scanned but not shown below are in state: closed)
PORT    STATE SERVICE
80/tcp open  http
MAC Address: 00:0D:88:A7:97:1C (D-Link)
Device type: WAP
Running: Linksys embedded, D-Link embedded
OS details: Linksys, D-Link, or Planet WAP
TCP Sequence Prediction: Class=trivial time dependency
                         Difficulty=0 (Trivial joke)
IPID Sequence Generation: Incremental

Nmap finished: 1 IP address (1 host up) scanned in 3.517 seconds
            Raw packets sent: 1679 (67.4KB) | Rcvd: 1677 (77.2KB)
root@l8:~ #
root@l8:~ #                                           9-6
```

Figure 9-5 Nmap results on a D-Link D-604 router

Some basic router attacks are listed below.

- Denial-of-Service (DoS) Attack—A denial-of-service attack on a router is similar to the DoS attacks that target a server. The hacker transmits a large quantity of packets to the router for it to determine an effective and efficient path for transfer. The router manages packets on a first-come, first-served basis, so a heavy DoS attack leaves the router unable to validate the path for the packets sent by valid users. The network slows down until the router has handled the DoS or until the administrator sets a rule for the router to filter traffic from the offending IP or IP range.

- Distributed Denial-of-Service (DDoS) Attack—**DDoS** works like a DoS, but the attack comes from many IP addresses, so the defense is more complicated. When 500 zombie (hacker-owned) PCs from residential ISPs like AOL and Earthlink start sending a DDoS to your router, you could block those IP ranges. But that would be like building concrete walls across the highway out of Cleveland, simply because somebody crashed a stolen car from Cleveland through your front window. Such a response is too strong and incorrect.

- Route Table Modification Attack—To decide the quickest, most efficient path for a packet to reach its destination, a route table is maintained within a router, just like on your PC. This route table must contain the IP addresses and related router addresses, as well as default paths. When a computer transmits a packet, it initially searches within its own route table to determine the path for the packets. If a match of the IP address with a router is not located, then the packets are forwarded to the default gateway. The gateway router will try to resolve the IP address to a different router that contains the closest possible match of the IP address available. An attacker hacks the gateway router and replaces the current paths in the route table with fraudulent ones. This can lead to all sorts of trouble, such as pharming attacks where the default path to a secure Web site runs though either the proxy server controlled by the hacker, a hacked duplicate Web site, or the hacker's own computer.

Figure 9-6 illustrates the hacking of routers.

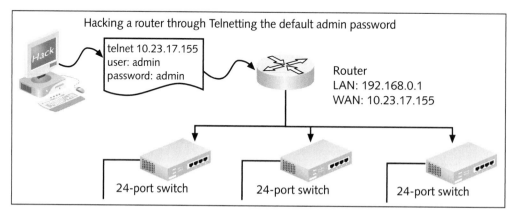

Figure 9-6   Hacking routers

FIREWALLS

Firewalls are often considered the ultimate one-point solution for securing networks from both internal and external threats. The main function of a firewall is to centralize access control for the network by keeping an eye on both inbound and outbound traffic and preventing unauthorized users and malicious code from entering a network. Compared to the IP packet filtering function of routers, which is performed on the IP layer, some firewalls can filter the packets on the application layer. This gives the network administrators an added advantage in protecting their network from hacking, worms, and even spam. Firewalls are designed to be transparent to authorized network users and very intrusive to unauthorized users. They provide a vigorous authentication system, block unauthorized traffic, and hide vulnerable network systems. There are many firewall vendors in the market, and their products have different features and different vulnerabilities. Figure 9-7 illustrates the concept of firewalls. Note in the figure that valid traffic, such as the order placed by Joe User to Buy.com, is allowed through the firewall. However, invalid traffic-whether it be the hacker's attempt to get into the network, or Worker X's attempt to reach a forbidden Web site-is blocked, or sent to a "bit bucket".

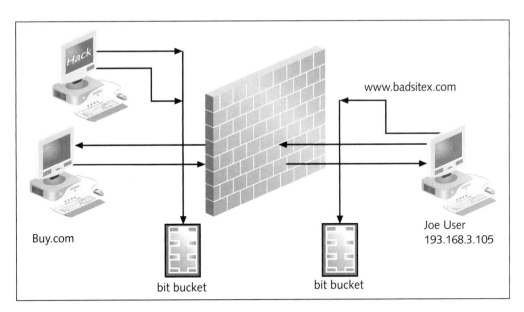

Figure 9-7   Firewall operation

This chapter covers general vulnerabilities that apply to firewall products from all vendors.

Limitations of Firewalls

To understand the vulnerabilities in firewalls, it is important to understand their limitations.

- Firewalls have a limited ability to check data integrity. It is not possible for them to check all the incoming and outgoing data on a network.

- Firewalls cannot filter packets that are not sent through them. Packets entering the network through modems, by laptops from outside plugged into network ethernet ports, and those sent to internal users from Web servers, are not validated by a firewall.

- Firewalls can encrypt a session. However, firewalls from different vendors may not work well together, and this can reduce the security level of the encrypted session.

- Firewalls do not provide robust support for application security. This increases the chances of the network being hacked. Network traffic that is executing vulnerable applications may pass through servers in the DMZ or in other network segments not protected by the firewall. Hackers look for opportunities like this to attack the network.

- Firewalls do not provide a complete solution for stopping malicious code from entering a network. This allows hackers to break into the network or create back doors.

- Firewalls may not detect attacks if they are not configured properly. Intrusion-detection tools that check for vulnerabilities in the firewall must be part of the organization's security policies, and must be used periodically to check the firewall.

- Firewalls cannot detect hackers using a valid username and password.

- Firewalls are effective only if security policies are established and enforced.

Types and Methods of Firewall Attacks

There are several ways to bypass a firewall, depending upon the type of firewall used in an organization's network and the quality of the configuration.

Firewall attacks can be organized into three categories:

- Spoofing—In this type of attack, the hacker appears as a legitimate user, which allows the hacker to send and receive packets to and from a network.

- Session hijacking—In this type of attack, the hacker intervenes in an active session. First, the hacker forges the identity of a host or a client. Next, the hacker ends the session of the user whose IP address has been forged by using session-ending packets. Then, the hacker continues the session and performs the hacking operations.

- Denial of service—In this type of attack, a hacker floods the target server with a large number of packets. As a result, the server is unable to communicate and respond to the requests sent by valid clients.

As new technologies and tools emerge, the methods that hackers use to break into a network protected by a firewall change. However, they use three basic methods to hack a firewall: back doors, root access, and through the Web.

Back Doors

Back doors are an alternate method used by hackers to access a network. After an attack, a hacker may leave an alternate route that can be used to hack the network again. For instance, a hacker may penetrate the network and leave a new user on the system with administrative rights, so that the hacker can return later. This allows the hacker to breach the firewall.

There are two ways to restore a computer after an attack:

- Format the computer and reinstall the data.

- Fix the bug used by the hacker to access the computer.

Formatting the hard drive closes all the back doors. It also prevents the hacker from using the same bug to penetrate the computer again. It is easy and relatively cheap to format or re-image a drive, compared with the time and thought required to find and kill the bug. This method is useful at a workstation level.

The second method is used for servers that are involved in a large number of transactions with multiple users. In this case, the cost of fixing the bug is less than the cost of formatting the computer. If a company uses a mail server to interact with both clients and employees, formatting the mail server can stop work and cause heavy losses. Compared to the first method, the chances of removing a back door using the second method are low. These methods may fix the immediate problem, but the source of the attack must be identified or the intruder may breach the firewall and break into the network again.

Consider the following example to understand how much damage a hacker can do to a network using a firewall. A hacker, who has either penetrated the firewall or entered the network using a back door, installs software on an internal computer. This software allows the hacker to interact with that computer, using a port authorized by the firewall, to interact with external entities. This may allow the hacker to penetrate the firewall again in the future.

Using various techniques, a hacker can lure or fool a user into creating a back door that allows the hacker to break into the network. A hacker can entice the user to create a back door in two ways. A hacker can send a program, such as Back Orifice, to gain remote access to a computer. The hacker can also put similar software on the Internet as an attachment to a downloadable file, and then provide it as a free download. This may provide the hacker access to the network. Figure 9-8 depicts the concept of a back door.

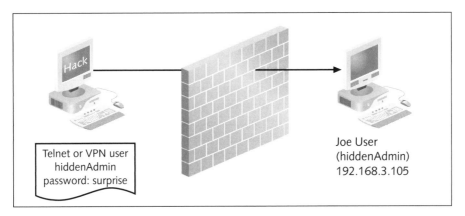

Figure 9-8   Back door

Root Access

This method is used when hackers want to return to a network and manipulate its data by using root or administrative access. A hacker attempts to gain this access by either using a back door to sniff the passwords or by using some other programming code to hijack a session and take control of the administrative sessions. The hacker has either already penetrated the firewall or is using a back door for root access. The hacker installs a rootkit that is used for a variety of purposes, such as password sniffing or injecting Trojans into the network after penetrating the root. Figure 9-9 shows the root access method.

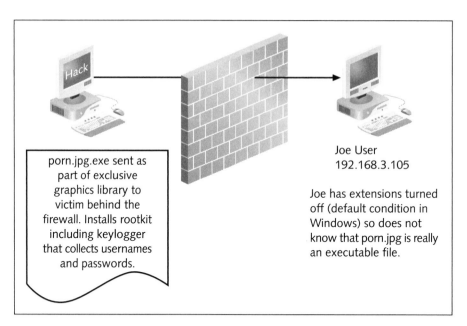

porn.jpg.exe sent as part of exclusive graphics library to victim behind the firewall. Installs rootkit including keylogger that collects usernames and passwords.

Joe User
192.168.3.105

Joe has extensions turned off (default condition in Windows) so does not know that porn.jpg is really an executable file.

Figure 9-9   Root access method

Through the Web

A hacker can break into a firewall through the Web in many ways since the majority of firewalls permit access to remote Web servers. The curious need only Google the term "Google Hacks" to find dozens of ways to get more information from Web sites than the owners intended. Hackers can access information on credit card numbers, usernames, passwords, and interesting code examples as well. Consider the following Google search:

```
"parent directory " /cgi-bin/ -xxx -html -htm -php -shtml -
opendivx -md5 -md5sums
```

This gets you directories of the interior of the CGI directories on lots of sites. This is one way hackers can find information logs on customers of the site. Change the search term that is highlighted above to find different lists. /users/ might be interesting.

```
allinurl:auth_user_file.txt
```

This Google hack gets pages like the DCForum's password file. This file gives a list of (crackable) passwords, usernames, e-mail addresses, country of origin, and phone numbers for DCForum and for DCShop (a shopping cart program).

```
MC Numbers: 5178000000000000..5178999999999999
```

This doesn't really work anymore, but in 2004 it was common for hackers to get credit card numbers and user information with this hack. Many or most vulnerabilities of this sort are plugged now, and the only pages this Google hack brings up are pages in blogs and forums, being passed around by people who don't know the hole has been plugged.

```
"# -FrontPage-" inurl:service.pwd"
```

This Google hack may return a list of pages containing Microsoft Frontpage passwords, useful for planting Trojan horses that will offer themselves as a download to every visitor. The passwords can also be used to add a script to the home page that will call to its hacker-controlled server from the unsuspecting user's browser, so the server can send a keylogger or some other small application. All of this traffic will appear to be normal, but the attacker will have access to at least one machine behind the firewall of the user's organization.

A firewall can be used to stop network attacks from happening, but it should be considered one piece of the multitier security solution for your organization, and not the final solution for all network security needs.

VPNs

A virtual private network (VPN) allows employees to access their company's network from a remote location using the Internet as a transport vehicle, rather than using the more expensive direct dial-up or dedicated WAN links. Using VPN, an external user can access a network and perform almost all the actions that users on the organization's internal network can perform. VPN uses protocols like point-to-point tunneling (encrypted data tunneling) to send and receive information over the network. VPN allows you to use pcAnywhere or other GUI-based terminal services. These show you a copy of your LAN-based computer (which has a pcAnywhere client installed) on your external PC (which also has a client installed). The VPN model is illustrated in Figure 9-10.

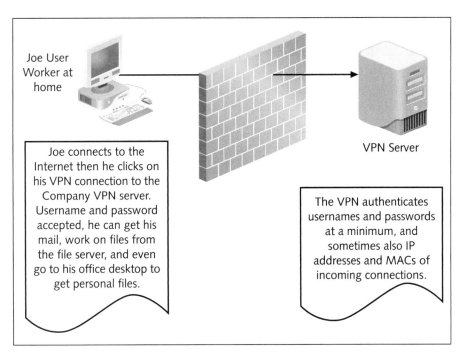

Figure 9-10   VPN model

Threats through VPN

Attacks on a company's network through a VPN are often indirect, and a result of successfully hacking a remote user's computer (or stealing a laptop). After successfully attacking the remote user's computer, the hacker can follow what that user does. If a VPN connection is sometimes used on the compromised computer, the hacker can acquire the necessary information and attempt to connect to the company network using the VPN connection. VPN connections are logged, but if the connection comes from a valid user and the passwords match, then the VPN server assumes the connection is valid.

A VPN connection of a valid user can be used to perform many attacks on a network, including DoS, session hijacking, and spoofing, as well as plain old theft, vandalism, and terrorism. Since the attacks are not considered a result of weaknesses in the VPN, they are deemed indirect attacks.

Ways to Safeguard the Network from Attacks through VPNs

Some basic steps can be taken to efficiently manage a VPN and prevent attacks while still allowing employees to safely access a network from any remote location. The basic steps for safeguarding the VPN links are listed below.

1. Protect your home computer's physical environment; do not put your laptop in harm's way. The stolen laptop is the easiest way to your company's VPN.

2. Do not use the "save" function for VPN passwords. Doing so would be like writing your pin number on your ATM card.

3. Install a host-based (personal) firewall on the remote computer. A firewall logs and stops attempts to break into a computer through its Internet connection.

4. Install a host-based intrusion detection system (IDS) on the remote computer to log or stop anomalous behavior on the machine. Configure the IDS to update its signature definitions at least every week.

5. Install antivirus software and configure it to update its virus definitions at least every week.

6. Perform more than one level of security checks to guarantee that the user trying to connect through the VPN is valid. Add a time factor to the allowed VPN connections, and never use the same user/pass combination for VPN, network access, and e-mail.

7. Audit the personal computers of remote users on a schedule (like weekly or every other day) to search for signs of intrusion.

8. Require username/password entry to remote computers. Maybe even consider a boot password or biometrics.

CHAPTER SUMMARY

❑ Network devices like proxy servers, routers, switches, firewalls, and VPNs are often targeted by attackers. The attacks are directed at the networking hardware or software.

❑ Networking software can be divided into three categories: security software, such as firewalls; connection software, such as VPN software; and transport software, such as proxy servers and router operating systems.

❑ Networking devices allow the computers on a network to interact with each other.

❑ Proxy servers restrict users from accessing specific Web sites, mask internal users IP addresses, maintain logs of Internet access, and maintain a cache of user-visited sites.

❑ Attacks made through proxy servers include buffer overflow attacks, denial-of-service attacks, and session-hijacking attacks. Most hackers access the Internet through the proxy server to keep their identities hidden.

❑ Routers and switches are used to segment a network; to filter packets; and, more recently, as gateway devices.

❑ If a hacker has access to the console port of the router, he can easily set a remote user for the router or switch, after which he can get into the router by Telnet until either the Telnet port is shut down or the attack is discovered.

❑ Attacks made on routers include DoS attacks, DDoS attacks, and route table modification.

❑ Firewalls centralize access control for the network, monitor inbound and outbound traffic, provide a vigorous authentication system, block unauthorized traffic, and hide vulnerable network systems.

❑ Firewall have several liabilities: firewalls cannot filter packets that are not sent through them; firewalls from different vendors may not work well together; firewalls do not provide robust support for application security; firewalls do not provide a complete solution for stopping malicious code from entering a network; firewalls may not detect attacks if they are not configured properly; firewalls cannot detect hackers using a valid username and password; firewalls are effective only if security policies are established and enforced.

❑ Types of firewall attacks include spoofing, session hijacking, and denial-of-service (DoS) attacks.

❑ Firewall hacking methods include back doors, root access, and Web access.

❑ Virtual private networks (VPNs) allow users to securely access their network from a remote location through the Internet.

9

❏ Threats through VPN are considered indirect attacks and include DoS attacks, session hijacking, spoofing, theft, vandalism, and terrorism.

❏ The basic steps for safeguarding the network from attacks through VPN are protecting the remote computer from theft; not using the "save" function for VPN passwords; installing a host-based (personal) firewall on the remote computer; installing a host-based intrusion detection system (IDS) on the remote computer; installing antivirus software and configuring it to update its virus definitions at least every week; performing more than one level of security checks; auditing the personal computers of remote users on a regular schedule; and requiring username/password entry to remote computers.

REVIEW QUESTIONS

1. What are the benefits of using a firewall?

2. What are the limitations of firewall software?

3. What are the benefits of using VPN technology?

4. What are the vulnerabilities of VPN?

5. What is the common vulnerability of all the devices covered in this chapter?

6. What is the common vulnerability of all the software covered in this chapter?

7. How is physical security a component of reducing attacks to routers and switches?

8. What is the transport function of a router?

9. Is a firewall the perfect security device for securing a network?

10. Can remote users disable the personal firewall on their computer?

Indicate whether the sentence or statement is true or false.

11. _____ Once your laptop is in your house, you can relax. Your company VPN cannot be stolen from your home.

12. _____ Always use the "password save" function for VPN passwords.

13. _____ A firewall logs and stops attempts to break into a computer.

14. _____ It is important to configure the IDS to update its signature definitions at least every week.

15. _____ Only install antivirus software if you also configure it to update its virus definitions at least every week.

16. _____ It is efficient to have every user on your business network use one password for network access, e-mail, and VPN.

17. _____ It is only important to do a network audit once a year at tax time.

18. _____ It might be a good idea to put a boot password on remote users' computers.

19. _____ Biometrics never work. There are too many false positives.

20. _____ Google hacks are illegal.

HANDS-ON PROJECTS

Set up one machine, for instance the central Linux server, behind a router inside the network. Cracking devices on the public Internet is unethical and illegal in many countries, so the safest way to practice is to set up a subnet. Make sure your router is set up to accept remote management, and that port blocking or ACLs are disabled.

**HANDS-ON
PROJECTS**

Project 9-1

1. As root, run *nmap* on the entire subnet to find out what you can about the subnet router, including what OS it is running. Here is an example *nmap* command—yours might vary based on your network configuration, so check with your instructor—and a portion of the output returned by *nmap*. The command shown scans the whole 192.168.0.*x* subnet and returns information about each host it finds. For this project, you are only interested in the information pertaining to the router.

```
nmap -vv -sS -O  192.168.0.1/24
```

The highlighted lines in the output shown below indicate that the device with IP address 192.168.0.1 is running a Linksys or D-Link embedded operating system.

```
Host 192.168.0.1 appears to be up ... good.
Interesting ports on 192.168.0.1:
Not shown: 1678 closed ports
PORT    STATE SERVICE
80/tcp open  http
MAC Address: 00:40:05:58:17:E3 (ANI Communications)
Device type: WAP
Running: Linksys embedded, D-Link embedded
OS details: Linksys, D-Link, or Planet WAP
OS Fingerprint:
TSeq(Class=TD%gcd=FA7F%SI=0%IPID=I%TS=U)
T1(Resp=Y%DF=N%W=2000%ACK=S++%Flags=AS%Ops=M)
T2(Resp=N)
T3(Resp=Y%DF=N%W=2000%ACK=O%Flags=A%Ops=)
T4(Resp=Y%DF=N%W=2000%ACK=O%Flags=R%Ops=)
T5(Resp=Y%DF=N%W=0%ACK=S++%Flags=AR%Ops=)
T6(Resp=Y%DF=N%W=0%ACK=O%Flags=R%Ops=)
T7(Resp=Y%DF=N%W=0%ACK=S%Flags=AR%Ops=)
PU(Resp=Y%DF=N%TOS=0%IPLEN=38%RIPTL=148%RID=E%RIPCK=E%UCK=E
%ULEN=134%DAT=E)
TCP Sequence Prediction: Class=trivial time dependency
                        Difficulty=0 (Trivial joke)
IPID Sequence Generation: Incremental
```

9

Print the contents of the network probe and highlight or circle for your instructor all the information that *nmap* was able to obtain about the router.

Project 9-2

1. Like many other home office routers, the router scanned in Project 9-1 (a D-Link DI-604) supports remote management, allowing hosts on the Internet to access its configuration screens via a Web browser, typically through port 8080. Remote management is disabled by default on DI-604 routers, but is often enabled on routers in larger business units. To connect to your router as a remote client on the Internet would, type the WAN-side IP address and port number, for example, 23.191.23.191: 8080. (Your instructor will provide you with the correct IP address and port number.) This will bring up a login dialog.

2. Log in using the known username/password, and print the display for your instructor.

Project 9-3

In Chapter 7, you learned about Ettercap, a tool used to perform man-in-the-middle attacks. In Projects 9-3 and 9-4, you will download and install Ettercap, and then use it to perform a man-in-the-middle attack.

1. Download the most recent version of Ettercap (ettercap-NG-0.7.3.tar.gz, as of this writing) from the central Linux server or from ettercap.sourceforge.net/download.php.

2. Extract the source folder to your desktop.

3. Open a root terminal and `cd` to `/home/`*yourusername*`/Desktop/etter*`.

(This puts you into the ettercap-NG-0.7.3 directory without having to type the whole name.)

4. Type `./configure` to verify that all required dependencies are installed and to configure Ettercap. The following dependencies are required for Ettercap to install and run successfully. (You will get an error message from the `./configure` command if any dependencies are missing.)

   □ libpcap should be version 0.8.1 or later

   □ libnet should be version 1.1.2.1 or later

   □ libpthread

   □ zlib

   If these dependencies are not installed, check with your instructor about how to install them before proceeding. This can often be accomplished using your Linux distribution's automated package installer. For example, to install libpcap in Fedora, you might only need to type `yum install libpcap-devel`.

5. Type the following:

```
make
make install
```

6. When this is complete, use a text editor to edit the /usr/local/etc/etter.conf file as follows:

   ◻ Set ec_uid and ec_gid to 0 (zero).

   ◻ Uncomment the two iptables scripts in the redir_command_on/off section of the file.

   Figure 9-11 shows the etter.conf file with the ec_uid and ec_gid set to 0.

```
black john - root@constantine:~                                      • ○ ✕
 File  Edit  View  Terminal  Tabs  Help
#####################################################################
#                                                                   #
#   ettercap -- etter.conf -- configuration file                    #
#                                                                   #
#   Copyright (C) ALoR & NaGA                                       #
#                                                                   #
#   This program is free software; you can redistribute it and/or modify #
#   it under the terms of the GNU General Public License as published by #
#   the Free Software Foundation; either version 2 of the License, or    #
#   (at your option) any later version.                             #
#                                                                   #
#   $Id: etter.conf,v 1.78 2004/10/12 15:28:38 alor Exp $           #
#                                                                   #
#####################################################################

[privs]
ec_uid = 0                    # nobody '65534' is the default. root=0
ec_gid = 0                    # nobody '65534' is the default. root=0

[mitm]
arp_storm_delay = 10          # milliseconds
arp_poison_warm_up = 1        # seconds
arp_poison_delay = 10         # seconds
arp_poison_icmp = 1           # boolean
arp_poison_reply = 1          # boolean
arp_poison_request = 0        # boolean
arp_poison_equal_mac = 1      # boolean
dhcp_lease_time = 1800        # seconds
port_steal_delay = 10         # milliseconds
                                                              9-14
```

Figure 9-11   etter.conf with uid and gid edited

Project 9-4

1. Read Ettercap's documentation. This application can cause sheer havoc in a private network and can cause your Internet connection to be blocked on the Internet, so be careful in using it.

2. On the command line, type the following:

```
su -
ettercap -G
```

The -G option brings up the gtk GUI. Figure 9-12 shows Ettercap's GUI Welcome page.

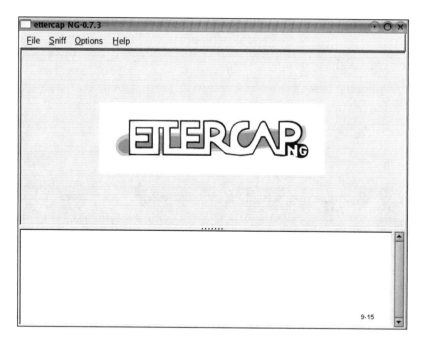

Figure 9-12   Ettercap GUI welcome page

3. The Welcome page doesn't let you do much but sniff. Set for unified sniffing by clicking **Sniff** on the menu bar and then clicking **Unified Sniffing**. Verify that the correct network interface (most likely eth0) is shown in the text box, and then click **OK**.

4. Before you add any targets, take a look at some of the views available in the program. Click **View** on the menu bar, and then click **Profiles**, to open the Profiles tab, as shown in Figure 9-13. You won't see any profiles yet.

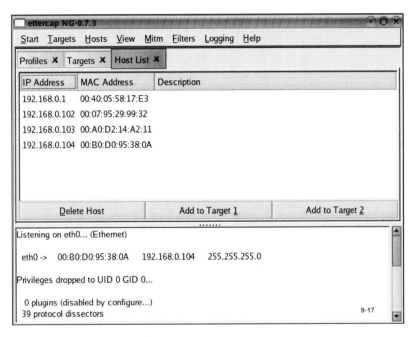

Figure 9-13   Profiles tab

5. Next, click **Hosts** on the menu bar and then click **Hosts list** to view the Host List tab. Figure 9-14 shows the Host List tab; again, yours will probably be empty at this point.

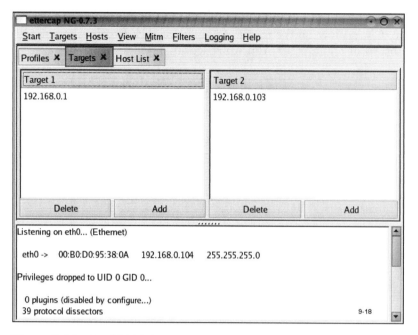

Figure 9-14   Host List tab

6. To set one or more target IP addresses, click **Targets** on the menu bar and then click **Current Targets**. Click the **Add** button below the Target 1 text area and type the IP address specified by your instructor in the IP address text box of the ettercap Input dialog box. Click **OK**, and then repeat this step using the Add button below the Target 2 text area. In Figure 9-15, 192.168.0.1 is the subnet's gateway.

7. Click **MITM** on the menu bar, and then click **Arp Poisoning**. Leave the optional parameters at their defaults and click **OK** to begin the attack. In the lower window, you can see the targets under attack. Figure 9-16 shows an ARP poisoning attack in progress.

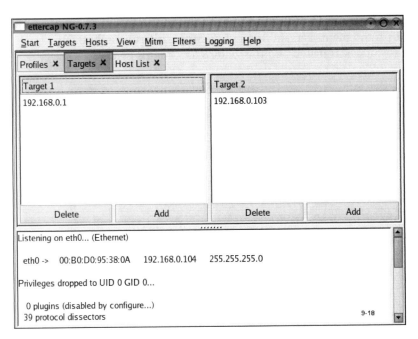

Figure 9-15   Targets tab

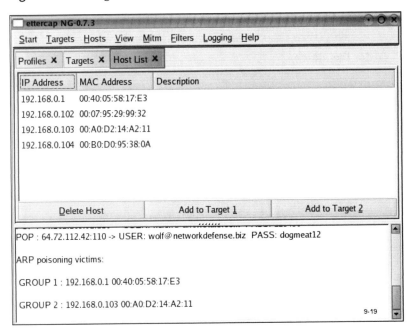

Figure 9-16   Poisoning in progress

8. Observe what happens to "normal" network traffic. When you are done, click
MITM on the menu bar, and then click **Stop mitm attack(s)**. As Figure 9-17
shows, the attack is halted and the victims are "re-ARPed."

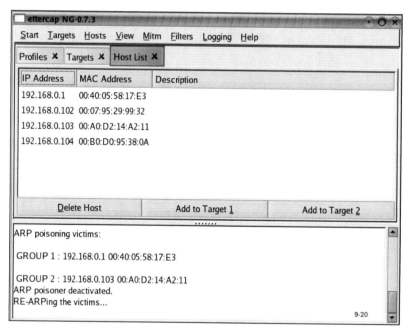

Figure 9-17   After the attack

10

TROJAN HORSES

> ## After reading this chapter and completing the exercises, you will be able to:
>
> ♦ Outline the evolution of the Trojan horse
> ♦ Name ways in which Trojans are deployed
> ♦ Identify risks associated with Trojans
> ♦ Name some well-known Trojans
> ♦ List Trojan attack prevention measures
> ♦ List Trojan detection tools

A Trojan horse is a type of application that uses trickery to get a user to install it, circumventing safety measures inherent in an operating system that might make it difficult for a covert installation to operate.

The original Trojan horse, shown in Figure 10-1, appears in Homer's *Iliad*. In the story, an alliance of Greek city-states is at war with the city-state of Troy over the love and person of Helen, the wife of Menelaus of Sparta. The Trojan prince Paris has abducted Helen from her home, and taken her to the strong and well-fortified city of Troy.

The Greeks lay siege to Troy, but death rates are high, and the Greek confederacy shows all signs of dissolving. The Greek warrior Odysseus has an artist create a large, inspiring statue with a hollow center and a secret door. The statue is built in the form of a horse, thus the term Trojan horse.

The Trojans are fooled into bringing the statue into the center of town, believing the Greeks have lost heart and created this gift to make amends. Then, under cover of darkness, the Greeks emerge from the statue and kill all the citizens of Troy.

The form of the statue was not as important as the payload of Greek soldiers hiding in its belly. The statue could have been shaped like anything with sufficient size to contain its dangerous secret cargo.

Figure 10-1   Trojan Horse

As modern citizens of the twenty-first century, we would not be taken in by this level of subterfuge in battle. But many computer users are enticed to introduce Trojan horse programs into their computers. And in doing so, they open a secret door for hackers to access their computers and their networks. Typical functions for a Trojan might include logging keystrokes, taking screen captures, accessing files on local and shared drives, or acting as a server where the client is the hacker. In short, a Trojan can perform almost any task on a computer that a human can. Trojan horse applications are usually masqueraded as games, utilities, or other useful applications, and they may even provide the advertised function while they perform their unadvertised functions. At this time, Trojans are not able to reproduce themselves like viruses or worms.

WORKINGS OF TROJANS

For Trojans to be a threat, they must be installed by the user and activated. Users who habitually log in as Administrator or root, or who have modified their user profile to have administrative powers, are most at risk from this sort of threat.

Installation

Users are tricked into installing Trojans using the oldest motivators in the world: fear, greed, habit, sloth, lust. Recent Trojan attacks have used several distribution vectors:

- E-mail attachments, either sent by a friend (who might have thought the attached program was useful or interesting), or sent by a worm that was propagating itself on vulnerable unpatched machines

- Scripts in HTML e-mails allowed to run automatically. If you have your e-mail set to show HTML, it will also run JavaScript code in the e-mail automatically

- Files on FTP servers (FTP servers are relatively easy to hack, so even legitimate sites are potential sources for Trojans)

- Scripts on spoofed Web sites

- Scripts on hacked legitimate Web sites

- Download opportunities on Web sites

- Files offered on bulletin boards and forums

- Social engineering, such as calling a network administrator as a legitimate user and talking him or her into loading a file of the caller's choosing

10

All of these vectors make use of a user's own mind to get him or her to do what the attacker wants.

Recent Trojan attacks have come through attached to spoofed Microsoft company e-mails disguised as a patch for Internet Explorer, and as an RPM package of `Linux-util` (which is a real utility package for Linux). Historically, these files have been sent as new computer games as well. Greed for the next best thing, or fear of an unpatched machine's vulnerability to attack, might cause unwary users to install this code so they can be ahead of all their friends. Or, the motivation could be a lack of motivation. Choosing not to validate the checksum that legitimate download sites provide for your protection is a good way to open yourself to a potential Trojan attack.

Functions of a Trojan

BO2K is a Trojan horse designed and used to make a horde of zombies to do the hacker's bidding. **Zombies** are machines that have been unobtrusively "owned" by a hacker. When a machine is **0wned**, the hacker can back door into it at any time and perform actions from that machine as if she were sitting at its keyboard. Consider the following quote from the BO2K Developer's FAQ (www.bo2k.com/dev/devfaq.html):

> *What are the design goals for BO2K?*
>
> *To be small, unobtrusive, and powerful. Pull out all the stops. Let the remote user control everything with confidence, and security. Let there be no single thing the user can't do from halfway around the world, that he couldn't do at the desktop. And keep it extensible. People should always be able to add new things to BO2K to extend the system. It should grow with people's needs, instantaneously supporting the demand. Control is the goal.*

Clearly, there could be a positive, beneficial use for such an application, and there is an obvious, intrusive reason for the application. This is that gray area of "is it a beneficial tool to be encouraged, or a dangerous weapon to be suppressed?" Network administrators may use something like this to automate audits of their networks, but it would need to be hardened so the attackers can't use the meta-network of remote-control clients to do illegal things. So the gray area expands. Remote control can be used for good and for evil. An ignorant or inexperienced remote administrator could make just as big a mess on the target machine as an evil, wicked **HaX0R** could. The heart of the model exists in several commercial remote-control products, including Terminal Server by Microsoft. Terminal Server allows remote desktop administration of Windows servers.

If you type the term "trojan" into the search engine at www.cert.org—a site owned by the Carnegie Mellon Software Engineering Institute, which tracks Internet threats—you get a list of over 400 advisories. There have been many Trojans developed over the years and they continue to be devised.

 Trojan horse attacks are not strictly a "Windows users' problem." Although Windows has a reputation for vulnerability to hacking, Trojans can be developed to run on any operating system. There are several UNIX threats on the list.

CAUTION

Trojans, like any commercial remote administrative application, can be written to perform almost any task that a legitimate user can perform:

- Sending and receiving files
- Viewing cached passwords
- Restarting the system

- Launching processes
- Modifying files
- Sharing files
- Modifying the registry keys

As you may know, random modification of system settings almost always crashes a target machine, so a remote administrator is statistically more likely to damage something than to improve anything. There have been a number of successful Trojans that are now famous, the specific functions of which are well-known. The value of notoriety is dubious, from the standpoint of a network administrator, as new users come onboard every day who have not heard of these "famous Trojans" and are enticed to install them anyway. The next sections give an overview of some of these well-known Trojans.

FAMOUS TROJANS

10

- PC-Write
- AIDS
- Back Orifice
- Pretty Park
- NetBus, SubSeven
- BO2K

PC-Write (1986)

This was the first known Trojan horse. The PC-Write Trojan masqueraded as version 2.72 of the shareware word processor PC-Write by Quicksoft (the company that made PC-Write; they did not release a version 2.72). When PC-Write 2.72 was launched, it wiped out the user's FAT (file allocation table) and formatted the hard drive, deleting all saved data. It was really a simple batch-file command, encoded as a binary .exe file.

AIDS.exe/PC Cyborg (1989)

This Trojan was distributed through the postal mail in 1989. It arrived on a floppy disk that allegedly contained information about AIDS (Acquired Immune Deficiency Syndrome) and HIV (Human Immunodeficiency Virus). The actual payload was aids.exe, which would encrypt the hard drive. The AIDS Trojan prompted the user to pay a fee for the password needed to decrypt the hard drive. The AIDS Trojan was unique because rather than destroy files, it held them hostage, demanding a ransom before the user could open and use the files again.

Back Orifice (1998)

Back Orifice is a remote administration server that allows system administrators to control a computer from a remote location. It was designed by a group called the Cult of the Dead Cow. During installation, it gives no indication of anything happening. Once installed, the server is intentionally difficult to detect, and it allows almost complete control over your computer by the remote attacker if he or she knows your computer's IP address.

Pretty Park (1999)

Called "PrettyPark.worm" by Symantec, this Trojan may be the first to use a worm to propagate itself. Once installed, this application would attempt to mail itself to anyone in your address book. When the attached program file, PrettyPark.exe, is executed, it may display the 3D pipe screen saver. It also tries to connect to an IRC server and join a specific IRC channel. This is where the Trojan function takes over. Pretty Park sends information to a pre-specified IRC every 30 seconds to keep itself connected and to retrieve any commands from the IRC channel. By connecting to IRC, the author or distributor of the worm can access information on your system including:

- Computer name
- Product name
- Product identifier
- Product key
- Registered owner
- Registered organization
- System root path
- Version number
- ICQ identification numbers
- ICQ nicknames
- Your e-mail address
- Dial-up networking username and passwords

In addition, being unknowingly connected to IRC opens a security hole in which your computer can potentially be used to receive and execute files.

NetBus (2001)

This Trojan was written by Carl-Frederik Neikter. Like Back Orifice, it allows anyone running the client portion (the attacker) to connect to and control the server portion of the target computer, using the same rights and privileges of the current user. This really randomizes who the remote administrator might be. According to the author, NetBus will perform the following functions:

- Open/close CD-ROM
- Show optional BMP/JPG image
- Swap mouse buttons
- Start optional application
- Play a .wav file
- Control mouse
- Show different kinds of messages
- Shut down Windows
- Download/upload/delete files
- Go to an optional URL
- Send keystrokes and disable keys
- Listen for and send keystrokes
- Take a screenshot
- Increase and decrease the sound volume
- Record sounds from the microphone
- Upload optional file
- Make click sounds every time a key is pressed.
- Scan Class C addresses by adding "+Number of ports" to the end of the target address

Figure 10-2 shows the NetBus Client setup screen.

SubSeven (1999)

SubSeven enables unauthorized people to access your computer over the Internet without your knowledge. In July 2003, Symantec Security Response received reports that people were receiving a spoofed e-mail, which claimed to be sent from Symantec, that encouraged the recipient to download and execute the SubSeven executable.

The e-mail was in Spanish and had the following characteristics:

From: SymantecMexico[update@symantec.com]

Subject: Urgente: Actualizacion Antivirus.

The e-mail offered a fix for the virus w32.HLLW.System@mm. This is not a real virus, and cannot be found on Symantec's search engine or by search on Google.

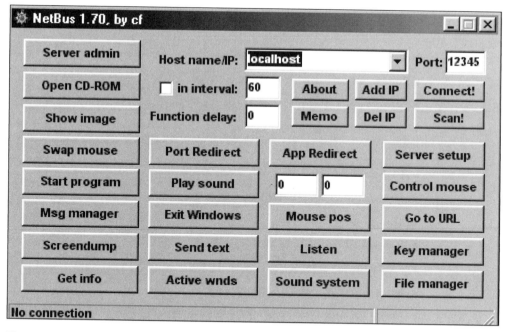

Figure 10-2   NetBus Client setup screen

When the server portion of SubSeven runs on a computer, the hacker remotely accessing the computer may be able to perform the following tasks:

- Set it up as an FTP server
- Browse files on that system
- Take screen shots
- Capture real-time screen information
- Open and close programs
- Edit information in currently running programs
- Show pop-up messages and dialog boxes
- Hang up a dial-up connection
- Remotely restart a computer
- Open the CD-ROM
- Edit the registry information

BO2K

Possibly "gone legitimate" as an open source project, Back Orifice 2000 is an interesting combination of fair and foul and is appealing as a concept for a network administrator with at-risk remote users. Wouldn't it be great to be able to enforce antivirus definition updates on these remote computers, as a functional security policy, and get that functionality for free? There is a commercial product called LANDesk that does this, so some conclude that it must be alright. The BO2K software allows you to use infected machines like a string of proxy servers. It also lets you set notifiers on the infected machines so that any client that wants to can log into your infected box. That means more random strangers mucking through your network. What fun!

DETECTION AND PREVENTION OF TROJANS

By far, the best way to deal with Trojans is to never get one.

- Never open an executable file that you have not verified.

- Never accept attachments that are not expected.

- Never allow anybody on your network to operate with root or administrator privileges.

- Make sure the standard user does not have permission to load or install programs.

- Install a software firewall so you can tell when a process on your computer is attempting to act as a server or otherwise access the Internet.

10

Ok, great! You can avoid getting infected by Trojans if you know how to avoid them. But until today, you didn't know how to do that. What now? There are several ways to check for Trojans, and some are recognized by antivirus programs if they come to the computer through an e-mail attack vector.

A widely used method that detects Trojans is called object reconciliation. This is similar to reconciling your check register every month to verify that the number of deposits and withdrawals match your bank statement. The term, object reconciliation, means "verification that things are the same." Objects, in this case, are files or directories, and reconciliation is the process of comparing the status of an object with its status at an earlier time. Therefore, object reconciliation is a technique that is applied to system files that are installed as part of the basic operating system. An example of this is when you compare the file size of a system file with a backup copy that was saved several months earlier. If no changes have been made to the system file since that time, then the file size should be the same. If you discover that the file size is different, it is quite likely that a Trojan has infected it.

Using this method, you can perform any or all of the following checks:

- Date and time—You can examine the most recent modification for a particular file. Whenever a file is opened and saved, a new date of modification is registered. Keep in mind that checking the status by using the date and time is considered a weak method because the system date is easy to modify. In some situations, such as when the original file has been copied or mailed to you, the original file remains unaltered. This is also not as useful if you didn't take a baseline snapshot at the start of the OS installation.

- Size—Using the size method, you are able to examine the size of the file and then compare it with the standard size. This method is not entirely reliable because when hackers replace the original content of a program, they often try to maintain the same file size.

- Checksum—This is used when you add the data elements of a file and execute an algorithm to calculate a value or checksum. The algorithm recalculates the checksum and compares it with the original value to perform an integrity check. If the checksum value is on the same system, then hackers may be able to tamper with it. Checksums should be kept on a separate system or on removable media that is not loaded on the possibly compromised computer. As an additional security step, these values should be accessible only to root or administrative users.

In addition to object reconciliation, the following measures can be implemented for detecting Trojans:

- Compare your system binaries to the original install files from your installation media to make sure that they have not been modified. Hackers typically change programs on UNIX systems. Some examples of these are: *login, su, telnet, netstat, ifconfig, ls, find, du, df, libc, sync,* any binaries referenced in /etc/inetd.conf, as well as other critical network and system programs and shared object libraries. Figure 10-3 shows the expected content of inetd.conf.

- Remember that it is important to check the backup files for Trojan programs because you don't know when the machine was infected.

- To detect Trojans on your Linux or Windows machine, you can use the Message-Digest algorithm 5 (MD5), Tripwire, and other cryptographic checksum tools. Trojan programs may produce the same checksum and time stamp as the legitimate version of the program, so just checking size and last modified time stamp is not sufficient to determine if the programs have been replaced. All these checksum tools are sufficient to detect Trojans, provided that they are kept secure in a location unavailable to attackers.

- Check for unauthorized services. Examine /etc/inetd.conf or /etc/xinetd.conf and its associated files and directories for unauthorized additions, updates, or modifications. Look for entries that execute shell programs, such as /bin/sh or /bin/csh, and verify all programs that are specified in /etc/inetd.conf or /etc/xinetd.conf to check that they are not Trojans masquerading as the legitimate programs.

- Check and examine legitimate services that you have commented out with # in /etc/inetd.conf or /etc/xinetd.conf. An attacker might begin a service that you thought you had terminated or may even replace the *inetd* or *xinetd* program with a Trojan program.

```
root@l8: /root                                                    ⬜⬜✖
File  Edit  View  Terminal  Tabs  Help
  GNU nano 1.3.8                File: /etc/inetd.conf

# /etc/inetd.conf:  see inetd(8) for further informations.
#█
# Internet server configuration database
#
# -- Lines starting with "#:LABEL:" or "#<off>#" should not be changed
# unless you know what you are doing!
# -- If you want to disable an entry so it isn't touched during
# package updates just comment it out with a single '#' character.
# -- Packages should modify this file by using update-inetd(8)
# <service_name> <sock_type> <proto> <flags> <user> <server_path> <args>
#
#:INTERNAL: Internal services
#echo           stream  tcp     nowait  root    internal
#echo           dgram   udp     wait    root    internal
#chargen        stream  tcp     nowait  root    internal
#chargen        dgram   udp     wait    root    internal
#discard        stream  tcp     nowait  root    internal
#discard        dgram   udp     wait    root    internal
#daytime        stream  tcp     nowait  root    internal
#daytime        dgram   udp     wait    root    internal
#time           stream  tcp     nowait  root    internal
#time           dgram   udp     wait    root    internal

#:STANDARD: These are standard services.
#:BSD: Shell, login, exec and talk are BSD protocols.
#:MAIL: Mail, news and uucp services.
#:INFO: Info services
#:BOOT: Tftp service is provided primarily for booting.  Most sites
# run this only on machines acting as "boot servers."
#:RPC: RPC based services
#:HAM-RADIO: amateur-radio services
#:OTHER: Other services
#<off># netbios-ssn      stream  tcp     nowait  root    /usr/sbin/tcpd /usr/sbin/smbd


^G Get Help    ^O WriteOut    ^R Read File   ^Y Prev Page   ^K Cut Text    ^C Cur Pos
^X Exit        ^J Justify     ^W Where Is    ^V Next Page   ^U UnCut Txt   ^T To Spell
```

Figure 10-3   Contents of inetd.conf

Table 10-1 lists a number of programs used to detect Trojan horses. Notice that in many cases, the commercial solutions for Trojan detection are for Windows platforms only. In those cases where the solution is good for other platforms, it is noted.

Table 10-1   Windows and Linux Trojan detectors

Tripwire	Tripwire Enterprise detects, reconciles, and reports on changes for millions of elements (e.g., files, directories, registry settings, directory server objects, and configuration files) on servers, network devices, desktops, and directory servers. It improves service quality by alerting you of any change and enabling quick remediation. Tripwire Enterprise agent platform support for Tripwire Enterprise/FS: • Solaris (SPARC) 8, 9, & 10 • Solaris (x86) 10 • Windows 2000 Server, SP2 • Windows Server 2003 • HP-UX 11.0, 11i v1, & 11i v2 • AIX 5.1, 5.2, & 5.3 • Red Hat Enterprise Linux 2.1, 3 & 4 AS, ES, & WS • SUSE LINUX Enterprise Server 9 Tripwire Enterprise agent platform support for Tripwire Enterprise/DT: • Windows XP Professional • Windows 2000 Professional, SP2 • Red Hat Desktop Linux 3 & 4 Tripwire is a very serious enterprise-level solution.

MD5	MD5 is a message-digest (MD) algorithm that was developed by Professor Ronald L. Rivest of Massachusetts Institute of Technology. It is used in digital signature applications to check the data integrity of a message or a file. MD5 creates a 128-bit hash value, which is a nonreversible, fixed-length number, converted from a message or text of any length by encryption. This method of finding Trojans is far more reliable than checksum and the other popular methods.
	
	   At the time the sender sends some data to a user, an MD5 calculation is performed on the message, as well as the secret key of the sender. Then the message is compressed in a secure manner, and it is signed with a private key. Finally, the resulting message digest and data are transmitted to the receiver.
	
	   The receiver performs an MD5 calculation on the data and the message digest. The result of the calculation is compared with the message digest that was sent by the sender. If these match, it implies that data has not been changed.

Table 10-1 Windows and Linux Trojan detectors (continued)

Spybot Search and Destroy	Spybot Search & Destroy can detect and remove spyware, adware, Trojans, and other sorts of unwanted applications from your computer. Spyware is a relatively new kind of threat that common antivirus applications do not yet cover. If you see new toolbars in your Internet Explorer that you didn't intentionally install, if your browser crashes, or if your browser start page has changed without your knowing, you probably have **spyware**. But even if you don't see anything, you may be infected, because more and more spyware is emerging that is silently tracking your surfing behavior to create a marketing profile of you that will be sold to advertisement companies. Spybot has a module called Tea Timer that alerts you when any activity will change your registry. Trojans like to change the registry so they can run as a service or be started up when the PC is rebooted or when the Internet is present.
TDS-3 (No longer produced)	Trojan Defense Suite (TDS) was an excellent software package for protection against Trojans. However, the maintenance costs were too high and sales were flat. It had many unique functions never seen in other anti-Trojan packages.
Hacker Eliminator	LockDown2000's newest anti-Trojan program. Hacker Eliminator only uses a small percentage of the system resources that the old LockDown versions used. Hacker Eliminator is not based on the previous source code for any of the older LockDown versions. This entire program and the methods that it uses are new.
TFAK	TFAK is a freeware anti-Trojan program for Windows that detects and removes the most commonly used Trojans. TFAK also provides several other features that help to remove and control Trojans. Three out of four of the known mirrors produce a 404 error, and the main site has not had an update since 2001.
Trojan Remover	Trojan Remover was written to aid in the removal of Trojan horses and Internet worms when standard antivirus software has either failed to detect the problem or is unable to effectively eliminate it. Written for Windows 95/98/Millennium/XP/Server 2003, it has been successfully used by Windows 2000 users, although this platform has not been officially tested.
Pest Patrol	Pest Patrol is a tool that scans for Trojans as well as programs known as "hacking tools" and spyware. Pest Patrol is currently being distributed by CA, which used to be called Computer Associates.
Anti-Trojan 5.5 (Now a-squared Personal version 1.6.5)	a-squared Personal is a malware scanner and remover of the latest generation, which specializes in Trojans, dialers, and spyware.
Tauscan	Tauscan is a powerful anti-Trojan horse tool capable of detecting and removing a wide range of malicious software that can damage your system.

10

Table 10-1   Windows and Linux Trojan detectors (continued)

The Cleaner	The Cleaner Professional is a system of programs designed to keep your computer and data safe from Trojans, worms, keyloggers, spyware, and all manner of malware. By actively monitoring files and processes on your computer, it can detect a virus in action and catch it before it has a chance to damage your valuable data.
PC DoorGuard	A couple of antiviruses may occasionally detect a Trojan, but this is only occasional and cannot give you any confidence that no one will steal your passwords using easily accessible Trojans like BO2000, NetBus, etc. Even having detected a Trojan, antivirus programs cannot offer any solution for removing the Trojan. PC DoorGuard has been designed to effectively fight Trojans. Most malicious viruses will also be caught, though. This way, PC DoorGuard offers you a complete shield from any Trojan, virus, or I-Worm (including Bagle, BugBear, Myparty, BadTrans, LoveLetter, SubSeven, etc). PC DoorGuard has been designed to work along with any other professional antivirus utility.
Trojan Hunter	TrojanHunter searches for and removes Trojans from your system. With an easy-to-use scanner and a guard that scans in the background, TrojanHunter is a must-have complement to your virus scanner.
Log Monitor	Log Monitor is a file- and directory-monitoring tool. The program periodically checks selected files' modification time and executes an external program if a file's time was changed or not changed. For directories, it handles such events as changes to files or addition and removal of files.
PrcView	PrcView is a process viewer utility that displays detailed information about processes running under Windows. For each process, it displays memory, threads, and module usage. For each DLL, it shows full path and version information. PrcView comes with a command-line version that allows you to write scripts to check if a process is running, kill it, etc.
AIDE	AIDE (Advanced Intrusion Detection Environment) is a free replacement for Tripwire. It generates a database that can be used to check the integrity of files on a server. It uses regular expressions for determining which files get added to the database. You can use several message-digest algorithms to ensure that the files have not been tampered with.
XNetStat	This is a GUI-based netstat tool for Windows that will help you monitor your machine for open ports.
ConSeal PC Firewall (Replaced by 8Signs Firewall)	A really good firewall for advanced Windows users with basic knowledge of TCP/IP and other protocols, this software will help you secure your PC. It has some major advantages over other Windows-based firewalls. The author of ConSeal formed a company called 8Signs in 2001. In August of 2003, 8Signs released the 8Signs Firewall.

The basic rule is that you should never open a file if you do not know what file type it is. If you are using a Windows machine, make sure you have configured the GUI to show you all the extensions. To determine whether a file might contain malicious code, you should be aware of some common (mostly safe) file types.

- Graphic image formats such as .jpeg, .jif, .bmp, .gif, .png, and .tif are usually legitimate formats and are probably safe to open.

- Text file formats such as .txt, .doc, and .rtf are legitimate.

If you receive any image files or documents other than these types, you should be wary as they could contain Trojans. There are a rather large number of executable file formats that you should not open or run unless you know the sender and know that he or she is sending you a file:

BAS – Visual Basic Class Module

BAT – Batch File

CHM – Compiled HTML Help File

CMD – Windows NT Command Script

COM – MS-DOS Application

CPL – Control Panel Extension

CRT – Security Certificate

DLL – Dynamic Link Library

EXE – Application

HLP – Windows Help File

HTA – HTML Applications

INF – Setup Information File

INS – Internet Naming Service

ISP – IIS Internet Service Provider Settings

JS – JScript File

JSE – JScript Encoded Script File

LNK – Shortcut

MDB – Microsoft Access Application

MDE – Microsoft Access MDE Database

MSC – Microsoft Common Console Document

MSI – Windows Installer Package

MSP – Windows Installer Patch

10

MST - Visual Test Source File

OCX - ActiveX Objects

PCD - Photo CD Image

PIF - Shortcut to MS-DOS Program

REG - Registration Entries

SCR - Screen Saver

SCT - Windows Script Component

SHB - Document Shortcut File

SHS - Shell Scrap Object

SYS - System Config/Driver

URL - Internet Shortcut (Uniform Resource Locator)

VB - VBScript File

VBE - VBScript Encoded Script File

VBS - VBScript Script File

WSC - Windows Script Component

WSF - Windows Script File

WSH - Windows Scripting Host Settings File

If you are using Linux or MacOS X, you have less chance of accidentally running a Trojan installer because your standard profile will not have permission to run an executable file, and you never run a session logged in as root with administrative permissions.

Chapter Summary

- ❑ Trojan horses use trickery to entice the user to install them. They are not currently self-reproducing, but some use worm-like tactics to distribute themselves.

- ❑ To be a threat, Trojans must be installed by the user and activated.

- ❑ Trojans act as remote administrative tools, and can be written to perform almost any task that a legitimate user can perform.

- ❑ There are several distribution vectors in common use, including e-mail attachments sent by friends, worms, or spoofed e-mail addresses; scripts in HTML e-mails; files on FTP servers; scripts on either spoofed or hacked Web sites; download opportunities on Web sites; files offered on bulletin boards and forums; and social engineering.

❏ Trojans can have many functions, such as logging keystrokes, taking screen captures, accessing files on local and shared drives, acting as a server, sending and receiving files, viewing cached passwords, restarting the system, launching processes, modifying and sharing files, and modifying registry keys.

❏ The first known Trojan horse was a fake version of PC-Write, developed in 1986. Today there are thousands of Trojans, and more appear all the time.

❏ Famous Trojans include PC-Write, AIDS, Back Orifice, Pretty Park, NetBus, SubSeven, and BO2K.

❏ To prevent receiving a Trojan, never open an executable file that you have not verified or open unexpected attachments; never allow anybody on your network to operate with root or administrator privileges; make sure that standard users do not have permission to load or install programs; install a software firewall; and configure Windows to show all file extensions.

❏ Trojans can be detected by various means, including software firewalls, IDS systems, some antivirus software, commercial programs, object reconciliation, and registry checkers.

10

REVIEW QUESTIONS

1. Define a Trojan horse application.

2. Explain why all attachments are possible Trojan suspects.

3. What is the difference between installation strategy and transmission vector as those concepts apply to Trojan horse applications?

4. Name four installation strategies.

5. Name six transmission vectors.

6. Is there any legitimate reason to use remote administration applications?

7. Name ten executable files (or extensions) for Windows platforms.

8. Short essay: In five to nine paragraphs, name and describe four famous Trojans.

9. Is Nimda a Trojan horse? Why or why not?

10. Is Zabbix a Trojan Horse? Why or why not?

Indicate whether the sentence or statement is true or false.

11. _____ Trojan horses are delivered via plain text files.

12. _____ It is unwise to habitually log into sessions as an administrator.

13. _____ TripWire, Tea Timer, and AIDE are registry checkers.

Match each date of appearance with the correct Trojan below.

    a. 2001

    b. 1989

    c. 1999

    d. 1986

    e. 2002

    f. 1998

    g. 1999

Famous Trojans

14. _____ AIDS

15. _____ Back Orifice

16. _____ BO2K

17. _____ NetBus

18. _____ PC-Write

19. _____ Pretty Park

20. _____ SubSeven

HANDS-ON PROJECTS

Since Trojan horses are easier to block than to remove, the following exercises focus on that aspect of network administration.

Three common encryption algorithms are described below. There are many more, but for the purpose of this project, you will be using only these three. In order of popularity, they are MD5, SHA1, and RIPEMD-160.

MD5 (Message-Digest algorithm 5) is a popular cryptographic hash function with a 128-bit hash value. As an Internet standard (RFC 1321), MD5 has been used in many security applications, and is often used to check the integrity of files. An MD5 hash is typically a 32-character hexadecimal number.

SHA1 is one of a family of SHA (Secure Hash Algorithm) hash functions. The rest of the family is SHA-224, SHA-256, SHA-384, and SHA-512. These hash functions were designed by the National Security Agency (NSA) and collectively published as a U.S. government standard. SHA-1 is employed in a large variety of popular security applications and protocols, including TLS, SSL, PGP, SSH, S/MIME, and IPSec. It is considered by some to be the successor to MD5.

RIPEMD-160 (RACE Integrity Primitives Evaluation Message Digest) is a 160-bit message-digest algorithm first published in 1996. It is an improved version of RIPEMD, which in turn was based upon the design principles used in MD4, and is similar in performance to the more popular SHA-1. The RIPEMD family also includes RIPEMD-128, RIPEMD-256, and RIPEMD-320. RIPEMD-160 was designed in the open academic community, in contrast to SHA-1. RIPEMD-160 is a less popular and less studied design.

HANDS-ON PROJECTS

Project 10-1

It is not always easy to detect whether you are downloading a program with a little Trojan tag-along. However, you can use a hash function to check the files you download from apparently legitimate locations.

1. Go to www.wireshark.org/download.html and download a copy of Wireshark Windows Vista installer version to your home directory. (You won't be installing Wireshark here, as this was already done in a previous chapter; in this project, you are simply going to check the integrity of the downloaded file.) Note that, under the "Verifying Downloads" header, the site states "File hashes for this version can be found in the signatures file. It is signed with key id 0x21F2949A."

2. Click the **signatures file** link and note the MD5, SHA1, and RIPEMD160 hashes for the version of Wireshark you have just downloaded (for example, wireshark-setup-0.99.5.exe). The hashes will look similar to the following:

```
MD5(wireshark-setup-0.99.5.exe)=6adee9c71780fbaf2a97deefd
f48f1b4
SHA1(wireshark-setup-
0.99.5.exe)=63c63af6fee52803715cbfc82e11fa42eddf86c5
RIPEMD160(wireshark-setup-
0.99.5.exe)=b6106ad29b39664c55aaf88984a6ca6114e13815
```

Download this file to your home directory and save it as hashes.txt.

3. Open a root terminal and change to your home directory.

4. Type md5sum wireshark-setup-0.99.5.exe (substituting the name of your downloaded file, if necessary) to view the file's MD5 checksum. Compare this to the appropriate MD5 checksum located in the downloaded file of hashes. If the file is legitimate, the checksums should match exactly.

HANDS-ON PROJECTS

Project 10-2

1. To make a properly formatted md5sum checksum file for any number of files, type the following at the root terminal, substituting the files of your choice for *FILE1*, *FILE2*, and so on:

```
md5sum FILE1 FILE2 FILE3 FILE4 > CHECKSUM.MD5
```

This will make a file, called CHECKSUM.MD5, with properly formatted checksum lines for each file.

2. To check your work, use the md5sum command as shown in Project 10-1.

10

Project 10-3

The simplest Trojan horse to create is a Windows batch file. Perform the following steps on a Windows machine.

1. Using Notepad, open a new document. Deceptively entitle the file "Lab-10-pix.gif.bat".

2. Using your DOS knowledge, write a short batch file to do some non-injurious thing, such as copying a known Windows file (for example, config.sys) to another file with a new name.

3. Run the file and make sure it has the intended effect on your Windows machine.

4. E-mail the file to yourself. Does your antivirus application recognize the file as possibly injurious? Note what happens when you run the application from the e-mail link. If the file did not have an effect, make the necessary changes so that it does.

11

DENIAL-OF-SERVICE ATTACKS

> **After reading this chapter and completing the exercises, you will be able to:**
>
> ♦ Define a denial-of-service (DoS) attack
> ♦ Describe causes of DoS attacks
> ♦ Describe several varieties of DoS attacks
> ♦ Define a distributed denial-of-service (DDoS) attack
> ♦ Discuss some known DoS and DDoS attacks
> ♦ Describe ways to prevent DoS and DDoS attacks

A denial-of-service attack (DoS) is a strategy designed to keep valid traffic from accessing the target of your attack. DoS attacks are mentioned throughout this text because DoS is an effective softening technique and is often used by hackers to break server security. One example of a DoS attack might be a user uploading 2 GB of files to your anonymous FTP server, or arranging to send five million spam messages to your mail server. In this chapter, you will learn about types and examples of DoS attacks.

The main targets of DoS attacks are:

- Web servers
- Application servers
- Communication links

DoS attacks deny access to legitimate network traffic, break and damage network connections between computers, prevent end users from accessing services of a computer, modify system configuration information, and can even destroy physical network components. These attacks can disable a network, lose data, and result in financial losses to an organization.

Causes of DoS Attacks

There are many defects and vulnerabilities found every week in operating systems, network devices, software, and applications. There does not appear to be a shortage of ways to exploit the openings found, so there is no shortage of employment for experts to design tools to plug the holes. Some major network defects and vulnerabilities include the following:

- Vulnerability of the network architecture
- Vulnerability of a specific server system architecture (Intel x86, AMD Opteron, etc.)
- Defects and bugs in the operating system or software
- Holes present within system security

Some vulnerabilities cannot be closed by patching because there is an inherent bandwidth limit or active connection limit on all physical equipment and all software. If your Web server can only accept 100 requests per second, then the 101st will be denied. In this case, you would need to upgrade the server software to a new version or even a different software product that can accept more requests. The upgraded server may not be able to run on the current hardware platform, which might need CPU and RAM upgrades. If the hardware is too old, the newest CPU might not work on it, so you might need to replace the machine the CPU is running on. The cost of updating the hardware may be higher than the potential loss to DoS. Therefore, in a sense, you are defining the DoS attacks as the lesser of two evils. There is also a network resource limit based on how big your pipe is. If you are running a cable modem at a home or satellite office, you may have a hard limit of between 3 and 6 Mbps (megabits per second) shared with an unknown number of other subscribers. But if your office is attached to the Internet by an OC-3 fiber-optic bundle, you are potentially able to accept 155.52 megabits per second. Table 11-1 shows the speed of some common connection technologies.

Table 11-1 Bandwidth comparison

Service	Bandwidth
Dial-up Modem	56 Kbps
ADSL	1.5 Mbps
Cable	3 to 6 Mbps
T-1/DS1	1.5 Mbps
T-3/DS3	1.5 Mbps
OC1	51.84 Mbps
OC3	155.52 Mbps
OC12	622.08 Mbps
OC24	1.244 Gbps
OC48	2.488 Gbps
OC192	10 Gbps
OC256	13.271 Gbps
OC768	40 Gbps

How your laptop's Ethernet card and your LAN equipment can run at the awesome bandwidth (often called "speed") of 100 Mbps is a function of how under-subscribed your LAN is. But this is a question for another time. In order to overcome these types of DoS attacks, you must monitor and upgrade the system security architecture at standard intervals.

Types of DoS Attacks

DoS attacks can be plotted on the matrix depicted in Figure 11-1.

X axis = Flood attacks or software attacks

Y axis = Isolated attacks or distributed attacks

Z axis = Voluntary or involuntary, on the part of the systems administrator

Voluntary DoS

A voluntary DoS occurs when the sysadmin has allowed (and sometimes laboriously designed) the system to perform a variety of services without considering the system's limitations. One example of a voluntary DoS attack is an administrator designing the VoIP system with 120 phones, projecting an average phone use of 20%, which is to say that only one out of five users will be on the phone at any given time. This works marvelously until the end-of-month company-wide marketing conference call from the company president. If 30% of the company's employees are in marketing, and they all attempt to call the conference bridge at the same time, the system will fail. Calls will be dropped and the repair tickets will flow in.

Involuntary DoS

An involuntary DoS takes place regardless of preparation and readiness by the sysadmin. For instance, an organization's system administrator receives notice that a particular printer is not working one day. When the administrator logs on to the print server, she discovers a large quantity of print jobs in queue from a user who has been on vacation for the last five days. All those jobs are malformed in such a way as to be unprintable. They have used up the available disk space, which denies access to other users. It is quite possible that there has been a DoS attack on that print server, and in any case, denial of service conditions exist there.

11

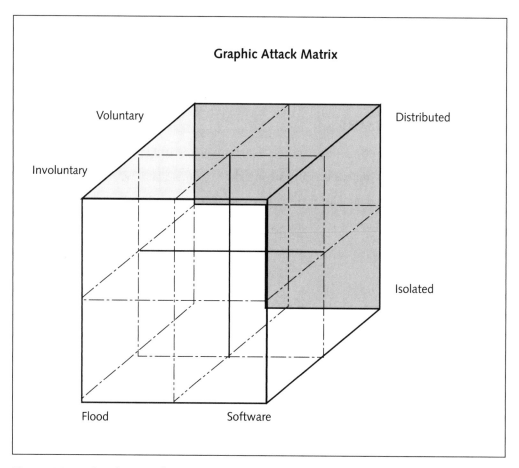

Figure 11-1 Graphic attack matrix

Flood Attacks

Processes running on computers or on network appliances need bandwidth, memory space, and disk space. They also need CPU time and data structures to operate. The majority of these devices are limited by design to a maximum packet-processing count. Flood attacks consume the limited resources of a computer or a network by transmitting a large number of packets as quickly as possible. This overloads the network, causing a resource gap for legitimate users.

A flood attack can occur under the following conditions:

- Sending connection requests
- Consuming the bandwidth
- Using your own resources
- Consuming others' resources

Sending Connection Requests

In this sort of attack, the target or victim receives a large quantity of connection requests. If it is a legitimate attack, and not merely a malfunctioning NIC card somewhere in the network, the attacker is probably using a spoofed IP address on the network to send the requests. Whether this is a malevolent act or not, it uses all the server's resources, causing a DoS condition that makes it impossible for the victim to process legitimate user requests. This condition is shown in Figure 11-2.

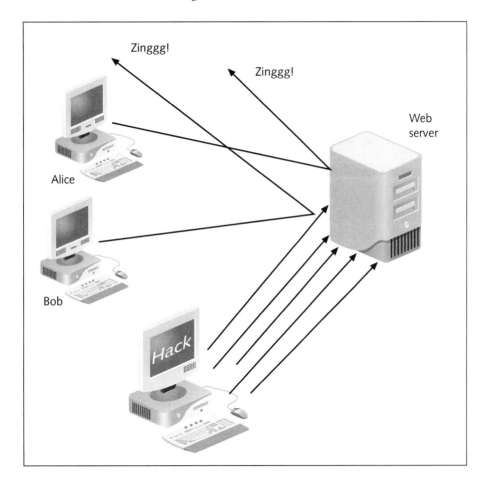

Figure 11-2 Connection request attack

If the organization has an active Telnet service on a router that permits a maximum of five connections, and a hacker opens five connections with this Telnet server, nobody else will be able to connect with this router using Telnet.

Consuming Bandwidth

In this kind of attack, all of a network's available bandwidth is consumed by sending a large number of packets. An example of this might be flooding a switch with 20 times more traffic than it can handle. All the available bandwidth is in use, so no legitimate packets can get through.

Using Your Own Resources

A hacker may use your own resources against you. To do this, a hacker uses forged User Datagram Protocol packets to connect the echo service on one computer to a service on another computer.

For instance, a hacker can transmit an echo request from a spoofed IP address. The response for this packet will automatically be sent to the computer whose IP address the hacker is using. Likewise, a hacker can send multiple echo packets by utilizing a spoofed IP address, as seen in Figure 11-3. The outcome is that the packets consume all the available network bandwidth, affecting network connectivity for all of the computers on the network.

Consuming Others' Resources

Hackers often try to consume resources on target systems, such as the memory or the hard disk. On many systems, a limited number of data structures are available to hold process information. A hacker may be able to consume these data structures simply by writing a program or a script that replicates itself.

For instance, the process table in UNIX permits only a finite number of entries. If a hacker has already created extra entries in the process table, a legitimate user will not be able to form any other valid processes. Furthermore, the larger the number of entries in the process table, the slower the speed of the existing processes in the CPU.

Hackers also attempt to consume disk space by sending an excessive number of e-mail messages, generating errors that must be logged, and placing files in anonymous FTP areas or network shares.

It is important to understand that any feature that allows data to be written to a system's hard disk can be used to execute a DoS attack.

Many user authentication applications and Web sites have policies to lock an account after a certain number of failed attempts to log in (commonly, three to five failed attempts). A hacker may be able to manipulate this policy to prevent legitimate users from logging on. In some situations, even privileged accounts, such as root or administrator, might be denied access.

Software Attacks

Software attacks exploit the existing software weaknesses. The effect is either degraded performance or crashes on the victim server. To perform these attacks, hackers generate a

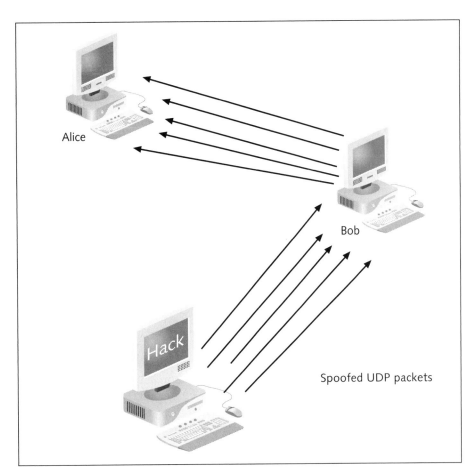

Figure 11-3   Echo request attack

small number of carefully malformed packets to exploit known software bugs. The bugs allow hackers to change or damage configuration files, and this interference may hinder valid users and even administrators from normal use of the applications.

For example, an attacker may be able to modify the route table on a network router, causing packets to be routed to illegitimate destinations. Or the attacker may be able to interfere with the registry of a Windows machine, opening possible back doors or making some services unavailable.

Software attacks, especially attacks by script-kiddies using old scripts they downloaded from so called "warez" sites or bulletin boards, are somewhat easier to prevent. The systems administrator can install available software patches as they are made available and also add firewall rules that drop malformed packets before they reach the target machine.

Among the most common software attacks are Ping of Death and DNS service attacks.

Ping of Death

Ping of Death is a historical DoS attack in which the hacker uses the Ping utility to acquire access to a system. The Ping utility is used to determine if a specific machine located at a specific IP address is online. Upon finding a likely target, the hacker then sends a packet to that computer. The packet size that can be sent to a computer through the Ping utility is limited to 64 KB. The hacker adjusts the packet size and sends through a larger packet.

Once the target computer receives a packet of more than 64 KB, the system may crash or restart. This occurs because the buffer overflows on the target computer. Some operating systems that are vulnerable to Ping of Death attacks are Solaris 2.4, Windows 3.11, Windows 95, MS-DOS, and Novell Netware. You must apply patches to these operating systems to help mitigate the effects of DoS attacks.

Most legitimate Ping utilities do not allow you to send a ping of more than 64 KB. The Ping utility on Windows NT and Windows 95 would let you send a larger ping. To test whether your machine is in danger, find a Windows 95 or NT box (3.51 or 4), and run the following command:

```
ping -l 65510 your.host.ip.address
```

The message on the Win95 box will be "Request Timed Out". This means that the ping wasn't answered, either because the machine is patched and ignoring you, or because it's dead. If you haven't seen a Win95 or NT4 machine for five or more years, don't lose heart. You can use Apsend to send an oversized packet. Figure 11-4 shows an attempt to send an oversized ping from a Linux box using the Ping command.

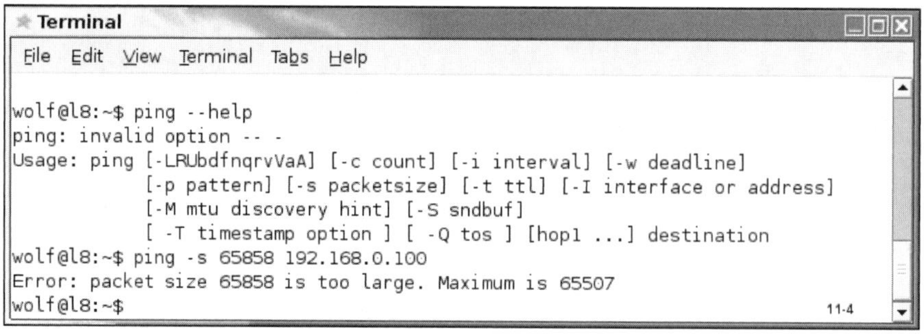

```
wolf@l8:~$ ping --help
ping: invalid option -- -
Usage: ping [-LRUbdfnqrvVaA] [-c count] [-i interval] [-w deadline]
            [-p pattern] [-s packetsize] [-t ttl] [-I interface or address]
            [-M mtu discovery hint] [-S sndbuf]
            [ -T timestamp option ] [ -Q tos ] [hop1 ...] destination
wolf@l8:~$ ping -s 65858 192.168.0.100
Error: packet size 65858 is too large. Maximum is 65507
wolf@l8:~$
```

Figure 11-4 Attempted Ping of Death

You can block pings on your firewall to save yourself from this class of attack. Any port that listens on the network is a likely target for an oversized packet, which could cause an overflow into the system kernel. This works by packets fragmenting in transit from the source to the destination. If your computer, router, switch, printer, or other equipment is not patched to prevent this overflow into the kernel, your machine may be hit.

The good news for systems administrators is that almost all operating systems have been patched to deflect this attack. In addition, the machines most likely to be used to perform this attack have been retired or updated to operating systems that do not allow an illegal enlarged packet to be sent.

DNS Service Attacks

Domain Name Service (DNS) is a database that maps domain names to IP addresses. Computers that are connected to the Internet utilize DNS to resolve URLs. Whenever users need a domain name resolution, they ask the DNS server. It then sends the required URL to the users. Two kinds of attacks are related to the DNS service: DNS spoofing and DNS overflow.

DNS Spoofing

An example of DNS spoofing might start with an organization launching a new product after comprehensive market research. The product is announced and its details are published on the company's Web site. Now that the product is being advertised, any user can view and buy the product by placing an order online. Eventually, one of the manufacturing firms calls, stating that they are unable to access the Web site. Whenever they try to log on, they are directed to a different Web site. Figure 11-5 depicts the effect of a hacker spoofing a DNS entry.

11

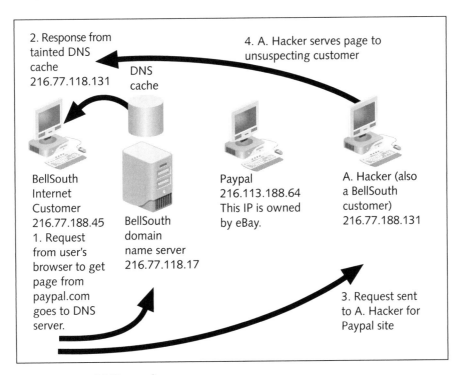

Figure 11-5 DNS spoofing

Apparently, a hacker has gained access to the Web server by sending false information. In this manner, users or customers may be redirected to Web sites other than their intended destination. This is not the same as phishing, which occurs when a spoofed e-mail is sent to a user, prompting the user to go to a fake site and log into what the user thinks is his or her bank's Web site or something of that nature. In phishing, the DNS service is working perfectly.

A DNS service attack may lead to customers giving their account information to hackers for use in identity theft schemes or abuse of credit cards or debit cards.

DNS Overflows

DNS overflows may happen when there is a failure to check and verify the length of the host name. If the host name length exceeds the allowed maximum, any excess data is sent to the DNS server, thus causing DNS buffer overflows on that DNS server.

Many `set-user-id` and `set-group-id` programs, as well as many network programs running with superuser privileges, make use of the `gethostbyname()` library function. Corrupting the program stack of these programs may allow arbitrary user-provided code to be executed inadvertently.

If successfully exploited, this buffer overrun condition could be used to gain superuser access to the system. Such an action could be initiated over the network from a remote system, or by a user on the local system. Penetration through a firewall may also be possible, depending on which services and applications are permitted by the firewall system.

Some of the other software attacks include Teardrop, Land, and Chargen. The Teardrop attack generates an IP packet overlap. This causes the target computers to crash or reboot. Derivatives of this attack include NewTear, TearDrop2, Nestea Bonk, Boink, and SYN Drop.

In a Land attack, a hacker sends to the target computer a packet that has the identical source and destination IP address as that of the target computer. This forces the target computer to crash or reboot.

Chargen attacks attempt to crash the server by making the server send packets to itself. As a result, the server becomes occupied with processing those packets and ignores valid users.

Isolated Attacks

An isolated attack comes from a single source, and is easily countered by blocking traffic from that source until the administrator of that domain can fix the problem. If it cannot be fixed, the user could block traffic from that site indefinitely.

Distributed Attacks

Distributed attacks come from multiple concurrent sources. This strategy is much more difficult to block with ACLs or firewall rules. Distributed denial-of-service, or DDoS, attacks depend on the hacker's ability to compromise information on a large number of systems.

First, the hacker exploits known vulnerabilities to gain access to a target system. Next, the hacker uses certain tools to direct future attacks on the system. The following components are engaged in a DDoS attack: the client, handler, and agent.

The hacker first attacks a system from the client computer.

The handler is the victim computer to which the attacks are directed. It is a compromised host with a special program running on it, and it is capable of controlling multiple agents.

The agent, also called a zombie, is a compromised host as well. A special program is running on it, similarly to the handler. The term zombie denotes a machine that has been unobtrusively "0wned" by a hacker. When a machine is 0wned, the hacker can back door into it at any time and perform actions from that machine as if she were sitting at its keyboard. An agent creates large numbers of crafted packets that are sent to the victim computer. Figure 11-6 shows the basic DDoS attack.

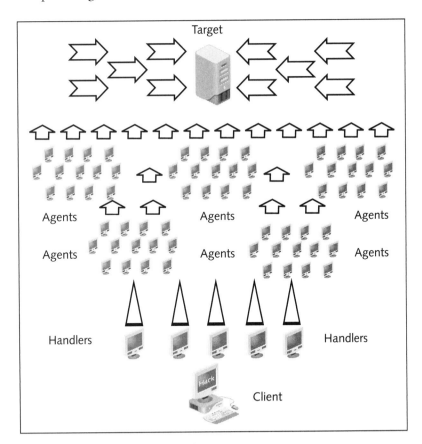

Figure 11-6 DDoS basic attack

Hackers may require hundreds or thousands of compromised hosts to make a DDoS attack successful. These compromised hosts are frequently computers with the Windows operating system. There are special tools that are used to attack a computer. They can be ported to other operating systems. The process of DDoS is fully automated and consists of compromising a host as well as installing tools on the host.

A DDoS attack occurs in the following sequence:

- The hacker identifies vulnerable hosts (100 or more is common).

- The hacker gets access to these hosts after they are compromised.

- The hacker installs the tool needed to attack each host.

- The hacker uses these compromised hosts for future attacks.

KNOWN DOS ATTACKS

Some known flood attacks are TCP SYN, SMURF, and Fraggle. The Denial of Service Database at http://attrition.org/security/denial/ has over 360 known DoS (and DDos) exploits used on different targets. The following list is general by class of attack, and does not specifically address single instances or exploits.

TCP SYN

In a TCP SYN attack, a client and server exchange a sequence of messages after establishing a TCP connection. The complete process uses the familiar three-way handshake of TCP. A TCP SYN attack uses the same three requests: SYN, SYN/ACK, and ACK.

In order to establish a connection, a client must send a SYN message to the server. Next, the server acknowledges the SYN message by transmitting a SYN-ACK message to that client. The client then completes the connection process by responding with an ACK message. After the connection between the client and the server has been established and maintained, they can exchange information.

The attack begins once the server has sent the SYN/ACK message back to the client, and is waiting for the client to respond. This is called a half-connection.

When there are too many clients establishing half-connections with the server, the data structure in memory that holds all the pending half-connections increases in size. Because this data structure is of a specific finite size, if there are an excessive number of half-open connections, the data structure can overflow in memory.

To assault a server on the network, a hacker only has to use the IP spoofing technique to send excess SYN requests to the server. The messages seem to be coming from legitimate users, but they are actually sent by a hacker. Figure 11-7 illustrates how multiple SYN requests overload a server.

The hacker transmits SYN requests to the server at a quicker rate than it can close incoming connections. Therefore, the memory and the processor of the server are kept busy. The server patiently waits for the ACK packets to arrive from the client. Consequently, the server

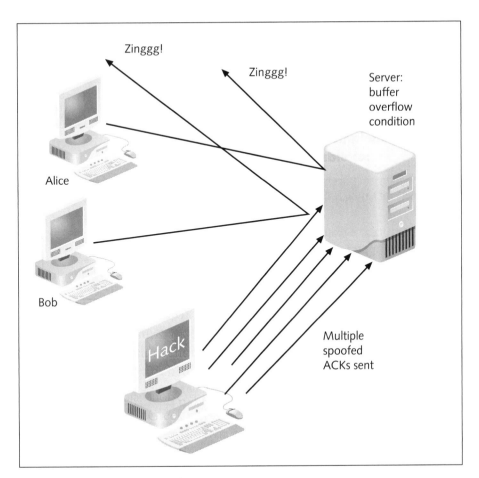

Figure 11-7   TCP SYN attack

is unable to accept any new connections or respond to the end-user requests. This may crash the server processes or even crash the hardware server, requiring a reboot.

SMURF

To understand how the **SMURF attacks** work, you first need to know about Internet Control Message Protocol (ICMP). ICMP is used to handle errors and exchange control messages on a network. ICMP can be used to verify whether a computer on the network is responding.

To check this, an ICMP echo request packet is sent to the computer. If the computer is alive and able to respond, it returns an ICMP echo reply. Figure 11-8 illustrates the ICMP implementation.

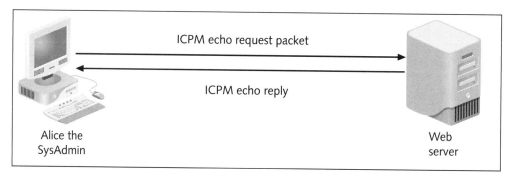

Figure 11-8   ICMP echo

The ICMP process is executed using the *ping* command. On IP networks, a packet is either sent to one computer or broadcast to the entire network.

The three main components involved in a SMURF attack are the hacker (attacking computer), packet amplifiers or intermediate devices, and the target computer (or victim).

In a SMURF attack, hackers broadcast ICMP request packets with a ping command throughout the network. When they do this, they forge the packet headers to contain the address of some other node on the network as originating the pings. This computer is the one that the hacker has chosen as her victim.

When the request packets are sent, the responding subnets, called packet amplifiers, receive them, and finally the packet amplifiers return ICMP echo reply packets. Figure 11-9 shows a SMURF attack in progress.

The packet amplifiers and computers on the network do not send the ICMP echo replies to the hacker's computer, because the hacker has used a spoofed address. The reply goes to the victim computer, which is the apparent origin of the pings. The victim receives multiple ICMP echo reply packets from all the computers and subnets on the network, clogging the network and making the victim machine unreachable.

Recently, automated tools have been developed that enable hackers to send these attacks simultaneously to several intermediaries. All the intermediaries direct their response, focusing on the same victim. Furthermore, attackers have developed tools that identify network routers that do not filter broadcast traffic, as well as networks to which multiple hosts respond.

Fraggle

Fraggle attacks are like SMURF DoS attacks, but instead of using ICMP packets, Fraggle attacks use UDP packets. The Fraggle attacker uses a spoofed IP address to broadcast hundreds of UDP packets to the computers on the network. Then the intermediate devices reply to the victim computer by sending hundreds of UDP echo reply packets. The hacker's best possible result is a system crash, and at the very least, the attack will produce excess network traffic.

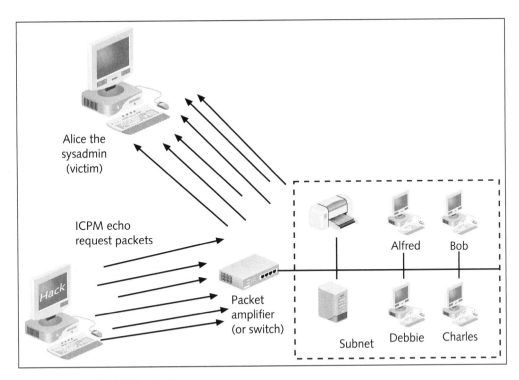

Figure 11-9 SMURF attack

Known DDoS Attacks

DDoS attacks are bound to the tools and strategies used to deploy them. DDoS tools use distributed technology to generate a large network of hosts. These hosts can attack thousands of computers via packet flooding. Some of the tools that can be used for DDoS attacks are Trinoo, Tribe flood network (TFN), and Botnets.

Trinoo

Trinoo is a distributed tool used to initialize coordinated UDP flood DoS attacks from multiple sources. A Trinoo network consists of a minute quantity of servers and a large number of clients. The two components are the Trinoo server and the Trinoo clients.

A hacker computer is connected to a Trinoo master computer in a DoS attack utilizing a Trinoo network. Then the hacker computer instructs the master computer to begin DoS attacks against one or more IP addresses. Next, the Trinoo master computer communicates with the Trinoo clients, giving them instructions to attack one or more IP addresses within a specified period of time.

TFN

TFN is also used to launch coordinated DoS flood attacks from multiple sources. These attacks can be against one or more targets. TFN has the capability to create packets with spoofed source IP addresses.

A TFN network can generate several DoS attacks such as:

- UDP flood attacks
- TCP SYN flood
- ICMP echo request flood
- ICMP directed broadcast

A DDoS attack using TFN follows the same principle as a Trinoo DDoS attack. A hacker's computer sends instructions to the TFN server, or the master program. Then the TFN server sends instructions to the TNF client pool. Finally, the TFN clients generate their DoS attack against one or more target IP addresses. During this time of sending instructions to TFN clients, the source IP addresses and ports can be randomized and packet sizes altered.

A TFN master program is executed from the command line to transmit commands to TFN clients. The TFN server communicates with TFN clients by utilizing ICMP echo reply packets. In the packet, 16-bit binary values are embedded in the ID field. In addition, arguments are embedded in the data portion of the packet. The binary values, which are defined at compile time, represent the different instructions sent between the TFN servers and clients.

Botnets

Botnets are a variety of software DDoS. A bot is a program that surreptitiously installs itself on a computer so it can be controlled by a hacker. A botnet is a network of robot, or zombie, computers, which can harness their collective power to do considerable damage or send out huge amounts of junk e-mail.

'Botmaster' pleads guilty to computer crimes – Reuters Published on ZDNet News: January 24, 2006, 5:38 AM PT

A 20-year-old accused of using hundreds of thousands of hijacked computers, or "bot nets," to damage systems and send massive waves of spam across the Internet, pleaded guilty to federal charges on Monday.

Jeanson James Ancheta, who prosecutors said was a well-known member of the "Botmaster Underground"—a secret network of hackers skilled in "bot" attacks—was arrested in November in what prosecutors said was the first such case of its kind.

The Los Angeles-area man pleaded guilty to charges of conspiracy, damaging computers used by the U.S. government, and fraud. He had been scheduled to stand trial later this year on a 17-count indictment.

Ancheta faces a maximum sentence of 25 years in prison, although prosecutors say federal guidelines recommend between five and seven years.

"Mr. Ancheta was responsible for a particularly insidious string of crimes," U.S. Attorney's spokesman Thom Mrozek said. "He hijacked somewhere in the area of half a million computer systems. This not only affected computers like the one in your home, but it allowed him and others to orchestrate large-scale attacks."

11

PREVENTION AND MITIGATION OF DOS AND DDOS ATTACKS

Prevention of DoS attacks is crucial for all systems. These attacks are designed to crash systems by using methods and techniques that appear to be normal network traffic. Network administrators can use packet filtering on the IP routers to give basic access control. However, this often slows router performance to an unacceptable point, so many common types of DoS attacks fail to be eliminated.

Prevention Methods

Traditional firewalls can stop specific IP addresses by using **Network Address Translation (NAT)**. This technique prevents DoS by refusing network traffic from specific TCP ports, limiting the network traffic coming from specific network addresses, and scanning the network traffic for viruses or undesirable applications.

These solutions were designed to prevent DoS attacks on LANs and subnet systems and were not meant for a Web environment. Placing additional firewalls in a network is not an effective solution for high network traffic in a Web environment.

The Cisco CSS 11000 series switches give comprehensive Web site and server–system security. They do not compromise scalability or performance, and successfully eliminate all DoS attacks without impact on the Web switch itself.

These switches provide site-level safety in the following ways:

- DoS attack prevention—Cisco CSS Web switches validate all session flow at the time of initial flow setup and eradicate all connection-based DoS attacks. Also, the switches eliminate other malicious or abnormal connections. This is performed without any impact on the performance of the Cisco CSS Web switch.

- Firewall security—Cisco CSS Web switches provide firewall services that include high-speed ACLs that block particular content requests by using an IP address, a TCP port, a URL, or a file type.

- NAT—Wire-speed NAT capabilities on the Cisco CSS Web switches appropriately hide the IP addresses of all the devices, such as Web servers and caches, positioned behind the Web switch. This reduces the likelihood of hackers attacking the servers directly by using explicit IP addresses.

- Load-balancing—In addition, the Cisco CSS switches offer security for server systems by providing firewall load balancing. When firewall security is required in the path from the Internet, or to guard mission-critical server systems or networks, Cisco CSS 11000 series switches can detect and counter bottlenecks. These switches can also abolish single points of failure by distributing the traffic among multiple load-balanced firewalls.

The Cisco CSS 11000 series switches will abandon frames if the:

- Length is short.

- Frame is broken and fragmented.

- Source IP address is similar to the destination IP address.

- Source address is not a unicast address.

- Source IP address is a loop-back address.

- Destination IP address is a loop-back address.

- Destination address is not a valid unicast or multicast address.

Other preventive measures that can be taken against DoS attacks include the following:

- Hackers frequently use source address spoofing to execute DoS attacks. To prevent these attacks, you need to implement router filters or ingress filtering on as many routers as possible in the network. These filters can restrict the IP addresses of the incoming packets, thus preventing packets that might come from spoofed IP addresses.

- Hackers usually attack weak and vulnerable computers. To hinder and prevent attacks, computers should constantly be updated with the relevant security patches. The more machines you are managing, the more important patch management automation becomes.

- Intrusion-detection systems on networks containing Web servers must be able to identify Trinoo or TFN attacks, based on communications between the master and client computers on the network. The network should be monitored to identify the signatures of the distributed attack tools in order to accomplish this.

- Disable any unnecessary services on your system to reduce the chances of intruders using them against you.

- If supported, enable quotas on the operating systems. Because disk space available to users across a network is limited, all legitimate users will have access only to the disk space allocated to them. In this situation, the hacker will not be able to use all of the available disk space. Another tactic is to put the /home directories or the Documents and Settings directory on a separate partition, and even on a separate hard drive from the operating system and applications.

It is important to establish baselines for activities. This helps in monitoring the disk activities, CPU usage, and network traffic. If the baseline is crossed, then some unauthorized activity could take place.

The following measures can be taken specifically for preventing DDoS attacks:

- Filter all the RFC1918 address space by using access control lists (ACLs)
- Apply ingress and egress filtering using ACLs
- Rate-limit ICMP packets, if they are configurable
- Configure the rate limiting for SYN packets

Mitigation of DoS and DDoS Attacks

Use a tool such as Tripwire to detect changes in the configuration information or on other files. The problem with mitigation of DoS attacks is that the attacks are easily mistaken for a small spike in network activity. If you become aware of an ongoing assault against a particular machine, operating system, or application, you can initiate blocking packets from the origin IP or to the victim. This is not usually a good fix. It might cause you to make larger restrictions than you want and cause a general shutdown of connections from your network to the Internet. Thus, you are performing a larger denial of service than the hacker did. Rather than manually turn back an attack in progress, it is much more effective to actively patch your machines and applications and stay current on new reports of DoS and DDoS attacks and systems. Run an IDS system that alerts you when the network is experiencing unusual traffic or activity.

CHAPTER SUMMARY

- ❑ A denial-of-service attack is any network event that restricts or denies valid uses of a resource. Main targets of DoS attacks are Web servers, application servers, and communication links.

❑ DoS attacks are caused by vulnerability of the network architecture, vulnerability of a specific server system architecture, defects and bugs in the operating system or software, and holes present within system security.

❑ There are three main groupings of DoS attacks: voluntary and involuntary attacks; flood and software attacks; and isolated and distributed attacks.

❑ Known DoS attacks include TCP SYN, SMURF, and Fraggle.

❑ Known DDoS attack tools include Trinoo, TFN, and Botnets. DDoS attacks require advanced tools to orchestrate the distributed agents attacking the victim machine.

❑ Methods of prevention for DoS attacks include using Cisco CSS Web switches; implementing router filters or ingress filtering; constantly updating computers with the latest, most relevant security patches; monitoring the network to identify attack tools; disabling unnecessary system services; and enabling quotas on the operating system.

❑ Methods of prevention for DDoS attacks include filtering all the RFC1918 address space by using access control lists (ACLs), applying ingress and egress filtering using ACLs, rate-limiting ICMP packets if they are configurable, and configuring the rate limiting for SYN packets.

❑ Attempting to mitigate DoS and DDoS attacks can end up causing more harm than an actual attack.

REVIEW QUESTIONS

1. What is a DoS attack and what makes it different from a DDoS attack?

2. If your network is experiencing a SMURF attack, what is the best response?

3. What is the best plan to prevent DDoS attacks?

4. What kinds of attacks could be classified as flood DoS attacks?

5. What kinds of attacks could be classified as software DoS attacks?

6. What kinds of attacks could be classified as isolated DoS attacks?

7. What kinds of attacks could be classified as distributed DoS attacks?

8. What kinds of attacks could be classified as voluntary DoS attacks?

9. What kinds of attacks could be classified as involuntary DoS attacks?

10. Where would a TCP SYN attack appear in the attack matrix?

11. Where would a SMURF attack appear in the attack matrix?

12. Where would a Fraggle attack appear in the attack matrix?

13. Can a malfunctioning Ethernet card cause a DoS condition?

14. Can a misconfigured firewall cause a DoS condition?

15. Can a coworker cause a DoS condition accidentally?

Indicate whether the sentence or statement is true or false.

16. _____ DoS attacks are not possible to mount from a dial-up Internet connection.

17. _____ Some DoS attacks are caused by honest mistakes.

18. _____ Trinoo is a tool for detecting DDoS attacks.

19. _____ The Ping of Death is unstoppable when used against a Windows NT 3.1 Machine.

20. _____ The machines most likely to be used to perform a Ping of Death have been retired or updated to operating systems that do not allow an illegal enlarged packet to be sent.

HANDS-ON PROJECTS

11

This chapter's projects are intended to show you how DoS attacks are initiated and how to tell you are under attack.

HANDS-ON PROJECTS

Project 11-1

1. Hping is a packet-crafting tool. Go to www.hping.org or to the central Linux server to download a copy of the hping3 source code for Linux and save it to your home directory. As of this writing, the file to download is named hping3-20051105.tar.gz.

2. In a terminal window, logged in as root, navigate to your home directory and expand the hping3-20051105.tar.gz file using the `tar` command:

```
tar xfv hping3-20051105.tar.gz
```

3. There is a known issue with hping3, in which the bpf.h file is not found during compilation. To work around this, make sure you are in the hping3-20051105 directory (created when you untarred the downloaded file), and use a text editor to edit the file libpcap_stuff.c. In that file, change the following line:

```
#include <net/bpf.h>
```

to:

```
#include <pcap-bpf.h>
```

4. Save the libpcap_stuff.c file and close it. Next, make the same change in the script.c file (located in the same directory), and then save and close it. You are now ready to continue with the installation of hping3.

5. Type the following commands to install necessary dependencies. (Type **y** and press **Enter** each time you see the "Is this ok?" prompt.)

```
yum install expect-devel
yum install tcl
yum install tcl-devel
```

6. Next, type the following commands to compile and install hping3:

```
./configure
Make
make install
```

7. Now you are ready to run the *hping* command. Type the following command, substituting the appropriate IP address of a machine designated by your instructor:

```
/usr/sbin/hping -1 -V 192.168.0.1
```

8. The output will look similar to a standard *ping* command. After about 10 seconds, stop the command by pressing **Ctrl+c**, and note that *hping* displays a summary of the ping statistics. Standard pings may or may not be accepted by the target machine, but for the purposes of this exercise, it is more important to get the implications of the act of packet–crafting and what can be done with it.

What is the standard ping, as shown by your machine, as each ping packet is sent?

_____

What are your statistics after 30 seconds of running?

_____

Project 11-2

Before proceeding with this project and the two that follow it, start Wireshark as root, and save the capture to a file named Chapter_11_Projects. You will use the results to see what happens when a node in your network is being subjected to a DoS attack.

1. In this project, you will launch a flood attack on a target machine (as specified by your instructor), using standard pings to random ports. You must be careful to note the time when you start the attack and run it for only 10 seconds. Enter the following command (substituting the correct IP address as necessary):

```
/usr/sbin/hping -1 --flood 192.168.0.1
```

2. Press **Ctrl + c** to end the torture. How many packets does *hping* report were transmitted and received?

_____

Project 11-3

1. The next attack is a half-open attack, which makes use of the standard TCP/IP three-way handshake. Recall that the three-way handshake requires the initiating machine to send a SYN packet. The receiving machine sends a SYN/ACK packet back, and the initiating machine sends a final ACK. A half-open attack sends a SYN, but does not send back the final ACK. The victim sits waiting for a few seconds, and finally clears the connection. If you send a large number of SYN packets, the victim can have its buffer filled with half-connections, and this keeps legitimate traffic from getting through. Note the starting time, and as the root user, enter the following command (substituting an IP address supplied by your instructor):

   ```
   /usr/sbin/hping -SV 192.168.0.103
   ```

2. Press **Ctrl + c** to stop the attack. What statistics does *hping* report after 10 seconds of attacking the target machine?

Project 11-4

11

1. This attack fills up the buffer of alternate ports. For instance, you could launch a DoS on the Telnet port or the FTP port of the victim machine. Run this attack on your central Linux server (or another machine designated by your instructor) for 10 seconds, noting the start time:

   ```
   /usr/sbin/hping --icmp-dstport 23 192.168.0.103
   ```

2. Press **Ctrl + c** to end the attack. What statistics does *hping* report?

Project 11-5

1. Stop the Wireshark capture and view the Chapter_11_Projects files to see the results of the capture. Note the start and end of each attack in your log in Wireshark.

2. Show your findings to the instructor.

12

BUFFER OVERFLOWS

After reading this chapter and completing the exercises, you will be able to:

♦ Describe buffer overflow

♦ List types of buffer overflows

♦ Identify techniques used to cause a buffer overflow

♦ Comprehend techniques used to detect buffer overflow conditions

♦ Understand methods used in preventing buffer overflows

Buffer overflow is a condition common to structured programming languages such as the "C" language, which was used to write utilities and operating systems, including UNIX and Windows. Thus, it is ubiquitous in the computing world. The C language uses files such as libraries of standard functions. Buffer overflow happens when input applied to a variable is larger than the memory allotted to that variable. Historically, programmers have not checked their programs for what happens after data overflows the memory allotment into other areas of memory. Buffer overflow techniques used by crackers exploit the interesting effects of these overflow conditions. After erroneous or anomalous data appears in the memory allotment of another function, it is difficult to tell what the outcome will be. What can be known is that something surprising will happen. When an attacker sends input in excess of the expected range of the value, the target system will either crash or execute the malicious code sent by the attacker. For this attack to make sense, one must comprehend the standard or typical sequence of events that occur when an application written in a structured paradigm programming language like C is executed.

Standard Execution of a C program

When a user requests to execute a file, such as the example below, the primary function referred to is the main function. This is the entry point to the detailed code in the application, which a programmer would have written to be executed completely, as well as to retrieve the required results. The main function is responsible for calling other functions, each of which executes a particular task, and may call other functions in turn. Functions use variables to store values that may be stored temporarily or permanently. Once a function has completed the sequence of events defined within the function, the program control returns to the calling or invoking function. Here is a small, simple program in C:

```c
#include <stdio.h> /* this is a standard library that
                      allows the keyboard, mouse and
                      monitor access to the program.
void print_converted(int pounds) /* Convert U.S. Weight to
                      Imperial and International Units.
                      Print the results */
{
    int stones = pounds / 14;
    int uklbs = pounds % 14;
    float kilos_per_pound = 0.45359;
    float kilos = pounds * kilos_per_pound;
    printf(" %3d %2d %2d %6.2f\n", pounds, stones, uklbs,
        kilos);
}
main()
{
        int us_pounds [10]; /* This line creates a
                      variable of integer type called
                      us_pounds. The [10] refers not to
                      how many pounds the user could
                      enter but to the number of
                      characters in the field and here
                      is where a buffer overflow could
                      easily happen in this program. */
        printf("Give an integer weight in Pounds : ");
        scanf("%d", &us_pounds);
        printf(" US lbs UK st. lbs INT Kg\n");
        print_converted(us_pounds);
}
```

The buffer overflow bug targets the variables that are used by functions to store values. The variables that are defined in a function accept values from the users or generate them automatically. These variables are assigned a fixed memory space to store the data specified for the variable. For instance, consider the code above that defines the variable us_pounds with a memory length of 10 characters assigned to it:

```
int us_pounds [10];
```

Buffer overflow has a goal of overloading the memory space provided to the variable. This might either allow the attacker to crash the computer or break into it. Whenever a value exceeding the memory assigned to the variable is specified, the extra characters are stored in a memory space that is not assigned to the variable, as shown in Figure 12-1.

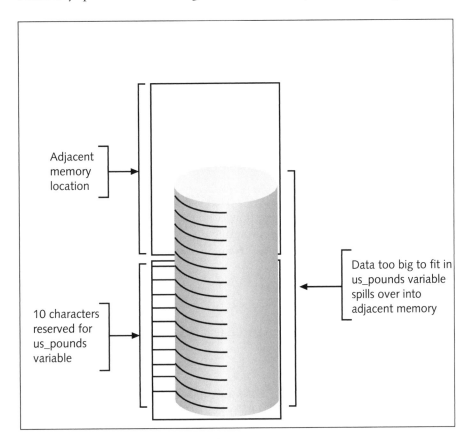

Figure 12-1 Simplified buffer overflow

The function with an overloaded variable is not able to determine the function that called it, so it may not be able to finalize the operation. If the function is unable to determine the last function that called the currently executing function, it could result in the crashing of the program. Hackers are able to manipulate the value provided to the variable in such a manner that it is stored in a specific memory space to execute some predetermined malicious code. This is similar to the programmer arranging a party for four people and having a hacker show up with six guests. The two extra guests either disrupt the party and cause it to fail or they quietly wander the halls rearranging stuff and maybe even breaking or stealing from the house.

When a function has completed, the program looks for a pointer, called an instruction pointer, to tell it where to go next. Since functions are blind to the greater application of which they are a part, these are necessary to keep the program on track. The pointers point to specific memory addresses. When hackers overflow the buffers, they can make the memory addresses that the pointers indicate become part of the string used to overflow the buffer. That new code may call for a download from a server of the hacker's choice.

Buffer overflows are not always intentional attacks. Programs may not allocate sufficient memory for certain types of variables, and functions may not exist to verify the length of data supplied to variables.

Buffer overflow can be avoided in two ways: by checking to see that no value greater than the memory assigned to the variable is specified for it, and by defining the sequence of steps that the program has to follow in case of a buffer overflow. Both of these solutions are programmatic, and in many cases, the only thing end users can do is continue to apply the patches to their operating systems and upgrade software as the upgrades become available. In certain cases, such as medical equipment and military weapons systems, the design process has been modified to catch more of these kinds of programmatic errors. If the application is keeping your heart beating, then 99.999% is not quite good enough, and there is no acceptable window of downtime.

On some specific operating systems, the kernel can be patched in such a way that running processes are not affected by buffer overflow conditions. This patch is called executable space protection, and it is available for Linux running on x86 architectures. Windows does not use a patch like this, so it is still susceptible to buffer overflows.

TYPES OF BUFFER OVERFLOWS

Buffer overflows can be divided into two categories: stack overflow and heap overflow.

Stack Overflow

Programs use a memory stack area to store values for variables. These values are either created by the application or specified by the user. A stack is intended to ensure that there is sufficient memory space for all functions to operate, and typically there is enough space in the stack if the memory is being purged properly.

Occasionally there are situations where the available memory defined in the stack is insufficient to complete the functions and an error is generated. Sometimes the functions are unable to verify the amount of memory available, and in that situation, the function keeps pumping new values into the stack, which overwrite other values in the stack. The stack becomes corrupt and this can lead to the application failing, or in some cases, to the computer failing.

In addition to defining allowed space for functions to operate, a stack stores details regarding the function that called the currently executing function. It stores this information as an instruction pointer, and this identifies the location where the program will go, or go back to, after the current function completes the tasks. The instruction pointers may lose the saved information after the stack is corrupted. They still point to the same piece of memory, but the function that was there has been garbled or moved. Hackers benefit from this by writing the code for a buffer overflow in such a manner that the code to which a function's pointers are indicating is code of the hacker's choosing and not the expected continuation of the program. After the functions finish searching for instruction pointers, the pointers then point to the code that a hacker has stored in the memory. This code may just disrupt the functioning of the computer, or it might transfer information from the target computer to the hacker's computer.

The following code gives an example of a buffer overflow through a stack.

```
#include <stdio.h>
#include <string.h>
    void check (char *x)
    {
        char var1[20];
            strcpy (var1, x);
            printf (var1);
    }
        int main (int argc, char* argv[])
    {
check ("Though tired, the explorer set off yet again on a
quest for a sandwich");
            return 0;
    }
```

In this code, the main function verifies the function by passing the value, "Though tired, the explorer set off yet again on a quest for a sandwich". The check function receives the value and copies it to the variable named var1. var1 has a memory equivalent to 20 characters assigned to it. A buffer overflow is inevitable when the 70-character string is copied to the variable (var1). Once this code is executed, a message "Segmentation failure" appears. This indicates that a buffer overflow has occurred. Plainly, the extra 50 characters are pushed into the memory area adjacent to that which was set aside for var1. In this example, the application would break, but no surprise code would be run. Text such as "…explorer set off yet again on a quest for a sandwich" would not do anything, but copy %user%\evil.exe %windir%\calculator.exe would run evil.exe, whenever the calculator program was called. This is not a common application to call for, so it would make it much harder to figure out what happened and when.

Process of an Exploit

First the hacker searches for a chance to overflow the buffer. Next the hacker determines the memory assigned to the variable. Finally, the hacker specifies a value greater than the maximum capacity of the variable and either the stack becomes corrupted, causing the computer to crash, or the instruction pointer directs the program to the memory space that is specified by the hacker.

Applications may not be able to avoid buffer overflows since the variables in the applications do not verify or ensure that input data is not larger than allocated memory. A hacker checks for some specific functions to ascertain the possibility of a buffer overflow. Some functions susceptible to buffer overflow include the following:

```
strcpy
scanf
fgets
wstrcpy
wstrncat
sprintf
gets
strcat
```

First, in the initial phase, a hacker searches the binaries for the existence of functions. This aids in determining the functions that must be targeted while assigning values to the variables.

The second step that a hacker may perform is to check the memory size assigned to the targeted variable by entering progressively larger strings until the application breaks or the program error handlers show a dialog indicating that there is code in the application to ensure the value of the output variable is of a specific size or smaller. This allows the hacker to determine the length of input string as well as the target function. This detail can be determined by various methods. The hacker could just follow the above procedure or get a copy of the source code for the application and search for susceptible functions. Applications created prior to the discovery of the buffer overflow bug and subsequent patching provide possible attacks to a hacker.

The next step is to pass a value that has a larger memory allocated to the variable. The values that are passed do not necessarily have malicious code. A hacker can design input values in such a manner that while the buffer is being overflowed, it is also overwriting the values that are in the instruction pointer. The result will be that the program may execute the hacker's surprise application instead of returning to the original function. The hacker gains control over the processor, and any number of interesting results may occur. Aside from crashing the computer or running unexpected code, the overrun may allow the hacker to avoid the passing of a NULL value to a variable. NULL values may act as terminators and end the execution of the stack overflow.

The last step in buffer overflow involves the variable accepting the value and then overflowing the stack. The stack overflows and becomes corrupt when a greater value is passed. The application will execute the function stored in the memory area that is pointed by the instruction pointer. This has been changed by the hacker to perform specific steps.

Heap Overflows

It is important to understand the use of a heap before understanding heap overflows. A heap is similar to a stack in that it provides memory to the application to allow for operation of the various functions therein to complete the application's tasks. A heap provides a permanent memory space unlike the temporary memory space that is provided by a stack. The data stored in a heap can be used throughout various functions and commands. A heap is randomly accessed because it stores values statically. If a variable is stored within the memory range 1289 – A200, all functions will be able to find that variable's value. This is useful if values of variables are required across functions. Even though the main function of a heap is to provide memory to the executing functions and their variables, the size of a heap usually grows as new variables' values are introduced. The two functions used to expand the heap manually are `malloc()` and `brk()`.

Various differences between a stack and a heap are presented in Table 12-1.

Table 12-1   Differences between stacks and heaps

Differentiation Points	Stack	Heap
Memory	High	Low
Use	Calling Functions Short-term storage of variables	Long-term storage for data
Access	Frequently accessed	Randomly accessed
Expansion	Automatically	Automatically and using `malloc()` and `brk()`
Sequence of value storage	LIFO	--
Grows	Grows from higher to lower addresses	Grows from lower to higher addresses

Figure 12-2 illustrates the structure of heaps and stacks. Heaps tend to expand into higher reaches of memory, and stacks tend to grow downward from a ceiling memory location.

A heap overflow is known as the corruption of the instruction pointer, which points to the memory area where the function to be executed is stored. An instruction pointer may be corrupted by using a second heap or by replacing the code in the classes or structures that are stored in the heap. Changing the code to corrupt the pointer is known as trespassing.

More Methods for Causing a Buffer Overflow

Traditional methods for causing the buffer to overflow include providing input values that are greater than the memory allocated for a variable. This section details two other methods:

- Character-set decoding
- Nybble-to-byte compression

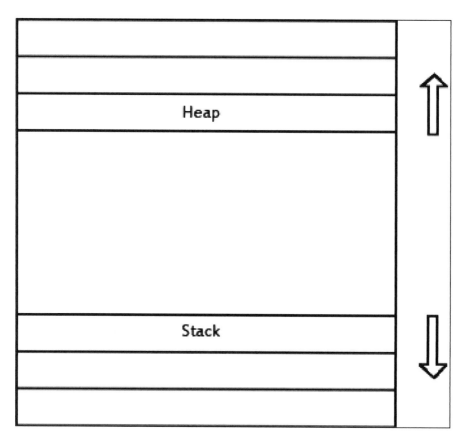

Figure 12-2   Structure of stacks and heaps

Character-Set Decoding

To circumvent stack buffer overflows, programmers create applications that do not allow extra characters to be accepted by a variable making the traditional buffer overflow method problematic. This check can be bypassed by using the character-set decoding method. This type of method uses the characters that are read differently by the computer and acquire larger space. While accepting the values, the variable first checks for the length of the input; after validation, it accepts the input. When the application reads these values, it will convert them into a different character set that uses more than one byte per character. Additional bytes of data may cause the input value to exceed the memory limitation of the variable.

Some examples of these characters are illustrated in Table 12-2.

Further examples of these character sets can be found at www.w3.org/TR/REC-html40/sgml/entities.html.

Table 12-2   Character conversions

Character Sign	Read As
Inverted exclamation sign	&#161
Cent sign	&#162
Pound sign	&#163
Currency sign	&#164
Section sign	&#167
Copyright sign	&#169
Degree sign	&#176
Right-pointing double angle quotation marks	&#187
Latin capital letter A with grave	&#192

Imagine a situation where an input string with a copyright sign and a section sign will be read as &#169&#167, yet considered as a 10-character string instead of a 2-character string, specified by the user. Even when a check is made for the length of the string, the value will be accepted by the variable because it is specified by the user as having only two characters. However, if the memory allotted to the character is only for two characters, it will ultimately lead to a buffer overflow. The code below could have been generated by using the concept of character-set decoding for stack overflow.

12

```
#include <stdio.h>
#include <string.h>
    void check (char *p)
    {
        char var1[3];
        if(strlen(p) >= 2){  printf( "\nError: The input
            value is more than 2 characters. Please enter a
            value that is fewer than 3 characters. \n\n");
        return;
    }
    strcpy (var1, p);
    printf (var1);
}
int main (int argc, char* argv[])
{
    char str[5];
    int result;
    printf( "Enter value:");
    result = scanf( "%s", str);
    check (str);
    return 0;
}
```

This code contains a verification that requests that the user specify a value. If the user specifies a string that exceeds two characters, the following error message will be generated: The input value is more than 2 characters. Please enter a value that is fewer than 3 characters. This shows that a check on the length of input is performed in this program. If the user specifies the value as ©§, the values will bypass the check with the variable accepting the value.

This code will not work because it must be compiled and executed in the same interface. The concept of character-set decoding is applicable to situations in which the user specifies a value from an HTML page. Character-set decoding becomes a weakness whenever a back-end script reads the code and, after expanding the value, results in a buffer overflow. The output of the following HTML code is shown in Figure 12-3.

```
<HTML>
PERSONAL INFORMATION FORM
<FORM METHOD="GET" ACTION = "http://172.17.68.154/cgi-bin/a.out">
Name: <INPUT TYPE="TEXT" SIZE="20" NAME="T1"><BR>
 <INPUT TYPE="SUBMIT" NAME="B1" VALUE="Submit">
 <INPUT TYPE="RESET" NAME="B2" VALUE="Reset"><BR>
</FORM>
</HTML>
```

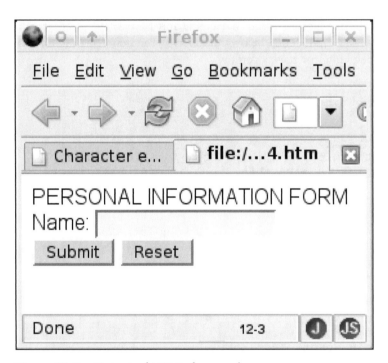

Figure 12-3 Output of HTML form code

When the HTML code is executed, the user must specify a value in the "Name" text box. A programmer has to code the page so that a check is made on the length of the specified string either in the front end, coded into the HTML, or in the back end, coded into the server-side CGI script that interprets the contents of the form's fields. This page has not been coded for verifying the length of the string, and that suggests that the character-set decoding method might work here.

The code below displays the back-end code that accepts the values specified by the user.

```
#include<iostream>
#include<stdio.h>
#include<string>
#include <signal.h>
void myfunc(int i)
{
cout << "Segmentation fault occurred";
exit(0);
}
int main()
{
signal (SIGSEGV,myfunc);
cout<<"Content-type:text/html"<<endl<<endl;
char input[20];
strcpy(input,getenv("QUERY_STRING"));
printf("The value of QUERY_STRING is: %s <BR>",input);
printf("The length of data stored in input variable is:
 %d <BR>",strlen(input));
return 0;
}
```

This code accepts the value specified by the user on the HTML page, and then saves it in the variable named input. This has a memory size of 20 assigned to it. If the user passes a value that requires a memory space that exceeds what the stack can handle, then the message Segmentation fault occurred is displayed. If a buffer overflow should occur, the key function has been coded to catch the SIGSEGV signal and call the myfunc function. The myfunc function may have been coded to take precautionary measures in the event of a buffer overflow. However, this code will show a segmentation failure message. The size of the stack is computer-dependent, and buffer overflow may not happen until a value that exceeds the stack size is specified.

Giving the value "öööööööööööööööö" for both the coded HTML page and the server-side script will generate a segmentation fault message because the data input will decode to fifty-eight characters.

The buffer overflow may occur when verification for the length of the input value is made at the client-side interface, and the back-end script accepts it without performing checks. Therefore, the client-side interface performs a check for the length of the string. If a user passes a value ©§, then the value will pass the check and reach the back-end script for more processing. If a check is not done by the server-side application, where the values read are &#169&#167 for a variable with a memory for only two characters, it will result in a buffer overflow. This can be avoided by performing double checks on the length of the input value supplied, as illustrated above.

Validation can be performed on the client side to increase server processing speed. However, client-side validation in HTML is extremely simple to defeat, so the server speed boost is at a potentially high cost. After the values have been checked by the client-side application, the server-side script then must perform another check. This double validation indicates to potential hackers that buffer overflow exploits are not possible on your Web site. To view this on a Web site, you must specify a search string with the aforementioned characters. The address bar will show the actual values that are read by the back-end application.

Figure 12-4 illustrates decoded input values as read by the back-end script in the address bar when the search term entered is @&^ as .%40%26%5E&.

Figure 12-4   Input as read by back-end script

Nybble-to-Byte Compression

This method involves compression of data that is passed as input value to the variables of the function that might be overflowed. This method is applied to use the buffer in a more efficient manner with a higher amount of data. It can be compared to zipping files to reduce traffic across the network. However, as a method to cause buffer overflows, it is not focused on reducing the traffic; rather, its focus is minimizing the size of the code so that hackers can double the amount of code in the buffer.

BUFFER OVERFLOWS: DETECTION AND PREVENTION

Now that you have been thoroughly impressed with the dangers of buffer overflow exploits, you may be interested to know how to identify programming practices and functions that are potentially vulnerable to buffer overflow.

Detecting Buffer Overflow

To identify the functions and variables that can lead to buffer overflows, the reaction of the application has to be checked whenever a large set of character data is supplied to a variable.

The function may include length verification, and thus return an error message if the data exceeds the expected size. This application is coded in a secure manner. A hacker may not be able to crack the computer with the buffer overflow method.

Checking the functions for buffer overflow can be a painstaking, tedious process because all variables that accept values must be checked. Additionally, precaution should be taken to ensure that the input data is provided in the correct format. Consider the following example: To check the possibility of a buffer overflow bug that is on an interactive Web page of a shopping mall, the expected format of data could be a name, date, item code, item name, or item details. Also, consider that the hidden data is also a part of the input that is given to the string. When specifying the input data, it is important to check that no NULL characters (empty fields) are being passed. This is important because they may discontinue the buffer overflow, thereby making it difficult to detect a buffer overflow bug.

Preventing Buffer Overflow

After a buffer overflow exploit has been detected, the probability of its existence in other applications by the same vendor is higher. A thorough check needs to be performed on those applications. The bug is typically fixed by programming the functions to perform an input validity check. This check refers to the code that checks for length data type in the string provided as input. Note that extra values should not be accepted. Also, the user should be asked to provide correct values for that variable. This is the wisest method to guard against a buffer overflow bug crashing the computer. One more method that can be applied is that of the function providing a null terminator after the values have been accepted. Providing a null terminator will prevent the buffer overflow even if additional values have been specified.

The destructive effect of the buffer overflow bug makes it crucial to verify that an application is not vulnerable to it. When creating new applications, you must verify the input string for accuracy on various parameters, which include length and format.

Consider developing specific programming guideline policies for your organization. Having, understanding, and applying secure-coding best practices may not be entirely foolproof, but they bring much value to the coding arena, including major protection against buffer overflow exploits.

Options are available to avoid the use of function calls that are vulnerable to buffer overflows. Table 12-3 illustrates such examples of unsafe function calls and their corresponding safe function calls.

Table 12-3 Alternative functions

Unsafe Function Call	Safe Function Call
gets()	fgets()
strcpy()	strncpy()
strcat()	strncat()
sprintf()	snprintf()

12

Checks must be made to validate the input values in both the new and old applications that were created prior to the buffer overflow bug being detected. The input values may have been specified by the user, automatically created by the computer, passed on from one function to another after processing, or calculated by performing certain operations like string concatenation and multiplication.

Software can be installed to keep a continuous check on a buffer overflow condition. This software must be updated with all available security patches.

CHAPTER SUMMARY

- ❑ Buffer overflow—a condition common to structured programming languages—happens when input applied to a variable is larger than the memory allotted to that variable. When an attacker sends input in excess of the expected range of the value, the target system will either crash or execute the attacker's malicious code.

- ❑ The buffer overflow bug targets the variables that are used by functions to store values. The variables that are defined in a function accept values from the users or generate them automatically. These variables are assigned a fixed memory space to store the data specified for the variable.

- ❑ The best ways to avoid buffer overflow are programmatic: keeping a check to see that no value greater than the memory assigned to the variable is specified for it, and defining the sequence of steps that the program has to follow in case of a buffer overflow.

- ❑ There are two main categories of buffer overflow: stack overflow and heap overflow.

- ❑ There are three main steps in the traditional process of buffer overflow: the hacker searches for a chance to overflow the buffer; the hacker determines the memory assigned to the variable; the hacker specifies a value greater than the maximum capacity of the variable.

- ❑ Two less-traditional methods used to cause buffer overflow conditions are character-set decoding and nybble-to-byte compression.

- ❑ To identify the functions and variables that can lead to buffer overflow, the reaction of the application has to be checked whenever a large set of character data is supplied to a variable.

- ❑ If a buffer overflow exploit has been detected, the probability of its existence in other applications by the same vendor is high.

- ❑ Buffer overflow can be prevented by programming the functions to perform an input validity check, having the function provide a null terminator after the values have been accepted, or using function calls that are not susceptible to buffer overflow conditions.

REVIEW QUESTIONS

1. Does a function in C automatically limit input larger than the memory buffer?

2. Will a null terminator prevent a buffer overflow?

3. What kinds of variables are stored in a stack?

4. What is a heap used for?

5. In running a buffer overflow exploit, does the hacker have to have a trusted relationship with the target PC?

6. What character decodes to the string "&#162"?

7. What does the error "A segmentation fault has occurred" mean?

8. How would a hacker go about defeating the client-side validation on a Web form?

Indicate whether the sentence or statement is true or false.

9. _____ UNIX was written in Java and rewritten later in C, which caused many buffer overflow problems.

10. _____ Bugs are typically fixed by programming the functions to perform an input validity check.

11. _____ Stacks are where user variables are stored.

12. _____ Heaps are where elastic variables used by more than one function are stored.

13. _____ Stacks cannot be increased and decreased automatically.

14. _____ Heaps are incremented automatically and manually by using the commands `malloc()` and `brk()`.

15. _____ You can purge heaps and stacks by running "Disk Cleanup."

16. _____ Validation performed on the client side decreases server processing speed.

The following functions are unsafe and subject to buffer overflows. Match them to the list of safe functions below.

    a. `strcpy()`

    b. `gets()`

    c. `sprintf()`

    d. `strcat()`

17. _____ `fgets()`

18. _____ `strncpy()`

19. _____ `strncat()`

20. _____ `snprintf()`

12

HANDS-ON PROJECT

As the most popular exploit on the Internet, buffer overflow may be the hardest exploit to avoid. As a vulnerability built into various programming languages, including the C language, it is just not possible to patch the problems on a wholesale, global basis. The C language is the basis of UNIX, Linux, and Windows, and was used to create most of the utilities you use today; thus, the fact that buffer overflow is a vulnerability inherent in the C language itself means that it affects many different types of systems worldwide.

**HANDS-ON
PROJECTS**

Project 12-1

1. Using a word processor, create a chart like the one below. In the middle column of your chart, explain the purpose of each of the vulnerable functions listed on the left. In the rightmost column, list the safer alternatives to use in place of these functions. These functions are part of the C programming language.

Vulnerable Functions	Purpose of Function	Safer Functions
Strcpy()		
Strcat()		
Sprintf()		
Gets()		

13

PROGRAMMING EXPLOITS

> **After reading this chapter and completing the exercises, you will be able to:**
>
> ♦ Describe the evolution of programming exploits
> ♦ Recognize vulnerabilities in ActiveX controls
> ♦ Identify steps to counter vulnerabilities in ActiveX controls
> ♦ Recognize vulnerabilities in VBScript
> ♦ Identify steps to counter vulnerabilities in VBScript
> ♦ Recognize vulnerabilities in HTML
> ♦ Identify steps to counter vulnerabilities in HTML
> ♦ Recognize vulnerabilities in Java and JavaScript
> ♦ Identify steps to counter vulnerabilities in Java and JavaScript

Programming exploits are the defects in various programming languages that are used to develop server-side and client-side applications. Some programming flaws are discovered accidentally, and some are detected by programmers who administer or run the applications. A very few are discovered by attackers.

During the early days of the Internet, most Web pages were static HTML, so programming exploits could only be aimed at the client-side browsers with which the users viewed the text Web content. This is still happening, and browsers are intensely scrutinized for vulnerabilities. As the technology has progressed, dynamic content became normal, with client-side and server-side scripts built into the HTML page code to add functionality to sites. This technology opened up more browser hacks and more server-side exploits. Current technology requires data-driven, interactive Web sites, where the content of the pages you see is the output of server-side technology. Data-driven sites contain thousands of pages of server-side code to provide a simple, useful interface for e-commerce, account management, and other site types across all categories. Some private photo album sites contain server-side, data-driven content and technology that if custom-coded would cost thousands of dollars to implement. Through open source, this technology is available for customization and modification for free. Interactive code is also vulnerable to hacking and can be prepared to attack browser vulnerabilities. Technologies and languages continue to emerge, and exploits continue to be found. Much has been done to improve security in transactions, but vulnerabilities within the languages and programming techniques have continued to surface.

In this chapter, you will become aware of programming exploits within ActiveX controls, VBScript, HTML, JavaScript, and the programming language Java.

The difference between a **script** and a programming language is that, for an application to be used, it needs to be compiled for the environment in which it is running. But a script runs uncompiled. Among compiled languages, Java is preferred for Web applications because applications designed in Java are platform independent. C++ or Python applications need to be compiled to run within specific operating systems. When compiled for a Microsoft Windows environment, the application is given an EXE extension and adjusted in myriad ways to run on Windows machines. The compiled application will not run in any other environment, and in some cases, it will only run in one specific version of Windows. Java, in contrast, is designed to run in a virtual environment called the Java Virtual Machine or Java Runtime Environment (JRE). The JRE is compiled for the most commonly used operating systems, and it is installed on most computers that are connected to the Internet. If you click on a link to a Java application, a file is downloaded to a cache on your computer, and started and run within your computer's Java Virtual Machine.

To be quite honest, platform independence is a misnomer. Java programs do not work without a JRE, so they are platform specific to the JRE. Java applications are not really acting independently, and this is one of the safeguards built into the Java language. C, C++, Fortran, and others, are all designed to interact more directly with the operating system and the hardware, and are more dangerous and powerful because of that. Thus, C++, Visual Basic, and other such compiled languages are very uncommon as Web page components specifically because of their potential to cause swift and irrevocable harm to the data stored on hardware or even to reconfigure the hardware itself without user interaction. The Java language is included in this chapter because of its prevalence on the Internet and the vast number of machines with JRE installed.

ActiveX controls are also compiled applications, though they are not as useful as Java applications because they were originally designed for use within a Windows environment within Internet Explorer. Though Mozilla-derived browsers ship with ActiveX support for a number of operating systems (running as a client on a JVM), Microsoft was contending as late as June 2006 that ActiveX is only optimized for Internet Explorer running on Windows XP.

ActiveX Controls

ActiveX controls are Component Object Model (COM) objects that can be embedded in a variety of applications. ActiveX controls are stand-alone compiled applications designed to make it possible to link and allow interactions between variously developed applications. ActiveX is a non-trivial part of most Windows applications, as ActiveX controls can invoke other applications through COM-defined interfaces. ActiveX controls can also be used on a Web page directly by using the Object tag or indirectly with script tags.

Web designers and Windows application developers can acquire all sorts of ActiveX controls from online vendors to make their applications work better. They can also produce their own customized ActiveX controls. Developers can make custom-built ActiveX controls available to other developers on the Internet. It is suggested that developers sign their ActiveX controls and not use controls that are not signed. A recent Google search for "Free ActiveX Controls" returned a list of almost 11 million pages.

13

From a developer's viewpoint, the perfect ActiveX control is not difficult to find, so almost any conceivable function can be built into a new application—from simple shell-scripting commands to program enhancements to stand-alone applications—to perform complex data manipulation. This wide range of functionality makes ActiveX controls interesting to attackers. It is critical for developers to use only authenticated controls, so it is important to get control components only from known and safe sources. With the awesome number of safe sources for ActiveX controls, there are still a number of ways that a hacked ActiveX control can get onto a user's machine. The page a control is on might be designed specifically to distribute the control, or perhaps the site was hacked and the malicious control was added without the knowledge of the site owner. It is also possible that the site developer was not careful in choosing ActiveX controls.

Up until 2006, when Microsoft issued the patch that disables autoplay of ActiveX controls, ActiveX was becoming a widespread way to perform surreptitious installation of spyware and adware on Windows machines. The method is still available because not all Windows machines have been patched to prevent it. But it is possible to imagine a time when the only way to distribute malicious ActiveX controls will be to include them in (presumably) safe, requested software.

Vulnerabilities in ActiveX Controls

The design flaw in ActiveX that allowed attackers to run arbitrary code was discovered in 1997 and published by Computer Associates (currently known only as CA) in 2000. Microsoft has been issuing patches in an application-by-application fashion since 2000. The patch for Internet

Explorer to curtail "silent autoplay of ActiveX controls" was issued by Microsoft in 2006. The design flaw in ActiveX is that ActiveX can do anything the user can do. If the user has administrative privileges, then the ActiveX control does as well. ActiveX does not, by default, operate in a "sandbox" environment as Java does, so the potential for damage, corruption, and general mayhem in any part of any Windows installation is very high.

Security threats from ActiveX controls occur whenever a user accesses a Web site with an ActiveX control that is registered on the user's computer. Prior to the patching of Internet Explorer, ActiveX controls were downloading silently from any Web page that contained them. The noticeable effect of this might be music playing automatically when a site is loaded in the browser, or a stock-ticker application updating automatically. All of this is exactly what one might expect, and is not a bad thing. The effect made Web sites easier to use, but it also made "drive-by installation" and activation of arbitrary code just as simple and effortless. Microsoft's Internet Explorer was entirely vulnerable to attack, by virtue of its tight integration with the Windows operating system and ubiquitous use of ActiveX and other COM controls. The default installation of IE allowed all ActiveX controls to run silently (with no notice to or input from the user). For many years, it has been possible to set the security preferences in Internet Explorer to require user input or disallow the use of ActiveX or scripts. But it is still possible to entirely disable protection based on page or domain. The most recent Internet Explorer versions check for the validity of ActiveX controls and authorization of controls provided by a trusted authority, as well as whether controls have been altered.

Attackers can use ActiveX to modify resources on an implementation of Windows in three ways. The first method is direct commands. An attacker specifies certain commands that the compromised ActiveX control executes upon download, such as editing the executable PATH or deleting/replacing a specific file. The second method is indirect attack, such as editing the preferences of Internet Explorer to make an unsafe site of the attacker's choice appear in the Trusted Sites list in Internet Options; or to change the default search engine to one of the attacker's choice; or, perhaps, to disable personal firewall software. These two attack modalities can be defeated by setting the security and privacy controls to disallow unsafe ActiveX behavior or unsigned components.

A third way is deceiving the browser security checks to indicate that an ActiveX control is secure. Initially, Internet Explorer checks for the signature of an ActiveX tool. If medium security settings are enabled on a computer, then a user is offered a dialog window where they are given the choice to download the component that is marked "Unsafe." An attacker can defeat security checks by marking their control as "Safe for Scripting." "Safe for Scripting" means the control can take any arguments or indicates that the ActiveX control is safe for any possible use of its property, methods, or events. If a browser detects a component that is marked safe, it downloads the component. Deceptive use of the "Safe for Scripting" value allows the attacker to successfully and silently hack the computer. Two examples of such inappropriate use of the "Safe for Scripting" flag are illustrated in the Microsoft Security Bulletin MS99-032, which describes a patch to correct two issues. This bulletin identifies the scriptlet.typlib and Eyedog components as illegitimately using this flag because of the following attributes:

> *scriptlet.typelib is a control used by developers to generate Type Libraries for Windows Script Components. It is marked as "safe for scripting", but should not be because it allows local files to be created or modified. The patch removes the "safe for scripting" marking, thereby causing IE to request confirmation from the user before loading the control.*

> *Eyedog is a control used by diagnostic software in Windows. It is marked as "safe for scripting", but should not be because it allows registry information to be queried and machine characteristics to be gathered. In addition, one of the control's methods is vulnerable to a buffer overrun attack. The patch sets the so-called "kill bit", which prevents it from loading within IE.[1]*

Security Measures

The COM architecture was first released with Windows 95, and soon after, developers realized its enormous potential to improve and standardize the many tasks that are executable by COM (Component Object Model), DCOM (Distributed or remote COM), and ActiveX (the preferred marketing term for COM). The simplicity and availability of these controls have also prompted malefactors to develop methods to access networked computers using the same technologies.

There are many security methods available to prevent attackers from using ActiveX maliciously. But to be effective, the methods must be embraced by both the developers and end users of technologies upon which ActiveX has an impact.

Application developers and ActiveX control developers must write tight, tense code so the more obvious vulnerabilities are absent—for example, requiring variable-boundary checks to avoid buffer overflow conditions, and not employing, as components of their work, controls and methods that are known to be compromised or easily defeated. The proper behavior and also the failure behavior of each component should produce predictable, not unexpected, results.

After the controls have been developed in adherence to secure coding guidelines, developers must guarantee that the tool enables the user's browser to properly identify it as safe to use and download. To ensure this, developers need to sign the tool and obtain a security certificate for the control from a certificate provider such as VeriSign and Thawte. The certificate contains important details about the developer. This helps users identify the developer in case the tool causes any problems. Browsers check for the validity of ActiveX controls as well as the integrity of the tool after the controls have been signed for validity. It will reduce the probability of attackers using ActiveX as a weapon when secure coding guidelines are standard and all valid ActiveX controls are signed and certified.

13

ActiveX controls are useful and offer expanded functionality to users. As an end user, one is wise to assume that the developers have ignored all security standards and that the tool is always suspect. To ensure that a downloaded tool is safe for use, users have to perform certain checks.

First, users must check that their Internet Explorer browser is the most recent and stable version available. Users still using Windows 95 or earlier are encouraged to upgrade their computer and operating system to later versions. You are probably having difficulties with many of the newer technologies available anyway, and you are susceptible to many annoying security risks and have no access to security patches.

People still using Windows 98 are encouraged to upgrade hardware and operating system as well, and for the same reason. If there is some compelling reason why you cannot or do not choose to upgrade, then use an alternative browser, such as Netscape, Mozilla Firefox, or Opera, none of which are susceptible to ActiveX exploits.

If you are running Windows 2000, make sure you are running Internet Explorer 6.0 and have the newest security patches in place. Then set your Internet Options security setting to High if you want no ActiveX control to be allowed, or to Medium if you wish to be informed when an ActiveX control is requesting permission for download.

If you are running Windows XP, make sure you are running IE6 or possibly IE7 (which has better security features), and set your Internet security level to at least Medium.

Figure 13-1 shows the Security Settings dialog box from the Internet Options dialog box, where you may set all of the scripting and ActiveX control settings to custom values. As depicted, the dialog box shows default Medium-level values.

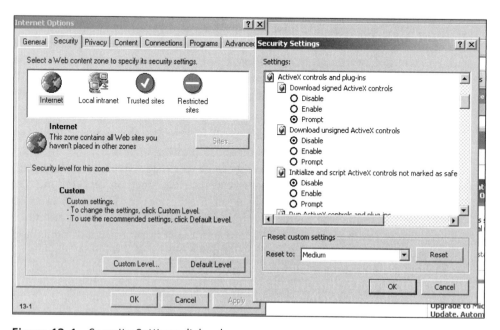

Figure 13-1   Security Settings dialog box

Properly configured security settings make browsing with Internet Explorer far safer. However, in many cases, the quickest solution for end users is to use a different browser, such as Firefox or Opera.

VBScript

VBScript, Microsoft's answer to Netscape's JavaScript language, is loosely based on the Visual Basic programming language, but is much simpler. It is supported by Internet Explorer and enables Web authors to add interactive controls such as buttons and scrollbars to their Web pages. These scripts can be run on any computer upon which the scripting engine has been installed. Microsoft provides a comparison of features that are supported by Visual Basic and left out of VBScript in the MSDN library.

Vulnerabilities in VBScript

VBScript is a one of the scripting languages that can be used within HTML tags to produce a dynamic HTML page. Internet Explorer and browsers based on IE are vulnerable to threats from VBScripts. The similarities between VBScript and Visual Basic make it easy for programmers and hackers to identify bugs and vulnerabilities in VBScript. Because this scripting language is used for client-side scripting, the code can help hackers get unauthorized access to the target computer quickly and efficiently. One of the most common exploits used on the Internet is a buffer overflow. Malicious VBScript can be used to produce a buffer overflow in an application, resulting in system failure or execution of arbitrary code on the victim computer. As a scripting language, it can also be used as a method to insert harmful code on the client computer.

An attacker who wants to use VBScript to insert a harmful ActiveX control can make an HTML page, which downloads an ActiveX control when opened by a user on his or her computer. The potential of VBScript to cause damage to a system may be understood through the functioning of the worm known as Love Letter.

The Love Letter worm used the Microsoft Outlook Address Book to replicate itself. An e-mail would arrive in the potential victim's inbox, from a known correspondent (who had been infected with the worm). The e-mail had an attachment, which when opened, executed a VBScript that infected the new victim and saved its VBScript to many places around the victim's hard drive, ensuring that it was reinstalled whenever the computer was restarted. Then it used the new victim's MS Outlook Address Book to send itself to all of the new victim's contacts. Finally, the worm placed a registry entry that caused the VBScript to run whenever the computer was restarted. It also added a registry key that launched a Trojan horse password stealer whenever Internet Explorer was launched.

13

Countering VBScript Vulnerabilities

If you are an end user, the most obvious method to avoid dangerous VBScripts is to use a browser in which VBScript does not run. You can either turn off scripts in Internet Explorer and disable auto-run features in Outlook, or you can use alternate browsers and mail clients. There is no way to check before you open the page to make sure the VBScript is safe. If you are unable to follow any of the preceding suggestions, you must at least uncheck the "Hide file extensions of known file types" check box in the File Options dialog box, accessible through the Tools menu of a Windows Explorer window or from Control Panel's window. After clearing that check box and clicking Apply, click the button that says, "Make all windows like this one", and click "Yes" when it asks if you are sure. At least you will not be fooled by a file with a doubled extension, like loveletter.txt.ocx, which is a common and sneaky way to get you to launch malicious attachments. This will save you from some worms using VBScript delivery systems.

If you are administering a network:

- Do not allow users to use IE or Outlook.

- Have standardized bookmark files of approved sites and an updated ACL of approved and unapproved domains on the gateway router.

- Run a centrally administered antivirus application across all of the Windows machines in the network.

- Run an intrusion-detection system that closes down the network access of any machine that starts mass-mailing anything.

If you are the administrator of a Web site:

- Run an antivirus application on your Web server to search for known bad ActiveX controls within the /home, /var/www, and c:\inetpub\ directories or any other directories where users have write and execute privileges.

If you are a Web programmer:

- Test your forms and other application code for possible buffer overflow vulnerabilities.

- Make sure your pages have not been hacked and modified.

HTML

Hypertext Markup Language (HTML) is the most basic script used to develop Web pages and uses a set of markup tags, such as <script> </script>, to define the structure of Web pages. Browsers represent pages by interpreting these tags. HTML is not a dynamic language, and cannot be executed successfully except within a Web browser. It was developed to present data or information in a platform-independent manner. A programmer cannot guarantee what machine or operating system Internet users might be using, so HTML provides a simple way to get one's information to the widest possible user base. Below is an example of an extremely simple Web page that could be written in notepad.exe or any other straight text editor. Our example page is titled Simple Simon the Pirate and contains the phrase, "Yo, ho, ho, and a bottle of water!"

```
<html>
<head>
<title>Simple Simon the Pirate</title>
</head>
<body>
<p>Yo, ho, ho and a bottle of water!</p>
</body>
</html>
```

HTML is essentially bulletproof and benign as long as it is used to display static text. But arbitrary requirements for more finished and sophisticated pages have required the development of many more tags and formatting conventions. HTML is not a formatting language, so much has been done to overcome the limitations inherent in HTML and browser configurations. End users can override any text or display color you define; they can turn off your background images and change the font size and color to fit their desires.

With increased complexity came increased opportunities for hackers to discover vulnerabilities. As password protection arose to restrict access to some areas within some sites, attackers learned search engine tricks to find unprotected areas within the protected sites; once inside unprotected areas, they could sometimes navigate to protected areas.

Vulnerabilities in HTML

HTML vulnerabilities are almost always vulnerabilities within applications that use HTML as a carrying protocol to transfer or display data. Transfer of data over networks by insecure plaintext protocols can also offer many opportunities for attackers to interfere with data delivery.

Buffer Overflow

This vulnerability exploits an unchecked buffer in Internet Explorer processing HTML elements such as FRAME and IFRAME elements. It is used by Internet Explorer, Outlook Express, and Windows Explorer and is performed using the res:// local resource protocol. Once the buffer overflow has been achieved, the attacker can run arbitrary code at the level of privilege enjoyed by the user on the victim machine.

HTML E-Mail

In 2001, when HTML e-mail was new and exciting, scripts within the pretty HTML e-mails were run silently and automatically, which led attackers to craft HTML e-mails to take advantage of that helpful feature. This helpful feature has since been patched in Internet Explorer (MS01-020), Outlook, and Outlook Express for Windows. This might be called a scripting exploit, but it has been treated as an HTML flaw in the literature.

Remote Access

In 2005, a vulnerability was found within Microsoft's HTML Help system that would allow a remote user to take complete control of a Windows PC (Microsoft Bulletin MS05-026). It is possible because the `window.showHelp()` function in Internet Explorer 5.x does not restrict HTML Help files (.chm) from being executed from the local host.

A similar vulnerability was discovered in 2005 in the Nikto application running in a Windows environment. If and when a Nikto operator could be tricked into scanning a malicious Web site, an unsanitized server header value returned in the HTTP response from a Web site. The information returned was used to generate an HTML-based vulnerability report. This can be exploited to execute arbitrary HTML and script code in the My Computer zone when the vulnerability report is viewed. Nikto is a security tool for finding vulnerabilities on Web servers.

Countering HTML Vulnerabilities

The most effective way to counter HTML-related exploits is to make sure you are up to date in your patching, and are paying attention when new exploits are reported. Perhaps it is uncomfortable for the average end user to keep up with the volume of errors and vulnerabilities found, but even that user can activate the automated patch management software that has been available since Windows 2000. It is also sensible to turn off services and features that you (1) know to be vulnerable to attack, (2) do not understand, or (3) do not use. If you find your Web surfing to be disrupted by setting the security slider to High, set it to Medium and ask for a dialog at every turn. Avoid known dangerous sites by installing and updating security software. An example of one is SpywareBlaster. This is a tool that automatically adds the URLs for known dangerous sites to your Internet security dialog as untrusted sites, so that scripts and downloads are always accompanied by a Windows dialog asking if you want to take anything from the known untrusted site. This is a simple function and one that you could do without a software utility, if you have the time. There are more than 30,000 suspect or known dangerous sites on the SpywareBlaster database.

Secure transfer of data has been made available by protocols such as Secure Sockets Layer (SSL). SSL encrypts the session, as well as the data that is being used in the session, using Public-Key Infrastructure (PKI). PKI uses public and private keys to encrypt and decrypt data. It is not possible to decrypt data within a reasonable time frame unless the keys are available. The way Internet Explorer handled SSL was discovered to be susceptible to a man-in-the-middle exploit, and tools such as sslsniff were developed to help script kiddies perform this exploit. Generating random encryption keys of 40 or 128 bits in length has solved this problem.

JAVA AND JAVASCRIPT

Although there are many similarities between Java and JavaScript, there are distinct differences between the two. Java is a programming language that is compiled into applications or applets. Java applications are stand-alone applications that either run on the server or are downloaded to the client machine. JavaScript is a scripting language that runs between <script> tags in a Web page. A JavaScript cannot operate on its own, and is not compiled to run.

Java

Java is an object-oriented programming language (OOP) developed by Sun Microsystems. Java is designed to run in a platform-independent manner using Java Runtime Environment (JRE) installed on the client computer as its sandbox. In Java, programs are not designed procedurally as they are in C++, which uses an if/then decision tree. In Java, each function is modularized. You may not have to design a printing subroutine for your Java program. There is a printing object that you can just plug into the new application. Java programmers can define objects and use them. OOP objects do not have feedback loops built in. A given object has specific, known inputs and outputs and the variable upstream in the process doesn't need to have feedback to know which kind of data to send to the object. The data sent to a particular object is always the same. With this low-level modularization, there is less of a chance that updating one piece of the application will break other parts. Comparing OOP to procedural programming is a bit like comparing the construction of a modular dwelling to that of a custom home. Java was intended to be developed quickly with pretested parts rather than requiring tests throughout to see if the whole construction will work. The tools supplied by Sun and other vendors provide an option to generate Java applets to provide functionality on the Internet. Java-enabled browsers may have built-in support to run applets, or they can run an applet through a plug-in.

Java is also designed to be machine-safe. Java can only act upon other objects within the JRE. Java has no access to write, modify, or delete files on the hard drive or to modify the operating system.

JavaScript

JavaScript is a scripting language developed by Netscape Communications Corporation, and is similar to VBScript in terms of implementation. However, it has far greater utility, as almost every browser on almost every platform is JavaScript-enabled. Viewing the source code of an HTML Web page may expose the structure of JavaScript used to provide interactive content within that page. In contrast to Java, JavaScript is not used to generate stand-alone applications. However, like Java, it does require a runtime environment. JavaScript can be executed in browsers like Netscape Communicator, Opera, Internet Explorer, Mozilla, Firefox, Galeon, Epiphany, Konqueror and others, which have a built-in JavaScript interpreter. As a script, the network bandwidth and client-side memory resource use is less than that required for the larger and more robust Java. It is comparatively easy to learn, yet can be used to develop complex scripts. The following code is an example of a simple JavaScript form:

13

```
<FORM method="POST" action="mailto:webmaster-email@yourdomain.
com" onSubmit="alert('Message being delivered');">
<B>Please type your name: </B><input NAME="username" size="35">
<B>Please type your address: </B><input NAME="address" size="40">
<B>Please type your favourite colour: </
B><input NAME="color" size="15">
<!-- Many more fields could be included -->
<input type=submit onBlur="doVerify()" value="Send Request!">
<input type=reset value="Reset">
<SCRIPT LANGUAGE="javascript">
    function doVerify()
{
   location.href = "http://www.yourdomain.com/forms/thanks-page.
htm"
//This can be directed anywhere  (a double-/
 comments out the line)
}
</script>
</form>
```

Security Vulnerabilities in Java

The vulnerabilities of Java are of three sorts: client-side malevolent applets, server-side cross-scripting, and server-side address spoofing. Of the numerous "Alerts" listed on the Sun Microsystems Support site, a substantial percentage are related to vulnerabilities in the JRE, which can result in applets arbitrarily giving themselves elevated privileges. Some are updates for Java Web Application Server and other Servers running on Sun operating systems, some are related to the Sun Java Desktop (a GUI environment for Linux and Solaris), and some are revisions of alerts from earlier years. McAfee's virus list (http://search. mcafee.com/) returns the following results for threats based on operating system and "Java Applet":

Category	Threats named	% of total
Linux	517	05.40%
UNIX	301	03.15%
Apple	36	00.38%
Mac	66	00.69%
Windows	8650	90.39%
All OS's	9570	100.01% (rounding error)
Java applet	43	00.45%
JavaScript	83	00.87
VBScript	305	03.19

The list above includes quite a lot of historical data, ranging back to 1999 and before. Patches are available for most (if not all) of the threats listed. As of this writing, all known Java applet threats are less than one-half of one percent of all named threats known to affect all of the popular operating systems, and most of them were low-level threats.

Because Java is a platform-independent technology, issues such as malevolent applets, which are really JRE vulnerabilities in disguise, can be used against any platform that has the JRE installed. There is one set of circumstances that might mitigate against the problem being a JRE issue, and that is in the event that the victim machine is using Microsoft's VM to run Java applets. The philosophy underlying Java is that it only works within the sandbox of the JRE. So it is a surprise any time an applet can break through the sandbox wall or trick a user into performing an action that allows code to be released into the operating system. Sometimes the error is within another program that uses Java applets in an unsafe way. Client-side attacks include:

- Attacks on file integrity—These attacks delete or modify files on the client, allowing the attacker to read, steal, damage, or delete other files on the client. This kind of attack can cause the victim to stop responding or add useful functionality for the attacker.

- Buffer overflow—Many variables in the predefined Java libraries do not look for buffer overflow vulnerability. As with other buffer overflow events, these may not actually be attacks, as they can be caused by innocent overloading of variables.

- Storm attacks—These attacks divert resources by sending large bursts of packets to the victim. They can also fill disk space with small files until the victim is unable to function, or create thousands of windows in the GUI to deplete resources and make effective work impossible.

- Denial-of-service attacks—These attacks divert the heavy traffic of a network to a particular server and overload that server's resources so it cannot process valid requests.

- Disclosure attacks—These attacks transfer information from a client computer to a remote computer. Attacks in this category include logging keystrokes of a computer and transferring the log file to another computer.

- Annoyance attacks—These attacks include any of a large number of amusing computer tricks, from playing audio files to ejecting and closing the CD-ROM drive at irregular intervals. There may be no malevolent payload to applets such as these, but they tend to unsettle the recipient in the same way as if you returned home to find that your 25-inch TV had been replaced with another of equal value and the den had been dusted. No real harm is done, but you know irrevocably that someone can plan and perform time-consuming and complicated entry into your personal space.

Vulnerabilities in JavaScript

The vulnerabilities in JavaScript are similar to and can be compared to those in VBScript because both scripting languages are delivered on HTML pages bracketed with <script> tags. However, the similarities in vulnerabilities do not mean that the same set of functions can be used to hack both the languages. Some of the tasks that can be performed due to

JavaScript vulnerabilities are: sending e-mail messages with information about the target computer to a client; opening and closing applications on the target computer; and modifying files on the victim's computer. The main threat posed by JavaScript is that it may be used to download components on a user's computer without his or her knowledge.

Countering Java and JavaScript Vulnerabilities

The best preventative measure for an end user is to perform all updates as soon as they are available, and to keep the virus definitions in their antivirus or security program updated. Then set the Internet Options Control Panel to ask for permission before running JavaScripts or downloading Java applets. Users are advised to check the authenticity of the validation signatures attached to applets and scripts, especially when the browser sends up a dialog stating that the script is suspect. It is possible for attackers to copy scripts and attach them to malicious code files. The victim's browser then might identify the script as safe. This can be avoided by double-checking the script's authentication. One further consideration: check for security of links available on the signed scripts. This is necessary because a client browser window may open signed scripts and the linked function, with the idea that all interactions with the signed scripts are secure. The pages the links point to could have been hacked or modified in an unsafe way.

Programmers are advised to develop and adhere to secure programming guidelines, and sign their scripts. Signing the scripts is a way to send a message to users' browsers that the script is safe, and it also prevents tampering by hackers, as that would be reflected in the signature. The creators of Java have plugged most of the holes in the JRE, and Microsoft has plugged the hole in the Microsoft VM.

CHAPTER SUMMARY

❑ Programming exploits are the defects in various programming languages that are used to develop server-side and client-side applications.

❑ ActiveX controls are stand-alone compiled applications designed to make it possible to link and allow interactions between variously developed applications.

❑ The design flaw in ActiveX is that it can do anything the user can do, allowing attackers to easily install and run arbitrary code.

❑ Attackers can use ActiveX to modify resources on an implementation of Windows in three ways: direct commands, indirect attack, and deceiving the browser security checks.

❑ To safeguard against attacks, end users should install the most recent and stable version of Internet Explorer available, upgrade their computer and operating system if using Windows 95, and upgrade their hardware and operating system if using Windows 98. Alternatively, end users can switch to a browser other than Internet Explorer.

❑ VBScript is loosely based on the Visual Basic programming language but is much simpler. VBScript can be used within HTML tags to produce a dynamic HTML page. Internet Explorer and browsers based on IE are vulnerable to threats from VBScripts.

❑ One of the most common exploits used on the Internet is a buffer overflow. Malicious VBScript can be used to produce a buffer overflow in an application, and can also be used to insert harmful code on a client computer.

❑ If you are administering a network, do not allow use of IE or Outlook; have standardized bookmark files of approved sites and an updated ACL of approved and unapproved domains on the gateway router; run a centrally administered antivirus application across all of the Windows machines in the network; and run an intrusion-detection system that closes down the network access of any machine that starts mass-mailing anything.

❑ If you are the administrator of a Web site, run an antivirus application on your Web server to search for known bad ActiveX controls within any directories where users have write and execute privileges.

❑ If you are a Web programmer, test your forms and other application code for possible buffer overflow vulnerabilities, and make sure your pages have not been hacked and modified.

❑ Hypertext Markup Language (HTML) is the most basic script used to develop Web pages. HTML is not a dynamic language, and cannot be successfully executed outside of a Web browser. HTML is essentially bulletproof and benign as long as it is used to display static text; however, the development of formatting conventions to overcome HTML's inherent limitations has opened the door to hackers.

❑ HTML vulnerabilities include buffer overflow, HTML e-mail exploits, and remote access exploits.

❑ The most effective way to counter HTML-related exploits is to keep up with the latest patches and pay attention when new exploits are reported. Secure transfer of data has been made available through such protocols as Secure Sockets Layer (SSL) and Public-Key Infrastructure (PKI).

❑ Java is an object-oriented programming language (OOP) developed by Sun Microsystems and designed to run in a platform-independent manner using Java Runtime Environment (JRE) installed on the client computer as its sandbox.

❑ JavaScript is a scripting language developed by Netscape Communications Corporation. It is similar to VBScript in terms of implementation, yet it has far greater utility, as almost every browser on almost every platform is JavaScript-enabled.

❑ There are three types of Java vulnerabilities: client-side malevolent applets, server-side cross-scripting, and server-side address spoofing.

❑ Client-side attacks include: attacks on file integrity, buffer overflow, storm attacks, denial-of-service attacks, disclosure attacks, and annoyance attacks.

❑ Tasks that can be performed due to JavaScript vulnerabilities include sending e-mail messages with information of the target computer to a client, opening and closing

13

applications on the target computer, modifying files on the victim's computer, and downloading components on a user's computer.

❑ The best preventive measure for end users is to perform all updates as soon as they are available, keep virus definitions in their antivirus or security program updated, and set the Internet Options settings to ask for permission before running JavaScripts or downloading Java applets. Programmers are advised to develop and adhere to secure programming guidelines and to sign their scripts.

REVIEW QUESTIONS

1. What is the difference between programming languages and scripting languages?

2. Does Visual Basic Script run on Mozilla browsers?

3. Is ActiveX just another Internet protocol?

4. What does COM stand for in reference to Windows COM controls?

5. Is ActiveX a scripting language?

6. How did Love Letter work?

7. What are the three sorts of Java exploits?

8. What is the difference between JRE and Microsoft's VM?

9. For an average Windows user, what is the best protection from programming exploits?

Indicate whether the sentence or statement is true or false.

10. _____ When the Internet was young, there were no servers.

11. _____ Data-driven sites contain thousands of pages of server-side code to provide a simple, useful interface for e-commerce and other site types across all categories.

12. _____ The difference between a script and a programming language is that a script runs under no control at all.

13. _____ Java is a script.

14. _____ C++ or Python applications need to be compiled to run within specific operating systems.

15. _____ Java is designed to run in a virtual environment called the Java Virtual Machine or Java Application Reservation (JAR).

16. _____ Java applications are not really acting independently, and this is one of the safeguards built into the Java language.

17. _____ Web designers and Windows application developers can acquire all sorts of ActiveX controls from online vendors to make their applications work better.

18. _____ ActiveX was becoming a great way to perform surreptitious installation of spyware and adware on Macintosh and Linux machines.

19. _____ Microsoft's answer to Netscape's JavaScript language was .Net.

20. _____ Malicious VBScript can be used to produce a buffer overflow in an application, resulting in system failure or execution of arbitrary code on the victim computer.

HANDS-ON PROJECTS

We will focus on Web programming exploits and the ways that they can be reduced. The most common exploits are designed around buffer-overrun vulnerabilities and known weaknesses in Web applications. As an administrator, your main resource is to update your patching promptly to keep incidents exploiting known vulnerabilities low. But as a Web designer, you might be able to do more.

HANDS-ON PROJECTS

Project 13-1

1. Research the "Get" and "Post" form submission methods.

   How does Get send form information? _____

   _____

   How does Post send information? _____

   _____

HANDS-ON PROJECTS

Project 13-2

1. Is it better to strip field input by inclusive or exclusive rules?_____

   Why? _____

   _____

2. Give an example of an inclusive validation rule (real HTML code, please).

   _____

   Does your code work? _____

13

Project 13-3

1. What are the dangers of client-side form-field validation? _____

   _____

2. What is the value of client-side validation? _____

   _____

REFERENCES

1. Microsoft Security Program: "Microsoft Security Bulletin (MS99-032)."
   21 March 2003, http://www.microsoft.com/technet/security/bulletin/
   ms99-032.mspx.

14

MAIL VULNERABILITIES

> **After reading this chapter and completing the exercises, you will be able to:**
>
> ♦ Define SMTP vulnerabilities
>
> ♦ Outline IMAP vulnerabilities
>
> ♦ Explain POP vulnerabilities
>
> ♦ Identify some specific server application vulnerabilities
>
> ♦ Lists types of e-mail-related attacks
>
> ♦ Identify some specific browser-based vulnerabilities
>
> ♦ Discuss protection measures

Some of the most common attacks are aimed at e-mail delivery and display systems and applications—this means e-mail servers and e-mail clients. Many of the vulnerabilities in e-mail systems are connected to HTML mail, with its beautiful graphics and background stationery. HTML vulnerabilities such as ActiveX exploits, scripting exploits, and application exploits have a strong effect on e-mail. Social engineering exploits such as phishing for passwords and 419 scams have an e-mail-based front-end. Spam, or unrequested commercial e-mail, has reached epidemic proportion, and in some cases, corporate mail servers are experiencing DDoS attacks from hundreds of residential zombies. In this chapter, you will learn more about various mail attacks, including SMTP attacks, IMAP attacks, and other e-mail-related assaults.

MAJOR MAIL PROTOCOLS

SMTP, IMAP, and POP are the main protocols supporting e-mail systems all over the world.

Simple Mail Transfer Protocol (SMTP)

Simple Mail Transfer Protocol (SMTP) is one of the most widely used upper-layer protocols in the Internet Protocol stack. SMTP is the method used to transfer e-mail messages from one server to another or from a client computer to a server. The mnemonic for SMTP is "Send Mail Today, Please" and this is a reasonable memory-link, as SMTP is used by most corporate mail servers to transfer mail from one server to another. An e-mail client using either Post Office Protocol (POP) or IMAP can recover the messages. For this reason, when configuring an e-mail application, service administrators can specify either the POP or IMAP server but must always specify the SMTP server.

SMTP uses the concept of spooling, as seen in Figure 14-1. Whenever an e-mail message is sent from a local application to the SMTP application, SMTP stores the e-mail message in a buffer known as the SMTP queue. The server checks the queue for messages periodically. When a message is found, it delivers it.

If the intended recipient of the e-mail message is unavailable, the server attempts to send the message later. If the e-mail message cannot be delivered because the recipient is not located, his box is full, or he is unknown, the message is discarded and the sender is notified. Holding all messages in the spool until they can be delivered is known as end-to-end delivery.

The SMTP Model

To deliver an e-mail message, the client computer must establish a TCP connection with port 25 of the destination computer. To accomplish this, the user's computer, operating as the client, sends an e-mail message to the server. Then, it waits for a response.

If the destination computer is unavailable, the server sends a single-line text message to the client computer, stating this fact, and then the client computer releases the connection and tries again later. If the server accepts the message from the client computer, it will send details about the sender and the receiver of the e-mail message. If the recipient exists at any of the destination mailboxes on the local mail server, the server will copy the e-mail messages into the appropriate mailboxes. If an e-mail message cannot be delivered due to problems such as the nonexistence of a recipient, an error report is returned to the client computer. If more e-mail messages have to be sent, the client computer continues with the connection to the server. When all of the e-mail messages have been exchanged between the client computer and the server, the connection is released.

SMTP Commands   The client computer communicates with the server by using specific commands. The most common commands that can be used are explained below.

HELO or *EHLO*—This command identifies the SMTP sender to the SMTP receiver and is the first command that the client computer sends to the server.

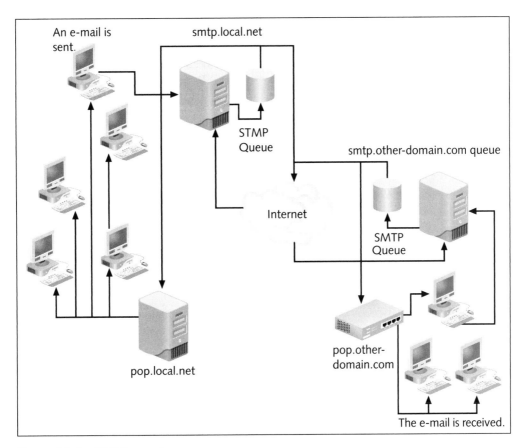

Figure 14-1 SMTP spooling

MAIL—This identifies the originator of the message.

RCPT—This command identifies the recipient of an e-mail message and can be used to send an e-mail message to a user. If there are multiple recipients, more than one *RCPT* command may be sent.

DATA—The client computer uses *DATA* to send the content of the e-mail message.

RSET—*RSET* ends the current e-mail transaction between the client computer and the server.

VRFY—This command asks the receiver to confirm when a user has been identified.

EXPN—This command requests that the receiver confirm that a mailing list has been identified.

QUIT—This command terminates the connection between the client computer and the server.

SMTP Vulnerabilities

Most attacks upon an SMTP server occur because the server has been configured incorrectly. Hackers scan the Internet for any incorrectly configured SMTP servers so that they can send an e-mail message to the server. By doing this, they can exploit the server in two ways:

- The attacker can send mail anonymously. The recipients of these e-mail messages will not be able to discover where the e-mail message came from because it will reach them anonymously through an authorized source and not directly from the hacker.

- Hackers can also send the SMTP server a single e-mail with the intention of reaching hundreds, thousands, or even millions of users. This method allows an attacker to send out megabytes of spam through the server's fast connection, even if the attacker is connecting through a dial-up modem.

Hackers can use several commands to exploit SMTP servers. Some of the SMTP commands which are often exploited by hackers are described below.

Buffer Overflows   A buffer overflow is one of the main types of attacks on the Internet. Hackers may try to overflow the buffer of the user's system. In this instance, a very long username, password, or file name is sent to the server. By doing this, a hacker may be able to disrupt a running process and insert malicious code to be executed on the server.

Hackers can create a buffer overflow on a system by sending a long *HELO* command, long e-mail names in *MAIL* or *RCPT* commands, or a long command. For example, a *HELO* argument of over 10,000 characters may overflow the buffer, and a *HELO* argument of over 12,000 characters may even crash the server.

Backdoor Entry   A backdoor entry permits hackers to take complete control of a mail system. By running a vulnerability scanner against a system and exploiting running services and protocols, SMTP commands such as *Debug* and *Wiz*, can open a back door for hackers.

Debug

The Morris worm created chaos on the Internet in 1988 by spreading through the sendmail program. This program supported a nonstandard command called *Debug* that permitted anyone to take control of the server. The Morris worm automated this process and was spread to the majority of the sendmail programs on the Internet. Today, it is highly unlikely that any of these old sendmail servers are found on the network.

Systems that use TCP to communicate can also be desynchronized by sending an enormous quantity of data packets. Such desynchronization may occur if a computer operator runs the server version of the product on a 486 system that processes a large number of e-mail messages.

Wiz

This command indicates an intrusion attempt. Systems that are more than 10 years old are likely to be vulnerable to the Wiz bug. The older versions of the sendmail command let a user connect to port 25 of the SMTP server by using a Telnet program. After being successfully connected to the SMTP server, the user only needed to type WIZ and a password. After this, the user would get a shell from which he or she could enter any command and take control of the system. Another vulnerability in the sendmail program permitted hackers to log on to the system without even typing a password.

Scanning E-mail Servers   Some standard SMTP commands like *EXPN* and *VRFY*, may allow attackers to acquire information from an e-mail server. The purpose of these commands is to locate user accounts and information about the e-mail system. It is feasible to Telnet into a SMTP server and send commands as if the hacker was a remote SMTP client. Attackers use this data to assault the user's computer.

In 1990, an attempt to scan an e-mail server was discovered. Hackers scanned a system by sending an e-mail message to an undefined user who was named decode. UNIX systems let this e-mail message be passed on to a program called uudecode instead of rejecting it or passing it to any user. This permitted hackers to crack into the system and overwrite system or configuration files.

Spamming E-mail Servers   In this kind of attack, an attacker sends a single e-mail message to a large number of recipients. The SMTP command *RCPT* is used to transmit an e-mail message to a user. This command can be specified either for sending a single e-mail message or multiple e-mail messages. A hacker attempts to attack a mail server by sending large numbers of *RCPT* commands to it. This may result in any of the following attacks on the mail server:

- A denial-of-service (DoS) attack—In this type of attack, a mail server may crash because it is not able to handle all of the incoming mail traffic.

- A user-account attack—In this attack, a hacker who may be looking for valid e-mail addresses sends e-mail messages to all possible combinations of e-mails. In this manner, all e-mail messages not rejected will probably reach legitimate users.

- A spam-relay attack—In this attack, a hacker may send an e-mail message to the server with multiple recipients. Then the server sends e-mail messages to each person. This allows a hacker to drastically slow down the performance of a system by loading it down and sending thousands of unwanted messages.

- Sending corrupt *MAIL* commands—To attack a system, an attacker may send a corrupt *MAIL* command to the SMTP server. This will hack the mail service. The attacker may also attempt to send a corrupted *RCPT* command to gain access over the e-mail service via a buffer overflow in the *RCPT* command.

- Manipulating commands such as *EXPN* or *VRFY*. This can cause a system to crash by damaging the mail transfer agent with a buffer overflow. Hackers can transmit

14

commands by posing as the network administrator of a network and exploiting the privileges of a sendmail program. Once the server is compromised, the attacker can perform all manner of hacker tricks, such as altering configuration files, overwriting system files, or placing Trojans on a mail server.

- Third-party mail relay—A third-party mail relay occurs when an external mail client found outside the organization sends e-mail messages to a mail server. The mail server processes, then delivers, the e-mail messages coming from the external mail client.

Most corporate mail servers do not allow third-party mail relaying. However, if a mail server allows third-party relay, anyone on the Internet can send e-mail messages to the server and the e-mail message appears to come from the mail server's domain, and not from the domain where the message actually originated. This is another way for an unauthorized user to remain anonymous.

Here is an example: Momlast.biz is an ISP that uses the e-mail domain user@momlast.biz. Momlast.biz users can use their e-mail clients to receive e-mail from their employers' POP servers. This works well in general; however, muletide@work.com wants to send e-mail out from home, and his work SMTP server is not accessible except from within the company's network. This is a setback until muletide tries using smtp.momlast.biz, and the mail goes out without a hitch. Momlast.biz has been used as a third-party relayer.

Internet Message Access Protocol (IMAP)

Internet Message Access Protocol (IMAP) is an e-mail client protocol which can be used to retrieve e-mail messages from a mail server. Essentially, IMAP allows users to access e-mail messages that remain on the mail server, as opposed to POP3, which downloads mail from the server to files on the local computer and erases that mail from the server.

Role of IMAP

An e-mail message stored on an IMAP server can be modified from any remote location with access to Internet, including a desktop computer at home, a workstation at the office, a notebook computer, a cellular phone, or a PDA. It is not necessary to download anything to the local computer and this is extremely useful if several local devices are used, or there is an issue of disk storage space on those local devices. Public devices, including school lab computers and library computers, are also at risk. Having 500 messages downloaded to a cellular phone or a 486 computer's disk drive may well crash the device and make recovery difficult.

The functions of IMAP include:

- Allowing users to read, edit, reply to, forward, create, and move e-mail messages
- Creating mailboxes
- Deleting mailboxes

- Renaming mailboxes
- Checking for new e-mail messages
- Deleting e-mail messages

In order to provide security to users while they are accessing e-mail messages, IMAP is designed to:

- Be compatible with Internet messaging standards
- Enable message access and management from more than one computer
- Permit access without depending on less efficient file access protocols
- Support concurrent access to all shared mailboxes

IMAP Vulnerabilities

Washington University (WU) IMAP and POP mail server code, version 2004b and earlier, are susceptible to buffer overflow conditions which give users super-user access on the mail server. Super-user access gives administrative rights to servers.

The first issue is this: IMAP supports various authentication mechanisms, including the Challenge Response Authentication Mechanism with MD5 (CRAM-MD5). A logic flaw in CRAM-MD5 could allow a remote attacker to gain unauthorized access to another user's e-mail. UW IMAP 2004b and earlier are affected by this vulnerability if CRAM-MD5 authentication is enabled, however CRAM-MD5 is not enabled by default.

Hackers are able to obtain super-user access to the mail server because the server process runs as root. This allows the process to run with full administrative access over the system without restriction.

To take advantage of this flaw, an attacker needs to connect to the server. Firewalls or filtering routers could protect the server from attacks, but users would need to firewall the server from possible external threats and (much more likely) internal threats.

Post Office Protocol (POP)

The venerable **Post Office Protocol (POP)** server delivers mail to users, downloaded to their local devices. This is a common (possibly the most common) way to distribute e-mail to users. The mail is downloaded through a mail client such as Outlook, Eudora, Netscape Mail, and Thunderbird as well as many other similar software packages that allow the user to do the following tasks:

- Read mail
- Move mail from one folder (directory) to another
- Add and edit e-mail accounts
- Create e-mail folders

- Delete e-mail folders
- Rename e-mail folders
- Check for new e-mail messages
- Delete e-mail messages

POP Mail Vulnerabilities

The IMAP and POP mail server buffer overflow above is one example of a widespread server vulnerability in POP mail. Another vulnerability exists in Outlook 2002 in how it processes POP e-mail headers. An attacker who can successfully exploit this vulnerability could send a specially malformed e-mail to a user of Outlook 2002 that could cause the Outlook client to fail because Outlook 2002 could not download the "special" e-mail. Outlook would experience this as a Denial of Service (DoS) because no other mail could be viewed until the special e-mail had been deleted, either using a different POP client, such as Eudora; by Telnetting into the server and using the Pine or Elm e-mail programs often included in a mail server installation; by using an alternate Web-based e-mail browser (very common in the mid 1990s); or by requesting an administrator to remove the offending message. The user's privacy is never compromised by this issue.

A more common issue for dial-up customers is to receive a 4MB message when an e-mail client or server setting allows messages no larger than 200K. The large message could clog the inbox and there is nothing to be done but Telnet in and delete it using the Pine or Elm utility, or have an administrator remove it. The other version of this vulnerability is to have dial-up access when a friend has broadband access, and multiple large e-mails of pictures and movies are sent. This is an effective DoS attack, because users cannot use a filter at the client level to block these messages from download. The messages have to download to be moved to the trash.

SERVER APPLICATION VULNERABILITIES

Some exploits are associated with specific mail-server applications. Below are some examples of exploits for two popular enterprise-level mail and messaging servers. These examples show that all server applications are vulnerable to one or another exploit.

Microsoft Exchange Server

These four vulnerabilities are from SecurityFocus.com and affect various versions of Microsoft Exchange Server, Windows 2000 Advanced Server, and Windows 2000 Datacenter Server:

- Microsoft Exchange Server Outlook Web Access Script Injection Vulnerability, 2006
- Microsoft Exchange Server Calendar Remote Code Execution Vulnerability, 2006

- Microsoft Exchange Server 2003 Exchange Information Store Denial of Service Vulnerability, 2005

- Microsoft Exchange Server 2003 Outlook Web Access Random Mailbox Access Vulnerability, 2004

IBM Lotus Domino Notes

These exploits are also from SecurityFocus.com and affect various versions of Lotus Domino:

- IBM Lotus Domino Multiple TuneKrnl Local Privilege Escalation Vulnerabilities, 2006

- iDefense Security Advisory 11.08.06: IBM Lotus Domino 7, 2006

- IBM Lotus Domino Web Access Session Hijacking Vulnerability (Vulnerabilities), 2006

- Session Token Remains Valid After Logout in IBM Lotus Domino Web Access, 2006

E-MAIL ATTACKS

Attackers can disrupt network services, spread viruses, and deny service to network users by exploiting the vulnerabilities of e-mail. E-mail attacks include list linking, e-mail bombing, spamming, sniffing and spoofing, e-mail attachments, 419s, scams, and phishing.

14

List Linking

List linking, as a technique, is quite similar to e-mail bombing. However, it is accomplished differently and involves enrolling potentially hundreds of target users through e-mail lists and distributed e-mail message systems.

Here is how listservers work: e-mail sent to a listserver doesn't go to a regular e-mail account. It goes to a database of users. The e-mail sent to that address is distributed to all members of the list. Figure 14-2 shows an example of how a list server operates.

The theory behind this voluntary mail-flooding is that the subjects of the messages are interesting to the member. E-mail lists produce more or less traffic depending upon how many people are involved and how much they have to say. Some lists produce fewer than ten messages per week, and some produce much higher traffic. I know of at least one list (Mandriva developers listserv) that produced as many as 500 discrete messages per day. Every member of the list receives every message, including a copy of those that the member sends themselves to the list. The example in Figure 14-3 shows what would happen if you set up only three list memberships.

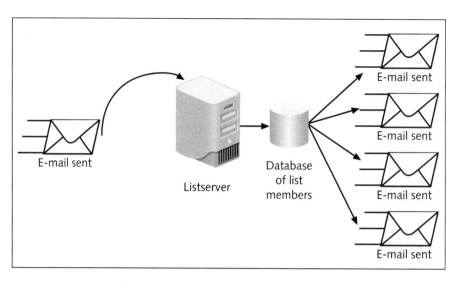

Figure 14-2   E-mail list operation

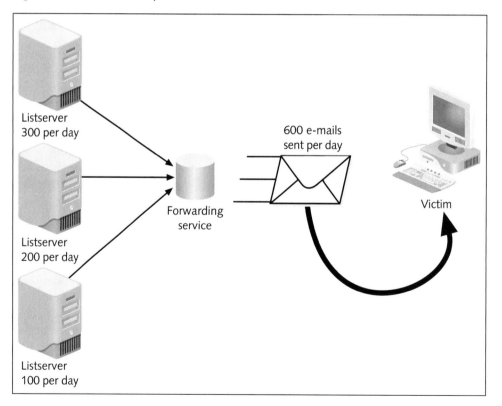

Figure 14-3   List-linking

E-mail Bombing

E-mail bombing is the practice of sending an identical e-mail repeatedly to the target user. This may exceed the storage or bandwidth of some e-mail accounts, making it impossible for legitimate mail to get through. Some mail services charge extra if accounts go over their storage limits and this moves the result from the annoyance category to the monetary losses category.

Some utilities are used on the Microsoft Windows platform for e-mail bombing. One of these is Mail Bomber.

Mail Bomber

Mail Bomber is an e-mail bombing utility that was distributed in a file called bomb02.zip. It is less available now than it was in 1997. Most of the entries about it are in cautionary Web sites covering historical threats. Certain e-mail bombing utilities are used on any system that supports SMTP servers. Other utilities are specialized, and may work only on systems like America Online. In the past, one could find an application called Doomsday which was designed to send mass e-mail on the AOL system, and was easily converted to an e-mail bomber. Mail bombing is simple on a Unix platform. A mail bomber could be written with just a few lines of code, presuming a user has some experience with a scripting language.

Today, hackers might be able to get a copy of Megasploit and use that to send e-mail bombs. Megasploit version 2.x runs on Unix, Linux, and Windows. Version 3.0 is in Alpha and works on Unix / Linux boxes only at this writing.

14

E-mail Spamming

Many people use the term spam to mean any e-mail they don't like or did not request. The specifications are defined on a case-by-case basis by each user. Though there is an act specifying penalties for entities who send spam and defines opt-out requirements for spam-mail (CAN-SPAM Act of 2003) there is a specific legal definition of spam in the act. My definition of spam, as a provider of e-mail services to several user communities, is as follows: **Spam** is commercial or nuisance e-mail with no effective opt-out system. By effective, I mean there has to be an opt-out link on the e-mail and it must actually opt the user off the list. Spammers tend to send from several false e-mail accounts, so it is difficult to filter the senders out. Spam is often sent from offshore servers for whom the U.S. laws governing spam do not presumably apply. Spam costs the ISP time and bandwidth. Current estimates suggest that over 80% of the e-mail traffic in the U.S. is spam or attempts to opt out of a spam sender's list. Corporations and governmental agencies that must archive all e-mail for regulatory reasons have to store all their spam for a period of several years and the costs of the storage are spiraling up.

E-mail spamming is nearly impossible to prevent because all users have their own definition of what constitutes spam when they are sending and what constitutes spam when they receive it. Legitimate marketers responding to requests for information are often accused of spamming because the recipients do not remember their request or have lost interest. The high quantity of spam messages inclines a user to assume that all commercial e-mail is unwanted or unrequested.

Spamming is sometimes considered a security hazard, especially if spammers use corporate e-mail servers to relay their messages.

E-mail Sniffing and Spoofing

Packet sniffers are able to collect all of the unencrypted data traveling on the Ethernet subnet that the sniffer is on, so all POP3 e-mail requests will show the attacker the username and password in plain text. If a user is running a sniffer on a corporate network, she will collect all of the usernames and passwords for all of her e-mail. Ethereal can also capture all the plaintext e-mails entirely. Graphics will not display in the Ethereal screen but all the text will. How useful could that be for a criminal? Just imagine what people put in e-mails every day, in the belief that it is safe. Student IDs, credit card numbers, phone numbers, "true confessions that might be admissible as evidence in court," etc. The sky is the limit, if a sniffer is on an active subnet. At the very least, the sniffer will have all of a coworkers' private information. Almost everything in this chapter is illegal to perform without permission.

E-mail spoofing is a way of tampering with e-mail so that the message received appears to be from a known and trusted person, when it is actually sent by an impostor. This is easy to pull off if the impostor also has a sniffer on the network. The imposter could read the mail on the server before the genuine user gets a chance to download it, and can send fraudulent e-mails from the authentic user's account with a different replyto: address. The person being imitated is not aware that it is happening.

E-mail Attachments

Most computer users now know that attachments to e-mail can contain worms and viruses. It has been known for just as long that some people will open any attachment. Worms can self-mail themselves to all the email addresses in your address book, leading all the recipients to think that the e-mail is from you. The e-mails to which worms attach themselves are often extremely poorly written and to an alert receiver they read nothing like a general level of discourse. Predictably, some people open them anyway, unaware that the attachment contains anything but vacation pictures, or work papers. If the hapless victim is using the operating system for which the worm was written, it quickly sends itself to all of the e-mail addresses in that victim's address book. Those who don't open the attachment, of course, don't get the virus or worm.

419s, Scams, and Phishing

These three e- mail attacks are varieties of unrequested e-mail that drop in your inbox, and they are included here because they are solvable by similar measures.

419 or Advanced Fee Fraud

"419s" are named after the relevant section of the Criminal Code of Nigeria referring to "Advance Fee Fraud." An advance fee scheme occurs when the victim pays money to someone in anticipation of receiving something of greater value—such as a loan, contract, investment, or gift—and then receives little or nothing in return. It is very common to get e-mails from people purporting to be government or bank officials who are attempting to move huge sums out of Nigeria (or other places). Somehow they have gotten the name (and/or e-mail) the victim and entice that recipient into trying to defraud the government or the bank out of a few million dollars. People who respond to the e-mail are then asked for small sums to move the process along, and are milked for larger and larger sums until they are tapped out or they resist the process. There are many such schemes that come as international lottery wins or pleas to help orphaned children of billionaires, for example. There are thousands of these scams launched every day, and there is no end to the number of different come-ons that will result in the victim needing to send money to move the project along.

Other Scams

Other types of scams include bad-check scams that look like job offers, where the victim is asked to agree to receive money for an offshore company who cannot get it otherwise. The victim is offered 10% of the money. This might seem reasonable unless the recipient knows that no legitimate offshore company has any trouble receiving cash and converting it to their currency of choice. If a victim responds to this offer, he starts receiving calls and letters and real forged checks for thousands of dollars. The audit process of the companies whose checks were stolen will discover the erroneous cashing of a check in a few months and be at the door asking for the money back. By then, the scammer is long gone with 90% of the money.

Phishing

Phishing uses e-mails from a purported financial institution (often eBay or Paypal) stating that there is something wrong with an account, and the account holder needs to log in to set it straight. They provide the account holder with a link which, if used, leads to a site that looks almost identical to the real company site. When the account holder logs in, the scammers capture the username and password.

Browser-Based Vulnerabilities

All browsers are applications written in some programming language by human beings. There is absolutely no such thing as a browser that does not have its share of bugs, coding errors, and vulnerabilities which might be exploited by an attacker. The following is a set of illustrative examples of browser-specific vulnerabilities. It is not meant to be an exhaustive list of all e-mail clients or all vulnerabilities specific to those clients. When choosing a browser, it is important to look at the larger picture including install base, operating system compatibility, and features required by use-patterns or the needs of an organization.

14

Microsoft Outlook Express 5.0

This is a historical issue, which means that there is already a patch for it. It is often used as an example of browser vulnerability because it is so well-defined and understandable to laypeople. Outlook Express is one of the most widely used e-mail clients on the planet, because it has come bundled with Windows since 1995.

Outlook Express 5.0 uses HTML pages as stationery for sending e-mail messages. This was a user-experience upgrade that many loved, however it was coupled with a feature that ran scripts coded into the HTML backgrounds automatically. Thus, a malicious script could be run to open an attachment without user interaction. This allowed such historical attacks as the "Love Letter" (aka "Lovebug") worm to propagate.

The issue was that scripts that run automatically in OE5.0 could act at whatever security level the user enjoyed. If the user had administrative privileges, then the script did too. Various annoyances could be contrived such as opening and closing the CD drive, opening a Web browser, starting a word processor, opening a spreadsheet, opening a new mail message (with or without preset contents), passing information about a recipient to a hacker, sending information about the compromised computer to a hacker, formatting the main hard drive or anything else somebody with the same user privileges as the user had. Here is yet another reason to use administrative privilege only when it is needed.

Microsoft Outlook 2000

Discovered by independent researchers, this is a historical exploit because there is already a patch for it available. It is a critical risk for both Exchange Server and Outlook 2000, 2002, and 2003. It is notable because it has probably existed since at least 2000. A remote code execution vulnerability exists in both Outlook and Exchange Server because of the way that they decode the Transport Neutral Encapsulation Format (TNEF) MIME attachment. A more common name for the TNEF format is Rich Text Format (RTF).

An attacker could exploit the vulnerability by constructing a specially crafted TNEF message that could potentially allow remote code execution when a user opens or previews a malicious e-mail message or when the Microsoft Exchange Server Information Store processes the specially crafted message. A successful attacker could take complete control of an affected system.

Mozilla Thunderbird 1.50

This is also a historical issue because a patch has been issued. A critical issue, patched by Mozilla on July 25th 2006, would allow a buffer overwrite in the case of a malformed VCard. This affected both Thunderbird 1.5.0.4 and SeaMonkey 1.0.2. A VCard attachment with a malformed base64 field can trigger a heap buffer overwrite. These have proven exploitable in the past, though in this case the overwrite is accompanied by an integer underflow that would attempt to copy more data than the typical machine has, leading to a crash.

OperaMail 8.54

This is a historical issue as there has been a major release that fixes the problem. No issues specific to the mail feature of the Opera browser are found. There is a JPEG image-handling remote integer overflow vulnerability issue with the browser by which an integer overflow error can happen when processing a specially crafted JPEG image with overly large "height" and "width" values. This could allow an attacker to take complete control of an affected system by convincing a user to visit a specially crafted Web page. The vulnerable versions are 8.54 and earlier. The solution is to upgrade to version 9.0.

PROTECTION

List linking, e-mail bombing, spamming, sniffing and spoofing, e-mail attachments, 419s, scams, and phishing are not connected with vulnerabilities in the code of e-mail distribution applications, or any particular e-mail client technology. They exist simply by virtue of having e-mail. There are a few fairly effective countermeasures to these threats and annoyances. These could be called personal and corporate measures.

Personal E-mail Security Countermeasures

The three personal e-mail security countermeasures covered here are segmenting mail, filtering mail, and using due diligence to ascertain whether the mail is safe before opening it or opening attachments. Due diligence would include antivirus software updated regularly.

14

Segmenting E-mail

Get two or more e-mail accounts and use them for specific purposes. For instance, you may have a personal e-mail account from your ISP, and a work account from your office, so you are aware of the value of segmenting work from home. To reduce the harvesting of e-mail accounts and subsequent increase in spam, get another account such as a Yahoo or Hotmail account that you as your reply address for lists or when you ask for information from an online company. If you are having huge spam issues with your current work account, have the network administrator give you a different username and close the old account. If you're having spam issues with your home account, just open a new username (most ISPs will help with this) and ignore the other account.

Filter Mail at the Client Level

All e-mail clients (Outlook, AOL, Netscape Mail, Mozilla, OperaMail, etc.) give users the tools to filter e-mails. I suggest filtering for whitelist rather than for blacklist terms. Most e-mail clients automatically whitelist the e-mails to which a user replies. One good strategy is to choose terms to whitelist and create new folders for those terms. Whitelisting gives few false positives, and makes it unlikely that I will ever miss e-mails from friends or colleagues, even if I have 192 e-mails appear in my inbox in an afternoon.

Blacklisting is often handled by the ISP and they typically place the suspected spam in the Bulk folder. Since spam comes from lots of randomly chosen accounts and the search terms are always changing, I choose not to spend a lot of time cleaning my list for spam. For instance, "Viagra" is blocked but "\/ | agr/\" is not.

Due Diligence

Due diligence is using the same amount of effort that a reasonably educated person would use. In this case, users should have antivirus software if there is any reason to suspect vulnerability to viruses or worms. It also makes sense to use a reasonable amount of consideration in evaluating the truth of e-mails, even those that apparently come from people known by the user. There is no reason to accept anything from unknown users or open attachments from them. There is also no reason to accept anything written by users you know, if you feel that it is not their usual style. A phone call to ask if a particular e-mail was sent is far quicker than cleaning the viruses off your computer. Even a real and important alert, such as "Dear Dad, Bill and I are getting married" will likely be repeated many times before the actual event.

Digital Signature and Certificates

A digital signature or certificate is a file that validates who a user is. Digital signatures are used by programs on the Internet (remote) and on a user's computer (local) to confirm the user's identity to any third party concerned. When a user gets an e-mail from somebody using PGP (which stands for "Pretty Good Privacy") or GPG (which stands for Gnu Privacy Guard), it has a key block at the bottom of the message. This is a sign that the message has not been tampered with or damaged during transmission. A browser can decrypt the e-mail before it is opened, but if it were diverted by a third party, they would be unable to read it, or edit it and send it on.

A digital certificate is issued by a third-party Certificate Authority (CA) authorized and accredited to issue such certificates. Thawte and VeriSign are examples of companies with this authority. The digital certificate includes information about the sender credited with signing the message. The CA verifies that the sender's e-mail address is owned by that sender. The e-mail address is then embedded in the digital certificate. It is this third-party verification of the ownership of the e-mail address that ensures the message content came from the address in the "From:" field of a digitally signed e-mail.

Corporate E-mail Security Countermeasures

Corporate e-mail administrators can offer more protection than the above personal measures. These include e-mail security policies; centrally administered antivirus and antispam tools; disclaimers; encryption; and firewall rules.

E-mail Security Policies

If a company does not have an e-mail security policy, the business should waste no time developing one that informs the entire organization of acceptable e-mail and messaging. Much of it might look like a sanitized version of the personal e-mail security countermeasures above. Employees of the organization will be encouraged to attend training about what constitutes an acceptable e-mail and what is suspicious. The organizational policy will also contain policies for infractions of the messaging protocols.

Provide Security Software

Make sure your organization's infrastructure is as secure as possible. Antivirus software ought to be implemented on all Windows and Mac machines, in case server-based solutions miss something. Software firewalls that prevent infections from spreading through network shares might be considered. Centralized patch management for all machines might be considered. Patching of the mail server itself is extremely prudent. Organizations may need to consider several software solutions to find the packages that best suit their requirements.

Important requirements may include transparency to the end-user, minor impact on network performance, and ease of implementation and administration.

Antispam Tools

Today's antispam tools are either software solutions which are loaded onto mail servers, or hardware solutions which are placed in the network. The wide variety of options available and the wide range of cost points make this a subject fit for its own book, but for this discussion, the same sort of research and requirements balancing as was required to choose a security application goes into this decision. All antispam tools are reactive and most are based on filtering algorithms. They look for any of a long list of words and phrases that are deemed high-probability of spam and block, sort, or delete the mail based on that list and algorithm.

These tools reduce storage requirements for regulatory purposes, and reduce time spent by employees in reading, analyzing, and processing the more obvious unwanted mail. Some advanced antispam tools include content-checking of incoming and outgoing e-mail.

Content-Checking

A content-checking tool can be installed on the e-mail system to monitor whether users are giving away trade secrets to unapproved recipients, or to check for offensive or inappropriate content such as racist remarks or pornography. This tool separates e-mail messages with suspect content and prevents them from being sent. An authorized censor within the organization must approve any suspicious messages.

Disclaimers

Disclaimers attached to each company e-mail are considered an effective way of controlling employees' propensity to send sensitive information to unapproved recipients. These disclaimers may have some effect upon some employees, but they are not going to stop malicious use, such as industrial espionage, nor will they stop ignorant misuse, such as sending a sensitive, personal mail.

Encryption

Encryption techniques such as PGP make gleaning useful information from packet-sniffing rather challenging. This encryption technique is based on paired keys and algorithms. Messages are encrypted by using a public key and can be decrypted with a paired, private key.

The two keys, public and private, are generated together. Each key can decrypt what the other key encrypts. The private key is intended to remain secret and is not transmitted to others, but the public key may be made widely available. If a user who has a public key encrypts a message, only a user with a copy of the unique private key is able to decrypt it within a useful time frame.

Virus Scanners

A reliable virus scanner checks all incoming and outgoing e-mail messages and attachments for e-mail viruses and worms. Server-based virus solutions cut the time users spend dealing with possible virus-laden e-mails. They should alert the mail administrators of the e-mail virus and how it was handled, or if it needs to be dealt with manually. In this manner, viruses can be stopped before they cause any harm to the system, and administrators are alerted before their systems become infected. Some antispam tools include virus protection based on their detection algorithm. It is wise to use multilayered defenses, and not use just one solution.

CHAPTER SUMMARY

- ❑ Mail system vulnerabilities are dependent on the major mail protocols, server software implementing those protocols, tendencies of users and attackers, and vulnerabilities in specific browser code.

- ❑ The major mail protocols are SMTP, IMAP, and POP.

- ❑ Simple Mail Transfer Protocol (SMTP) is used to transfer e-mail messages from one server to another or from a client computer to a server.

- ❑ Most SMTP vulnerabilities occur because the SMTP server is not correctly configured. Hackers scan the Internet for any incorrectly configured SMTP servers so that they can send an anonymous e-mail message to the server.

- ❑ Some standard SMTP commands can be used by attackers to create a buffer overflow, open up a backdoor entry, scan an e-mail for information, or spam an e-mail server.

❑ Internet Message Access Protocol (IMAP) is an e-mail client protocol that retrieves e-mail messages from a mail server. An e-mail message stored on an IMAP server can be modified from any remote location with access to the Internet.

❑ Older versions of IMAP and POP are susceptible to buffer overflow conditions, which give attackers administrative rights to servers.

❑ Post Office Protocol (POP) delivers mail to users, downloaded to their local devices.

❑ In addition to the buffer overflow vulnerability, e-mail clients are vulnerable to over-sized messages, especially in cases where Internet access is by phone modem.

❑ All mail-server applications—including Microsoft Exchange Server and IBM Lotus Domino Notes—are vulnerable to exploit.

❑ E-mail attacks include list linking, e-mail bombing, spamming, sniffing and spoofing, attachments, 419s, scams, and phishing.

❑ All e-mail browsers have their share of bugs, coding errors, and other vulnerabilities.

❑ Three personal e-mail security measures are segmenting mail, filtering mail, and using due diligence to ascertain whether mail is safe before opening it or its attachments.

❑ Corporate e-mail security measures include implementing an e-mail security policy, providing security software and virus scanners, installing antispam and content-checking tools, attaching disclaimers to all company e-mail, and using encryption.

14

REVIEW QUESTIONS

1. What does SMTP stand for and what does it do?

2. What does IMAP stand for and what is it for?

3. What is the POP (or POP3) protocol and what is it for?

4. What is the most common cause of SMTP server vulnerability?

5. What is the most common e-mail vulnerability (or complaint)?

6. What e-mail client has the largest install base?

7. Who makes the Thunderbird e-mail client?

8. What is an e-mail and messaging server from Microsoft?

9. Name a messaging server from IBM.

Indicate whether the sentence or statement is true or false.

10. _____ Microsoft will give you a penny for every e-mail sent out for the Red Cross.

11. _____ POP mail cannot be stored on the server after downloading it.

12. _____ IMAP mail is stored on a server to be retrieved and read from any Internet-connected computer.

13. _____ Viruses leave a local computer through POP mail, so POP should be disabled.

14. _____ In Thunderbird's Inbox, e-mails are stored in one long file, called INBOX.

Match the following port numbers with the protocols below.

a. 465

b. 995

c. 25

d. 143

e. 110

f. 993

15. _____ SMTP e-mail server

16. _____ POP3 e-mail server

17. _____ IMAP(4) e-mail server

18. _____ SMTPS wsmtp protocol over TLS|SSL

19. _____ IMAPS SSL encrypted IMAP

20. _____ SPOP SSL encrypted POP

HANDS-ON PROJECTS

Here we will look at mail server vulnerabilities, as well as how to tell if a message is spoofed. In these hands-on exercises, you will learn how to set up a mail server on your Linux machine, and use a Web-based GUI to administer it.

HANDS-ON PROJECTS

Project 14-1

According to SMTP, an e-mail must have a point of origin. However, due to the very nature of TCP/IP, that point of origin can be spoofed in several ways. Using the *whois* and *nslookup* commands, discover all of the fully qualified domain names of all of the IP addresses (in bold type) in the e-mail headers shown below. Compare these to the apparent senders' fully qualified domain names.

```
Return-path: <info@hi5.com>
Envelope-to: wolf@networkdefense.biz
Delivery-date: Fri, 03 Nov 2006 08:05:54 +0200
```

```
Received: from [204.13.50.162] (helo=mailman162.hi5.com) by
        allhyper.com with esmtp (Exim 4.50) id 1GfsBd-0007DP-
        QP for wolf@networkdefense.biz;
        Fri, 03 Nov 2006 08:05:53 +0200
Received: from sfapp089 (10.100.10.188) by mailman162.hi5.com
        id h9be4409c7s3; Thu, 2 Nov 2006 22:05:54 -0800
        (envelope-from <info@hi5.com>)
Message-ID: <1110398059.1162553953228.JavaMail.root@sfapp089>
From: hi5 <info@hi5.com>
To: wolf@networkdefense.biz
Subject: =?ANSI_X3.4-1968?Q?Nun_Yabiz_has_sent_you_a_hi5_
Message?=Mime-Version: 1.0
Content-Type: multipart/alternative;  boundary="----=
_Part_88475_970375511.1162553953227"
Date: Thu, 2 Nov 2006 22:05:54 -0800
X-Evolution-Source: pop://wolf%40networkdefense.
        biz@networkdefense.biz/


Return-path: <karpaasi68@luukku.com>
Envelope-to: wolf@networkdefense.biz
Delivery-date: Fri, 03 Nov 2006 08:54:18 +0200
Received: from [220.129.70.110] (helo=mail.allhyper.com) by
        allhyper.com with smtp (Exim 4.50) id 1GfswT-0004cC-
        WC for wolf@networkdefense.biz;
Fri,
        03 Nov 2006 08:54:18 +0200
Reply-to: "kari Raatikainen" <karpaasi68@luukku.com>
From: "kari Raatikainen" <karpaasi68@luukku.com>
Date: Fri, 3 Nov 2006 14:39:26 +0800
Message-ID: <646911281857346742.263120022900054170@luukku.com>
To: "wolf@networkdefense.biz" <wolf@networkdefense.biz>
Content-type: text/html; Charset=Windows-1251
Subject: Get a huge sexy bulge on your head with Ear Enlarge
        Patch.
X-Evolution-Source: pop://wolf%40networkdefense.biz@
        networkdefense.biz/
Mime-Version: 1.0


Return-path: <Ann_Onnymus@aol.com>
Envelope-to: wolf@networkdefense.biz
Delivery-date: Fri, 03 Nov 2006 08:43:12 +0200
Received: from [64.12.137.3] (helo=imo-m22.mail.
        com) by allhyper.com
        with esmtp (Exim 4.50) id 1Gfslk-0003PR-
        44 for wolf@networkdefense.biz;
        Fri, 03 Nov 2006 08:43:12 +0200
Received: from Ann_Onnymus@aol.com by imo-m22.mx.aol.com
        (mail_out_v38_r7.6.) id 4.beb.62c492e
        (29672) for <wolf@networkdefense.biz>;
        Fri, 3 Nov 2006 01:42:57 -0500 (EST)
```

14

From: Ann_Onnymus@aol.com
Message-ID: <beb.62c492e.327c3ef0@aol.com>
Date: Fri, 3 Nov 2006 01:42:56 EST
Subject: Re: As the Urn Turns
To: wolf@networkdefense.biz
MIME-Version: 1.0
Content-Type: multipart/alternative;
        boundary="----------------------------
        1162536176"
X-Mailer: 9.0 SE for Windows sub 5032
X-Spam-Flag: NO
X-Evolution-Source: pop://wolf%40networkdefense.
        biz@networkdefense.biz/

From Hanne Palencia Wed Nov 1 05:30:44 2006

X-Apparently-To: bill@yahoo.com via **216.252.100.158**;
        Fri, 03 Nov 2006 02:28:34 -0800
X-YahooFilteredBulk: **84.6.72.147**
X-Originating-IP: [**84.6.72.147**]
Return-Path: <jos@a1s.com>
Authentication-Results: mta143.mail.re3.yahoo.com
        from=a1s.com;
domainkeys=neutral (no sig)
Received: from **84.6.72.147** (HELO bitterseas.com)
        (**84.6.72.147**) by mta143.mail.re3.yahoo.com with SMTP;
        Fri, 03 Nov 2006 02:28:34 -0800
Message-ID: <000001c6fdb9$ef2711d0$a8b9a8c0@exaxho>
Reply-to: "Hanne Palencia" <jos@a1s.com>
From:"Hanne Palencia" <jos@a1s.com>
To:bill@yahoo.com Subject:
Re: 482
Date: Wed, 1 Nov 2006 05:30:44 -0800
MIME-Version: 1.0
Content-Type: multipart/alternative; boundary="----
=_NextPart_000_0001_01C6FD76.E103D1D0" X-
Priority: 3 X-MSMail-
Priority: Normal
X-Mailer: Microsoft Outlook Express 6.00.2800.1106
X-MimeOLE: Produced By Microsoft MimeOLE V6.00.2800.1106
X-Antivirus: avast! (VPS 0645-3, 02/11/2006),
        Outbound message
X-Antivirus-Status: Clean Content-Length: 494
From Channel Watch Wed Nov 1 10:40:00 2006
X-Apparently-To: bill@yahoo.com via **216.252.100.162**;
        Thu, 02 Nov 2006 14:22:04 -0800
X-YahooFilteredBulk: **205.162.43.7** X-Originating-IP:
        [**205.162.43.7**]
Return-Path: <channel-watch@eweek-zannounce.com>

```
Authentication-Results: mta265.mail.re2.yahoo.com from=eweek-
        zannounce.com; domainkeys=neutral (no sig)
Received: from 205.162.43.7 (HELO 3.7.omessage.com) (205.162.
        43.7) by mta265.mail.re2.yahoo.com with SMTP;
        Thu, 02 Nov 2006 14:22:04 -0800
From:"Channel Watch" <channel-watch@eweek-zannounce.com>
To:BILL@YAHOO.COM
Subject: Channel Watch: Easy Does It: Buiilding the Future
        with Managed
Services
Date: Wed, 1 Nov 2006 12:40:00 -0600
Content-Type: multipart/alternative; boundary="----
_NextPart_kqr9kiqoVpOwnsXH2mQZWLx84Y8ABXdbAAM8CAE="
MIME-Version: 1.0 X-MailSessionID: kqr9kiqoVpOwnsXH2mQZWLx84Y8
ABXdbAAM8CAE=
Content-Length: 2561
```

Outgoing message – Note that the routing information is not there yet:

```
Subject: Bug Report: Base uses all available cpu cycles to
        perform any operation
From: Wolf Halton <wolf@networkdefense.biz>
To: users@openoffice.org
Content-Type: multipart/alternative; boundary="=-
        721rdUs6DGH5MQ21VB8C"
Message-Id: <1161190654.9891.3.camel@localhost>
Mime-Version: 1.0
X-Mailer: Evolution 2.6.1
Date: Wed, 18 Oct 2006 12:57:37 -0400
X-Evolution-Format: text/html
X-Evolution-Account: 1160504578.15909.0@yossarian
X-Evolution-Transport: smtp://wolf@smtp.comcast.net/;use_
        ssl=never
X-Evolution-Fcc: mbox:/home/wolf/.evolution/mail/local#Sent
```

14

Project 14-2

1. Using your own e-mail account, try to find five e-mails in which the "From" e-mail address and the HELO mail server IP address are different.

2. For each e-mail you found, ask yourself whether it is possible to surmise from the message headers whether the e-mail is a legitimate message sent using a relay (such as a work e-mail sent from home) or a spoofed e-mail sent by a spammer or malicious hacker. Write a paragraph describing how you would try to determine this.

Project 14-3

In this project, you will explore how to spoof an e-mail using the command-line in Windows. Essentially, you will be manually issuing commands that your e-mail program normally issues behind the scenes when you send an e-mail. To complete this project, you will need to connect to a mail server. Ask your instructor for the name of the mail server you should use. In this example, you will send the spoofed message to your own e-mail address; keep in mind that you should never send a spoofed e-mail to anyone but yourself.

1. Click **Start**, click **Run**, type **cmd**, and then press **Enter** to open a command prompt window.

2. Recall that port 25 is the well-known port used to send SMTP messages. Connect to port 25 on the mail server by typing the following command:

   ```
   telnet mail_server 25
   ```

3. A welcome message appears; this varies, depending on the mail server. Next, introduce yourself to the mail server by typing the following command:

   ```
   HELO mail_server
   ```

4. Now type the following command, using the email address shown. This will make it appear to the recipient that the e-mail is coming from the indicated address. (Type carefully, as the backspace key will not work when issuing these commands.)

   ```
   MAIL FROM:penguin@southpole.com
   ```

5. Next, type the following command to address the e-mail to yourself:

   ```
   RCPT TO:your_email_address
   ```

6. Type the following commands to forge the message header:

   ```
   data
   from:penguin@southpole.com
   Date: Sat, 10 Dec 1863 8:15:11 -0500
   Subject: Greetings from down below!
   ```

7. Press **Enter** and then type the following, which is the body of your message:

   ```
   It's cold down here!
   ```

8. Press **Enter** to create a blank line, type a period (.), and then press **Enter** again to end your message.

9. Type **quit** to exit the server.

10. Check your e-mail account for the message and verify the sender and header information that you forged.

# CHAPTER 15

WEB APPLICATION VULNERABILITIES

> **After reading this chapter and completing the exercises, you will be able to:**
>
> ◆ Recognize Web server vulnerabilities
>
> ◆ Discuss ways to protect Web servers against vulnerabilities
>
> ◆ Pinpoint Web browser vulnerabilities
>
> ◆ Understand session ID exploits
>
> ◆ List several protective measures for Web browsers

The Internet is a collection of interconnected networks. Users can access many different kinds of servers, from very primitive FTP servers to very complex application servers such as corporate intranets and commercial portals. Most users are not aware of the sort of applications they are contacting and there is a good reason for this. Web servers are not intended to be the star of the show. They are expected to be as unobtrusive as the wheel bearings on a supermarket shopping cart. The only time you notice the shopping cart wheel bearings is when they are not working, and the only time the average user is aware of a Web server is when she sees error messages, such as those in Table 15-1.

Table 15-1 HTTP error messages

Error code and text	Meaning and response
400 Bad File Request	Usually a syntax error in the URL. This is rarely seen, as most browsers interpret text they cannot parse as being a search term.
401 Unauthorized	Server is looking for an encryption key from the client or is responding to a bad password entry.
403 Forbidden/Access Denied	Special permission needed to access the site. Used for password-protected areas or private zones to which the Webmaster is not giving any access, such as /cgi-bin/ data storage directories.
404 File Not Found	"Gone to Atlanta" So called because of Atlanta, Georgia's 404 area code. A very common error message, returned when a page has been moved, renamed, or deleted.
408 Request Timeout	Client stopped the request before the server finished retrieving it. Sometimes this means your firewall closed the connection, sometimes it means the user hit the Stop button, attempted to close the browser, or clicked on a link before the page loaded. Usually seen when network connections or servers are slow and file sizes are large.
500 Internal Error	Server configuration errors prevent the page from being displayed. Contact the site administrator to report the error, if you can.
501 Not Implemented	The host Web server doesn't support a requested feature.
502 Service Temporarily Overloaded	Server congestion; too many connections; high traffic.
503 Service Unavailable	Server busy; site may have moved, or you might have lost your dial-up Internet connection.
Connection Refused by Host	Password-protected page to which you have not been granted access, or your password was typed incorrectly.
File Contains No Data	Data-driven application unable to produce the requested data. The request might have been malformed, the table formatting might be unsuitable to the requested data, or the IP headers might have been stripped of needed information. Sometimes a resend will clear the issue.
Bad File Request	Browser may not support the form or other coding you're trying to access. If your browser is of recent vintage, the problem may lie at the server side.
Failed DNS Lookup	The Domain Name Service can't translate your domain request into a valid Internet (IP) address. The DNS server may be busy or down, or an incorrect URL may have been entered. This condition often returns a search page rather than an error.
Host Unavailable	Error returned by the user's browser. Host server may be down, or swamped with requests (includes DoS attacks).

Table 15-1   HTTP error messages (continued)

Error code and text	Meaning and response
Unable to Locate Host	Error returned by the user's browser. Either the Host server is down, the Internet connection is lost, or the URL was typed incorrectly.
Network Connection Refused by the Server	The Web server is busy.

Along with the convenience of transparent Web services comes the possibility of having potentially valuable information lost, stolen, corrupted, or misused. Information that has been recorded on Web sites is vulnerable to duplication in other places on the Web, as a snippet in e-mails, or for inclusion—cited or not—in school papers. If the site was loaded by remote FTP access, that FTP user and password can be guessed or hacked. If the site is data-driven, attackers can use the complexity of the site programming to their benefit, looking for openings in the application software. Sites can be hacked to insert destinations for phishing exploits. Intranets can be attacked to glean customer information. Files can be altered and removed. Some of these attacks are obvious to the victim, such as when the user's home page is replaced with alternate content, but some are almost impossible to detect.

Why the Web Is Vulnerable

The protocols upon which the Internet rest are, by nature, insecure. The TCP/IP protocol suite contains some secure protocols; however, the expected function and proper behavior of TCP and IP were developed among people who knew each other. The Internet has evolved, but the forces driving Web development in the last 30 years have involved new, commercially viable features like higher throughput—so that more complicated multimedia could be presented; and transparency of controls—so that untrained, or minimally-trained, individuals could use the Internet. There have also been advances in industrial computing, grid computing, and SIP Voice over Internet. Although many recognize that security is important, speed and transparency are the watchwords of today's Internet, and these sometimes come at the expense of better security. It is easy to see how the absence of a fundamentally secure infrastructure, coupled with the above set of user expectations, would result in Web attacks being quick, easy, and inexpensive, and detection being complicated and difficult.

Most Web users place a great deal of trust in the infrastructure of the Internet. This could well be because most of them are not knowledgeable about the structural support underlying the Internet. Organizations hire experts who may or may not be given the authority to plug the known holes in the organization's network. The general public seem to believe they have nothing to steal, so they have nothing to lose either. Surprisingly, many Webmasters and server administrators seem to believe that their servers or sites are so well-protected or insignificant that they would never be the target of an attack. Technology improves constantly, so yesterday's secure patch is tomorrow's script-kiddie exploit. Thinking that you are "done" with patching your Internet-facing servers or even your home computer is a weakness that hackers have

15

exploited over and over. Changing to a more active patching methodology may be more costly than merely retreating, but it is far cheaper than fixing the damage, once your site has been hacked.

Some factors that lead to vulnerability of data and applications on the Web are the following:

- Weak passwords

- Insecure software configurations

- Ease of information distribution of new vulnerabilities and exploits

- Increasingly sophisticated hacking tools available

- Increasing number of people with access to and interest in the Internet for criminal endeavors

Weak Passwords

The Internet is rife with usernames and passwords. Users must supply authentication to get on the Internet at all. This is masked by the "transparency" requirement of Internet use. Even if you are using T1 access, and as a user, you never see the username/password transaction, your ISP and your LAN administrator are aware of your organization's authentication keys which allow you access. DSL accounts employ client applications to authenticate their access, and dial-up access accounts use usernames and passwords to grant access. All e-mail accounts have username/password authentication, though many users use the transparent "saved password" systems on their computers and forget that they even have passwords. Many Web sites use authentication schemes, and these schemes are of varying levels of security. As a user, it is difficult to ascertain whether a site has a strong passwording system. It is the responsibility of the Webmaster or sometimes the server administrator to make a site or server secure. The only thing that a user can do to maintain security is to choose a set of strong passwords. A set of passwords is better than just one password because even the strongest password can be cracked, given sufficient time. A password like **W9oO0wWrefgr7&** would be difficult to guess. Were you to leave it lying about, and have it fall into a cracker's hands, it would probably be comforting to know that the cracker could only access your music file-sharing account, and not use it to access your online bank account or credit-card accounts.

Insecure Software Configuration

Microsoft server operating systems are shipped using an easy-to-implement, but unsecured, configuration which allows Web sites to be hosted on the computer quickly. These servers are wide open—meaning they are not properly secured by default—so it is not surprising that Web sites hosted on such computers might be open to attack. In 2007 the average time between bringing an unsecured server (or client) onto the Internet, and its being infected by one of the thousands of circulating Internet worms, is less than 20 minutes.

Furthermore, the majority of network traffic on the Web is not encrypted. A very simple packet sniffer can discover a new Web server as quickly as it can make its presence known to the closest DNS server.

More and more servers are entering the Internet every month and new users increase at a higher rate. The applications used on Web servers, from the implementation of the HTTP server to advanced data-driven, server-side applications, are already complicated and already require very specialized knowledge to configure properly. But to make matters worse, these applications increase in complexity and in implementation. The open-source Mambo project, a content management system built on PHP, was recently found to have a vulnerability based on a common error of letting the configuration.php file be writable. This is an easy hole to plug, but in the last several years, hackers have searched for that file and, upon verifying that it is writable, have uploaded their own HTML to the site. The result is that every page, on a site so afflicted, shows the inserted HTML. Some Webmasters panic when this happens, and rebuild their entire sites by uploading backup files to replace the hacked files.

Ease of Information Distribution

The Internet is primarily an avenue for distributing information, and so it follows that the news of novel exploits and newly discovered vulnerabilities are widely known upon disclosure.

Increasingly Sophisticated Hacking Tools Available

Network security professionals and hackers alike develop and discover new tools and innovative methods of attacks that apply to new features of security systems and software. They have sophisticated tools and techniques to monitor the Internet for new connections. Systems which are newly connected to the Internet are often not properly configured, thus becoming susceptible to damaging attacks.

15

Network security tools available to attack (or test) a system or a network have also become more effective, easier to use, and more accessible. GUI front-ends for the tools and even Windows-based tools make it possible to play with hacking tools without much knowledge of operating systems or command-line mumbo-jumbo. Those lacking in technical skills are still able to break into vulnerable systems. Certain tools can give a hacker the ability to examine programs for vulnerabilities, even without their source code. These tools are designed to assist system administrators in identifying problems, but hackers can use them to exploit the problems discovered and break into systems. The tools used by hackers have increased in automation, allowing hackers to rapidly collect information about thousands of Web hosts with minimal effort. These tools are able to scan entire networks from a remote location and identify individual Web hosts with specific weaknesses.

Some tools can even automate multiple attacks, such as a denial-of-service attack. An intruder can use a packet sniffer to obtain passwords for a router or firewall. The intruder can then disable filters in the firewall and read data from a secure server. Some of the tools used to exploit Web vulnerability are:

- Network scanners
- Password-cracking tools

- Packet sniffers

- Trojan horse programs

- Tools for modifying system log files

- Tools for automatically modifying system configuration files

Access Increasing

An ever-increasing number of people are accessing the Internet every year, and fast access through cable or DSL is also increasing. The general increase of population brings with it an increased number of people with access to and interest in the Internet for criminal endeavors. The often-inflated numbers quoted by companies that advertise that they have been hacked is in itself a motivation for criminally-minded people to work on hacking into these computer "gold mines." It may be said that the number of people sufficiently trained or self-taught to use available exploits outnumber the security professionals who are charged with defending corporate networks. Most crackers are not technically sophisticated pro-grammers, but they have gotten the pieces they believe they need to understand network topology, security, protocols, and operations. The attacks that overwhelmingly populate the Internet are worms and viruses, and are often the work of newly minted hackers. Real damaging hacks are still very seldom achieved and are usually inside jobs.

WEB SERVER VULNERABILITIES

There are hundreds, perhaps thousands, of varieties of Web server software. Many of these are custom code developed for a single narrow implementation, but the two most widely used are Apache and Microsoft Internet Information Server (IIS). The best numbers we have on Web server populations come from Netcraft.com, and a fleeting look at their data shows that it is not without ambiguity. "IIS" shows up 8 times on the list, and "Apache" shows up 27 times. According to the June, 2007 survey[1], IIS is running on approximately 38 million Web servers and Apache is running on about 65 million Web servers. (Note that this does not mean that there are twice as many Unix/Linux servers as Windows servers, since Apache also runs on Windows.) There are myriad reasons why a Web server might be vulnerable. These vulnerabilities may be due to engineering and design errors or just faulty implementation. A few of the most important Web server vulnerabilities are as follows:

- Insecure network

- Unsecured hardware

- Threats from insiders

- Weaknesses in site administration tools

- Weaknesses in application or protocol design

- Weaknesses in operating system software

Insecure Network

When the network of an organization is not secure, no data transmission over the Internet or local area network (LAN) is secure. Users who have access to the network can intercept messages over the network with the use of packet sniffers. Most unencrypted traffic—including usernames and passwords, email messages, Web page requests, and VoIP calls—is vulnerable to a packet sniffer set within the network segment.

Unsecured Hardware

If the Web server hardware is not securely protected from unauthorized physical access, no amount of software security can protect that server's data. A Web server in an open room or in some common area, where all users can access it, is not secure. After 10 unmonitored minutes, a cracker with the right tools can leave your server wide open to external hacking later. In such a case, which is the vast majority of cases, no amount of protection from external threats to the network can save the organization from an internal breach of security.

Threats from Insiders

It is an ongoing myth that outsiders perpetrate most computer crimes. Discounting worms and viruses, which are generally self-perpetuating, most effective computer crime originates within the organizations targeted. It is a mistake to assume that everyone in the organization who has access to system resources will follow the organization's security policies. It is easy to tamper with documents. Network administrators—just like police officers, CFOs, and others charged with the protection of some facet of an organization's upkeep—can be motivated to bend or break their promise to uphold the law or company policy, and they are far better able to bring an exploit to a successful conclusion than others who do not have the access or specialized knowledge. Their motives might include boredom, idle curiosity, the challenge, revenge, or financial reward. A large organization may have several different Web servers for its marketing, accounting, and sales divisions. Any or all of these servers might be assaulted by employees, consultants, or contractors working within the company.

Weaknesses in Site Administration Tools

Web sites are designed to be dynamic, and content of a successful site is updated and renewed often. Therefore, a server upon which Web sites are hosted is also regularly monitored. An administrator should monitor her log files for information about the users visiting the site—for the kinds of browsers these users have; for their FTP accesses, especially uploads; and for additions of new files and directories to unexpected areas within the site's structure. Knowing user demographics and the software they use tells you the way to tweak the site so that it runs best for the users. If 38% of your visitors use a specific browser or operating system, you might consider testing the site on that browser/OS, to ensure that they can properly access and use your site. If many users are coming from two different countries with different base languages, you might want to consider forking your site to be language-friendly to both large supported language groups—or at least to test the second-highest language group to see if they want a native language area in your site. If you see that new directories are being added to your site, it's possible that someone is adding landing pages for phishing exploits on your site. This is extremely simple to plug, if you are paying attention, but it puts you in a difficult position if legal authorities are the ones who bring it to your attention.

If you administer your server locally, it is simple to keep your administration tools secure. As soon as you decide to open the server up to remote administration, or in those cases where you host many sites with many administrators, the challenge of securing the admin tools goes up geometrically. Several administrators may monitor the same Web server for different Web sites. In this situation, the server must allow remote editing and authoring. Some Web sites are updated from client computers on the server's LAN, and others access the server from the Internet. The easier you make it for authorized users to access their sites, the easier it becomes for unauthorized users to access pieces of the Web server.

Weaknesses in Application or Protocol Design

At the time that software is designed, security is often not of the highest priority. Frequently software developers plan to consider the security aspect of the system at some later stage of development. This kind of developmental strategy typically produces software that presents unexpected vulnerabilities because the security components were an add-in rather than being fundamental considerations in the design process.

Because protocols define the rules and conventions for computers to communicate over a network, if a protocol has a fundamental design flaw, then it is vulnerable to various exploits, essentially forever. Each time a new application is developed using that flawed protocol, the same flaw has to be patched. One ubiquitous example is buffer overflow, which is a design flaw in the C and C++ languages, and by extension, a perennial favorite, as those languages underlie almost all of the operating systems used as platforms for Web servers.

Weaknesses in System Software

All operating system software has vulnerabilities due to the nature of the software life cycle, the languages used to program the software, and the philosophy and focus of development organizations. System software is very complicated and intended to supply the base for all subsequent application layer and presentation layer software. Figure 15-1 shows the basic architecture of all operating system design. The operating system and the kernel (where system calls emanate) sit at the heart of a system, right above the hardware; the applications surround that, and the interfaces surround that. As a user, you never interact with an operating system directly; you are always dealing through two layers of abstraction. You interact directly with hardware when you plug things in, type on the keyboard, hit the *on* button, disconnect a cable, etc. There are questions as to whether the device drivers are separate from the kernel (microkernel architecture, e.g., AIX and AmigaOS) or whether they are incorporated therein (monolithic architecture, e.g., Linux, Windows, and UNIX)—but this is for another text.

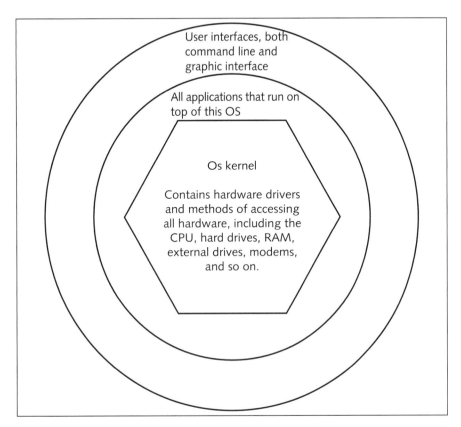

Figure 15-1   Computer architecture

The point of this example is to demonstrate that even with the best software in the world and unlimited time to develop it, the system software is the foundation upon which the software is laid. Since system software, including the hardware driver packages, is subject to the same time constraints and emphasis on transparency and ease of use, the same issues of security as an afterthought apply to system software as they do to application software. In the case of Windows system architecture, the network services and remote configuration facilities are enabled by default, and policies for accessing system files are liberal. This is a philosophic holdover from when Windows was designed as a GUI interface for Microsoft DOS. Windows has integrated the GUI and disk operating system into one large indivisible package, to the point that DOS is now but a virtual machine operating as an application above the OS in Windows Server 2000 and later versions. UNIX and Linux systems, on the other hand, were created as multiuser, multiprocess operating systems, and thus ship with networking security in mind—network systems are disabled by default and require some setup and configuration before they are used.

System software vulnerabilities can be divided into coding and implementation categories, which hackers often exploit using their own tools.

Coding Vulnerabilities

- API abuse—An API is a contract between a caller and a receiver. The most common forms of API abuse are caused by the caller failing to honor its end of this contract. For example, if a program fails to call `chdir()` after calling `chroot()`, it violates the contract that specifies how to change the active root directory in a secure fashion.

- Access control vulnerability—Various access-related vulnerabilities include unsafe mobile code, unsafe privilege, unverified ownership, user management errors, ACL errors, and race conditions.

- Authentication vulnerability—Password policy issues, including password aging, weak passwords, and retained default passwords.

- Code permission vulnerability—Weak access controls in code. For example, a method or variable might be `public()` rather than `private()`.

- Code quality vulnerability—Poor code quality leads to unpredictable behavior. From a user's perspective, this may appear as poor usability, but an attacker might use it as an opportunity to stress the system in unexpected ways.

- Cryptographic vulnerability—For instance, choosing poor or weak encryption algorithms or keys that are too short or too obvious.

- Environmental vulnerability—This category covers everything external to the source code, such as insecure compiler configuration, physical security of the packaging, and the delivery process.

- Error-handling vulnerability—Code does one of two things when an error happens in a process, either the error is handled by a subprocess, intended for that purpose or it stops the process. An error-handling vulnerability exists when the process fails and doesn't then exit cleanly.

- General logic error vulnerability—A logic error is a bug in a program that causes unexpected results or operation but not failure. Logic errors are usually the hardest to debug because they do not cause the program to fail completely. A common technique in solving logic errors is to print the program's variables to a file or the console in order to isolate where the problem is.

- Input validation vulnerability—The most common input validation vulnerability is buffer overflow, which is a condition that allows excess data in a field to overwrite the memory adjacent to the space set aside for the expected field input. The overflow runs into other areas of RAM, overwriting the data pointers that would take the subfunction back to a higher-level function.

Implementation Vulnerabilities

- Improper Web server access configuration—A Web server is itself treated as a user of the operating system and hardware on a physical server. It has required rights and access privileges, just like a human user. A properly configured Web server has only the rights and privileges that are required for it to operate effectively.

- Administrative privileges—If a Web server user profile has administrative privileges, or on a UNIX/Linux system is "running as root," then all users are able to access all files on the physical server, including all private and protected files including system files.

- Default user accounts—Default user accounts—such as the "guest" user on Windows servers, or default users on applications that are later installed on the server—can create vulnerabilities, especially if they are forgotten by the system administrators. These accounts should be deactivated or deleted if they are not being used.

  Another way that default user accounts can be a problem is in situations where administrators set up all new users with the same password. In most cases this kind of practice is harmless, and makes life easier, but what if there are users set up who never log in and change their default password? Network protocol analyzers can return to an attacker the list of users who have never logged in. This can lead to a huge vulnerabilities in the system.

- Misconfigured file permissions—Many multiuser operating systems use account privileges to uphold security to users on a network. All users on a network have a user account associated with a group access policy and every account is associated with a specific set of rights and privileges based on group or role policy plus individual special access. For instance, some accounts may be given the right to read or write certain files, open network connections, or access device drivers. Group policies allow user setup to be easy. If a user is accidentally associated with a group possessing permissions that the user really should not have, it can cause security issues. Or, if a group is given widened access because of a specific individual's requirements, then every new member of the group is given the access.

15

PROTECTION AGAINST WEB APPLICATION VULNERABILITIES

This section details certain measures that you can take to secure your Web server from being exploited. Note that the physical server must be protected, the network architecture must be protected, the operating system on that server must be protected, and the Web server application also must be protected. There may also be systems and applications—such as Java Runtime Environment, Web-hosting software, PHP, Visual Basic.NET infrastructure, JAS, Cold Fusion servers, and e-mail applications—required on your server, in addition to many other narrow-focus Web applications, which will need to be patched and protected as well. It is expected that some of your security solutions may overlap in area of effect.

Securing the Operating System and the Web Server

Place your Web server in a demilitarized zone (DMZ). A DMZ is a neutral zone between the private LAN and the public network of an organization. It is designed to prevent external users from gaining direct access to any internal servers or workstations that have confidential data. This protects your LAN from the possibility that your Web server will be hacked by some insider or some outsider. However, this does not, by itself, protect the Web server from network-borne attack.

Next, check for all default configurations in the operating system and in the Web server. Dump any default user profiles and shutdown or even uninstall any services that the server does not need to be running. Modify user groups to guarantee that authorized users have only as much access as they require. Shut down Telnet and anonymous FTP. Use encrypted services like secure shell (SSH) and authenticated FTP. Set your network firewall to ignore HTTP connections to all ports except HTTP and HTTPS ports, and automate OS patch updates so that patches are installed as soon as they are available.

Monitoring the Server for Suspicious Activity

Learn what suspicious traffic looks like and monitor system logs for it. Install Snort on your server to search for signature attacks. This can involve constant monitoring. It is also a good idea to install some scripts to watch for attacks on the server. Use Snort as a base and add filters to search for new exploits. Generate scripts or use tools such as Tripwire, that can run unattended, to maintain the integrity of password files and registry entries. If any of these tools detect a change at the threshold that you configure, you can set them to send an e-mail to the server administrator or a page to her cell phone.

Controlling Access to Confidential Documents

Limit the number of users having administrative or root-level access. Allow only secure shell encrypted remote administration, or authenticated user access through the GUI control panels built into your hosting software, if you sell hosting to other site managers.

Always maintain your Web page on a server on the intranet, and make all changes to your Web pages from there. Then upload the Web pages to the public server through an SSL connection. This will prevent having the LAN exposed for any length of time, and gives you a complete "book version" of the site in case your public server goes down for any reason. It will be quick to update a replacement server if the public server burns down or is hacked irretrievably.

Setting Up Remote Authoring and Administration Facilities

Remote authoring and administration facilities allow you to monitor all user activity on your private development machine and also to keep a record of Web server logs on a protected machine. Whether you keep your logs on the Web server or on a separate machine, keep them encrypted.

Frequently remove unnecessary files from the scripts directory and also remove default documents that were shipped with your Web servers.

Protecting the Web Server on a LAN

Prior to connecting the Web server to the Internet, make certain that it has been hardened and cannot be used as a staging area to attack other computers on the network. If it is at all possible, put the Web server in a DMZ or put a hardware firewall between it and the rest of the LAN.

If the organization has several Web servers and they are maintained by different departments, remove trust relationships that might exist between them. If one of your servers is attacked successfully, it does not help the attackers to get at any of your other servers.

Checking for Security Issues

Periodically, scan your Web server with tools such as Nmap or Nessus to check for possible new vulnerabilities. Add a software firewall such as Zone Alarm Pro to your Windows machine to monitor for unexpected internal traffic and to monitor unexpected connections to the Web server.

WEB BROWSER VULNERABILITIES

On the client side, the main issues are similar to the server side. Physical tampering and operating system vulnerabilities do exist and ought to be controlled; however, for most users, the main focus is the Web browser. This is the main access to Internet resources and so it is the primary place where client vulnerabilities appear. The most common source of Web-browser exploits is physical tampering. At home or at work, the best way to avoid physical tampering is to password-protect your screensaver and always lock your screen if you are leaving the station. If they cannot look at anything on your computer but the login screen, most casual hackers will move on to easier pickings.

15

Cache File

When a Web site is accessed, the browser receives files from the Web server which the browser interprets as a displayable Web page, music file, or other type of file, and it then presents the data to the best of its ability. For instance, in an average HTML page, the code received to make a word italic is <i>Word</i> The browser displays this as *Word*.

Everything you access on the Internet is copied to a cache file. If you happen to access this page later, your browser checks to see if you have the file. If the file is available in the cache, then the browser displays it in preference to displaying the file available on the server. There is a significant time savings and also a bandwidth savings. If the page has been updated, the browser compares the page in the cache file to the page on the server and loads the latest page. You can force the browser to download a new page by hitting the Reload or Refresh button on your browser.

The information saved in the cache files, history file, or bookmarks on a browser might pose a threat if accessed by someone intending to gather information about the user. This information gives a physical intruder a good idea of your habits and may even give them lists of passwords and usernames for access-controlled sites.

If your browser supports HTML 3.0 extensions and Java, and you are not properly configured, your history file, cache, and other files can be copied from your hard drive and directly uploaded to an attacker's server by using Java, JavaScript, or ActiveX. Your system can later be used to attack other resources behind your LAN's firewall.

History File

The history file dialog in a browser allows you to view the pages you have visited in the last user-defined number of days. The next time you open a page that is listed in your History, the followed links on the page will be purple, not blue.

Any queries submitted to search engines is also stored in the history file. In addition, all information regarding the forms you submit on a Web page is also included in the history file. Furthermore, the history file may include credit card details, user name, or password.

Figure 15-2 shows the History tab and dialog tab in the Preferences dialog box in Firefox 1.5.0.5

Bookmarks

Bookmarks are similar to history files because they store information about the Web pages you have visited; however, bookmarks do not expire like history files.

If you bookmark a Web site that requires entering a password, for convenience, the username and probably the password may also be stored in the cache, and you are given the option to save the username and password (available in Firefox by looking at the Preferences | Privacy | Passwords | [View Passwords] dialog box). An attacker who can access your machine may be able to access your controlled-access sites by going into your computer, looking for the Bank of My Town, and going to the site. If you saved the password, it will be filled in * * * and the attacker can access your data there.

Cookies

A cookie is a small text file, stored on your computer by Web servers, that contains information about the last session when you visited the site. Cookies store followed link information and may store username and password information for some sites, so that you can go back to a site within a short amount of time and not have to log in again. Cookie files are stored in C:/Documents and Settings/Username/Cookies on a Windows 2000 or XP machine. On a

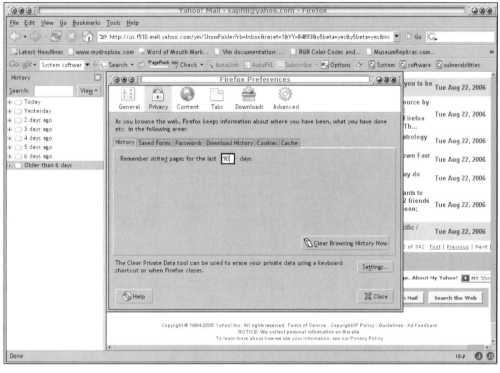

Figure 15-2   History tab in Firefox

Win95/98 machine, they will be in a subdirectory of the $Windows$ directory. On a Linux box, they are stored in the /home/user/.mozilla/firefox/profilename/ directory.

There are two flavors of cookies:

- Session cookies —Temporary cookies that are erased when you close your browser at the end of your session. The next time you visit that site, it will not recognize you and will treat you as a completely new visitor as there is nothing on your computer to let the site know that you have visited before. Session cookies maintain state while you are connected to a given site, keeping track of which pages you have visited on that site and maintaining the followed/unfollowed color-markers of links within the site.

- Persistent cookies—These remain on your hard drive until you erase them or they expire. How long a cookie remains on your hard drive depends on how long the visited Web site has programmed the cookie to last. Persistent cookies are sometimes used by advertisers to track your behavior on the Internet.

Figure 15-3 illustrates the location of cookie files on a Linux user's computer, along with an example of a cookie's contents. Note that the browser and operating system are visible near the top of the `cookies.txt` file. The .mozilla directory is generally hidden. An attacker would have to know to make hidden directories and files visible to steal the information there.

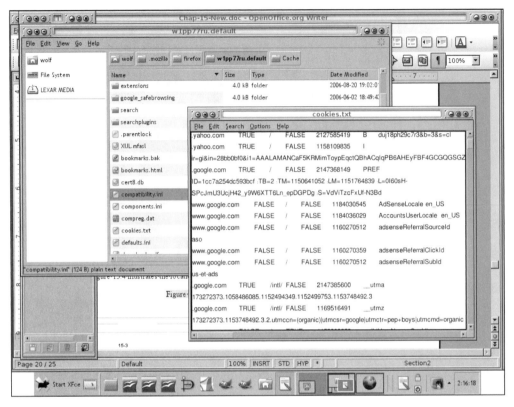

Figure 15-3   Linux cookie files

Location of Web Files Cache

The cache information is located in various directories, depending on the operating system, the browser, and the version of the browser. The cache information is typically stored in a subdirectory of the Web browser's working directory. On a Windows 2000 or XP box, the Temporary Internet Files directory is located in the C:/Documents and Settings/username/ Local Files/Temporary Internet Files directory. The Local Files directory is a normally hidden folder. To unhide all folders, go to Start | Control Panel | Folder Options dialog box, click View, and then click the appropriate check box to unhide hidden files and folders. Click Apply and then close the Folder Options dialog box. Next, open the Internet Options dialog box to set Internet Explorer to configure your system to cache information according to your requirements. You can set the browser to update the cache every time a page is visited, every time Internet Explorer is started, automatically, or never. If you do not make a choice here, all page information will be stored by default in the cache automatically.

Browser Information

Whenever you log onto a Web site, the browser automatically sends information. This is why logon credentials that are sent to a Web server may compromise the privacy of a computer. The purpose of this feature is to allow the server to send the level of content viewable by your hardware and software setup, but it might also be used by an attacker to exploit a vulnerability known to be present on your browser version on your operating system. This is really useful information for attackers. One of the sites that can be used to acquire information from the Web browser is BrowserSpy (www.gemal.dk/browserspy/). This site can provide all types of detailed information about you as well as your browser.

Every time a Web site is visited, the browser automatically sends the following data to the Web server on which it can be compiled and analyzed:

- Host address
- Web browser's version
- Web browser's language
- Files the Web browser accepts
- Characters your Web browser accepts
- Browser encoding
- Username
- HTTP port of the computer

It is possible that the following information about a computer's settings may be acquired if JavaScript is enabled on the user's Web browser:

- JVM or Java plug-ins
- FTP password
- Current resolution
- Maximum resolution
- Version
- Color depth
- Platform
- Anti-aliasing fonts

Session ID Exploits

Once establishing a connection with a server, a user provides authentication information. The username, password, or any other account details is given to the server. Based upon this data, a session is established between the user's computer and the server. At this time, a session ID is generated and then sent to the client. The session ID is used as a key between the client computer and server. This shows that the user can communicate with the server until that session expires. Based on the session ID, the client computer is given access to a variety of services on that server. The session ID maintains the user-state information until the session expires or one of the nodes terminates the session. If the session ID happens to expire prematurely, the user must to establish the session with the server again in order to access its services.

A typical scenario could involve a user needing to withdraw some amount from a bank through an online account. In order to properly withdraw the amount, the user needs to establish a connection with the bank's server. Once a session is established between the user's computer and the bank's server, the user will be able to execute the transaction with the server.

Sometimes, when sessions expire, servers permit the same session ID to be used for the next session between the client and the server. In this case, the initial setup for establishing a session between a client and server is bypassed. When the client computer sends the same session ID to the server, the server may accept it and use it for the new session, thus saving considerable session setup time.

When a session is reused in this way, all access controls based on client information are given to the user. This is based on the assumption that the original session has already made the necessary authentication checks. An attacker can use the same server behavior to access account details by borrowing the session key and connecting to the server. The server recognizes the session ID and accepts it as valid. Then the server provides access to its services assuming that a legitimate user has requested the session. This is one way an unauthorized user with access to a user's machine or a sniffer on the user's network gets account details of a user.

The problem of a session ID being used by an unauthorized user affects servers that support session reuse and also have multiple virtual hosts served from a single server. Some of the virtual hosts use differing client/server verifications which include either no verification or little verification.

For instance, a Web cache or a proxy server that is not configured properly may cache either the initial cookie header or the cookie itself. Therefore, an unauthorized user who requests the same URL from the server may gain information from the cache rather than establishing a new connection. This user may acquire another user's session on subsequent requests. Consequently, the unauthorized user may access the Web site by using a valid user's details.

WEB BROWSER PROTECTION

Hackers are able to learn a lot about individuals and organizations due to browser vulnerabilities. A site may capture information about an operating system, browser, e-mail address, hostname, and last site visited because of various logon options. For protection from various browser vulnerabilities, consider taking the following precautions. You could disable the cache, or set its size to zero. This will require the browser to always load the page from the Internet and may, at times, degrade system performance. Alternately, you could set your browser to clear your cache every time you close the browser, and look into the file system to see if it is actually doing that. One interesting feature of Windows 2000 and later is that the Temporary Internet Files are kept in subdirectories which are not visible in the right pane of Windows Explorer, only in the left pane. This means that you must always use the Explorer option when you are looking at the files there. This is true, even if you have used File Options to make all files and folders—including hidden system files—visible. Internet Explorer does not always empty these double-hidden files at the close of a session or before visiting a Web site.

In addition, set the History preference to save for 0 days or, even better, delete the file at the end of the session.

Furthermore, do not set vulnerable pages in your bookmarks, and either do not save passwords or set the master password (if this option is available in your browser). Remember to clear your cookies file to remove cookies, and make the cookie.txt file read only. Another step might be to disable JavaScript support and cookies on your browser, although this may be annoying as it will prevent you from properly viewing and using many Web sites. A less drastic step might be to use Firefox as your browser, set your browser to accept only cookies from trusted sites and the originating Web site, and set your Internet security to High, requiring all scripts to ask for permission to run.

CHAPTER SUMMARY

15

- The protocols upon which the Internet rest are insecure. Speed and transparency are the driving forces of Internet development, often coming at the expense of security.

- The absence of a fundamentally secure infrastructure, coupled with constantly evolving user expectations, results in quick, easy, and inexpensive Web attacks.

- Factors that lead to vulnerability of data and applications on the Web include weak passwords, insecure software configuration, readily available information about new vulnerabilities and exploits, availability of increasingly sophisticated hacking tools, and more people with access to and interest in the Internet for malicious purposes.

- There are hundreds, even thousands, of Web server programs. Many—including the most popular, Apache and Microsoft IIS—are custom-programmed for specific uses.

- Web server vulnerabilities include an insecure network, insecure hardware, threats from insiders, weaknesses in site administration tools, weaknesses in application or protocol design, and weaknesses in operating system software.

- System software vulnerabilities can be divided into two categories: coding and implementation, which hackers often exploit using their own tools.

- Several layers require protection in relation to Web services: the physical server, the network architecture, the operating system, the Web server application, and any additional systems and applications required on your server.

❏ Actions to take for protecting Web servers include securing the operating system and Web server, monitoring the server for suspicious activity, controlling access to confidential documents, protecting the server on a LAN, and checking for security issues.

❏ Primary Web browser vulnerabilities include physical tampering, operating system vulnerabilities, and vulnerabilities inherent in the browser itself.

❏ Hackers can learn a lot about individuals and organizations due to browser vulnerabilities. A site may capture information about an operating system, browser, e-mail address, host name, and last site visited through various logon options.

❏ A session ID serves as a key between a client computer and a server. Sometimes, when sessions expire, servers permit the same session ID to be used for the next session between the client and the server, bypassing the initial setup. An attacker can use this server behavior to access information about the user by borrowing the session key and connecting to the server.

❏ To protect against various browser vulnerabilities, password-protect your screensaver, lock the screen when you are away from your computer, disable the cache, set History preference to save for 0 days, do not bookmark vulnerable pages, do not save passwords, and delete cookies. Alternatively, use Firefox as your browser, set it to accept only cookies from trusted sites and the originating Web site, and set your Internet security to High.

REVIEW QUESTIONS

1. Does placing a Web server in a DMZ protect it from network-borne threats?

2. What are the five classes of attack possible on a Web server?

3. If cookies are so dangerous, why don't valid Web servers discontinue their use?

4. Can a Web server session ID be stolen over the Internet?

5. Is there any valid reason for servers to collect information about their visitors?

Indicate whether the sentence or statement is true or false.

6. _____ Wget is a tool that can be used to retrieve HTTP, HTTPS, and FTP files over the Internet.

7. _____ Namedroppers is a tool that can be used to capture Web server information and possible vulnerabilities in a Web site's pages that could allow exploits such as SQL injection and buffer overflows.

8. _____ Some cookies can cause security issues because unscrupulous people might store personal information in cookies that can be used to attack a computer or server.

9. _____ To limit the amount of information a company makes public, you should have a good understanding of what a competitor would do to discover confidential information.

10. _____ Network attacks often begin by gathering information from a company's Web site.

11. _____ The HTTP CONNECT method starts a remote application-layer loopback of the request message.

Match each term with the correct statement below.

    a. HTTP 400 Bad Request

    b. HTTP 403 Forbidden

    c. HTTP 404 Not Found

    d. HTTP 405 Method Not Allowed

    e. HTTP 408 Request Timeout

    f. HTTP 500 Internal Server Error

    g. HTTP 502 Bad Gateway

    h. HTTP 503 Service Unavailable

12. _____ Request not understood by server

13. _____ Server received invalid response from upstream server

14. _____ Request not allowed for the resource

15. _____ Server is unavailable due to maintenance or overload

16. _____ Request could not be fulfilled by server

17. _____ Request not made by client in allotted time

18. _____ Server understands request but refuses to comply

19. _____ Unable to match request

15

Hands-On Projects

This is a potential legal minefield. Skill in this area must be carefully used. The main Linux server will have several vulnerable Web applications to test—pre-patch versions of applications with known vulnerabilities, and so on. It is not illegal to search for particular versions of Web applications or servers on the Internet, but it might well be illegal to run an exploit against a server you do not control. The ethical way to do penetration tests starts with a signed permission to do so. Security companies that have started their tests before they acquired signed permission have been taken to court for criminal hacking.

Hackers search security sites on the Web first for new vulnerabilities and exploits, and then start searching the Web for sites with the vulnerability. Security specialists, with permission from clients or their employers, do the same things but specifically to the sites owned or controlled by the client or employer.

Project 15-1

XSS or CSS is the most common attack on Web applications, beating out buffer overflow, possibly because there are so many new sites built around Microsoft .Net, PHP, Cold Fusion, Java Server Pages, and the like. In this lab, we will look for sites that use the different applications by searching the Web for their signatures. The pages returned by data-driven site applications are not identical to the pages that produce them.

1. Try searching on google.com for

```
document.location.href='index.php'
```

This is a code snippet from a Mambo or Joomla PHP portal page. Searching google.com gets you one set of results, but it is much more fruitful to search google.com/codesearch, as follows:

```
http://www.google.com/codesearch?hl=en&lr=&q=document.
location.href%3D%27index.php%27&btnG=Search
```

Project 15-2

1. The following search will produce xls files containing the terms "login" and "password". See if you can find five such sites. Record the sites you do find in a text document and submit to your instructor.

```
"login: *" "password: *" filetype:xls
```

This is a legal search; however, use or transfer of the information found using the data discovered in the search is unethical and probably illegal.

CAUTION

REFERENCES

1. Netcraft.com, "June 2007 Web Server Survey." http://survey.netcraft.com/Reports/0706/.

16

WINDOWS VULNERABILITIES

After reading this chapter and completing the exercises, you will be able to:

♦ Give an overview of the main Windows operating systems

♦ Understand the vulnerabilities of Windows 2000/XP/Server 2003

♦ Identify the current vulnerabilities of Windows Vista

The security of the applications running on a computer is partially dependent on the security of the main operating system. Currently, the most commonly used microcomputer operating systems are Microsoft Windows, MacOS, and Linux. The most widely used operating systems on larger servers is one of the many versions of UNIX.

Microsoft's Windows operating systems have been well-received since the release of Windows 3.11. The chief reason for their popularity is Microsoft's large marketing budget and sophisticated distribution system. This popularity comes at a price, however, as there arise new security flaws in Windows systems every day.

Part of the belief that Windows is less secure than other operating systems stems from the ubiquity of Windows. It is such a big target, with such a large installed base, that attacks on Windows are more satisfying because of the impact they can have. Another reason that Windows appears less secure is that the philosophy underlying the design of the original Windows systems was that these machines would be stand-alone, single-user devices, like toasters or television sets. Microsoft originally introduced this fork of the UNIX X Window system at a time when most operating systems required users to memorize lots of commands. With the amazing GUI features of Windows operating systems, and the far more effective marketing structure of Microsoft's marketing apparatus, in comparison to the academic style affected by other operating-system providers, Windows became a standard on millions of PCs.

Windows Operating Systems

The important Windows operating systems are:

- Windows 95
- Windows 98
- Windows NT 4.0
- Windows Millennium Edition (ME)
- Windows 2000 (NT 5)
- Windows XP
- Windows Server 2003
- Windows Vista

Windows 95

Windows 95 is a multitasking, single-user, GUI-based operating system. It supports the Plug-and-Play feature, which helps Windows 95 automatically detect and configure devices. In addition to the above features, Windows 95 is a 32-bit operating system and is designed to support 16-bit Windows 3.1x applications.

Windows 98

Windows 98, an enhanced version of Windows 95, has more customized GUI features. Its file protection and Plug-and-Play features are enhanced as well.

Windows New Technology (NT) 4.0

Windows NT 4.0 was the first popular network operating system developed by Microsoft. It was designed for enterprise use and had far more security features than any previous Windows versions. Windows NT took full advantage of the Intel and AMD 32-bit processors. By the time NT 4.0 came about, support for multiple languages increased the popularity of Windows. Similar to Windows 95 and Windows 98, Windows NT 4.0 also supports Plug-and-Play.

Windows Millennium Edition (ME)

Windows ME was designed to be the successor to Windows 98, after Microsoft's engineers had failed to bridge Windows 98 and Windows NT with Windows 2000. Windows ME was a package of updates to Windows 98, along with a few poorly designed application programs that many people contended were meant to unfairly use Microsoft's monopoly position to knock off better products made by other companies. Many experts call ME a dismal failure, because it had many device-driver issues. It was an effective system if it was used for its designated purpose: single-user, stand-alone PC with very standard peripherals.

Windows 2000

The name Windows 2000 (Win2K) was a marketing decision, not a technology change. The "new technology" name was aging and the idea of NT 5.x and so on appeared to accentuate the effect of that aging. Windows 2000 is a multiuser, multitasking operating system, like Windows NT 4.0. It is more secure and stable than Windows NT 4.0. Windows 2000 provides wizards which simplify several activities. This is an OS from the early Microsoft philosophy of "One OS for business and another for home use." Windows 2000 comes in four versions: Windows 2000 Professional, Windows 2000 Server, Windows 2000 Advanced Server, and Windows 2000 Datacenter Server.

Windows XP

Windows XP (WinXP) is a multiuser, multitasking operating system based on Windows 2000. There exist both "home" and "work" versions of XP—called XP Home and XP Professional, respectively—and there are some significant differences between the two, as Windows XP Home is a cut-down version of Windows XP Pro. After Service Pack 2 was delivered, Windows XP Pro started to show some real promise, as it offered improved security and better wireless network support.

Windows Server 2003

Windows 2003 (Win2K3) was developed after XP, and was meant strictly for enterprise use. It was intended to get users to update their NT 4.0 servers, and has been pretty successful in that goal since NT 4.0 support ended. Windows Server 2003 comes in eight versions: Small Business Server, Web Edition, Standard Edition, Enterprise Edition, Datacenter Edition, Computer Cluster Edition, Storage Server, and Home Server.

.

16

Windows Vista

Windows Vista was released in 2006 for home and business users. Microsoft's primary stated objective with Vista was to improve the security in the Windows operating system. Vista comes with built-in antispyware software, and new account profile file privileges that may keep users from installing malware. The top-end versions come with a feature called BitLocker that encrypts a computer's hard drive in the case of a lost or stolen machine. Vista comes in five versions: Ultimate, Home Premium, Home Basic, Business, and Enterprise.

VULNERABILITIES IN WINDOWS 2000/XP/2003

Currently, Windows 2000, XP, and 2003 are the predominant versions of the Windows operating systems, although after 2007, Vista may take the lead. All of these operating systems are useful for building large corporate networks. All three have good networking features and user-friendly interfaces for those who are used to Windows. Microsoft continues to support these with new security patches.

As with all previous versions of Windows, Windows 2000, XP, and 2003 are not remotely secure with their default installation settings. The slightest negligence by a systems administrator can make these operating systems extremely vulnerable. In addition to the existing vulnerabilities, new flaws appear regularly. Windows systems administrators must ever remain vigilant and actively pursue protective measures to secure their networks.

There are several vulnerabilities which exist in Windows 2000, XP, and 2003. Some of these vulnerabilities are common to all of these operating systems, whereas others are specific to just one or two.

Passwords

Since the security of passwords is very important to the security of any system, encryption algorithms and hash values are used to secure them.

The easiest way to break password security on a Windows 2000 or later machine is to use a password-burning program which can set the administrator password to a blank. It is not necessary to decipher the password if it can be replaced. This is the device that network administrators would use, as stealth is not a feature with this tool.

Windows 2000 and later applications store passwords in the form of hash values in a database called Security Accounts Manager (SAM), which has a default location of C:\WINNT\ system32\config. The operating system locks the SAM database, making it impossible to read the SAM database from within a Windows operating system. Nevertheless, hackers are able to crack these passwords by using password-cracking tools. To decipher passwords, these tools access the SAM database. At this point, hackers can import passwords from the Windows registry. Hackers are only able to import passwords from the Windows registry of a target computer if remote registry access is enabled on that computer. They might also copy the SAM database and use the password cracker on the file. Hackers can start an operating system from a "**Live Disk**" of an operating system that supports the NTFS (or possibly the FAT32) file system and then copy the SAM file from the target computer. It is important to note that only hackers who have physical access to the target computer can use this method to obtain passwords.

TIP

The NTFS file system is more secure than the FAT32 file system.

The Microsoft utility SYSKEY safeguards passwords from cracking activities. The SYSKEY utility encrypts passwords with a 128-bit algorithm, making it very difficult to crack. The SYSKEY utility is active by default in Windows 2000 and newer operating systems. Newer password crackers like Cain and Abel can crack 128-bit encryption.

A program named *pwdump3* gives remote access to the SAM database on a computer in which the SYSKEY utility is active. However, to use *pwdump3*, hackers need to have administrator privileges on the target computer.

Although all the Windows operating systems since NT 4.0 are susceptible, it still requires administrative privilege to exploit this vulnerability. For this reason, system administrators must be careful about who they grant access rights to for users of a Windows 2000 and later operating system. The administrator accounts should also be protected with strong passwords and most computer use should be done with lower privileges.

Default Accounts

At the time of installation, Windows 2000 makes a default account with the name "Administrator". By default, the password is blank. Nobody can delete the administrator account from a Windows 2000 computer, but it is possible to change the password of this account at the time of installation.

To acquire access to a target system that is running either of these operating systems, hackers attempt to use the account named Administrator. To avoid this, users can change the name from Administrator to something else. After changing the name, make a new account named Administrator but give it no special access privileges.

Windows 2000 and later operating systems also create a default account labeled "Guest". This allows nonregular users to access the system. The guest account has a blank password by default. When enabling the guest account, hackers may use that account to access a Win2K, WinXP, or Win2K3 computer.

Win2K, WinXP, and Win2K3 also create a default account called "default" with full administrative rights at installation. This is often used as the main or only account by users who do not know to run lower access privileges generally and to use administrative privileges only when they are needed.

16

The main thing that is wrong with having known default names for accounts is that it makes a password cracker's life much easier. If they have to come up with both the username and a password, it multiplies the difficulty involved.

File Sharing

Files in a folder may be shared to allow other users on the network to access those files. In Windows 2000, XP, and 2003, users can share files in a folder by using the Properties dialog box. To open the Properties dialog box, right-click the icon of the folder that is to be shared, then select the Sharing option from the shortcut menu.

After the Properties dialog box is displayed, select the "Share this folder" option to enable the sharing feature. The default setting for sharing is "all access" so there is a definite risk there. To set the permissions more tightly, click the Permission button in the Properties dialog box. "Full Control" access to all users means that any user on the network can change the contents of the files in the shared folder. Access can be restricted based on user or group, and for the sake of maintaining security, it is important to set the access rights rather than leave the default sharing settings.

Windows Registry

Windows 95 was the first version of Windows to use a registry, though it was not the source of all its system settings. WinNT 4.0 and its successors use the registry as the source of all system settings information. Changing settings in the registry without understanding the effects can easily render a Windows installation inoperable. The registry of Windows NT 4.0 and later Windows operating systems stores system and user related information under different keys. Examples of these are, HKEY_LOCAL_MACHINE and HKEY_USERS. Poorly configured registries have certain flaws which permit hackers to access Windows computers.

One critical vulnerability in the registry is related to the registry information about an action performed by a user during login. The Windows registry maintains this information in a key called HKEY_LOCAL_MACHINE\SOFTWARE\Microsoft\Windows\CurrentVersion\Run.

Automatically, every user of a Windows 2000 and XP computer has a "Set Value" access to this registry key. The "Set Value" access lets any user who has access to the system, make modifications. Therefore, a user who does not have administrator privileges can alter this key to obtain unauthorized access. For instance, a worm that infests the computer can add entries to it. To prevent hackers from exploiting this vulnerability, the "'Set Value" access should be restricted to specific users, such as administrators.

Trust Relationship

Windows 2000, XP, and 2003 operating systems authenticate only the users who access resources within the domain. Yet all of these operating systems have a feature that is known as trust relationship. It allows the authenticated users of a Windows domain to access resources on another domain, without being authenticated by it. The domain that trusts the users of another domain is known as the trusting domain and the domain with trusted users is the trusted domain.

These operating systems authenticate users by means of verifying their Security Identifiers (SIDs) in the access control list. Each user and group has a SID, and the access control lists store SIDs and the user rights related to each SID. Each of the various resources on a Windows machine maintains an access control list. Whenever a system administrator grants rights to a user for a resource, the access control list of that resource is updated with the SID and rights of that particular user. If a user attempts to access a resource, the operating system compares the SID of the user with the SIDs in the access control list of that resource and grants only authorized users to use that resource.

When the user of a trusted domain tries to access a resource on a trusting domain, that trusting domain allows the trusted domain to authenticate users. If the trusted domain authenticates the SID of the user, then the trusting domain permits the user to access the resource without any re-authentication.

There is a risk that a cracker can hack a network and add unauthorized SIDs into that domain's ACL. The trusting domain asks for no authorization. If hackers are successful in this activity, they may be able to access critical resources on the trusting domain without any evidence that they are unauthorized.

Hackers require administrator privileges on the trusted domain in order to exploit this. Furthermore, they need strong technical knowledge to change low-level operating system functions and data structures. To insert SIDs in a Windows operating system, hackers must develop customized programs which allow them to modify the authentication details. The Windows 2000 operating system has a mechanism named "SIDHistory". It allows users with administrator privileges to insert SIDs into the authentication details. However, this mechanism lacks a programming interface. Therefore, to exploit this vulnerability in a Windows 2000 operating system, hackers must create binary modifications to the data structure of SIDHistory.

Microsoft provides patch programs for Windows 2000, known as SID filters, that solve this issue. For Windows 2000 operating systems, administrators can install SID filters from Windows 2000 Security Roll-up Package 1, but must install SID filters on the domain controller of the trusting domain. After installing the SID filter, it must be activated for specific trusted domains. Once activated, it filters all SIDs included in the authentication details of the trusted domain and removes all SIDs that are not related to the trusted domain.

Windows 2000 Event Viewer Buffer Overflow

Event Viewer is a tool of Windows operating systems that shows all event logs. The logs found in the Event Viewer are Application, System, and Security. Based on the category of the event, an event is appended to one of these logs. All users can see the Application and System logs, but only users with administrator privileges can view the Security log.

16

In the Event Viewer tool of the Windows 2000 operating system, a buffer overflow occurs in the operating system section that shows the properties of event log records. This buffer overflow happens when a user views the properties of an event record that has been made with some malicious content.

The Event Viewer buffer overflow can produce two different results; first, the Event Viewer may stop functioning, otherwise, with a carefully crafted overflow, it may be possible to run arbitrary code and use the target computer to perform hacking activities.

The use of this vulnerability depends upon the privileges that the hacker has on the target system. If hackers have administrator privileges on the target system, then they will be able to do serious damage. Microsoft introduced a patch for this vulnerability, and the vulnerability does not appear in XP or Win2K3.

NBNS Protocol Spoofing

Windows operating systems use the NetBIOS Name Server (NBNS) protocol to help computers on a network manage name conflicts. The NBNS protocol does not support the authentication process; rather it has two mechanisms which aid computers in solving name conflicts.

The first mechanism is the Name Conflict mechanism. All the computers in the network use this mechanism. The name server uses it to verify if there is a name conflict when a computer registers or refreshes a name in the network. Clients within a network use the Name Conflict mechanism whenever they communicate with other clients.

The second mechanism is the Name Release mechanism. It helps the computers on a network release names when they are not needed any more.

Hackers are able to exploit NBNS mechanisms to conduct a denial of service attack to a computer on a network. With this technique, hackers spoof NBNS traffic and mislead a computer in a network to conclude that its name has conflicted on the network. Consequently, the target computer does not register a name in the network. If a name is already registered, then the target computer cancels that network name. When the other computers on that network try to communicate to the target computer, their messages cannot reach the target because the imaginary name conflict has gotten rid of the name. This issue was fixed in Windows 2000 Service Pack 3.

RPC Service Failure

The Remote Procedure Call (RPC) service of Windows operating systems does not validate inputs that are submitted to it for processing. This vulnerability permits hackers to deny legitimate services of the system to the users.

Hackers can easily send RPC requests with invalid inputs to computers running these operating system. When a computer receives these invalid inputs, the operating system processes them. Depending on their nature, invalid inputs lead to the system services stopping for a period of time.

This vulnerability is also apparent in other Microsoft products, such as Microsoft SQL Server 7.0, Microsoft SQL Server 2000, Microsoft Exchange Server 5.5, and Microsoft Exchange Server 2000.

To minimize the chances of such attacks, the latest service packs should be installed on Windows computers.

SMTP Authentication Vulnerability

A bug in the authentication process of the SMTP service of Windows 2000 Server lets the SMTP service authenticate unauthorized as well as authorized users. Hackers exploit this flaw and use the SMTP service of a target Windows 2000 server to send unauthorized e-mail messages. They cannot use this vulnerability to obtain administrator privileges on the target system. If a user is not using the SMTP service, it should be disabled. Users should make sure the latest patches are being used.

Telnet Vulnerabilities

The Windows 2000 Telnet service has various flaws and vulnerabilities. Some of them enable denial-of-service attacks, while others allow unauthorized access to Windows 2000 computers.

The Telnet service of the Windows 2000 operating system lets users execute system commands that terminate the service. Hackers can use this feature to perform denial-of-service attacks against the Telnet service. Win2K Telnet also lets a user start idle sessions. Hackers work at configuring the Telnet service in order to start multiple idle Telnet sessions. In this situation, the Telnet service processes these idle sessions, not allowing legitimate users to start a Telnet session. Hackers can also execute logon commands with some specific, yet incorrect, information. When hackers execute this type of logon command, it causes access violation in the Telnet service.

These vulnerabilities not only deny services to legitimate users but can compromise any privileges or data on the target system. In most cases, restarting the Telnet service or the Telnet server solves the problem until it is attacked again.

A further vulnerability is that the Telnet service helps hackers gain unauthorized access on the target system. When starting a session, the Telnet service generates a named pipe and uses it for the initialization process. However, if the Telnet service finds an existing named pipe, it uses that named pipe rather than creating a new one. The vulnerability is that hackers are able to predict the name of this pipe. If hackers replace or create a named pipe with specific malicious content on the server, then the Telnet service uses that pipe for the initialization process. After creating a named pipe, hackers associate it with a program that permits them to access the target system remotely. Consequently, when the named pipe is used by the Telnet service, the associated program is executed, and hackers get the unauthorized access.

16

To effectively exploit this vulnerability, hackers need the ability to code and load programs on the Telnet server. Furthermore, they are able to exploit this vulnerability only if the Telnet service is started and running on the target system. Microsoft has patched these vulnerabilities. This patch can be downloaded by installing the latest service pack. If users are not using the Telnet service, it should be shut down. If a computer user is using the Telnet service, consider using a secure protocol like SSH instead.

IP Fragments Reassembly

A bug in the Windows 2000 code component that handles the reassembly of IP fragments causes the target system to spend all the CPU time to process IP packets that have been modified by hackers. The processing of such packets can deny the services of a system to the users for some time. In some critical stages, this vulnerability may even cause a system to crash. Hackers can use this vulnerability to perform denial-of-service attacks on a computer that is running Windows 2000. However, it is very difficult for a hacker to exploit this vulnerability on computers that are protected by firewalls and proxy servers. In most cases, they exploit this vulnerability on computers where Web servers are installed. Patches for this vulnerability are available in the latest service packs of Win2K.

ResetBrowser Frame Vulnerability

Windows operating systems have a protocol that is called Computer Browser. This protocol permits a user of one of these systems to browse contents of other computers that are in the network. There is a Master browser in a network that manages the browsing activities of all other browsers. In addition to this browser management, the Master browser also keeps a list of computers in the network and their services.

The browsers in a network communicate to each other by using frames. This type of frame command is known as ResetBrowser and allows a Master browser to close the other browsers in a network. Master browsers use the ResetBrowser frame to close browsers that are out of contact with other browsers. Users cannot configure the browsers on their computers to avoid the ResetBrowser frame. However, hackers can use the ResetBrowser frames to close the browsers in the network. This sort of activity denies the browser services to legitimate users and allows the attacker to configure the browser on her own computer as the Master browser in the network.

Users can download and install the Microsoft patch programs to stop hackers from exploiting this vulnerability by installing the latest service pack.

There are more vulnerabilities not listed here. However, Microsoft releases a new patch on the second Tuesday of each month to fix new vulnerabilities as they arise. Protect the Windows operating system installed on computers by regularly installing patches and service packs. To obtain information about the latest vulnerabilities and their patches, go to www.microsoft.com/technet/security/tools.

VULNERABILITIES IN WINDOWS VISTA

Windows Vista was designed with a greater emphasis on security than previous Windows desktop operating systems. It includes a number of new features to protect computers from attack. However, known vulnerabilities do exist, and as Vista becomes more widely deployed, more vulnerabilities are likely to be discovered.

Vista Speech Attack Tactic

Vista's speech recognition feature can be used to force a PC into executing some commands. A malicious Web site could host an audio file that shouted out commands to shut down the system, if the system had the speech-recognition application running and was equipped with speakers and microphone. The commands understood by the system include copy, delete, shutdown, etc. A carefully crafted audio file could download an application from the Internet and install it on the victim computer without user intervention. To reduce the chance of this application being run on a computer, users might mute the microphone for general use or disable automatic loading of the speech-recognition application when the operating system loads.

Apple: Vista May Corrupt iPods

Upgrading from Windows 2000 or XP might result in iTunes Desktop player not allowing playback of purchased tunes. iPod users may also encounter difficulties ejecting their digital music players from a desktop port using the "Safely Remove Hardware" feature found on the Vista system tray. This may corrupt a user's iPod. Apple says the safe way to undock an iPod from a Vista-equipped PC, until a patch to the iTunes software is installed, is to use the "Eject iPod" control in the iTunes software.

CHAPTER SUMMARY

- ❏ Microsoft Windows is the most common preinstalled operating system in the world.

- ❏ The security of the applications running on a computer is dependent on the security of the main operating system. As is true of all operating systems, new security flaws appear in Windows systems every day.

- ❏ The belief that Windows is less secure than other operating systems stems in part from the sheer ubiquity of Windows and from the philosophy underlying the design of the original Windows systems: that these machines would be stand-alone, single-user devices.

- ❏ The main Windows operating systems include Windows 95, Windows 98, Windows NT 4.0, Windows Millennium Edition (ME), Windows 2000 (NT 5), Windows XP, Windows Server 2003, and Windows Vista.

- ❏ As with all previous versions of Windows, Windows 2000, XP, and 2003 are not remotely secure in their default installation settings, and new flaws appear regularly.

- ❏ Vulnerabilities affecting one or more of these systems include password security, default accounts, file sharing defaults, Windows registry security defaults, trust relationships between domains, Event Viewer buffer overflow, NBNS protocol spoofing, RPC service failure, SMTP authentication, Telnet vulnerabilities, IP fragments reassembly, and Reset-Browser frame vulnerability.

- ❏ Although Vista places a greater emphasis on security than its predecessors, some known vulnerabilities do exist (and more are likely to appear as Vista becomes more widely deployed). Two of these are the Vista Speech Attack Tactic and an iTunes bug that may corrupt iPods or cause problems with playback of downloaded tunes.

16

REVIEW QUESTIONS

1. What Windows operating systems are supported with security patches?

2. List and describe three Windows 2000 vulnerabilities. Short essay (no more than two pages, please).

3. Why is any Windows installation "insecure by default"?

4. What was the original design philosophy of Windows?

5. What is the largest difference between Windows 2000 and Windows XP?

6. What year was Windows 2000 released?

7. What year was Windows XP released?

8. What year was Windows Vista Released?

9. Where is the default location of the SAM file?

10. What Windows utility encrypts passwords with a 128-bit algorithm?

11. What is wrong with having known default account names?

12. What is the default password of the Windows Administrator user?

13. The Event Viewer buffer overflow exploit affects which Windows operating system?

14. What day is Microsoft's patch release day?

15. Which Windows release has a "speech recognition" feature which can be used to force a PC into executing some commands?

16. Who may adjust the access privileges of shared folders on a Windows machine?

17. Windows Server 2003 was developed and released for what purpose?

18. The easiest way to break password security on a Windows machine is to use a password burning program which can set the administrator password to a blank. It is not necessary to decipher the password if you can just replace it. What is the downside to using a tool such as this?

19. What are the five versions of Vista?

20. What are the versions of Windows 2000?

HANDS-ON PROJECT

Operating system vulnerabilities can be classified as being either default vulnerabilities or utility vulnerabilities. Default vulnerabilities are the result of a standard installation. Utility vulnerabilities are those exposed by use. In this project, you will investigate default vulnerabilities in Windows.

HANDS-ON PROJECTS

Project 16-1

1. Writing Assignment: Citing data on the three current Windows desktops (Windows 2000, XP, and Vista), discuss what the default vulnerabilities of each version are and how the list has changed over time. Does the list remain the same from version to version or are some holes opening and others closing over time? Why do you think this is?

17

LINUX VULNERABILITIES

> **After reading this chapter and completing the exercises, you will be able to:**
> - Identify UNIX-based operating systems
> - Identify Linux operating systems
> - Identify vulnerabilities from default installation
> - Identify various vulnerabilities in Linux and UNIX-based utilities

Linux, the second most widely used Intel-based microcomputer operating system, was derived from UNIX by an engineering student from Finland named Linus Torvalds in 1991. Torvalds began the project that became Linux as a bare-metal terminal-emulator that ran on an 80386 chip. Linux code is not proprietary, though the standard for the Linux kernel is still maintained by Linus Torvalds.

Ken Thompson and Dennis Ritchie at Bell Labs developed a general-purpose operating system they named UNIX in 1969. The name is a pun on Multics, another operating system then being developed by Bell Labs. The first version of UNIX was written in assembly language. In 1973, the developers of UNIX revised it by writing it in C language. After that, several vendors, such as IBM and HP, bought the source code of UNIX and developed their own versions of UNIX. The majority of UNIX users believe that UNIX-based operating systems are quite secure. However, this is not entirely true. UNIX-based operating systems are not totally secure when installed using the default installation procedure.

A discussion of the various UNIX-based operating systems is detailed below.

UNIX-Based Operating Systems

Some of the most popular UNIX-based operating systems are BSD, HP-UNIX, AIX, and SCO Unix. SunOS and Solaris arose, mostly, from BSD code. Most of them are proprietary and maintained by their respective hardware vendors. Because the source code is not freely available, developers, users, and systems administrators sometimes have to wait for the release of bug fixes.

Linux Operating Systems

Linux source code is available free of cost, and some Linux distributions (distros) are also free. The basic architecture and features of Linux are the same as those of the UNIX-based operating systems. Linux follows the open-development model, and the source code of the Linux kernel is available for study and modifications on the Internet.

There are many distributions of Linux. As of the writing of this text, the most commonly searched-for distro is Ubuntu. Red Hat, which used to be the 800-pound gorilla of Linux distros as recently as a year ago, comes in at a mousey 27th place. Table 17-1 displays the top 20 distros—ranked by average number of hits per page (HPD)—according to www. distrowatch.com, as of mid-2007.

Table 17-1   Top 20 Linux distros

Rank	Distribution	HPD
1	Ubuntu	2648
2	openSUSE	1910
3	PCLinuxOS	1505
4	Fedora	1450
5	MEPIS	1107
6	Debian	963
7	Mandriva	940
8	Damn Small	742
9	Sabayon	737
10	Slackware	641
11	Gentoo	579
12	KNOPPIX	566
13	Zenwalk	530
14	Mint	525
15	Kubuntu	473
16	CentOS	454
17	FreeBSD	431
18	Puppy	430
19	Freespire	402
20	Vector	397

One of the main differences between Linux distros is whether they use one of two different packages in their automated package installation technology. Either they use Red Hat Package Manager (RPM) technology or they use Debian packages (DEBs). Ubuntu uses DEBs while Mandriva, Fedora Core, and Red Hat use RPMs. All general distributions of Linux allow the use of both the command line interface (CLI) and the graphical user interface (GUI).

As with the UNIX-based operating systems, Linux is not fully secure in a default installation. For this reason, you need to analyze the possible vulnerabilities that may affect either Linux or UNIX-based operating systems.

VULNERABILITIES FROM DEFAULT INSTALLATION

With the installation of Linux, certain steps must be taken to secure the computer. Most services are off by default upon installation of Linux or UNIX-based operating systems, and they must be configured to run. This is one of the main reasons that Linux/UNIX-based operating systems are considered safer than Windows.

Most Linux/UNIX vulnerabilities appear to be essentially voluntary because of laziness or ignorance on the part of system administrators. A few of the known vulnerabilities of Linux operating systems are discussed below.

Basic Exploits

The basic hacks for a Linux system start with physical access, so the first security measure is to lock down physical access to your Linux servers. It is a good idea for all servers to be kept in a room with good security and restricted access. If this is impossible, then you must take care in selecting start-up options in your basic input/output system (BIOS) setup.

Even if you protect your operating system with complex passwords and other security measures, the system is still vulnerable to hacking attempts. Set your computer to start only from the hard drive, and set a BIOS password so an attacker cannot easily boot your computer from a floppy disk or a CD-ROM. This is actually a hardware hack and not related to the operating system you have installed. You can hack into any x86 architecture machine if you have a bootable floppy or CD-ROM.

17

Login Passwords

Some Linux and UNIX-based operating systems store encrypted login passwords in a file called /etc/passwd. This file also contains the logon names in the more vulnerable, cleartext format. Since all users have read permission to the /etc/passwd file, a hacker who has access to such a system will be able to read the file. This vulnerability is a critical weakness because the hacker can obtain logon names, which can then be used to gain illegal access to systems. The majority of UNIX password-cracking tools can decrypt the passwords stored in the passwd file.

Some UNIX and Linux distros store passwords in a file called /etc/shadow, which is readable only to root. root is the default and unchanging administrative user for UNIX/Linux systems. It is possible to reset the passwd file as the password repository during installation, and this could open an unnecessary vulnerability on your system.

There are many password-cracking tools available to decode UNIX passwords. Users generally choose passwords that mean something to them, and are memorable, but these passwords are the easiest to guess or decrypt. All the users of a Linux system are obliged to select strong passwords with six or more characters, including numbers and special characters. The password for root must be especially strong, because every cracker knows that the default administrative user is root.

Bad System Administration Practices

Upon the installation of Linux, the default configuration and accounts are vulnerable to hacking attempts. These will be discussed in further detail below.

Root Account Mismanagement

The root account is the most important user account in Linux and other UNIX-based operating systems. Knowing this, hackers almost always first attempt to gain access to the root account because it can provide all access privileges on the system. It cannot be reiterated enough that choosing an extremely complex password is a key defense strategy. Strong passwords are best for the root account.

Use root access only when you actually need root access. Almost everything that a user needs to accomplish can be accomplished in regular default user mode. Most other user accounts do not have permission to perform critical activities, cannot look at critical system files, and cannot write to much of anything in the /etc directory, where the system settings are kept. If other users are able to perform certain administrative functions, such as backups, the system may display warning messages about how dangerous the activity may be. The system performs all activities without warning messages while a user is in root user mode. The operating system assumes that users with root account access are fully aware of the functions being performed.

Another obvious vulnerability is leaving a system unattended after logging on with the root account. An alert hacker within an organization can quickly exploit this careless situation to perform any type of hacking activity. Thus, one should always log out of root access when the task requiring it is complete, or if the computer is going to be idle or unattended.

A true command line interface (Terminal mode using tty1 through tty6) never goes into screen-saver mode. Your CLI is too little to be left alone, so specify a time-out period for root account access in the CLI, which minimizes the risk if you happen to be distracted and pulled off-station.

An organization that grants special access to users or groups should not grant any root privileges to them. This includes situations in which employees are highly trusted, such as the CEO or the CFO of the company. Most system administrators will agree, the fewer individuals who have root access, the better.

A Linux system configured in a way that allows remote login is more vulnerable to hacking activities. Hackers have safe, private time to guess root passwords and access the system. If an illegal cracker can work from a distant location, they have less chance of being caught, and time is on their side. To avoid this, remote login of the root account should not be permitted. If you want to access the Linux system from remote locations with root privileges, you can log in by using a normal account. Next, use the /bin/su – command to work with root privileges.

Default Account Mismanagement

Some special accounts are created by default while installing a Linux operating system. The vendors provide these accounts to perform specific system activities. If you do not need the service, disable it and also disable its user account. The default Linux accounts include adm, lp, halt, sync, news, uucp, operator, games, ftp, and gopher.

The root account is most preferred by hackers, but the next preference is the default accounts. Thus, as the number of active default accounts in a Linux system increases, so does the security risk.

Some default groups, such as adm, lp, and popusers, are also present in the Linux operating system. Like default accounts, default groups are also vulnerable to hackers. To prevent hackers from manipulating default accounts to access your Linux system, all unnecessary default accounts and groups should be deleted immediately. For instance, if you do not use the ftp service, you need to delete the ftp account. If you intend to use the service someday, then just disable the account instead of deleting it.

To delete an account, use the following syntax:

```
userdel account_name
```

Use the following syntax to delete a group:

```
groupdel group_name
```

File Export Mismanagement

If you use the NFS, or Network File Sharing service, for exporting files, be aware that there is a risk to the integrity of data in the files. If the access of the /etc/exports file is not restricted to read-only, then hackers can access confidential and valuable information from your Linux system.

17

Console Program Access Mismanagement

Some of the console programs that could be exploited include *shutdown*, *poweroff*, *reboot*, and *halt*. These programs are critical to the integrity of Linux systems, and generally root access is required to execute them. This is another exhortation to restrict root privilege.

Resource Allocation Mismanagement

If every user of a Linux system has unlimited access to resources, like core files and memory, then malicious users can conduct denial-of-service attacks on that Linux system by engaging all of the resources available. To avoid these types of attacks, you need to apply resource limits to all users. To do this, you use the /etc/security/limits.conf file. This file permits you to prevent users from creating core files, to restrict the number of processes they can use, and to restrict the use of memory.

su Command Mismanagement

The *switch user (su)* command helps users of a Linux operating system temporarily switch the current privileges available to those of the root account. If access to this command is not restricted, then users may try to log in as root and then execute commands that are restricted to normal users. This is why you must restrict the access of the *su* command to avoid the misuse of root privileges. The best administration practice is to use the *sudo* utility rather than the *su* command.

Unnecessary Services

When you install the Ubuntu Linux operating system, you will notice that various networking services are available as a series of check boxes. Some of these services include telnet, IMAP, POP3, and ftp. Although they are helpful for communicating with other computers, these services are highly vulnerable to unauthorized access. If you are not using the service, do not install it. Some services such as POP3 are difficult to remove after they are installed. Hackers attempt to gain unauthorized access to Linux systems by connecting to network services.

UTILITY VULNERABILITIES

You can utilize different utilities in Linux and UNIX-based operating systems for various activities. For instance, the *grep* utility can be used for finding strings within files. Weaknesses within some utilities allow hackers to breach the security of a Linux or UNIX-based operating systems.

r Utilities Vulnerabilities

The *r* utilities permit users to access Linux and other UNIX-based operating systems from remote locations. The two important *r* utilities are *rlogin* and *rsh*. The *rlogin* utility lets a user connect to a remote host from the terminal of a local host. The *rsh* utility is used to permit trusted users to execute commands on a local host from a remote host.

The *r* utilities use an insecure mechanism called rhosts. In addition to rhosts, the *r* utilities transmit data in the plain text form. Attackers can exploit the insecure medium and the transfer of *r* utilities plain text data. This enables them to gain access to a Linux or UNIX system. It is a good practice to disable the *r* utilities to avoid exploitation of their vulnerabilities, and to use SSH or some other secure protocol.

Sendmail Vulnerabilities

Linux and UNIX-based operating systems use the sendmail daemon to send e-mail messages by employing Simple Mail Transfer Protocol (SMTP). Several versions of sendmail are available. However, every version has vulnerabilities that permit intruders to intercept e-mail messages. For instance, sendmail open source version 8.13.5 and all similar commercial versions have a vulnerability that lets remote hackers deliver commands on a target system. If a UNIX system has any version of sendmail from 8.13.5 and earlier, then attackers can send malformed e-mail messages to that system, and then carry out commands with root privileges on the target system.

To avoid security risks, it is necessary to install the latest version of sendmail from ftp://ftp.sendmail.org/pub/sendmail/. You can also use qmail or postfix instead of sendmail to avoid the known sendmail hacks.

Telnet Vulnerabilities

Telnet is a popular service that allows users to connect to a UNIX, Linux, or Windows computer from remote locations. Hackers love this because it sends data unencrypted over the network and they can easily take advantage of this service by using brute-force and dictionary attacks to connect to a target system. Therefore, to increase the security of a UNIX or Linux server, *telnet* must be disabled. Use *ssh* instead, if you need to get a command line interface from a remote computer.

17

Trivial File Transfer Protocol (TFTP) Vulnerability

UNIX and Linux systems use Trivial File Transfer Protocol, or TFTP, to start diskless computers. This service allows routers to get system configuration details without having to logon to a Linux system. Also, the TFTP does not require any type of authentication. Hackers can use these vulnerabilities to acquire unauthorized access to a Linux system that uses this service.

groff Vulnerability

groff is a package that is used in Red Hat Linux for document formatting. There is a buffer overflow vulnerability in the preprocessor of this package prior to version 1.7.3. This enables attackers to gain access rights to the lp account in the target system.

In order to exploit this vulnerability, hackers need to invoke *groff* in the LPRng printer spooler. This vulnerability usually affects Red Hat Linux versions 7.0, 7.1, and 7.2. To find a resolution to this threat, updated *groff* packages can be obtained for different versions of Red Hat Linux from www.redhat.com/support/errata/RHSA-2002-004.html. After installing the updated package, you need to make sure that all of the RPMs on your Linux system are updated. The vulnerability has been patched. The vulnerability does not affect Debian stable version or Ubuntu, which is based on Debian.

Printing Vulnerability

The printing security feature of Red Hat Linux 7.2 is vulnerable to attacks. This weakness permits remote users to print any file on a Red Hat Linux 7.2 system for which the lp account has the read permission. You can prevent hackers from using this vulnerability by updating the affected Ghostscript package. You may install the updated Ghostscript from www.redhat.com/support/errata/RHSA-2001-138.html. This is of historical value only. Current Red Hat versions are not affected.

passwd Command Vulnerability

There is a design error in Ubuntu 5.04 through 6.06 LTS. The *passwd* command in *shadow* in Ubuntu 5.04 through 6.06 LTS, when called with the -f, -g, or -s flag, does not check the return code of a *setuid* call, which might allow local users to gain root privileges if *setuid* fails in cases such as PAM failures or resource limits. A standard *apt-get dist-upgrade* will apply the patch that nullifies this error.

sudo Vulnerability

The *sudo* package allows system administrators to grant some or all root privileges to users listed in the sudoers text file. As well as being a feature for granting privileges, *sudo* logs user activities. Whenever an unauthorized attempt to access *sudo* occurs, the package will send an e-mail warning to the root account. The oldest *sudo* versions, before *sudo* version 1.6.4, had a functionality bug that allowed hackers to gain root privileges. Therefore, these versions did not clear environment variables before sending warning e-mail messages. Hackers can pass parameters to the *sudo* package. This activity may permit them to gain root access.

This vulnerability of *sudo* affects Red Hat Linux versions 7.0, 7.1, and 7.2. Download the RPM from www.redhat.com or use the CLI utility Yellowdog Updater, Modified (*yum*) to update your system.

mutt Buffer Overflow Vulnerability

mutt is a text-based e-mail client package that you can use in any Linux or UNIX-based operating system. You can use the *mutt* package in conjunction with MIME and PGP. *mutt* also supports POP3 and IMAP e-mail messages. If you use a *mutt* package version earlier than mutt-1.2.5.1, a weakness allows hackers to overwrite the data stored in the system memory. The reason for this vulnerability is a buffer overflow in these versions of *mutt*.

Attackers sometimes send e-mail messages with malformed content to the target system. This malformed content permits these remote hackers to change the arbitrary bytes in the memory. This vulnerability affects all Red Hat Linux operating systems, from versions 6.2 to 7.2. This has been patched on newer versions of Red Hat.

The UseLogin Vulnerability of OpenSSH

SSH is a program that provides a secure connection to a distant, remote computer. You can use it to execute commands on remote computers, move files to computers, and transfer files from computers. OpenSSH, an implementation of SSH1 and SSH2, provides protection to the network traffic from all possible unauthorized access attempts by implementing authentication and by monitoring network sessions. Usually, sshd servers control user logins. There is a directive in OpenSSH, UseLogin, which you can use to maintain control of user login attempts by using the */usr/bin/login* command. Nonetheless, this directive is not enabled with the default installation of OpenSSH.

If you enable the UseLogin directive in the earlier versions of OpenSSH, a vulnerability allows remote hackers to gain root access to the Linux operating system. If OpenSSH is installed on a computer running Linux, users who have SSH connection to the computer can execute commands on it from any remote location. When a user executes a command from a remote location, OpenSSH drops root privileges and then executes the command. In some situations, however, OpenSSH fails to drop root privileges. This vulnerability lets the hacker gain the root access to the system. The UseLogin vulnerability does not affect OpenSSH 2.1.1. In order to prevent remote hackers from exploiting this vulnerability, you need to update the latest version of OpenSSH.

17

WU-FTPD Exploits

wu-ftpd is an ftp server that allows users to organize files on the server to perform ftp actions. When a user sends an ftp command, the *wu-ftpd* server allocates some area of the memory space to process the command. The *wu-ftpd* server allocates memory by using a function called `malloc()`. After processing the command, the *wu-ftpd* server allocates the memory to some other command.

In case of an error while processing a command, the server does not allocate any section of the memory to that command request. In such situations, the *wu-ftpd* server stores this error information in a variable. However, for some specific file patterns, the *wu-ftpd* server fails to set the variable with the error information. This failure causes the server to attempt to allocate some memory for the process. This vulnerability of the *wu-ftpd* server may allow attackers to execute arbitrary code on the *wu-ftpd* server. This has been resolved in the newer versions of *wu-ftpd*.

GID Man Exploit

A buffer overflow occurs in the `ultimate_source()` function of a few early versions of the GID man package. Hackers often use this buffer overflow to gain root access to a target system. To exploit this vulnerability, hackers generate man pages that contain filenames with escape characters.

This vulnerability affects all Red Hat Linux versions ranging from 5.2 to 7.1. To safeguard your Red Hat Linux operating system from this vulnerability, you just need to update the GID man package from www.redhat.com/support/errata/RHSA-2001-072.html., or update your operating system to the current version of Red Hat or Fedora.

There are many more vulnerabilities in the thousand-odd Linux distros and the three-score UNIX flavors. This gives you a few vulnerabilities for Red Hat and Ubuntu.

CHAPTER SUMMARY

- Derived from UNIX in 1991 by Linus Torvalds, Linux is the second most widely used Intel-based operating system today.

- In 1969, Ken Thompson and Dennis Ritchie developed UNIX—a general-purpose operating system.

- Some of the most popular UNIX-based operating systems are BSD, HP-UNIX, AIX, and SCO Unix. SunOS and Solaris arose out of BSD code.

- Linux source code is free, as are some Linux distributions (distros).

- The basic architecture and features of Linux are the same as those of UNIX-based operating systems.

- There are many software distributions built around the Linux kernel. As of the writing of this text, the most commonly searched distro is Ubuntu.

- All general distributions of Linux allow the use of both the command line interface (CLI) and the graphical user interface (GUI).

- Most services are off by default upon installation of Linux or UNIX-based operating systems, and they must be configured to run. This is one of the main reasons that Linux and UNIX-based operating systems are considered safer than Windows.

- Categories of vulnerability for Linux operating systems include basic exploits, login passwords, bad system administration practices, and unnecessary services.

◻ Basic hacks for a Linux system begin with physical access, so great care must be taken to lock down physical access to your Linux servers.

◻ Some Linux and UNIX-based operating systems store encrypted login passwords in a file called /etc/passwd, which also contains logon names in the more vulnerable, cleartext format. A hacker who gains access to such a system can obtain logon names, which can then be used to gain illegal access to systems.

◻ Some UNIX and Linux distros store passwords in a file called /etc/shadow, which is readable only to root. It is possible to reset this file as the password repository during installation, which could create an unnecessary vulnerability on your system.

◻ Users of a Linux system should select strong passwords—especially the password for root, because every hacker knows that the default administrative user is root.

◻ Upon the installation of Linux, the default configuration and accounts are vulnerable to hacking attempts due to root account mismanagement, default account mismanagement, file export mismanagement, console program access mismanagement, resource allocation mismanagement, and *su* command mismanagement.

◻ Various networking services are available as part of some Linux operating systems; however, these services are highly vulnerable to unauthorized access.

◻ Weaknesses within some utilities in both Linux and UNIX-based operating systems allow hackers to breach the security of the system.

◻ Utilities known to be vulnerable include *r* utilities, *sendmail*, *telnet*, Trivial File Transfer Protocol (TFTP), *groff*, the printing security feature related to Ghostscript, the *passwd* command, the *sudo* command, *mutt* buffer overflow, the UseLogin feature of OpenSSH, *wu-ftpd*, and GID Man.

17

REVIEW QUESTIONS

1. What is a "voluntary vulnerability"?

2. Did Linus Torvalds invent Linux?

3. What is a good hardware hack for an x86 system?

4. Describe a utility vulnerability, and what makes it different from a kernel vulnerability.

5. What is root account mismanagement?

6. What is default account mismanagement?

7. What is console program access mismanagement?

8. What is *su* command mismanagement?

Indicate whether the sentence or statement is true or false.

9. _____ *dir* is a Linux command used to locate files.

10. _____ Linux is not an operating system.

11. _____ If you are not using *telnet* on your Linux box this week, you should delete the telnet user.

12. _____ If there are no Windows machines on your network, you must set up the Samba server to talk to other Linux and UNIX machines.

13. _____ All other things being equal, the default installation of Fedora Core 6 is not entirely secure.

14. _____ /etc is where files go when you delete them.

Match each term with the correct statement below.

    a. place for temporary files

    b. root user home directory

    c. configuration files are stored here

    d. standard users have their personal files here

    e. lilo or grub configuration files are stored here

    f. standard location to find system logs

15. _____ /boot

16. _____ /tmp

17. _____ /var/logs

18. _____ /home

19. _____ /etc

20. _____ /root

HANDS-ON PROJECTS

Linux has several known vulnerabilities that we can classify as being either default vulnerabilities (all of the exploits available after a standard or default installation) or utility vulnerabilities (vulnerabilities that appear as a result of use). In Project 17-1, you'll make a change to a system setting in Fedora to address a known default vulnerability.

HANDS-ON PROJECTS

Project 17-1

1. **Setting Shell Session Timeout.** Setting a time-out feature for root is critically important, if there is a possibility that a user with remote access or local access might use the root account to do any work on the computer. Using the *vim* editor, you can add lines to all profiles as follows.

(You will need root access to make this change to /etc/profile.) At a command prompt in a Terminal window, type:

```
vi /etc/profile
```

2. Add the following lines to the /etc/profile file:

```
export TMOUT=600 //this sets the timeout to 10 minutes
readonly TMOUT //This makes TMOUT unwritable by root users,
               //so a remote hacker cannot set the timeout
               //to some arbitrarily high number or
               //disable it.
```

TIP

Inside a bash script, there are two common ways of adding comments to the code: starting a line with a # or typing a double slash, //. UNIX and Linux operating systems do not execute anything after the comment marker on the line.

HANDS-ON PROJECTS

Project 17-2

1. **Linux Default Vulnerabilities.** Writing assignment: Using knowledge gained in this and previous chapters, summarize the default vulnerabilities in Fedora Core 6 when it is set up with standard server packages.

HANDS-ON PROJECTS

Project 17-3

1. **Linux Utility Vulnerabilities.** Suppose the Fedora Core 6 server from the previous exercise is being used as an application server and is running the following applications: Apache Web Server, Tomcat Application Server, PHP, PERL, and SSH. Using an Internet search and/or a library search, try to find five current vulnerabilities for each of these services.

Server Application	Count	Exploit	How to Fix or Avoid
Apache Web Server	1		
	2		
	3		
	4		
	5		
Tomcat Application Server	1		
	2		
	3		
	4		
	5		
PHP	1		
	2		
	3		
	4		
	5		

17

Server Application	Count	Exploit	How to Fix or Avoid
Perl	1		
	2		
	3		
	4		
	5		
SSH	1		
	2		
	3		
	4		
	5		

18

INCIDENT HANDLING

> **After reading this chapter and completing the exercises, you will be able to:**
>
> - Identify the necessity of incident handling
> - Identify different types of incidents
> - Recognize the various phases of incident handling
> - Note the phases in preparing for incident handling
> - Describe the steps in the identification of incidents
> - Understand the need for incident reporting and communication
> - Describe the steps in removing a bug
> - Identify the steps in recovering from an incident
> - Identify the importance of following up after incident handling
> - Understand the process of tracking hackers
> - List emergency steps that follow an incident

An incident in a computer-security environment is an event that tests the security solutions in place on a network or, in the case of a stand-alone machine, on that machine itself. An incident can have one or more of several outcomes. Fraud, information leakage, or the destruction of network resources are just some examples of the negative consequences of a security incident.

Incidents take many forms. The most common incidents that affect network security are attacks from malicious code such as viruses and Trojans, and inside jobs by employees, contractors, and consultants. The most rare, but most widely publicized, attacks are those from outsiders, and these are handled as incidents as well.

Any incident can be a serious threat to an organization's network. Sophisticated risk management allows organizations to predict the extent of damage that could be expected in many cases. Damage can range from a small disruption of work to a major network outage with recovery periods spanning days or even weeks.

The following is a list of common events that may indicate an attack in progress, which in turn may lead to reporting a security incident:

- The execution of an unusual process using network resources could be a sign of a denial-of-service (DoS) attack.

- A pattern of many employee complaints of computer malfunctions on their systems may herald a virus or worm attack.

- Resource requests may increase in an unusual way and result in the slowing down of a network. This could also be an indication of a denial-of-service attack.

- An authentication request by an IP address that is not a part of the network may indicate an intrusion attempt. This may be an attempt by a hacker trying to access the network in search of confidential information.

To prevent the occurrence of such incidents, and to quickly and properly respond to such threats, an administrator must develop three documents:

1. A predictive document describing the possible threats to the network and the potential losses such risks would cause the organization to incur.

2. A "hot list" of what to prevent, what to patch, and what to endure. This document recommends whether training, added physical security, or added technology are the proper preventive measures; identifies the organization's response team; and defines the chain of command or information.

3. An incident response policy to ensure the smoothest possible response to any threat.

TIP   Individuals and organizations can obtain incident-response and incident-handling templates from several sources online, including www.sans.org/resources/policies/, www.dir.state.tx.us/security/policies/templates.htm, and http://sbc.nist.gov/PDF/NASA%20Security%20Policy%20Templates.pdf.

Need for Incident Handling

Many people are learning how to break into networks illegally for many reasons, from fun to potential income. Crackers are increasing in numbers, as more people enter the Internet and information about networks and computers becomes more commonplace. Organizations large and small are relying on computer processing to run their businesses and are using the Internet as a critical part of their business process. It is also true that more partially trained administrators are entering the ranks of IT every year. The potential for attacks on data or hardware naturally rises with these trends. Businesses may suffer losses if system administrators are not aware of potential problems. Consequently, an organization must follow the lead of experts and use industry best practices to prepare to handle incidents with minimum effort and cost.

There are many reasons to develop effective incident handling policies:

- If an organization is familiar with its security policy and procedures, there is less flailing about and confusion when an incident occurs.
- The number of attempted breaches that become security incidents are reduced when organizations take preventative measures.
- Organizations that handle and document incidents may be less likely to have repeat occurrences.
- Proper incident handling helps organizations assess the strengths and weaknesses in their system and their staff.
- Documented handling of incidents using industry standard practices safeguard an organization from potential legal ramifications related to the incidents.
- Properly trained incident-response teams give upper management time to prepare a factual and community-involved official response to the aftermath of a security breach.

Types of Incidents

Every organization has its own unique mix of resources and vulnerabilities, which are ranked by the cost it would require to replace the resources and the effort it would take to recover from an incident. A risk assessment orders an organization's vulnerabilities by severity and urgency. There are various types of incidents that can occur on a network or a computer. Here are some common incidents:

- Defaced pages
- Denial-of-service attacks
- Errors and omissions
- Fraud and theft
- Intrusion
- Quiet intrusion
- Malicious code

18

Defaced Pages

This type of incident means an attacker has hacked your Web server. Defaced-page incidents result in loss of revenue, reputation, and morale of a company. Hackers may deface pages as a gentle warning that a Web server is not entirely secured, or as revenge, political protest, or a practical joke. Imagine if you typed in a Web address to a dry cleaner's and the home page listed exorbitant prices, showed images of damaged clothes, or provided faulty contact information. This type of attack, if done subtly, may go unnoticed for several hours or days.

Denial-of-Service Attacks

Denial-of-service attacks are geared toward servers that process user requests or provide services to users on a network. These attacks send a large quantity of packets to a server so that resources are overutilized. Consequently, servers are not able to process legitimate requests sent by valid users.

A denial-of-service attack is typically caused by malformed packets, errors, and omissions in the server application design, or by TCP/IP vulnerabilities. A denial-of-service attack can be divided into three subcategories: buffer overflow conditions, network flooding, and stack errors.

Buffer Overflow   These attacks send input data of a greater size than the capacity of an unchecked variable in the server application. They often result in the failure of the application or execution of malicious code. This action forces the server to deny any requests sent by the computers on the network.

Network Flooding   This is the most basic form of a DoS attack. Large numbers of requests are sent to the server. This results in the slowing down or failure of the network.

Stack Errors   These attacks aim at the TCP/IP stack. Hackers use the known vulnerabilities of TCP/IP to corrupt the stack, resulting in the failure of server applications.

Errors and Omissions

This phrase is shorthand for any intentional or unintentional misconfiguration of any resource on the network, from a gateway router to automated patch installation on a server. It also refers to errors or omissions in the code base of any and all applications and system software anywhere in the network. Errors and omissions do not always lead to incidents, but to ensure that errors and omissions are reduced, a professional or an experienced technician must audit the software throughout its development life cycle and after deployment. Intentional errors and omissions are often made to create a back door in the software program, as a long-term troubleshooting aid. This should be removed before the software is certified for shipment, but often isn't. Hackers find information like this and use it to prepare targeted attacks. Errors and omissions often lie undetected for weeks before they are used in an exploit, and sometimes remain for weeks after that.

Fraud and Theft

These incidents can be performed either by traditional practices or by using new tools, targeting the loopholes in security and planning. Statistics reveal that most incidents of fraud involve "inside" individuals who possess knowledge of the hierarchy and workings of the target organization. These white-collar criminals may practice their deceit for decades before being caught. It is possible that they may never be caught, if they have a deep enough understanding of the system and sufficient power within the organization.

Intrusion

Intrusion simply refers to any attempt to gain unauthorized access to a network. Typically, the intruder is an insider who has gained access to the authentication information of a user with higher access privileges than he or she has. However, the intruder can also be an outsider who has used stealth or skill to obtain the authentication details of a valid user. In addition, the intruder probably has a valid network IP address from which to access the network. In case of outsider attacks, the administrator initially must verify that the attempt was actually made by an outsider. The administrator should consider the possibility that an employee of the organization is trying to access the network remotely. An employee intruding from the outside is not always done with ill intent. Careful guidelines must ensure that employees may access some areas of the company network, yet be restricted from others.

Quiet Intrusion

These attacks may be the most devastating for organizations. Quiet intrusion occurs when a hacker intrudes undetected into the network of an organization, and leaves little or no trace of his actions. This type of hack may be categorized three ways:

- Retrieving information—The attacker retrieves classified information. Much of this can be done using a packet sniffer. Sniffers are passive devices and are practically undetectable, if the attacker knows how to configure her attack. Network administrators may never notice the presence of the hacker.

- Corrupting data—The attacker corrupts data on a network. Unless the sensitive machines are running software that monitors changes in file size, the administrator may not be aware of the attack until the system crashes or the corrupted data is requested and the application fails. The administrator may not properly classify this condition as an attack, and the vulnerability may not be patched.

- Creating or identifying back doors—The attacker is planning to attack the target network at a future time. To make that attack smoother and more effective, the attacker attempts to use or create a back door into the system or the network. The network administrator may not notice the attacker doing reconnaissance on the network and will be surprised when the attack is executed on the future date.

18

Malicious Code

Malicious code is used for destructive purposes only. Malicious code includes worms, viruses, and Trojan horse programs. There are many reasons for someone to write malicious code. This code can be used to penetrate a system to retrieve confidential information, disrupt the network, or create a back door. Malicious code is designed to enter the network unnoticed. Such code can also be designed to be executed at a specific time or by remote control, when the system administrators are on low alert. Many malicious code attacks are especially dangerous because they are designed to replicate and distribute themselves automatically.

PHASES OF INCIDENT HANDLING

Figure 18-1 shows a basic flowchart of incident handling.

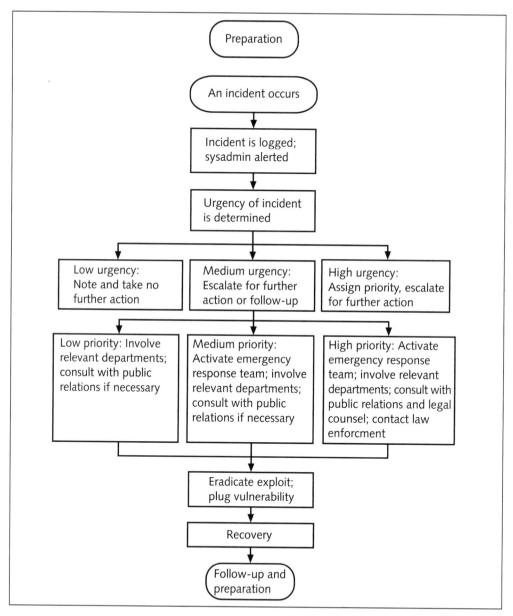

Figure 18-1   Flowchart: phases of incident handling

The key phases of incident handling are:

- Preparation
- Identification
- Reporting (Logging)
- Setting urgency
- Setting priority
- Eradication
- Recovery
- Postmortem

Preparation for Incident Handling

Preparation for handling incidents starts with knowing the resources and their vulnerabilities, *baselining* the network to discover all the assets involved, and developing systems and policies, including creating the incident-response team. In a perfect world, this project would be done long before there are any incidents; however, with the current state of technology, if an organization has not done this preparation, they have probably been hacked at least once already. The only place to start is from where you are, so now is the perfect time to start preparing to handle security incidents.

Planning an Incident-Handling Policy

All organizations should devise a formal incident-handling policy. The policy should be written in clear and concise language, and needs to include at least the following sections:

- Purpose and sponsor—This defines the purpose of the policy and indicates who the sponsors are within the organization.

- Network and system details—The better and more exhaustive the baseline of the system and known vulnerabilities, the more it will be useful to an incident-handling administrator for responding to an incident quickly.

- Policy—This section should list the chain of command or chain of information. It includes top policy-makers and identifies the person(s) assigned to fix incident-related issues. It also defines the steps that the person who identified the problem should follow. References to any external organizations that need to be informed are also included in this section.

- Procedures—As the most important section, this includes all the intricate details of the steps that an incident handler must take. This section defines all possible incidents as well as the methods to fix them in the quickest safe manner.

- Responsible organizations—This section lists information about organizations that can provide the incident handler with information and skills to fix the problem.

18

This list must contain details regarding the organizations' names, contact method, and contact people.

- History—This section describes how incidents should be logged and what information is to be included in that history file. It should also tell where these history documents are stored. History of similar incidents gives useful background to aid the response team in choosing tactics to address the current incident.

The organization should then identify the skill sets required to address the expected range of vulnerabilities. This is used as a guide to develop an emergency response team or to train the members of an existing team.

Incident-Handling Team

Incident-handling teams are responsible for identifying incidents and responding to them in the most effective manner possible. The skills represented in an emergency response team cross department lines, from security to technical to management to communications. Depending upon the size of the organization, the team may be small or large.

Minimally, the team needs somebody with experience and skill at identifying attack signatures and responses; somebody who has enough clout within the organization to make sure the security policies are not ignored by management; and somebody who can systematize communications within the team and with outside entities. In a very small organization this could be a single person. If this is the case, this one-person team needs wide latitude within the organization.

Incident-handling teams should practice exercises and drills to make sure the team members are able to coordinate well in the event of a real emergency. Besides being trained in the various phases of handling a security incident, the team should be trained to retain the evidence of an incident—for example, by taking snapshots of the affected systems or securing the physical area to stop evidence from being hauled away.

The more efficient and effective the incident-handling team is, the lower the losses in productivity, time, money, and labor.

IDENTIFYING INCIDENTS

The first step in an incident response is to identify whether an incident is actually occurring. A properly prepared network infrastructure has IDS and firewalls in place and may well have Snort or Tripwire installed. These applications provide the administrators with alert messages. These messages, such as "packets originate from outside the network with headers listing an origin within the network," derive from filters. The security application is set to choose whether to log the incident or to log and notify. There are such things as unimportant network traffic anomalies, and the applications probably won't notify about such an incident. Notifications can also be sent because of incidents that are organic and accidental, such as a NIC going bad and continuously sending random data onto the network as a broadcast (255.255.255.255). Such errors or bugs can look like an attack. Some false positives are the result of user error, such as accidentally sending to a printer 45 copies of a 300-page document. This causes a denial of service condition, but it does not require scrambling the response team. System administrators can easily troubleshoot such false emergencies. Ascertaining whether there has been an attack is not the same as identifying an incident.

First, the administrator has to confirm that the issue is an actual security incident, and not just another network traffic event. The possible incident is logged, then a security expert is informed as to the details of the event. That expert chooses whether to alert the incident-response team. The expert must be well suited to the event. A Windows security expert might not be the one to ask about an event involving a Linux server.

Next, the network services that may have been affected must be identified. It is important to determine the extent to which the incident has affected or might still be affecting the network. If there are chances that the incident may replicate, the network officials should be informed and steps should be taken accordingly.

Next, the appropriate historical documents and current vulnerability alerts ought to be reviewed. The organization's incident-response policy is a good document to review, as it outlines the required action steps and identifies who should be notified of the incident.

Finally, the incident-response team performs forensics to determine the type of incident and the possible responses. The security experts use the following tools to make their determinations:

- Approach to incident detection
- Assessing the severity of the incident
- Risk assessment
- Systems and network logging

Approach to Incident Detection

How one approaches incident detection can seriously impact the number and kinds of incidents that are detectable. The first step is called watching. It is important that a network be monitored for unusual activity. Monitoring, or watching, can be performed in an ad hoc way, by checking occasionally for unusual activity based on a perception that the network is not working normally, or in response to a user's complaint. This is essentially reactive, and probably not the best choice for a large network. Watching can also be done using "always on" monitoring tools. The next step is checking the details of a possible incident, and the last step is taking action. If the possible incident cannot be easily explained as a benign anomaly, then the incident-response team may be called in.

In addition to the aforementioned steps, there are specific procedures that may be incorporated to ensure that incidents are detected prior to damaging the network or a specific computer.

A large part of the detection process is to ensure that the proper monitoring tools are available on the network, that they are updated frequently with the newest patches, and that they have not been compromised.

Confidential files must be stored in a secure area. This secure site should be checked at regular intervals.

The network administrator must learn to read the system logs of the resources on the network, and get in the habit of comparing and collecting the information from many logs to look for possible attacks.

Detection Tools

Detection tools are installed on the network to make early detection possible. There are tools available that can scan for viruses, monitor and inspect log files, and check the integrity of data files.

System-monitoring tools monitor the events of attacks made on specific computers, such as password cracking or executing unauthorized programs. Network analysis tools record any unusual activities on a network, which can simplify the analysis and identification of incidents. User-analysis tools record unusual activities performed by users, such as repeated attempts to connect to the server or attempts to access restricted resources. Log-analysis tools check the log files and report any exceptional entries.

Assessing the Severity of an Incident

Understanding the severity of incidents is important because the scale of response changes based upon the scale of the problem. The severity of an attack upon a given vulnerability is different for different organizations. Part of the risk assessment of an organization's initial security policy is to set the level of risk for each vulnerability. Potential damage from an attack may include monetary loss, but it can also result in a loss of productivity, company standing, or customer trust.

Severity is also determined by the number of network resources involved, both directly and indirectly. If a large number of machines are affected, it might raise the severity level and trigger a higher level of response.

Many types of attacks are capable of replicating themselves. A virus that can replicate itself through e-mail is a common yet serious threat. This sort of attack makes it difficult to determine the number of computers that may have been affected. Attacks with replication capabilities are often considered high-severity attacks.

Severity level may also be affected by the motive of the attacker. If an attacker is merely proving they he can break into a network, and his motivation is not to damage or steal data, then the severity level may be reduced.

Risk Assessment

Ongoing risk assessment is done for each incident in order to determine whether to use the affected computer on the network. There are three options for dealing with the affected computer: shut it down, disconnect it from the network, or continue incident-handling operations and enable the computer to remain on the network.

Systems and Network Logging

When an incident is discovered, the first sources for information are the log files on the affected machine and general network traffic logs from routers and switches. These log files can contain useful data about suspicious or unusual activities on the network. They often provide solid evidence that can be used to trace a hack. The data in the log file may also provide information about the extent of the damage. The type of attack may be detectable by the "attack signature" available in the log files. Some examples of the log files available in Linux and Windows are listed below.

UNIX and Linux Log Files

Some essential Linux log files live in the /var/log directory. What follows is a partial list of log files that includes some of the more useful logs:

- syslog, which is a dumping ground for automated CRON jobs, as well as various logged functions by applications that do not maintain their own log files (**CRON** is an automated scheduler utility, and a CRON job is any task assigned to CRON.)

- auth.log, which keeps track of successful and unsuccessful login attempts

- checksecurity.log, which tracks root accesses to devices

- mail.err, mail.log, and mail.warn, which together keep track of mail server behavior

- apache (or apache2), which keeps track of Web server error messages

Logs also exist for monitoring tools such as Snort and Nessus.

Windows Log Files

To view Windows system logs, you open the GUI Event Viewer in the Administration Tools control panel. You can look at system, security, and application logs. Web server logs contain data regarding the connections to applications such as Cold Fusion, IIS, and Microsoft FrontPage.

Additionally, a check needs to be performed for suspicious files. In the case of an incident, a check must be initiated for recently created files. The names of these files probably include an "executable" extension, such as pif, dll, exe, or drv (or perhaps another 20 or so choices).

18

REPORTING AND COMMUNICATING INCIDENTS

All users on the network should know how to report a possible incident. Even apparently minor incidents should be noted, as it may help to prevent serious incidents later. The appropriate people to be notified should be listed in an organization's security policy. Incidents must be reported in a uniform way. Automated intranet forms are often a good way to ensure uniformity of reporting, and the uniformity makes it easier to quickly understand and classify the report.

Reporting the Incident

If an incident has been observed, the following experts may need to be informed:

- System administrator
- Senior management
- Legal counsel
- System and network users
- Human-resource department
- Public-relations department
- Federal, state, or local law-enforcement agencies

The person reporting the incident needs to report it in direct and clear language outlining the facts. This helps the experts react efficiently.

All information of the incident should be reported. Concealing or omitting facts may result in more confusion, effectively slowing the investigation. The incident should be reported with neutral tone, using nontechnical language in reports to upper management or non-technical staff, who might misunderstand the use of jargon. Organizations having employees who use several languages in the course of business need to take extra measures to ensure that all employees understand the situation and policies.

The hacked resource is not the best tool for spreading information about the attack. If your mail server was hacked or infested with worms, it would not be wise to use e-mail to update the employees on the progress of the incident. Workers will naturally feel more helpless if they cannot send e-mails, therefore all employees must be trained to understand this key concept before an incident occurs. Resolution will be far more difficult if all the hacker has to do to keep up with the progress is to read company e-mail.

Communicating the Incident

Incident communication refers to the official communication with the individuals fixing the incident. It is quite different from incident reporting. It refers to the in-house instructions that must be sent to appropriate people to fix the incident. Properly communicating an incident includes the following tasks listed below:

- Identifying people with skills that make them useful in handling the incident
- Determining how much information should be communicated to the relevant experts
- Determining the amount of responsibility to be delegated to individuals
- Determining the mode of communication, and securing communications
- Identifying an incident-handling team leader to be responsible for bringing the incident to successful closure

ERADICATING THE BUG

One of the key steps that incident-handling teams need to perform while eradicating bugs is to create backup copies of files. This is the preliminary step following initiation of the eradication process. Making backup copies refers to taking snapshots of the system to store and preserve. Backup copies are useful for such purposes as tracking the hacker after the incident has been fixed and retrieving data while resuming work. It is very rare for a hacker not to have left a back door while performing an attack. For this reason, taking snapshots makes it possible to trace the hacker. It is vital to understand that the hacker may have modified the commands that need to be used. To view the data, a separate CD-ROM supporting the command execution should be used. The following set of information must be retrieved:

- A report of the process status with the parent process ID of each process
- A report of all the open connections
- A backup copy of the temp directory, which is deleted if the computer is restarted

18

All of these reports and files should be stored in a backup file. In Linux, you may use the following archival commands to make backup copies:

tar—This is used just when data needs to be saved.

dump—This is used when the disk image needs to be archived. This image may be required to obtain forensic information.

dd—The disk-to-disk program is required to make quick backups.

Correcting the Root Problem

Correcting the root problem is another essential step. In order to properly clear the network of problems caused by the incident, an analysis should be performed, and knowledge obtained from previous incidents should be consulted. At this crucial stage, accuracy of analysis of the problem is important. The steps that should be taken to repair the problem chiefly depend on the type of problem being repaired. It is important to remove all traces of the incident from the network. If this is not done, the problem may resurface.

Identifying and Implementing the Steps to Fix the Problem

Several kinds of problems occur due to attacks. A few of these are listed below, along with their solutions.

Virus and Worm Attacks

The chief difference between a **worm** and a **virus** is that worms replicate in a network and viruses do not. Because of the replication factor, worms can cause much more damage than viruses. If there is any difficulty distinguishing whether the attack is a worm or a virus, it is smart to treat the incident as if it is a worm attack.

Handling a worm or virus incident:

- Isolate the computers that have been affected.
- Disconnect the affected computers from the network to stop the virus or worm from spreading. If it is a worm, then completely disconnect the server from the Internet. This is the best, easiest way to stop the worm from spreading outside the network, however, it means that getting the patches to fix the problem is more difficult.

Once the problem is ready to be fixed, the appropriate people must be informed and backup copies of the affected hard drives should be made. Always check for "signature" affected files.

Hacker or Cracker Attacks

Incidents by hackers or crackers have to be treated differently from the way attacks by viruses or worms are handled. Viruses and worms are executable files, but they are able to do only one thing or one set of things to attack your network. A dedicated cracker has a much larger selection of attacks to try out on your network, and often the attacker can monitor what you do to combat the attack. The hacker may also be an expert programmer and so may take care of the intricate details to avoid being caught, such as changing dates and times on files, or erasing or modifying log files.

A hacker attack may be made in three different ways: activating a new session, terminating an active session, or hijacking an active session.

An unskilled hacker's actions can be tracked by viewing the log files. Log files reflect activities such as login attempts or SSH authentication failures. In these situations, information regarding the hacker can be derived from the network address used, or from other information logged in the various log files.

If the hacker has ended the session, the first step for the incident-handling team is to identify the part of the network that was affected. After taking the snapshots, the incident-handling team needs to fix the problem by using the appropriate commands.

The best chance to catch a cracker is when she is working through an open session. There may be but a few minutes for the incident-handling teams to take action, identify, and stop the hacker. If the appropriate subject-matter experts are not available, the easiest solution is to block the hacker from working on the network. This may not lead to an identification of the hacker, but it can prevent the hacker from gaining any information from the network or corrupting it further.

Denial-of-Service Attacks

Denial-of-service attacks are implemented to flood network servers with large numbers of useless packets, thus blocking the processing of valid requests. This flood fills all of the network connections of which a server is capable. Although these types of attacks do not pose a direct threat to an organization's data, stopping network services harms the organization and the reputation of the network security team.

The following is a checklist for managing a denial-of-service attack:

1. Identify areas that would be affected if the attack is successful.

2. Determine the attack method used by the hacker.

3. Locate a point where the attack can be stopped that will cause minimal disruption.

4. Implement the procedures that need to be taken to block the attack.

5. Reestablish normal network conditions.

6. Analyze any loopholes in network security.

7. Identify permanent solutions to cover security loopholes.

8. Implement the chosen solutions.

18

RECOVERING FROM INCIDENTS

After an incident, recovery without permanent damage is the goal. The network should be made functional so that the organization will face no further revenue loss.

Phases of Recovery

The four phases of recovery from incidents are reinstallation, reauthentication, scanning to check eradication, and resuming work.

Reinstallation

After the errors have been fixed, all infected computers must be either reinstalled or fixed with a patch. All the computers that were not infected should be patched as well. Reinstalling is safer than patching because it involves formatting the hard disk and leaves no chance for any back doors. Reinstalling a system takes far longer than updating a patch, and reinstallation of all the computers on the network is liable to take quite a lot of time. During reinstallation, check for the following:

1. Verify that no traces of the incident are left.

2. Implement security checks on the network so the problem does not arise again.

3. Change the administrative password and users' passwords before the system is reconnected to the network.

4. Make a backup copy of the newly installed settings so that if a hacker attacks again, the process of reinstalling is faster.

If a patch is used to fix a problem, first test it by simulating the method that the hacker had used. If the tester is unable to penetrate because of the presence of the patch, it can be considered safe to use. Too often, a patch is applied but the problem is not retested. If the patch does not work, the system will fail again, wasting time and money.

Reauthentication

It may be necessary to disable all accounts and then reenable the accounts, pruning the unknown or unused accounts. If a hacker cracked into the system using authentic details, he may have entered into the system with secret user information and a valid password. Disabling and then reenabling accounts takes care of this problem.

Scanning

Scanning checks should be performed after the repair, reinstallation, and reauthentication. Administrators need to perform scanning checks to ensure that no security holes were left open. This prevents vulnerabilities from being overlooked accidentally.

Resuming work

Users may resume their work after all steps have been completed. If system administrators have done their job well, the chance of a repeat attack is less likely.

Postmortem

It is important to learn from successes as well as from mistakes. After the problem has been fixed, the next step is to derive lessons that can be implemented in the future. To learn from the hacking problems, the teams must analyze the incident to identify the possible root cause of the problem. This helps the organization to avoid similar problems in the future, identifies the weak areas in network security, and implies a roadmap to the next continuing vulnerability to be fixed.

The following steps should be followed to derive accurate lessons from hacking incidents. These steps are identifying the root cause of the problem, incorporating short- and long-term changes, incorporating actions for unpredictable incidents, and learning from the problem.

Identifying the Root Cause of the Problem

Understanding the root cause of the problem or at least the root actionable cause is a very important step. Incident-handling teams need to perform this step in a predetermined way by using one of several methods. One of these methods is root cause analysis.

In order to determine the cause, teams must ask how and why a problem occurred. Agree to keep the tone of your root cause analysis (RCA) neutral. Excitement, resentment, anger, and frustration may actually lower your ability to think clearly, and this can lead to ignoring the obvious. The objective in identifying the problem should move from generic to specific, so that learning can be measured and implemented. It is important to perform your RCA as soon as possible after the bug has been eradicated, to avoid losing important information.

Some of the questions to be addressed in the root cause analysis include:

1. How did the hacker manage to hack into the network in the first place, or how did the worm/virus get into the network?

2. How can the network have more security to avoid more incidents in the future?

3. What tools and patches were missing that permitted the hacker to detect a loophole in the network?

4. What processes or technology could have helped the incident-handling team fix the issue quickly and efficiently?

5. Are there any changes that need to be made in the incident-response policy; is more expertise or a different organizational model needed?

6. Is there a better network design that will not allow the hacker to perform operations, even if the hacker manages to break in?

18

Identifying Short-Term and Long-Term Changes

After the analysis of the root cause has been completed, an action list should be developed. The results from the RCA may provide points that are generic and not translatable into immediate action. For instance, if we just scrapped the TCP/IP system and put in something that was more secure, many of the security issues we see today would disappear. As nice as this seems, it is probably not something a single, small organization, such as Jack's Fish Mart, is going to achieve in a reasonable time frame. A logical progression of economically feasible steps should be generated and then converted into action. Then the action list needs to be divided among different, appropriate groups. Tasks for the incident-handling teams should be provided to only the members of the incident-handling teams. IT, training, public relations, and human resources may also have tasks on the list.

Identifying Actions for Any Unpredictable Incident

The knowledge obtained from the RCA should be implemented in areas that were affected by the previous incident as well as other areas vulnerable to attacks. Hackers exploit vulnerabilities, and so no area of the network can be left undefended.

Implementing the Learning

This, the last step of the postmortem phase, is where the people involved get to implement the learning derived from the incident. A postmortem is of no value if the lessons learned are not translated into action.

Tracking Hackers

As covered in Chapter 1, unethical hackers are often educated people with malicious intentions. These hackers can be roughly divided into two categories, amateurs and experts. Amateur hackers are more easily traced, because they are unaware of the methods used to trace hacking behavior. Therefore, they lack the knowledge to remove their tracks. The experts have detailed knowledge of various hacking techniques to ensure they are not caught. The difference in depth of knowledge also explains why the harm caused by experts is higher than that caused by amateurs.

Tracking hackers requires patience and coordination, as well as support from people and organizations all across the world. Obtaining information regarding a specific packet type and tracing the origin point of a hacker may require a tedious data-searching process. For this reason, the coordinator needs to ensure that the data analysis is performed correctly.

To pin down a hacker, a combination of both technology and psychology must be applied. Technical experts can identify the security loopholes and methods used by hackers. It takes an expert in forensic psychology to provide valuable input regarding the hacker's mindset and the possible geographical location of the hacker. The team that attempts to trace the origin of the malicious code should perform the hacking procedure in reverse order. It might be more effective to spend the time developing more secure network protocols than to chase individual crackers. There might be simple ways that would take the profit out of malicious hacking, making the career criminals look elsewhere for their prey. There is a peculiar mindset that would rather punish criminals than make crime unprofitable, and this mindset among the enforcers actually encourages criminal behavior.

There are two approaches to tracking hackers: "generic to specific" and "specific to generic to specific." The approaches are based on the type of information used.

Generic to Specific

This refers to data whose outline is broad in the beginning, yet, with the use of evidence and logic, the output is specific. Consider the location of the hacker. Initially, the hacker-tracking team knows only that an attack was performed. Later they discover the details about the technology used. After using data collected over the Internet, and then performing an analysis on that data, the team may be able to locate the individual.

Specific to Generic to Specific

This approach may be confused with the generic-to-specific approach. However, what differentiates this approach is that information collated before tracking the hacker is very specific and leads to a generic analysis about the hacker. Specific data should be detailed and circulated to the group handling the incident. These people perform analyses by using various assumptions, then they attempt to locate the hacker. The specific-to-generic-to-specific approach may be compared with the integration concept in mathematics. In integration, first the problem question needs to be expanded. Later, by applying various logical mathematical concepts, it is reduced to the answer statement.

Documents, such as log files, ISP server data, and assessments of existing vulnerabilities, provide information regarding the hacker. The choice of technology and techniques used to trace a hacker after an incident is case-specific, and it does not make sense to list all the specific choices. There are some generic steps that can be followed to trace a hacker:

- Analyze log files for signatures regarding the hacker. Complete analysis can uncover information that could lead to identifying the hacker directly or at least provide important information about the hacker. The analysis phase continues until the hacker is caught.

- Analyze the attacker's possible motivation based on the results of the hack.

- Divide timelines. Segregating technology and methods used by a hacker in relation to timelines can help identify the time period when the hacker could have created and tested the tool. This might also indicate the time period for which the log files should be verified, and may even give some idea of in which time zone the hacker resides.

- Define geographical sectors. The Internet should be divided into different geographical sectors based on the inputs from the log files and psychological analysis. Using evidence and assumptions, one sector can be selected for defining the possible location of the hacker. The process of defining geographical sectors can be compared to an Internet Global Positioning System (GPS).

- Identify any links that transmitted similar data. When creating and testing code, the hacker may have transmitted data across the network in either a zipped or encrypted format. A search must be made for files transmitted in such formats in order to identify the location of the computers that were used by the hacker.

18

- Pinpoint the location of the hacker. With data retrieved by various analysis reports, the hacking code should be addressed so that it provides complete evidence that points to a specific individual.

EMERGENCY STEPS

The following is an emergency guide for use in case of an attack.

Important Emergency Steps

- Stay calm—Getting emotional only adds to the problem. The nontechnical employees may be panicking because they do not understand the situation. It is incumbent upon the technician to maintain composure in a fast-changing situation.

- Take accurate and comprehensive notes—Note as much as you can for use later in the incident-response process.

- Notify the relevant set of people—You should already have a list of people to notify in your incident-handling policy form. Concise communication to the proper people in the chain of command adds to the necessary sense of calm and makes it easier to make the right decisions. This is NOT the time for internecine political posturing.

- Confirm that it is an incident and not an event—Do not automatically assume a problem is a security incident. Many employees panic and ignore the possibility that the event is benign or merely one more computer glitch. Let the expert officially confirm that there is an incident.

- Use secure modes of communication—It is not advisable to use a mode of communication that a hacker could be monitoring. When a computer on a network is used to communicate, the hacker might be able to see that communication. The hacker may have the power to stop or change the communication before the team has an opportunity to start working on the resolution.

- Avoid spreading the problem—Once a problem has been identified on a specific computer, that computer should be removed from the network. This may appear to be the only logical course of action, but if the machine provides one or more critical services to the network, taking it offline may be another problem. Best practice: Have redundant machines to handle critical services, and have one service per server. Your Web server, your e-mail server, your application server, and your authentication server are better if hosted on separate machines.

- Make backups—Snapshots of the incident should be taken to aid in analyzing the incident. Hackers may attempt to edit or delete information later. By preserving data, the situation can be archived for future use and research.

CHAPTER SUMMARY

◘ An incident in a computer security environment is an event that tests the security solutions in place on a network or, in the case of a stand-alone machine, on that machine itself. Negative consequences of a security incident include fraud, information leakage, or the destruction of network resources.

◘ The most common incidents are attacks from malicious code—such as viruses and Trojans—and inside jobs by employees, contractors, and consultants. The most rare but best publicized attacks are those from outsiders.

◘ Damage from incidents could range from a small disruption of work to a major network outage, with recovery periods spanning days or even weeks.

◘ Common events that may point to an attack in progress include the execution of an unusual process using network resources; a pattern of employee complaints of computer malfunctions on their systems; an unusual increase in resource requests; or an authentication request by an IP address that is not part of the network.

◘ To prevent and properly respond to incidents, an administrator must develop a predictive document, describing potential threats to the network as well as potential losses; a "hot list" of what to prevent, what to patch, and what to endure; and an incident-response policy.

◘ Every organization has a unique mix of resources and vulnerabilities, ranked by the cost it would require to replace the resources and the effort it would take to recover from an incident. A risk assessment orders an organization's vulnerabilities by severity and urgency.

◘ Incidents that can occur on a network or computer include defaced pages, denial-of-service attacks, errors and omissions, fraud and theft, intrusion, quiet intrusion, and malicious code.

◘ The key phases of incident handling are preparation, identification, reporting (logging), setting urgency, setting priority, eradication, recovery, and postmortem.

◘ All users on a network should know how to report a possible incident. Even apparently minor incidents should be noted.

◘ When eradicating bugs, incident-handling teams need to create backup copies of files by taking snapshots of the system.

◘ After an incident, recovery without permanent damage is the goal. The network should be made functional so that the organization will face no further revenue loss.

◘ The four phases of recovery from incidents are reinstallation, reauthentication, scanning to check eradication, and resuming work.

◘ It is important to learn from successes as well as from mistakes. The following steps should be followed to derive accurate lessons from hacking incidents: identifying the root cause of the problem, incorporating short- and long-term changes, incorporating actions for unpredictable incidents, and learning from the problem.

18

❏ There are two approaches to tracking hackers: "generic to specific" and "specific to generic to specific."

❏ In an emergency, stay calm, take accurate and comprehensive notes, notify the relevant set of people, confirm that it is an incident and not an event, use secure modes of communication, avoid spreading the problem, and make backups.

REVIEW QUESTIONS

1. Why is an incident-handling policy needed?

2. What are some different kinds of incidents?

3. What are the phases of incident handling?

4. What are the phases in preparing for incident handling?

5. What are the steps in identifying incidents?

6. Why are secure communication channels important?

7. What are the steps to remove a bug?

8. What are the steps to recover from an incident?

9. What is the point of a postmortem investigation after the incident is fixed?

10. What are the basic steps to respond to an incident?

Indicate whether the sentence or statement is true or false.

11. _____ The first person to call in the event of an apparent incident is the CEO of the company.

12. _____ Your incident-handling policy will contain the proper procedures for all eventualities.

13. _____ If you discover an anomaly in the network logs, the first thing to do is to stay calm.

14. _____ Most hackers leave some clues. It is up to you to keep the scene clean so the forensics specialists have a chance to discover them.

Arrange the steps involved in tracking hackers in their correct order.

a. Identify any links that transmitted similar data

b. Divide timelines

c. Analyze the attacker's possible motivation based on the results of the hack

d. Define geographical sectors

e. Analyze log files for signatures regarding the hacker

f. Pinpoint the location of the hacker

15. Step one _____

16. Step two _____

17. Step three _____

18. Step four _____

19. Step five _____

20. Step six _____

HANDS-ON PROJECT

Disaster recovery, incident-handling, and business continuity policies are documents that should be created during an organization's planning phase to ensure a business or organization's continued health. With a *known* policy in place, any disruption of normal operations is mitigated and reduced in severity. This is analogous to the 911 emergency notification system in many areas in the United States. A complicated powerful system in place, with all of the money, people, and technological resources it implies, can do nothing whatsoever if potential users are not aware of the procedure required to access the services.

HANDS-ON PROJECTS

Project 18-1

1. Writing assignment: Develop an incident-handling document for the Weezle Corporation plastic molding company. Weezle has been hacked once, and some amount of data has been stolen or corrupted. There was no incident-handling policy in place, and the stockholders are in an uproar. They do not know if their network has been hacked several times or whether it was an isolated incident.

   Weezle Corp.'s president, Ima Weezle, has requested that you create a disaster-recovery plan for the company. Weezle Corp. has two locations, one in Ableton and one in Brazelton, separated by 20 miles. The Ableton facility consists of a warehouse and factory with 20 injection-molding lines, and 590 employees. All the lines are connected to the IP network, and there are 20 networked PCs and 4 networked high-speed Okidata printers. The Brazelton facility consists of the main offices, 12 warehouses, and a factory area with 15 blow-molding lines. There are 85 networked PCs, two RS6000 mini-computers (tape backups done daily on each RS6000), and four legacy HP and DEC mainframes carrying historical data only.

   The plan should cover incident handling, data recovery, logging requirements, chain of command notifications, bug eradication, incident recovery, and emergency steps. Submit the plan to your instructor when it is completed.

18

Glossary

./configure – The first step of compiling and installing an application on a computer running a Linux operating system. The "./" part tells the OS that the file "configure" is to be executed as a program rather than opened within another application.

0wned – Yes, the initial character of this word is a zero. This is a common way that hackers and wannabes use written language, using characters that approximate the letter. This is also used in word mangling for passwords. When a machine is 0wned, the hacker can backdoor into it at any time and perform actions from that machine as if she were sitting at its keyboard.

Active Spoofing – A method of spoofing in which the hacker can see both parties and is in a position to observe the responses from the target computer and then respond accordingly.

Advanced Encryption Standard (AES) – An encryption standard that replaced DES (the Data Encryption Standard) around the turn of the 21st century.

Algorithm – A precise rule (or set of rules) specifying how to solve some problem.

ARP Spoofing – Modifying the Address Resolution Protocol (ARP) table for hacking purposes. When a packet arrives on the network, the router searches the ARP table for the destination computer's MAC address. If the address is not detected, the IP address is broadcast, and the computer with the matching IP address replies with its MAC address. After the MAC address has been received, the packets are transmitted to the destination computer. An ARP spoofing attack involves detecting broadcasts, faking the IP address, and then responding with the MAC address of the hacker's computer. After the router has received the MAC address, it assumes that the received MAC address is correct and sends the data to the hacker's computer.

Asymmetric Key Algorithms – Asymmetric key algorithms use two keys for encrypting and decrypting data. Each user has a public key and a private key. Public key algorithms effectively solve the biggest drawback to secret key schemes: the distribution of the proper keys to the proper people. Public key algorithms allow public keys to be sent unencrypted over insecure media.

Asynchronous Transfer Mode (ATM) – A high speed (up to 155 Mbps), controlled-delay, fixed-size packet switching and transmission system integrating multiple data types (voice, video, and data). Uses fixed-size packets also known as "cells" (ATM is often referred to as "cell relay").

Authentication – Verifying the identify of a user that is logging onto a computer system or verifying the integrity of a transmitted message.

Back Door – In the security of a system, a secret means of accessing the system deliberately left in place by designers or maintainers. May be intended for use by service technicians. Also called a trap door.

Blind Spoofing – Any spoofing attack where the cracker cannot see the results of the attack directly, and must guess or infer those results.

Block Cipher – Block ciphers operate on blocks of data. The algorithm breaks the plaintext document into blocks (usually 8 or 16 bytes long) and operates on each block independently. For example, the first 16 bytes are converted to a 16-byte block of encrypted text using the key table, then the next block is encrypted, and so on, until the whole document is encrypted.

Blowfish – An encryption algorithm developed by Bruce Schneier of Counterpane Systems.

Botnet – Botnets are a variety of Software DDoS. A bot is a program that surreptitiously installs itself on a computer so it can be controlled by a hacker. A botnet is a network of such zombie computers, which can harness their collective power to do considerable damage or send out huge amounts of junk e-mail.

Brute-Force Attacks – Brute-force attacks use all possible combination of letters, numbers, and special characters to determine the target password. They are very time consuming and require patience, yet the use of brute-force can extract the most difficult passwords given sufficient time. Brute-force attacks are slow compared to dictionary attacks. The speed of the operation depends on several factors, but chiefly on the length of the password.

Caesar Cipher – Devised by Julius Caesar, the Caesar Cipher consists of transposing forward three characters. C becomes F, A becomes D, and so on until reaching the end, at which point the letters wrap back around and X becomes A.

Ciphertext – A coded or encrypted document.

Clipper (and Capstone) Chips – The Clipper Chip was a cryptographic device purportedly intended to protect private communications while at the same time permitting government agents to obtain the "keys" upon presentation of "legal authorization." The "keys" are held by two government "escrow agents" and would enable the government to access the encrypted private communication.

Command Line Interface (CLI) – Terminal-based or terminal emulator-based user interface, characterized by text-only interface style and single-line entry of commands to a computer's operating system.

Connection Hijacking – An attacker may be able to control an existing connection between source and destination computers using connection hijacking. To do this, an attacker desynchronizes a series of packets between the source and destination computer.

Cracker – One who breaks security on a system. Coined by hackers in defense against journalistic misuse of the term "hacker." The term "cracker" reflects a strong revulsion at the theft and vandalism perpetrated by cracking rings. There is far less overlap between hackerdom and crackerdom than most would suspect.

Cracking – The act of illegally hacking into a computer system without the permission of the system's owner.

CRON Jobs – CRON is an automated scheduler utility in Unix and Linux, and a CRON job is any task assigned to CRON.

Cryptanalysis – (1) Operations performed in converting encrypted messages to plaintext without initial knowledge of the crypto-algorithm and/or key employed in the encryption. (2) The study of encrypted texts.

Cryptography – The process or skill of communicating in or deciphering secret writings or ciphers. Cryptography is a common way of protecting passwords. Cryptography uses an algorithm to encrypt a ciphertext document from a plaintext document, and when the information is needed again, the algorithm is used to decrypt the ciphertext back into plaintext.

Cyberattack – An assault against a computer system or network.

Cybercrime – Computer-based crimes, often having to do with online fraud.

Cyberterrorism – An illegal incursion into a computer system that alters files and data in order to cause damage by some other means. Such an incursion into air traffic control systems has often been cited as a cyberterrorism example, in which the system's computers are altered to malfunction in some manner.

Cyclic Redundancy Check (CRC) – A method for detecting errors in data transfers. A special polynomial algorithm that produces and uses a coefficient and a remainder (16 or 32 bits long) to check if the transmission proceeded without problems. CRC values change even if only one bit in the file changed, which makes it extremely reliable for checking integrity of files transmitted between computers.

Data Encapsulation – A process of enclosing higher-level protocol information in lower-level protocol information.

DES (Data Encryption Standard) – A widely used encryption algorithm that was selected as an official standard by the U.S. government in 1976. Has been superseded by AES.

Decrypt – The act of decoding a ciphertext document and producing from it a plaintext document.

Demilitarized Zone (DMZ) – A term borrowed from the military defining an area in which no troop movement is allowed through by either side. In terms of computer security, a demilitarized zone (DMZ) is a network area (a subnetwork) that sits between an organization's internal network and an external network, usually the Internet. The DMZ allows contained hosts to provide services to the external network, while protecting the internal network from possible intrusions into those hosts.

Denial of Service – A condition in which a system can no longer respond to normal requests. Legitimate users are unable to access the services provided.

Denial-of-Service Attack – An assault on a network that floods it with so many additional requests that regular traffic is either slowed or completely interrupted. Unlike a virus or worm, which can cause severe damage to databases, a denial of service attack interrupts network service for some period. See **Distributed Denial of Service Attack (DDOS)**.

Dictionary Attacks – The process of guessing passwords by using a list of common words. This method of password cracking systematically enters every word in a dictionary in order to deduce the password by comparing each word in the dictionary against the user's password. Dictionary attacks have the capability to determine the key necessary to decrypt an encrypted document. This works especially well against weak passwords.

Diffie-Hellman – Diffie-Hellman is a commonly used public-key algorithm for key exchange. It is generally considered to be secure when sufficiently long keys and proper prime generators are used. The security of Diffie-Hellman relies on the difficulty of the discrete logarithm problem (which is believed to be computationally equivalent to factoring large integers). The Diffie-Hellman algorithm is very slow and is generally used for distributing secret keys over an insecure channel, not to encrypt whole documents.

Digital Signature Algorithm (DSA) – A digital signature connects documents with the holder of a specific key. The algorithm is considered too slow for general encryption.

Digital Signature Standard (DSS) – DSS stands for the United States government's Digital Signature Standard. Its security is based on the discrete logarithm problem (like Diffie-Hellman), although its design has not been made public.

Digital Time Stamps – A digital time stamp connects a document with a specific time of origination.

Distributed Denial-of-Service Attack (DDoS) – A distributed denial-of-service attack uses multiple computers throughout the network that it has previously infected. All of these "zombies" work together to send out bogus messages, thereby increasing the amount of phony traffic.

Domain Name Service (DNS) – (1) A distributed database on servers and routers that direct the flow of messages on the Internet. (2) Information pertaining to those servers, that service, or the data within the database.

Elliptic Curve Cryptosystems – Elliptic curves are mathematical constructions from number theory and algebraic geometry, which in recent years have found numerous applications in cryptography.

Encrypt – To encode data for security purposes.

Enigma – During World War II, the German Army used this machine to send encoded commands and orders from headquarters to the battle lines.

Ethernet – A computer network cabling system designed by Xerox in the late 1970s. Originally, transmission rates were 3 Megabits per second (Mbs) over thick coaxial cable. Media today include fiber, twisted-pair (copper), and several coaxial cable types. Rates are up to 10 Gigabits per second or 10,000 Mbs.

IP Address Exhaustion – A theoretical time when the number of unallocated IP addresses is equal to zero. Currently thought to be early 2011. At this point, all IPv4 addresses will be in use, and presumably IPv6 will be the standard addressing mode.

IP Security Architecture (IPSec) – A collection of Internet Engineering Task Force (IETF) standards that define an architecture at the Internet Protocol (IP) layer to protect IP traffic by using various security services.

Federal Information Processing Standards (FIPS) – Documents published by the National Institute of Standards and Technology. AES is described in FIPS-197.

Fiber Distributed Data Interface (FDDI) – FDDI is a 100 Mbps fiber-optic networking technology. It is an ANSI standard. It uses a "counter-rotated" token ring topology. An FDDI network is typically known as a "backbone" network. It is used for joining file servers together and for joining other LANs together.

Firewall – A method for keeping a network secure from intruders. It can be a single router that filters out unwanted packets, or it may comprise a combination of routers and servers that each perform some type of firewall processing. Firewalls are widely used to give users secure access to the Internet as well as to separate a company's public Web server from its internal network. Firewalls are also used to keep internal network segments secure.

Fully-Qualified Domain Name (FQDN) – This name fully identifies the server program that an Internet request is addressed to. The FQDN includes the top-level domain name, the second-level domain name, and additional levels as necessary. An FQDN should be sufficient to determine a unique Internet address for any host on the Internet. The prefix "http://" added to the fully-qualified domain name completes the URL.

Google Hacks – Search strings to be used in Google or other search engines that return useful information for hackers who are looking for known vulnerabilities in various Web applications and architectures.

Graphical User Interface (GUI) – A visible two-dimensional representation used to receive user input and to display the device's output.

Hacker – A person who writes programs in assembly language or in system-level languages, such as C. Although it may refer to any programmer, it implies very tedious "hacking away" at the bits and bytes. Since it takes an experienced hacker to gain unauthorized entrance into a secure computer to extract information and/or perform some prank or mischief at the site, the term has become synonymous with "cracker," a person that performs an illegal act. This use of the term is not appreciated by the overwhelming majority of hackers who are honest professionals (sometimes called "ethical hackers"). See HaX0r.

Hash Functions – A cryptographic hash function generates a fixed-size hash value from a message of any length.

HaX0R – A common way for hackers or wannabes to refer to themselves or others. This uses word mangling to disguise the word "Hacker," and at the same time makes an internal pun on the XOR function. See XOR.

Hybridization – The process of deriving new words through the addition of letters and/or numbers to every word in a dictionary. The hybridization practice performed the most is to add a range of numbers—for instance, 0 to 100—to both the beginning and the end of a word in the dictionary.

IEEE 802.3 – IEEE 802.3 is a collection of IEEE standards defining the physical layer and the media access control (MAC) sublayer of the data link layer of wired Ethernet. This is generally a LAN technology with some WAN applications. Physical connections are made between nodes and/or infrastructure devices (hubs, switches, routers) by various types of copper or fiber cable.

Installed Base – The number of devices known to be running a specific software product.

International Data Encryption Algorithm (IDEA) – IDEA is an algorithm developed at ETH Zurich, in Switzerland. IDEA is considered one of the best and most secure algorithms available today. It uses a 128-bit key to encrypt 64-bit blocks, and the same algorithm is used for encryption and decryption. IDEA is a fairly new algorithm, but it has already been around for several years, and no practical attacks on it have been published despite numerous attempts to analyze it.

Internet Control Messaging Protocol (ICMP) Attacks – In this form of attack, packets are used to send fraudulent or deceptive connection information among computers. ICMP is validly used to test for connectivity using utilities such as the ping command. ICMP does not authenticate packets, so it is easy to intercept them and transmit spoofed ICMP packets.

IP Spoofing – This is a technique attackers use in which they send packets to the victim or target computer with a false source address. The victim is unaware that the packet is not from a trusted host, so it accepts the packet and sends a response back to the indicated source computer.

ISN – See Sequence Number.

Key – The key is a number, word, or phrase generated in an algorithm to both encrypt and decrypt.

Key Escrow – An arrangement whereby government authorities would hold encrypting keys "in escrow." allowing them to decrypt encrypted communications, provided they had the proper legal authority.

Kernel – The kernel is the heart of a computer's operating system. The kernel communicates with the user, the hardware, and the software through utilities and hardware drivers.

Keylogger – A keylogger program can easily be installed on a computer by an inside cracker or by trickery from an e-mail attachment. The unsuspecting user does not realize that this program is recording every key he or she presses. The hacker or cracker then examines the file generated by the program, and determines the passwords by examining the keylogger log.

less – less is a Linux CLI command that takes the output of some other command and presents that output in a screen-by-screen format, rather than streaming the information as fast as possible. This is very important in cases where the information takes up more than one screen, as is the case where the *locate* or *ls* commands are used.

Live Disk – Some operating systems, notably several flavors of Linux, can be booted directly from the CD-ROM drive, allowing troubleshooting and forensics to be performed upon a hard drive without adding or removing data from that drive. Starting an OS from the hard drive always changes the drive, as new session information is added and pagefile space is overwritten.

locate – The locate command shows all of the displayable file and folder names containing the designated string.

Loopback – A diagnostic mode built into a network interface card in which data transmitted through the interface is received back into the same interface. The common TCP/IP loopback address is 127.0.0.1.

ls – ls is the Linux or Unix CLI command to list the files in a directory.

make – The second step in compiling and installing an application on a computer running a Linux operating system. make is an application that runs the "makefile" configured by the "configure" application. In some applications, this is the last step.

make install – The third and final step of compiling and installing an application on a computer running a Linux operating system. make install is a subcommand of the "make" command. It places all the pieces of the application in the path where the operating system can find them.

Media Access Control (MAC) – The hard-coded address of the physical layer device that is attached to the network. All network interface controllers must have a hard-coded and unique MAC address. The MAC address is 48 bits long.

Message Digest Algorithm 5 (MD5) – Message Digest Algorithm 5 (MD5) is a secure hash algorithm developed at RSA Data Security, Inc. It can be used to hash an arbitrary-length byte string into a 128-bit value. MD5 is in wide use, and is considered reasonably secure.

more – Linux CLI command that presents data in a paged format allowing for easy reading of large data sets. Similar to the less command.

Modulo – Given two numbers, a (the dividend) and n (the divisor), a modulo n (abbreviated as a mod n) is the remainder, on division of a by n. For instance, the expression "7 mod 3" would evaluate to 1, while "14 mod 7" would evaluate to 0.

NCSC – National Computer Security Center. The arm of the U.S. National Security Agency that defines criteria for trusted computer products.

Netstat – The netstat command allows all the Transmission Control Protocol (TCP), User Datagram Protocol (UDP), and IP connections on a computer to be viewed.

Network Address Translation (NAT) – Allows one IP address, which is shown to the outside world, to refer to many IP addresses internally, one on each client station, and performs the translation back and forth.

Network Security – The authorization of access to files and directories in a network. Users are assigned an ID number and password that allows them access to information and programs within their authority. Network security is controlled by the network administrator.

One-Time Pad – In cryptography, a random key that is combined with the plaintext only once.

Open System Interconnection Model (OSI Model) – This is a paradigm established by the International Standards Organization (ISO) for communications worldwide. It divides the networking process into seven logical layers, starting at the cable and interface card level

and ascending to the operating system level. The layers are: Physical, Data Link, Network, Transport, Session, Presentation, and Application.

Operating System (OS) – An operating system is the software that acts as an interface between the user and the hardware and the applications (programs) on a computer. The operating system consists of a kernel and a variety of specialized utility programs.

Packet Filter – Blocks traffic based on a specific Web address (IP address) or type of application (e-mail, FTP, Web, etc.), which is specified by port number. Also known as a "screening router."

Packet Sniffing – Packet sniffers are used to inspect all the traffic in a network or subnet. This information assists network administrators as well as attackers. Use of a packet sniffer allows easy access to all plaintext information being transferred in the network. Encryption techniques defeat sniffing techniques, though they sometimes affect network performance.

Password Cracking – Password crackers are programs that are used to decrypt or decipher encrypted passwords. Some cracking programs use comparative analysis to match encrypted versions of passwords with the original. Some, called "brute-force" engines, test against a large dictionary file.

Phishing – Phishing relies on mass exposure of ads, pop-ups, or e-mails purported to be from legitimate companies. These notices warn of impending issues and request that users click a link to "verify" their account information. The verification site collects the information and uses it to steal from the victim, or to perpetrate identity theft to steal from companies.

Phreaking – (1) The art and science of cracking the phone network (so as, for example, to make free long-distance calls). (2) By extension, security cracking in any other context (especially, but not exclusively, on communications networks).

Plaintext – A plaintext document is an unencrypted or unencoded document that is readable by a human with ordinary comprehension.

Ping of Death – A ping request that crashes the target computer. It is caused by an invalid packet size value in the packet header. There are patches for most operating systems to prevent it.

Point-to-Point Protocol (PPP) – A protocol used to send data over serial lines. PPP provides error checking, link control, and authentication, and can be used to carry IP, IPX, and other protocols. PPP is superseding SLIP as the leading dial-in protocol.

Port Scanning – Examining the local network and also remote hosts with a scanning utility for vulnerabilities based upon which ports are open and what applications are listening at those ports. Scanners, developed by security professionals, help system administrators evaluate the security of their networks, and assist them to choose a course of action to close the vulnerabilities. Attackers use these tools for the same reason, but their motive is to gain illegitimate access to the network or the computers on it.

Post Office Protocol (POP) – Protocol concerned with e-mail delivery from the mail server to the client (local) computer to be read by a user within an e-mail application.

Pretty Good Privacy (PGP) – PGP is both a protocol and the name of the program that most widely implements that protocol. The PGP protocol, documented in RFC 1991 and expanded into the OpenPGP proposal (RFC 2440), is a presentation layer protocol that defines a standard to cryptographically secure e-mail messages. RFC 2015 describes how various kinds of PGP messages should be encapsulated using MIME.

Promiscuous Mode – A sniffer on any node on a network can record all the traffic that travels across this network by using the native NIC behavior of examination of packets. An administrator or a hacker can use a sniffer in the promiscuous mode to capture all network traffic.

Quantum Cryptography – Quantum cryptography is a method for secure key exchange over an insecure channel based on the nature of photons. Photons have a polarization, which can be measured in any basis, where a basis consists of two directions orthogonal to each other.

Reconnaissance – Attackers use reconnaissance techniques such as social engineering, dumpster diving, and Internet footprinting to collect information to potential target computers.

RC4 – RC4 is a cipher designed by RSA Data Security, Inc. The main advantage of RC4 is its speed; the algorithm is very fast. Several GB per second can be encrypted on a Pentium 4 PC.

RIP Attacks – RIP attacks take advantage of RIP, or Routing Information Protocol. This information protocol is an essential component in a TCP/IP network and is responsible for the distribution of routing information within networks.

RSA (Rivest, Shamir, and Adleman) – The RSA public-key cryptosystem is the most popular public-key encryption standard. RSA develops keys that are the product of two 1024-bit prime numbers.

S-boxes – Substitution Boxes (or S-boxes) are a basic component of symmetric key algorithms. In a block cipher, they are used to obscure the relationship between the plaintext and the ciphertext.

Script – A short, uncompiled application that works within a shell, such as a bash script; or a runtime environment, such as perlscript or PHP.

Script-Kiddies – A subset of hacking enthusiasts who, having little knowledge or experience, find and run scripts that others have made available through various media. Script-Kiddies are universally despised by experienced programmers. When an individual is singled out as being or acting like a script-kiddie, this is a derogatory usage.

Secure Hash Algorithm (SHA, SHS) – Secure Hash Algorithm (SHA), also known as Secure Hash Standard (SHS), was published by the US Government. It produces a 160-bit hash value from an arbitrary length string. SHS is structurally similar to MD4 and MD5. It is roughly 25% slower than MD5 but may be more secure, because it produces message digests that are 25% longer than those produced by the MD functions.

Secure Sockets Layer (SSL) – SSL is an application layer protocol created by Netscape for managing the security of message transmissions in a network. SSL uses the public- and private-key encryption system from RSA, which also includes the use of a digital certificate. Most e-commerce sites use SSL to secure their transactions.

Secure/Multipurpose Internet Mail Extensions (S/MIME) – A MIME-compatible protocol that adds security and authentication to documents sent via e-mail.

Secure Shell (SSH) – SSH is a secure way of transferring information (including files) between computers on a network.

Sequence Number – Also called Initial Sequence Number (ISN). A unique number for every packet on a particular connection maintained by a reliable transport layer service. The sequence number allows the transport layer to see if any packets were lost or delivered out of sequence by the underlying network and data layers.

Serial Line Internet Protocol (SLIP) – Predecessor of PPP. Allows a user to connect to the Internet directly over a high-speed modem.

Serial Optical – The Serial Optical interface is for use with optical point-to-point networks using the Serial Optical Link device handler.

Side-Channel Attack – A side-channel attack is any attack based on information gained from the physical implementation of a cryptosystem, rather than theoretical weaknesses in the algorithms.

Skipjack – Skipjack is an NSA-developed encryption algorithm for the Clipper (and Capstone) chips.

Smurf Attack – An assault on a network that floods it with excessive messages in order to impede normal traffic. It is accomplished by sending ping requests (ICMP echo requests) to a broadcast address on the target network or an intermediate network. The return address is spoofed to the victim's address. Since a broadcast address is picked up by all nodes on the subnet, it functions like an amplifier, generating hundreds of responses from one request and eventually causing a traffic overload.

Social Engineering – Social engineering, including phishing, is a term to describe how hackers deceive individuals into voluntarily giving out passwords and privileged data by pretending to be someone else, such as a bank official.

Source Routing – A sender using source-routing can specify the return path through which the destination computer will send its reply. Typically, this feature is used for either troubleshooting a network or improving its performance.

Spam – (1) Unrequested commercial e-mail messages. (2) An attack vector for denial-of-service (DoS) attacks. (3) Any unwanted e-mail message.

Spoofing – Spoofing is a method for gaining unauthorized access to computers by sending packets or messages with forged headers indicating that the information comes from a trusted source. Attackers use various techniques to find an IP address of a trusted host. Then they modify their packets so that they appear legitimate.

Spyware – Software that sends information about your Web surfing habits to a different Web site, without your knowledge. Often built into free downloads from the Web, it transmits information in the background as you move around the Web. The license agreement that you often accept without reading may say that the information is anonymous. Anonymous profiling means that your habits are being recorded, but not your personal information. This information is used to create marketing profiles.

Stream Cipher – Stream ciphers use a key stream to encrypt and decrypt a plaintext message. A key stream is similar to a one-time pad.

Substitution – The replacement of a letter or group of letters with another letter or group of letters.

Switch User (su) – This Unix / Linux command allows a user to perform a specific task as a different user.

Symmetric Key – Symmetric key algorithms use the same key to encrypt and to decrypt the data. Both the sender and the recipient must have a copy of the key.

SysAdmin – Systems administrator.

Time Domain Reflectometry (TDR) – A technique for measuring cable lengths by timing the period between a test pulse and the reflection of the pulse from an impedance discontinuity on the cable.

Token Ring – Token ring local area network (LAN) technology was developed in the late 1960s. US patents were awarded in 1981 and token ring was developed and promoted by IBM in the early 1980s and standardized as IEEE 802.5 by the Institute of Electrical and Electronics Engineers. Initially very successful, it was eclipsed by 10BASE-T for Ethernet and the EIA/TIA 568 cabling standard in the early 1990s.

traceroute – A request for a Web page that resides on a remote server must pass through several servers or routers on its way. In a UNIX-based operating system, you can track all of the intermediate servers by using the traceroute command. In Windows operating systems, it is possible to use the tracert command to trace the route of a request.

Transmission Control Protocol/Internet Protocol (TCP/IP) – A suite of protocols that underlie the Internet. The TCP/IP suite is comprised of many protocols and applications that focus on two main objectives. IP has the tools to provide the correct routing of packets and any device-to-device communications, and the Transmission Control Protocol, TCP, is responsible for safe and reliable data transfer between host computers. It is the common language of networked computers and makes transferring information fast and efficient.

TCP Packet Flags – There are six possible packet flags: URG, ACK, PSH, RST, SYN and FIN. Packets can have more than one flag set, and this is indicated by the flag names being separated by a slash ("SYN/ACK") or a comma ("ACK,FIN"). SYN/ACK says the packet is attempting to synchronize with the sender and also acknowledge the received packet. Normally, a packet will have only one flag sent except in the case of SYN/ACK or FIN/ACK.

 URG: Urgent Pointer field
 ACK: Acknowledgment field
 PSH: Push function
 RST: Reset the connection
 SYN: Synchronize sequence numbers
 FIN: No more data from sender

TCP SYN Attack – A TCP SYN attack takes advantage of the way that most hosts implement the TCP three-way handshake. When Host B receives the SYN request from A, it must keep track of the partially opened connection in a queue for at least 75 seconds. Most systems are limited and can only keep track of a small number of connections. An attacker can overflow the listen queue just by sending more SYN requests than the queue can handle. This is why SYN attacks are also called SYN-Flooding.

Transposition – An alteration of the positions or order of letters or words, as in an anagram.

Tripwire – A computer program from COAST that detects and reports changes in key system files.

3DES (Triple DES) – Triple DES is the technique of encrypting plaintext with DES and then taking the ciphertext and encrypting it again with another DES key, and then taking the result and encrypting it yet again with yet another DES key.

Trojan Horse – A program that appears legitimate, but performs some illicit activity when it is run. It may be used to locate password information or make the system more vulnerable to future entry, or it may simply destroy programs or data on the hard disk. A Trojan horse is similar to a virus, except that it does not replicate itself. It stays in the computer doing its damage or allowing somebody from a remote site to take control of the computer. Trojans often sneak in attached to a free game or other utility.

Turing Bombe – Alan Turing, as a member of the British government's Code and Cypher School at Bletchley Park, developed a machine called the Turing Bombe to crack the "Enigma Code."

Uniform Resource Locator (URL) – The FQDN combined with the protocol of the page or resource sought. An example of a URL is http://www.google.com.

User Datagram Protocol (UDP) – The User Datagram Protocol (UDP) is a transport layer protocol defined for use with the IP network layer protocol. It is defined by RFC 768, written by John Postel. It provides a best-effort datagram service to an End System (IP host).

User Interface – All applications have a user interface or interfaces, through which the application accepts input and displays results. On modern operating systems on microcomputers, PDAs, and cellular phones, the interface is usually a Command-Line Interface (CLI) or a Graphical User Interface (GUI). Keyboards, mice, cameras, microphones, and other input devices sit on the User side of the interface.

Virus – Software used to infect a computer. After the virus code is written, it is buried within an existing program. Once that program is executed, the virus code is activated and attaches copies of itself to other programs in the system. Infected programs copy the virus to other programs.

Voice over Internet Protocol (VoIP) – May refer to any one of several IETF protocols designed to allow users to make voice-based "telephone" calls over an Ethernet connection.

Virus Hoaxes – Considering the speed with which messages can be copied and sent via e-mail on the Internet, pranksters love to spread phony warnings just to upset as many people as they can. Virus hoaxes such as the Good Times virus tell people that if they open their e-mail, their hard drives will be erased or some such catastrophe will occur. The Department of Energy maintains the Computer Incident Advisory Capability Web site that identifies current virus hoaxes. For information, visit *http://hoaxbusters.ciac.org*.

Wannabe – A person new to an area of endeavor within a given field. This person often adopts the style of dress or communication of people who appear to be successful members thereof. Sometimes called Newbees or Newbies.

War Dialer – A war dialer is a script that tells the modem to dial a range of phone numbers and then identifies those that are connected to remote computers. The phone number range is defined by the user, and then the program proceeds to dial these numbers, one after the other, attempting to establish a remote connection.

Warez – Warez are malware, hacking scripts, or other software that produce antisocial results. The term also refers to commercial software that has been illegally copied or distributed.

whereis – The Linux CLI command, whereis shows you where the files appear in your PATH (the directories in which you are allowed to read, write, or execute an application or other file).

which – The Linux CLI command **which** displays the location of the application that will execute when you type its name on the command line. There are many reasons why you might find multiple executable files with the same name—for example, you might be developing an application and have multiple versions in test. However, the default copy of an executable will be in the PATH of almost all users.

Word Mangling – A way of transposing or substituting letters in regular words to create passwords that are stronger than regular dictionary words. For example, "Fiddle" is an easy word for a cracker to guess, but "elddiF", "FiddleelddiF", "Fid23dle", or "F1ddl3" might be harder.

Worm – A destructive program that replicates itself throughout disk and memory, using up the computer's resources and eventually shutting the system down.

XOR (eXclusive OR) – A Boolean logic operation that is widely used in cryptography as well as in generating parity bits for error checking and fault tolerance. XOR compares two input bits and generates one output bit. The logic is simple. If the bits are the same, the result is 0. If the bits are different, the result is 1. Various symbols are used to designate the XOR operation including a + sign inside a circle, an underlined "V", and the caret (^).

Zombies – Zombies are machines that have been unobtrusively 0wned by a hacker. When a machine is 0wned, the hacker can back door into it at any time and perform actions from that machine as if the hacker was sitting at its keyboard.

Index